Economic Issues Today

Alternative Approaches

FIFTH EDITION

POL 57

4pm

Thurs. June 1.

Rm F319

ECONOMIC ISSUES TODAY

Alternative Approaches

Fifth Edition

Robert B. Carson

STATE UNIVERSITY COLLEGE
ONEONTA, NEW YORK

St. Martin's Press
NEW YORK

Senior editor: Don Reisman
Project management: Caliber Design Planning, Inc.
Cover design: Judy Forster

Library of Congress Catalog Card Number: 89-63887
Copyright © 1991 by St. Martin's Press, Inc.
All rights reserved. No part of this book may be reproduced by any form or by any means, mechanical, electronic, photocopying, recording, or otherwise, except as may be expressly permitted by the applicable copyright statutes or in writing by the Publisher.
Manufactured in the United States of America.
54321
fedcb

For information, write:
St. Martin's Press, Inc.
175 Fifth Avenue
New York, NY 10010

ISBN: 0-312-03714-7

ACKNOWLEDGMENTS

"BROTHER CAN YOU SPARE A DIME?" Lyrics by E.Y. Harburg. Music by Jay Gorney. © 1932 Warner Bros., Inc. Copyright renewed. All Rights Reserved. Used by permission.

Figure 14.1: From Michael I. Boskin, ed., *The Crisis in Social Security*. San Francisco: Institute for Contemporary Studies, 1977, p. 8. Reprinted by permission.

*This book is dedicated to my mother,
Catherine Postlewaite Carson.*

PREFACE

While the fifth edition of *Economic Issues Today* remains firmly committed to the general objectives and philosophy of earlier versions, the topical coverage of particular issues and the shadings of focus of the new edition reflect some significant revising. It could be no other way. As the United States enters the last decade of the twentieth century, both the economic agenda before the nation and the world and the processes of economic reasoning are undergoing extensive changes. Simply put, the issues and ideas that dominated throughout the 1980s are not precisely the same as those that will dominate in the 1990s.

Among the changes that longtime users of *Economic Issues Today* will notice are:

1. A modest revision of the Introduction, emphasizing the altered "mood" of economics, economists, and the general public from that which existed only a few years ago.
2. An extensively revised and broadened examination of the issue of consumer protection.
3. An elaborate updating of the deregulation issue that takes account of the recent rise of "reregulation" advocacy.
4. A recasting of the productivity issue within the context of American "competitiveness" in world markets.
5. The addition of a brand-new issue, "Income Distribution and Public Policy."
6. An extensive rewriting of the several issues dealing with stabilization policy to reflect new thinking in this area that has been prompted, on the one hand, by a long period of steady, if not especially spectacular expansion, and on the other, by fears that we are losing control of our domestic economy.
7. A virtual rewriting of the unemployment issue to focus more clearly on the impact of structural shifts within the American economy.
8. An entirely new discussion of the military spending issue, setting the arguments within the context of new realities imposed by changes in cold war politics.

9. A new issue, "America in the World," that examines the impact of
the new international economy on the United States.
10. A reconstruction of the debate over economic planning, with the
respective arguments for and against it developed in light of the
recent changes in Eastern Europe and the Soviet Union.

Throughout the book, I have used the most recent available references and data as well as added new tables and figures so that the
information is as current as possible.

These changes, extensive as they may be, are designed to
enhance, rather than alter the pedagogical approach of the earlier edi-
tions. As before, the book requires no background in the methods of
economic analysis, and as much as possible it avoids the use of economic jargon in favor of everyday language. This edition of *Economic
Issues Today*, like previous ones, stresses the ideological choices that
exist in economic thought and that often cause ordinary citizens to be
confused about what economists *do* and what economists *believe*. As
ever, it is meant to be a provocative book, more interested in provok-
ing discussion and thought than in presenting "right" solutions to
problems. It remains committed to the belief that real economic solutions are possible in a democratic society only when all alternatives
are known and considered.

Although longtime users are familiar with the text's philosophy
and perspectives, new readers might benefit from an explanation of
why I undertook this project in the first place and how, in fact, the
book is organized.

All too frequently, students begin their study of economics with
the impression that economists are bland and monolithic when discussing important issues confronting the general society. We may as
well admit that the profession sometimes exhibits a tendency to bland-
ness in its public utterances, but surely any supposed unanimity
toward social policy questions has vanished. With the rise of an influential Radical caucus within the discipline, beginning in the late 1960s,
and the more recent resurgence of variations of laissez-faire ideology,
any facade of consensus has clearly been broken down. The application of economic theory to issues of public policy more and more
reflects a range of choice from Conservative to Liberal to Radical.

For the student struggling with basic theory and analytic tools, as
well as for the ordinary citizen overwhelmed by economic data in the

newspapers and on the TV evening news, it is hard to avoid confusion over what economists really think about the problems facing the nation. This book begins with the assumption that the answers economists give to policy questions can be usefully compared and analyzed according to the particular biases of their arguments and the probable outcomes of their proposals. In other words, differences in economic logic and interpretation of evidence are not so much a function of skill mastery as they are the expression of strongly held social and political opinions. The text also assumes that economics as a body of knowledge takes on greater meaning and is more readily comprehended when it is viewed in this way.

For each issue, a Conservative, Liberal, and Radical analysis and proposed solution are presented in turn as the valid approach to the problem. On one page, there may be a vigorous and unyielding defense of laissez-faire and the market economy; on another, a program for the elimination or modification of the free market. This is not the way economic analysis and theory are usually taught, but it is what the practice of economics is about. In the real world, the citizen and the economist make public policy choices that protect, attack, or modify the market mechanism. We may defend our positions in terms of economic logic, but behind our proofs lies our political and ideological view of the world. This book attempts to examine the relationship between ideological values and the economic theories and policies that are their outcome.

Since the text presents a wide range of perspectives on a number of currently sensitive issues, it should provoke disagreement, controversy, and discussion. In itself, the book does not urge a particular ideological position or a particular variety of economic analysis. The decision to select or reject this or that point of view is left—as it should be—to the reader.

Each chapter is self-contained and may be assigned in any order the instructor chooses. There are relatively few footnotes or direct references to specific economists, although the ideas of many contemporary economists and schools of economic thought will be apparent. The bibliography at the end is offered for anyone wishing to dig a little deeper into an issue or a particular economic perspective or approach.

The decision to minimize the explicit discussion of technical terms and specific economic concepts in the discussion of contemporary policy issues does not mean the author rejects the importance of formal economic analysis. For instructors using *Economic Issues Today* along with a conventional principles of economics text, the Instructor's Manual supplies an outline of the pertinent economic concepts. Even instructors using this book as collateral reading may find the manual quite useful.

The basic outline of this textbook grew out of discussions with Irving Rockwood and my own earlier experience with editing two collections of readings in economics. As the work developed, I received further encouragement in very early stages from Tony Dick and Murray Curtin, and at a later and most critical juncture from Bertrand Lummus.

For this fifth edition, I am indebted to Don Reisman of St. Martin's press for his editorial encouragement and support. Once again, Emily Berleth, who from the book's inception has had to deal with the author's idiosyncracies, occasional forgetfulness, and always inadequate typing skills, served brilliantly and good-humoredly as project coordinator.

Finally, there is the special debt I owe to my students. Their constant questioning and demanding of answers to "the great economic problems of the day" initially inspired the writing of the book and continue to serve to keep me alert to contemporary economic trends and events. Alas, I have probably learned much more from their questions than they from my answers.

CONTENTS

Economic Issues Today

Alternative Approaches

FIFTH EDITION

PART 1

INTRODUCTION

Alternative Economic Philosophies
A Survey of Conservative, Liberal, and Radical Critiques

The ideas of economists, both when they are right and when they are wrong, are more powerful than is commonly understood. Indeed, the world is ruled by little else. Practical men, who believe themselves to be quite exempt from any intellectual influences, are usually the slaves of some defunct economist. Madmen in authority, who hear voices in the air, are distilling their frenzy from some academic scribbler of a few years back.

John Maynard Keynes, 1936

The Contemporary Economic Paradox

A perplexing paradox dominates economic thinking in contemporary America. On the one hand, public appetite for information on economic matters has never been greater. Subscriptions to and reading of a wide variety of business, financial, and general publications on the state of the economy is a matter of habit with a growing number of Americans. Ordinary citizens' attention usually heightens as the evening television news presents its "Business Briefs" and "Economy Watch" segments. Whereas earlier epochs turned to religion as a daily compass, our era turns to economic reports, projections, and analyses in an effort to obtain both a personal and historical sense of direction. The monthly report of the "leading economic indicators" by the U.S. Department of Commerce compels the same kind of attention once reserved in earlier civilizations for observing the stars or examining the entrails of sacrificed sheep.

On the other hand, for all the interest in economic matters, the public reserves no special status for economists, the high priests of this new secular faith. Indeed, a good case can be made that in recent years an inverse relationship has existed between the public's interest in economic affairs and its respect for economists. If pondered at some length, the phenomenon becomes particularly puzzling. *After all, how can the nation really be absorbed in the "stuff" of economic study and reporting and not be interested in the analytical and theoretical efforts of those most closely related to the actual study of economic events?*

Explanations are not easy, but the most serviceable one seems to be that the American public finds economic reasoners confusing and contradictory in their pontifications about the state and direction of economic affairs. Not only does the advice of the practitioners of the "dismal science" frequently seem to be inconsistent with the available evidence, but, taking the same evidence, economists may render entirely different judgments about its meaning.

Paraphrasing George Bernard Shaw, an exasperated President Kennedy, then soliciting economic advice on ways to stimulate a sluggish economy, lamented, "If you laid all economists head to feet, all you would reach is confusion." It is doubtless a view shared by many contemporary evening news watchers. However, the president missed the point. Really what you would reach wouldn't be confusion, it would be different points of view (economists will assure the uninitiated that there is a difference between "confusion" and "different points of view"). Economists, as a group, have rarely been noted for their single-mindedness. Indeed, as one wag noted, if they were, they and their work would not enjoy much attention. Nothing, after all, is quite as dull an area of intellectual activity as one in which everyone agrees with everyone else.

Were it not for the gravity of the subject matter and the fact that so much depends on "being right" in economic affairs, it might be sufficient to account for diversity and disagreement in economic matters as a simple matter of human perversity. Alas, we are compelled to dig a bit deeper in searching for an explanation.

Why Economists Disagree

Essentially there are two reasons for economists' holding contrary perspectives on matters of economic theory and policy. First of all, there is the possibility that while there may be fundamental agreement on economic values and perspectives and on methods of studying specific data, men and women of essentially the same views and training may still honestly differ in interpretation of the data. Such was the case in the winter of 1984–1985, when "economist bashing" briefly became a popular indoor sport of the Reagan administration. Many economists outside the administration who had previously been enthusiastic supporters of most of the president's programs took a more pessimistic view of the economy's expected future performance than did Reagan. Some began to talk openly about an impending recession. As recession failed to materialize and the economy blossomed, Reagan supporters, including a number of administration economists, gleefully poked fun at certain other economists whose sophisticated models seemed decidedly less accurate than Ronald Reagan's hunches.*

*Reagan in fact toyed with abolishing the President's Council of Economic Advisors composed entirely of his own appointees—on the grounds that considering the kind of advice he had been getting, it would be a useful reduction in governmental expenditures. The president might have been better served by taking a longer view on the value of having consensus among economists irrespective of their immediate predictive accuracy. Consensus had not helped Hoover much in 1929 when few conventional economists saw any weakness in the bull market, nor had the consensus on the CEAs of Johnson and Nixon in the 1960s prepared the nation for the stagflation of the 1970s.

Although this first type of disagreement within the economics fraternity, and sometimes between economists and political leaders, is "good front-page news" and may actually have significant consequences, it is not nearly as important as the kind of disagreement that reflects different fundamental ethical and political perspectives. In our second instance, disagreement begins with the very way in which economic facts and data are gathered, perceived, and measured and therefore carries through to very different expectations about the outcome of particular economic policies. The tremendous economic scare the nation experienced in the late fall of 1987 is a useful recent illustration of this type of disagreement.

On October 19, 1987, the New York Stock Exchange posted its largest one-day decline in financial values in nearly sixty years. Not since Black Tuesday—October 29, 1929—had the financial community and the economy in general been rocked by so calamitous an event. Of course, Black Tuesday was an awesome and frightening benchmark to use in any historical comparison since that date is burned deeply in the collective historical consciousness of the nation as the beginning of the Great Depression epoch.* Overnight, October 19, 1987, became "Black Monday." As the ripple effects of the New York Stock Exchange's nosedive were felt throughout the world's financial and political centers, the media rushed to press and to air with special reports and analyses of the causes and meanings of Black Monday's events. Accordingly, the public was treated to lengthy discussions by economic experts and, not surprisingly, to a wide variety of interpretations.

Although most economists did agree that the events of Black Monday were particularly distressing, there was great disagreement over their causes, expected effects, and possible cures that might be undertaken to mitigate them. The overall economic analysis that the public was treated to reflected much more than mere differences of opinion over "the facts" or the meaning of "the facts." This kind of disagreement was certainly present in the post–Black Monday debates; however, the sharper divisions among economists turned on matters of fundamental disagreement in philosophy or in outlook on

---

*At the time, however, the collapse of the 1929 bull market, while certainly seen as a major financial catastrophe, was not viewed as it presently is. Two years were to pass before the nation slumped into depression, and, at the end of 1929, the New York Times was to select Admiral Byrd's trip to the South Pole as the "news story of the year."

economic matters generally. The varying perspectives were especially evident when economists looked toward the future. Some, after laying the blame for the crisis on government deficits, saw recovery possible only if the nation moved immediately to balanced budgets. Others worried that budget balancing could only make matters worse, pushing the United States and ultimately the world into a new "Great Depression." A few saw no cures at all, and more or less accepted the prospect that the United States and the world were slipping into economic Armageddon.

Of course, the urgency of the post–Black Monday arguments receded with the passage of time when none of the grimmer economic scenarios took shape, but the debate itself remains as an illustration of how economists' differing basic outlooks and values can come into conflict when attention is focused on a particular economic event. This category of "professional disagreement" is far more perplexing—to economists as well as to the general public—than our earlier case of Ronald Reagan's "economist bashing."* Within the profession, there is a strong tendency to avoid discussion of this more basic reason for disagreement among economists. The best-selling introductory economics textbook tries to bury the question this way:

> A reasonable summary of the state of disagreement in economics today would be: Economists are quite divided on central issues of macroeconomics, particularly the role of money. A substantial amount of accord is seen in the microeconomic theory of prices and markets. But on the broad political and ethical issues of economics, economists are as divided as their parents or cousins.†

*A good case can be made that the Black Monday debate is an important contributory factor to the "economic paradox" we cited earlier. Time, not policy changes, made public concern over the meaning of Black Monday disappear. The various economic arguments and their predictions of a dark economic future were mostly forgotten within a year. The presidential election of 1988 proceeded with scarcely a reference to Black Monday—or virtually any other item on economists' agendas.

†Paul A. Samuelson and William D. Nordhaus, *Economics*, 12th ed. (New York: McGraw-Hill, 1985), p. 7. The traditional technique has been to divide economics as a science into two parts: *positive economics*, which deals purely with factual relationships such as the level of national output, unemployment, prices, and so on; and *normative economics*, which interprets these facts into goals, merely reflecting individual value judgments. The trouble is, as most economists admit, that these distinctions have blurred. For instance, is the decision not to count those who have "given up" looking for jobs as part of the unemployed a *positive* or *normative* judgment? There are few purely factual relationships that don't require some amount of value judgment.

While such a disclaimer may serve its immediate purpose—to simply get on with the conventional theoretical "stuff" of introductory economics by shoving economic values into the realm of personal politics—it is an evasion not unnoticed by the sharp-eyed student as well as by many ordinary people seeking hard answers to hard economic questions. The necessity for making so-called personal value judgments always keeps sneaking into real-world economic discussions: What is the solution to the farm problem? Does the federal deficit really matter? Who should pay how much in taxes? The fact is that economists not only offer opinions but construct programs dealing with these questions, and they do it as economists, not as "parents and cousins" of economists. Meanwhile, it is perfectly evident that politicians, the "madmen in authority," as John Maynard Keynes described them, are indeed listening to the advice of these "academic scribblers."

The frequent squabbling among economists over desired policy objectives can scarcely be hidden from the public, and such disagreement can be downright unsettling. It often comes as a rude surprise to the person on the street, who, although paying due professional respect to economists, still sees the economist as a kind of mechanic. When one's car does not start, the car owner expects (at least hopes) that the diagnosis of mechanical trouble given at one garage is exactly the same as what will be heard at any other. If there is one mechanical problem, there should be one mechanical solution. The moral of this comparison is that the study of economics is more than studying a repair manual, and economists are not mechanics.

The Role of Ideology

How is such disagreement possible? Isn't economics a science? Economists' answers to that question vary. A common and reasonable enough response is simply that scientists disagree too. While there is much truth to such an answer, it really begs the question. Plainly, the "dismal science" of economics is not a science like physics. Whereas economists may sometimes talk about the laws of supply and demand as if they were eternal verities like the law of gravity, there is abundant anthropological and historical evidence that many societies have behaved quite contrary to the laws of supply and demand.

To be sure, economists employ (or at least should employ) the rigor of scientific method and quantitative techniques in collecting data, testing hypotheses, and offering reasonable conclusions and predictions. However, economists deal with different "stuff" from that of their colleagues in the exact sciences. Their data involve human beings and their laboratory is a world of behavior and perception that varies with time and place. On top of this, economists, like all social scientists, are called on to answer a question not asked of those in the "pure" sciences: "What *ought* to be?" Astronomers, for instance, are not asked what *ought* to be the gravitational relationships of our universe. That would be a nonsense question. Economists, however, cannot evade making some determinations about optimal prices, optimal income distribution, and so forth. Their decisions, while perhaps based on a genuine effort at neutrality, detachment, and honest evaluation of the available evidence, finally must be a matter of interpretation, a value judgment based on their own particular world views. To put the point directly: *Economics, as a study of human behavior, cannot avoid value judgments. Struggle as it may, economics as a discipline is never free from ideology.*

The early economists of the eighteenth and nineteenth centuries— Adam Smith, David Ricardo, John Stuart Mill, and especially the heretic Karl Marx—perceived economics as merely part of a broader political-economy context, but this view had largely been abandoned by the end of the nineteenth century. In the middle of the twentieth century, the economics profession generally approached "ideology" as if it were a dirty word, unprofessional, or, at the very best, too troublesome to deal with. The emphasis was on theoretical tools, considered both universal and neutral. All this changed in the 1960s and 1970s when well-known American economists thrust themselves into the powerful debates then sweeping American society. Their views on the war in Vietnam, poverty, civil rights, the extent of government power, the environmental crisis, the oil embargo, the causes of "stagflation," high technology versus smokestack industries, and much more could be heard regularly on television talk shows and miniseries or read in the columns of weekly newsmagazines. Often there was the pretension that this "talking out of church" had little impact on the body of "professional" theory and judgment, but the pretension was unconvincing. For good or ill, the genie was out of the bottle, and the economics profession had again become involved in politics and in recommending political courses of action to pursue economic objectives.

Initially, through the 1960s and into the early 1970s, prevailing opinion among economic reasoners upheld a Liberal perspective on political economy, advocating an active interventionism by government to "correct and improve" the workings of the economy. However, during the late 1970s, this consensus began to break down as the national economy slipped into a long period of sagging growth, rising unemployment, and escalating inflation. In its place, a new consensus began to build on behalf of a Conservative, minimum-government approach to political and economic matters. As the Liberals' star fell and the Conservatives' rose, the intensity and bitterness of economic and political argument sharpened. Although the shrillness of the ideological debate calmed a bit during the Reagan years—no doubt a by-product of the long economic expansion that began in late 1982—the past three decades of shifting ideological perspectives have left their mark on the economics profession. To a considerable extent, the ordinary economics textbook illustrates this point. While economics texts continue to do what such books have always done, namely, to introduce the reader to a generally agreed-on body of theoretical and analytical techniques and tools that constitute the study of economics, most have also found it necessary to identify and discuss the alternatives of Liberals, Conservatives, and, sometimes, even Radicals in the practical extension of economic analysis to actual policy-making situations.

The significance of all this should not be lost on the beginning student of economics. Though many economists may stress the value-free nature of their studies, and of economics in general, common sense and observation suggest that this is at best a vastly exaggerated claim. The content and application of economic reasoning are determined ultimately by the force of what economists believe, not by an independent and neutral logic. But to say that economics is a matter of opinion is not to say that it is just a study of relatively different ideas: Here's this view and here's that one and each is of equal value. In fact, opinions are not of equal value. There are good opinions and there are bad ones. Different economic ideas have different consequences when adopted as policy. They have different effects—now and in the future. As we confront the various policy solutions proposed to deal with the many crises now gnawing deep into our economy and society, we must make choices. This one seems likely to produce desired outcomes. That one does not. No other situation is consistent with a free and reasoning society. Granted it is a painful situation, since choice always raises doubts and uncertainty and runs the risk of wrong judgment, but it cannot be evaded.

This book is intended to focus on a limited number of the hard choices that we must make. Its basic premise is that economic judgment is fundamentally a matter of learning to choose the best policy solution among all possible solutions. The book further assumes that failure to make this choice is to underestimate the richness and importance of the economic ideas we learn and to be blind to the fact that ideas and analysis do indeed apply to the real world of our own lives.

On Sorting Out Ideologies

Assuming that we have been at least partially convincing in our argument that economic analysis is permeated by ideological judgment, we now turn to examine the varieties of ideology common to American economic thought.

In general, we may characterize the ideological position of contemporary economics and economists as Conservative, Liberal, or Radical. These, the same handy categories that evening newscasters use to describe political positions, presumably have some meaning to people. The trouble with labels, though, is that they can mean a great deal and, at the same time, nothing at all. At a distance the various political colors of Conservative, Liberal, and Radical banners are vividly different. Close up, however, the distinctiveness blurs, and what seemed obvious differences are not so clear. For instance, there is probably *not* a strictly Liberal position on every economic issue, nor are all the economists who might be generally termed "Liberal" consistently in agreement. The same is true in the case of many Radical or Conservative positions as well. Unless we maintain a certain open-endedness in our categorizing of positions, the discussion of ideological differences will be overly simple and much too rigid. Therefore, the following generalizations and applications of ideological typologies will attempt to isolate and identify only "representative" positions. By doing this we can at least focus on the differences at the center rather than on the fuzziness at the fringes of these schools of thought.

We are still left with a problem. How do you specify an ideological position? Can you define a Radical or a Liberal or a Conservative position? The answer here is simple. As the British economist Joan Robinson once observed, an ideology is like an elephant—you can't define an elephant, but you should know one when you see it. Moreover, you should know the difference between an elephant and a horse or a cow without having to resort to definitions.

There is a general framework of thought within each of the three ideological schools by which we can recognize them. Thus we will not "define" the schools but merely describe the salient characteristics of each. In all the following, the reader is urged to remember that there are many varieties of elephants. Our specification of a particular ideological view on any issue is a representative model—a kind of average-looking elephant (or horse or cow). Therefore, the Conservative view offered on the problem of federal deficits, for instance, will probably not encompass all Conservative thought on this question. However, it should be sufficiently representative so that the basic Conservative paradigm, or world view, can be distinguished from the Radical or Liberal argument. Where truly important divisions within an ideological paradigm exist, the divisions will be appropriately noted and discussed.

THE CONSERVATIVE PARADIGM

What is usually labeled the Conservative position in economic thought and policy-making was not always "conservative." Conservative ideas may be traced to quite radical origins. The forebears of modern Conservative thought—among them England's Adam Smith (1723–1790)—were not interested in "conserving" the economic order they knew but in destroying it. In 1776, when Smith wrote his classic *Wealth of Nations*, England was organized under a more or less closed economic system of monopoly rights, trade restriction, and constant government interference with the marketplace and individuals' business and private affairs. This system, known as mercantilism, had been dominant in England and, with slight variations, elsewhere on the Continent for over 250 years.

Adam Smith's Legacy   Smith's remedy was simple enough: Remove all restrictions on commercial and industrial activity and allow the market to work freely. The philosophical basis of Smith's argument rested on his beliefs that (1) all men had the natural right to obtain and protect their property; (2) all men were by nature materialistic; and (3) all men were rational and would seek, by their own reason, to maximize their material well-being. These individualistic tendencies in men would be tempered by competition in the marketplace. There, men would have to compromise with one another to gain any individual satisfaction whatsoever. The overall effect of these compromises would ultimately lead to national as well as individual satisfaction. Competition and self-interest would keep prices down and production high and rising as well as stimulate product improvement, invention, and steady economic progress. For this to happen, of course, there would have to be a minimum of interference with the free market—no big government, no powerful unions, and no conspiring in trade. Smith's position and that of his contemporaries and followers was known as "Classical Liberalism." The Conservative label now applied to these views seems to have been affixed much later, when Smith's heirs found themselves acting in the defense of a status quo rather than opposing an older order.

Thus modern capitalist economic thought must trace its origins to Adam Smith. While this body of thought has been built on and modified over the past 200 years, the hand of Adam Smith is evident in every conventional economics textbook. Common sense tells us, however, that a lot has changed since Smith's day. Today business is big. There are labor unions and big government to interfere with his balanced free market of equals. His optimistic view of a naturally growing and expanding system is now replaced by growth problems and by a steady dose of pessimism in most glances toward the future. Nevertheless, modern Conservatives, among contemporary defenders of capitalism, still stand close to the ideals of Adam Smith.

Modern Conservative thought is anchored in two basic philosophic ideas that distinguish it from Liberal and Radical positions. First, the market system and the spirit of competition are central to proper social organization. Second, individual rights and freedoms must be unlimited and uninfringed.

Conservatives oppose any "unnatural" interference in the marketplace. In particular, the Conservative views the growth of big government in capitalist society as the greatest threat to economic

progress. Milton Friedman, Nobel laureate and preeminent figure in
the Conservative Chicago school, has argued that government has
moved from being merely an instrumentality necessary to sustain the
economic and social order to becoming an instrument of oppression.
Friedman's prescription for what "ought to be" on the matter of
government is clear:

> A government which maintained law and order, defined property rights,
> served as a means whereby we could modify property rights and other
> rules of the economic game, adjudicated disputes about the interpreta-
> tion of the rules, enforced contracts, promoted competition, provided a
> monetary framework, engaged in activities to counter technical monopo-
> lies and to overcome neighborhood effects widely regarded as suffi-
> ciently important to justify government intervention, and which
> supplemented private charity and the private family in protecting the
> irresponsible, whether madman or child—such a government would
> clearly have important functions to perform. The consistent liberal is not
> an anarchist.*

The antigovernment position of Conservatives in fact goes further than merely pointing out the dangers to individual freedom.
To Conservatives the growth of big government itself causes or worsens economic problems. For instance, the growth of elaborate government policies to improve the conditions of labor, such as minimum-
wage laws and social security protection, are seen as actually harming
labor in general. A wage higher than that determined by the market
will provide greater income for some workers, but, the Conservative argument runs, it will reduce the total demand for labor, and
thus dump many workers into unemployment. As this example
indicates, the Conservative assault on big government is seen not
simply as a moral or ethical question but also in terms of alleged economic effects.

Another unifying feature of the representative Conservative argument is its emphasis on individualism and individual freedom. To be
sure, there are those in the Conservative tradition who pay only lip
service to this view, but for true Conservatives it is the centerpiece of
their logic. As Friedman has expressed it:

*Milton Friedman, *Capitalism and Freedom* (Chicago: University of Chicago Press,
1962), p. 34.

We take freedom of the individual . . . as the ultimate goal in judging social arguments. . . . In a society freedom has nothing to say about what an individual does with his freedom; it is not an all-embracing ethic. Indeed, the major aim of the liberal [here meaning Conservative as we use the term] is to leave the ethical problem for the individual to wrestle with.*

Modern Conservatives as a group exhibit a wide range of special biases. Not all are as articulate or logically consistent as Friedman's Chicago school. Many are identified more readily by what they oppose than by what they seem to be for. Big government, in both its microeconomic interferences and its macroeconomic policy-making, is the most obvious common enemy, but virtually any institutionalized interference with individual choice is at least ceremonially opposed.

Some critics of the Conservative position are quick to point out that most modern-day Conservatives are not quite consistent on the question of individual freedom when they focus on big business. In fact, until comparatively recently, Conservatives usually did demand the end of business concentration. Like all concentrations of power, it was viewed as an infringement on individual rights. The Conservative Austrian economist Joseph Schumpeter argued that "Big Business is a half-way house on the road to Socialism." The American Conservative Henry C. Simons observed in the depressed 1930s that "the great enemy to democracy is monopoly." Accounting for the change to a more accommodating position on big business is not easy. Conservatives offer two basic reasons. First, big business and the so-called monopoly problem have been watched for a long period of time, and the threat of their power subverting freedom is seen as vastly overstated. Second, by far the larger problem is the rise of big government, which is cited as the greatest cause of business inefficiency and monopoly misuse. Another factor that seems implied in Conservative writing is the fear of communism and socialism. To direct an assault on the American business system, even if existing business concentration were a slight impediment to freedom, would lay that system open to direct Radical attack. How serious this supposed contradiction in Conservative logic really is remains a matter of debate among its critics.

*Ibid., p. 12.

The Recent Resurgence of Conservative Economic Ideas In the United States, until the drab years of the Great Depression, what we now call "Conservative economics" *was* economics, period. Except for an occasional voice challenging the dominant wisdom, usually to little effect, few economists, political leaders, or members of the public at large disagreed greatly with Adam Smith's emphasis on individual freedom and on a free market economic condition.

The Depression years, however, brought a strong reaction to this kind of political and economic thinking. Many—perhaps most—of the millions of Americans who were out of work in the 1930s and the millions more who hung on to their jobs by their teeth came to believe that a "free" economy was simply one in "free fall." While most staunch Conservatives complained bitterly about the abandonment of market economics and the "creeping socialism" of Franklin Roosevelt's New Deal, they had few listeners. For thirty-two of the next forty-eight years after FDR's election in 1932, the White House, and usually the Congress, was in "Liberal" Democratic hands. For Conservatives, however, perhaps the greater losses were in the universities, where the old free market "truths" of Adam Smith and his disciples quickly fell out of style. In their place, a generation of professors espoused the virtues of the "New Economics" of John Maynard Keynes and the view that a capitalist economy "requires" government intervention to keep it from destroying itself.

Driven to the margins of academic and political influence by the 1970s, the Conservatives seemed in danger of joining the dinosaur and the dodo bird as an extinct species. However, by the late 1970s, in the aftermath of Vietnam and the Watergate scandal and in a period when nothing government did seemed able to control domestic inflation and unemployment problems, there developed a growing popular reaction against government in general. As more and more Americans came to believe that government economic and social interventions were the cause of the nation's maladies, the Conservative ideology took off again under its own power.

In 1980, the Conservative economic and political paradigm succeeded in recapturing the White House. Ronald Reagan became the first president since Herbert Hoover to come to office after a private-sector career. There was no doubting Reagan's philosophical commitment to the principles of a free enterprise economy.

As might be expected, Conservatives found themselves facing a difficult situation. Implementing a free market policy was, of course, much easier to accomplish in theory than in the real world— especially in a world vastly more complex than that envisioned by Adam Smith. "Reaganomics," the popular catchword for the new brand of Conservative economics, was quickly and sorely tested as the economy slipped into a deep recession in late 1981. To both friendly and hostile critics, Conservatives responded that quick solutions were not possible since the economic debris of a half-century needed to be swept aside before the economy could be reconstructed. Despite the fact that Reaganomics proved to be somewhat less than an unqualified success (indeed, a good many Conservatives would now call it a failure), the Reagan years were a time of moderate but sustained economic boom—the longest peacetime boom in American history. Despite some dark clouds—the near-tripling of the federal debt, a worsening international trade situation, and Black Monday— the Reagan–Bush 1980s remained, in economic terms, a comparatively bright period in American economic history. Meanwhile, the collapse of communism in Eastern Europe and the Soviet Union's shift toward a more open economic and political system in the last years of the decade could only be counted as frosting on Conservatives' ideological cake. As America entered the last decade of the century, Conservatives basked in the sunlight of success. Important for our study is the fact that a wide range of Conservative economic ideas and political perspectives that had been shunned in serious academic debates for over forty years have again made their way back into economics textbooks.

THE LIBERAL PARADIGM

According to a national poll, Americans tend to associate the term *Liberal* with big government, Franklin Roosevelt, labor unions, and welfare. Time was, not too long ago, when Liberal stood not just as a proud appellation but seemed to characterize the natural drift of the whole country. At the height of his popularity and before the Vietnam War toppled his administration, Lyndon Johnson, speaking of the new Liberal consensus, observed:

After years of ideological controversy, we have grown used to the new relationship between government, households, business, labor and agriculture. The tired slogans that made constructive discourse difficult have lost their meaning for most Americans. It has become abundantly clear that our society wants neither to turn backward the clock of history nor to discuss the present problems in a doctrinaire or partisan spirit.*

Although what we will identify as the Liberal position in American economic thought probably still dominates the teaching and practice of economic reasoning (as we shall see, even some Conservatives have adopted elements of the Liberal analysis), the Liberal argument is undergoing considerable changes. These changes, however, are more cosmetic than basic, and the central contours of Liberal belief are still visible.

The "Interventionist" Faith Whereas Conservatives and Radicals are comparatively easily identified by a representative position, Liberals are more difficult to identify. In terms of public policy positions, the Liberal spectrum ranges all the way from those favoring a very moderate level of government intervention to those advocating broad government planning of the economy.

Despite the great distance between the defining poles of Liberal thought, several basic points can be stated as unique to the Liberal paradigm. Like their Conservative counterparts, Liberals are defenders of the principle of private property and the business system. These, however, are not categorical rights, as we observed in the Conservative case. Individual claims to property or the ability to act freely in the marketplace are subject to the second Liberal principle— that social welfare and the maintenance of the entire economy supersede individual interest. In a vicious condemnation of what we would presently call the Conservative position, John Maynard Keynes directly assaulted the philosophy that set the individual over society. Keynes argued:

> It is not true that individuals possess a prescriptive "natural liberty" in their economic activities. There is no "compact" conferring perpetual rights on those who Have or on those who Acquire. The world is not so governed from above that private and social interest always coincide. It is

*The Economic Report of the President, 1965 (Washington, D.C.: U.S. Government Printing Office, 1965), p. 39.

not a correct deduction from the Principles of Economics that enlightened self-interest always operates in the public interest. Nor is it true that self-interest generally is enlightened; more often individuals acting separately to promote their own ends are too ignorant or too weak to attain even these. Experience does not show that individuals, when they make up a social unit, are always less clear-sighted than when they act separately.*

To the Liberal, then, government intervention in, and occasional direct regulation of, aspects of the national economy is neither a violation of principle nor an abridgment of "natural economic law." The benefits to the whole society from intervention simply outweigh any "natural right" claims. The forms of intervention may vary, but their pragmatic purpose is obvious — to tinker and manipulate in order to produce greater social benefits.

Government intervention in the economy dates from the very beginnings of the nation, but the Progressives of the early twentieth century were the first to successfully urge an extensive and systematic elaboration of governmental economic powers. In response to the excesses of giant enterprises in the era of the Robber Barons, the Progressives followed a number of paths in the period from 1900 to 1920. One was the regulation of monopoly power, to be accomplished either through antitrust prosecutions to restore competition or through the use of independent regulatory commissions in cases where a "break them up" policy was undesirable (for instance, railroads and other firms possessing *public utility* characteristics). A second was indirect business regulation effected by such Progressive developments as legalization of unions, the passage of social legislation at both the federal and state levels, tax reforms, and controls over production (for example, laws against food adulteration) — all of which circumvented the power of business and subjected it to the public interest.

Although the legislation and leadership of the administrations of Theodore Roosevelt, William Howard Taft, and Woodrow Wilson went a long way in moderating the old laissez-faire ideology of the previous era, actual interference in business affairs remained slight until the Great Depression. By 1933 perhaps as many as one out of

*John M. Keynes, "The End of Laissez Faire," in *Essays in Persuasion* (New York: Norton, 1963), p. 68.

every three Americans was out of work (the official figures said 25 percent), business failures were common, and the specter of total financial and production collapse hung heavy over the whole country. In the bread lines and shantytowns known as "Hoovervilles" as well as on Main Street, there were serious mutterings that the American business system had failed. Business leaders, who had always enjoyed hero status in the history books and even among ordinary citizens, had become pariahs. Enter at this point Franklin Roosevelt, the New Deal, and the modern formulation of "Liberal" government–business policies. Despite violent attacks on him from the Conservative media, FDR pragmatically abandoned his own conservative roots and, in a bewildering series of legislative enactments and presidential decrees, laid the foundation of "public interest" criteria for government regulation of the marketplace. *Whatever might work was tried.* The National Recovery Administration (NRA) encouraged industry cartels and price setting. The Tennessee Valley Authority (TVA) was an attempt at publicly owned enterprise. At the Justice Department, Attorney General Thurman Arnold initiated more antitrust actions than all of his predecessors combined. And a mass of "alphabet agencies" was created to deal with this or that aspect of the Depression.

Intervention to protect labor and extensions of social welfare provisions were not enough to end the Depression. It was the massive spending for World War II that finally restored prosperity. With this prosperity came the steady influence of Keynes, who had argued in the 1930s that only through government fiscal and monetary efforts to keep up the demand for goods and services could prosperity be reached and maintained. Keynes's arguments for government policies to maintain high levels of investment and hence employment and consumer demand became Liberal dogma. To be a Liberal was to be a Keynesian, and vice versa.

Alvin Hansen, Keynes's first and one of his foremost proponents in the United States, could scarcely hide his glee in 1957 as he described the wedding of Liberal Keynesian policies with the older government interventionist position this way:

> Within the last few decades the role of the economist has profoundly changed. And why? The reason is that economics has become operational. It has become operational because we have at long last developed a mixed public-private economy. This society is committed to the welfare

state and full employment. This government is firmly in the driver's seat. In such a world, practical policy problems became grist for the mill of economic analysis. Keynes, more than any other economist of our time, has helped to rescue economics from the negative position to which it had fallen to become once again a science of the Wealth of Nations and the art of Political Economy.*

Despite the Liberal propensity for tinkering—either through selected market intervention or through macro policy action—most Liberals, like Conservatives, still rely on traditional supply-and-demand analysis to explain prices and market performance. Their differences with Conservatives on the functioning of the markets, determination of output, pricing, and so forth lie not so much in describing what is happening as in evaluating how to respond to what is happening. For instance, there is little theoretical difference between Conservatives and Liberals on how prices are determined under monopolistic conditions. However, to the Conservative, the market itself is the best regulator and preventive of monopoly abuse. To the Liberal, monopoly demands government intervention.

Varieties of Liberal Belief   As noted before, the Liberal dogma covers a wide spectrum of opinion. Moreover, the Liberal position has shifted somewhat in response to the 1970s' economic disappointments and certain successes of the Reagan years.

On the extreme "left wing" of the Liberal spectrum, economists such as Robert Heilbroner and John Kenneth Galbraith have long argued that capitalism as the self-regulating system analyzed in conventional economic theory simply does not exist. Heilbroner contends: "The persistent breakdowns of the capitalist economy, whatever their immediate precipitating factors, can all be traced to a single underlying cause. This is the anarchic or planless character of capitalist production."† For a time, this critical defect led Heilbroner to flirt with "central planning" as the only possible "cure." However, he has recently backed away from this position, holding instead that capitalism plus government regulation to provide periodic corrections has proved to be more durable than central planning efforts.

To the left-leaning and always iconoclastic John Kenneth Galbraith, who sees problems of technology rather than profit dominating the

*Alvin H. Hansen, *The American Economy* (New York: McGraw-Hill, 1957), p. 175.
†Robert Heilbroner, *The Limits of American Capitalism* (New York: Harper & Row, 1966), p. 88.

giant corporation, a more rational atmosphere for decision making must be created. In brief, the modern firm demands a high order of internal and external planning of output, prices, and capital. The interests of the firm and state become fused in this planning process, and the expanded role of Liberal government in the whole economy and society becomes obvious. While Galbraith has in the past maintained that he was a socialist, the Liberal outcome of his program is obvious in that he (1) never explicitly takes up the expropriation of private property, and (2) still accepts a precarious social balance between public and private interest.

Although Galbraith's Liberalism leads to the planned economy, most Liberals stop well before this point. Having rejected the logic of self-regulating markets and accepted the realities of giant business enterprise, Liberals unashamedly admit to being pragmatic tinkerers — ever adjusting and interfering with business decision making in an effort to assert the changing "public interest." Yet all this must be done while still respecting basic property rights and due process. Under these arrangements, business regulation amounts to a protection of business itself as well as the equal protection of other interest groups in pluralist American society.

In the not-too-distant past, business itself adapted to and embraced this position. Whereas certain government actions might be opposed, the philosophy of government intervention in the economy was not necessarily seen as antibusiness. The frequent Conservative depiction of most Liberals as being opposed to the business system does not withstand the empirical test. For instance, in 1964 Henry Ford II organized a highly successful committee of business leaders for Liberal Lyndon Johnson, while Conservative Barry Goldwater, with Friedman as his adviser, gained little or no big-business support. However, the extent of government regulation soon reached a level that was wholly unacceptable to the private sector. In the late 1960s and early 1970s, a blizzard of environmental, job safety, consumer protection, and energy regulations blew out of Washington. Added to what was already on the ground, the new legislative snowfall seemed to many observers at the end of the 1970s about to bring American business to a standstill. Many who a decade before frankly feared the economic "freedom" of the Conservative vision now embraced that position.

The distress of economic "stagflation" in the 1970s (lower growth, rising unemployment, *and* price inflation), for which the Liberals seemed to have no programmatic cures, along with a growing popular sentiment against "big government" in general, drove Liberals from positions of political influence. Even within universities, the Liberal consensus began to collapse, with some former Liberal theorists deserting to the Conservative camp and most others adopting a lower profile in their teaching, writing, and research. Yet by the end of the 1980s, most of the analytical and policy positions associated with Liberal economic reasoning still survived—a bit subdued from the high-flying days of Kennedy's New Frontier and Johnson's Great Society but distinguishable nonetheless. Among the more reform-minded Liberal reasoners, the old economic agenda items— income distribution, discrimination, the environment, consumer protection, monopoly abuse, labor unions, structural shifts in the economy and their resulting dislocations—remained vital concerns in any policy-making effort. However, Liberal hopes for a fairly swift and sweeping resolution of these problems had diminished greatly from the expectations of the 1960s and early 1970s. The new realities of a slow growth economy, massive federal deficits, reduced American competitiveness in world markets, and costly entitlement programs put serious constraints on even a visionary reformer's dedication to interventionism. But this commitment had not been extinguished. When the Eastern European Communist states toppled like dominoes and the long time cold war confrontation with the Soviet Union seemed to move steadily toward a peaceful end, there was brave talk among Liberals of the prospects for a "peace dividend." The ending of the cold war was envisioned as freeing up vast sums for favored social agenda items that had long been shelved.

Meanwhile, in the business community, the old propensity to enlist government on the side of "improving" the stability of domestic markets was given new life in the face of rising foreign competition, the decline of certain basic industries, and the double frights provided by Black Monday and the savings-and-loan industry crisis. In particular, the last two events seemed to show that too much market freedom might not be as desirable as it sounded.

The present-day ambivalence of Liberals on the degree and type of intervention will be evident in our survey of economic issues in this book; nevertheless, this tendency should not be misunderstood. Specific Liberal approaches to problem solving may be debatable, but the essence of Liberal economics remains unchanged: The capitalist economy simply requires pragmatic adjustment from time to time to maintain overall balance and to protect particular elements in the society.

THE RADICAL PARADIGM

Specifying a Radical position would have been no problem three or four decades ago. Outside of a handful of Marxist scholars, some socialists left over from the 1920s and 1930s, and a few unconventional muckrakers, there was no functioning Radical tradition in American economic thought. However, the two-sided struggles of the 1960s over racism and poverty at home and the war in Vietnam produced a resurgence of Radical critiques. By the mid-1970s, the Radical caucus within the American Economic Association had forced on that body topics for discussion at annual meetings that directly challenged conventional economic thought. The Union of Radical Political Economics (URPE) boasted over 2,000 members and its own journal. Meanwhile, basic textbooks in economics began to add chapters on "Radical economics."

The Marxist Heritage By the early 1970s, Radical economics had arrived—but what, precisely, was it? To many non-Radicals, it was simply Marxist economics warmed over, but this explanation, though basically true, is too simple. To be sure, the influence of Marx, the leading critic of capitalism, is pervasive in most Radical critiques. But Radical economics is more than Marx. Marx's analysis of capitalism is over a hundred years old and deals with a very different set of capitalist problems. (In Marx's time, capitalism was only in the beginning stages of industrial development and was still characterized by small entrepreneurs carrying on essentially merchant capitalist undertakings.) With this qualification in mind, we will argue, however, that no study of current Radical thought is possible unless one starts with, or at least touches on, the ideas of Karl Marx. Although a few iconoclastic Radicals will reject a close association with Marxism, the evidence is overwhelming that Marxist analysis is central to understanding the representative Radical position in America today.

Since the Marxist critique is likely to be less familiar to many readers than the basic arguments of Conservatives or Liberals, it is necessary to be somewhat more detailed in specifying the Radical position. As will be quickly apparent, the Radical world view rests on greatly different assumptions about the economic and social order than those of the Conservatives and Liberals.

According to Marx's view, the value of a commodity reflects the real labor time necessary to produce it. However, under capitalism workers lack control of their labor, selling it as they must to capitalists. The workers receive only a fraction of the value they create—according to Marx, only an amount sufficient in the long run to permit subsistence. The rest of the value—what Marx calls "surplus value"—is retained by capitalists as the source of their profits and for the accumulation of capital that will increase both future production and future profit. As the appropriation of surplus value proceeds, with the steady transference of living labor into capital (what Marx called "dead labor"), capitalists face an emerging crisis. With more and more of their production costs reflecting their growing dependence on capital (machines) and with surplus labor value their only source of profit, capitalists are confronted with the reality of not being able to expand surplus appropriation. Unless they are able to increase their exploitation of labor—getting more output for the same, or less, wages paid—they face a falling rate of profit on their growing capital investment. Worse still, with workers' relatively falling wages and capitalists' relatively increasing capacity to produce, there is a growing tendency for the entire capitalist system to produce more goods than it can in fact sell.

These trends set certain systemic tendencies in motion. Out of the chaos of capitalist competitive struggles for profits in a limited market there develops a drive toward "concentration and centralization." In other words, the size of businesses grows and the number of enterprises shrinks. However, the problems of the falling rate of profit and chronic overproduction create violent fluctuations in the business cycle. Each depression points ever more clearly toward capitalist economic collapse. Meanwhile, among the increasingly impoverished workers, there is a steady growth of a "reserve army of unemployed"—workers who are now unemployable as production decreases. Simultaneously, increasing misery generates class consciousness and revolutionary activity among the working class. As the economic disintegration of capitalist institutions worsens, the subjective consciousness of workers grows to the point where they successfully overthrow the capitalist system. In the new society, the workers themselves take control of the production process, and accumulation for the interest of a narrow capitalist class ceases.

The Modern Restatement of Marx Of necessity, the modern Radical's view of the world must lack the finality of Marx's predictions. Quite simply, the capitalist system has not self-destructed and, in fact, in a good many respects is stronger and more aggressive than it was in Marx's day. Although the present-day Radical may still agree with Marx's long-run predictions about the ultimate self-destructiveness of the capitalist order, the fact is that *relevant* Radicals must deal with the world as it is. While the broad categories of Marx's analysis are retained generally, Radical thought must focus on real-world, current conditions of capitalist society and present an analysis that goes beyond merely asserting the Marxist scenario for capitalist collapse. Useful economic analysis must be offered in examining contemporary problems.

The beginning point for modern Radical critiques, as it was also for Marx over a hundred years ago, is the unquenchable capitalist thirst for profits. This central organizing objective of all capitalist systems determines everything else within those systems. The Radical analysis begins with a simple proposition about how capitalists understand market activity:

Total sales = total cost of materials and machinery used up in production + total wages and salaries paid + (− in the case of losses) total profits

Such a general view of sales, costs, and profits is, thus far, perfectly consistent with traditional accounting concepts acceptable to any Conservative or Liberal. However, the Radical's analytic mission becomes clearer when the proposition is reformulated:

Total profits = total sales − total cost of materials and machinery used up in production − total wages and salaries paid

It now becomes evident that increasing profits depends on three general conditions: (1) that sales rise, *ceteris paribus* (all things being equal); (2) that production costs (composed of wage costs and material and machinery costs) decline, *ceteris paribus*; or (3) that sales increases at least exceed production cost increases. The capitalist, according to the Radical argument, is not simply interested in total profits but also in the "rate of profit," or the ratio of profits to the amount of capital the capitalist has invested.

With capitalist eyes focused on raising profits or raising profit rates, it becomes clear to Radicals which individual economic policies and strategies will be advanced by capitalists: *Every effort will be made to keep costs low*, such as reducing wage rates, speeding up the production line, introducing so-called labor-saving machines, seeking cheaper (often foreign) sources of labor and materials, and minimizing outlays for waste treatment and environmental maintenance. At the same time, *efforts will be made to keep prices high*, especially through the development of monopolistic price-making power on both a national and an international scale. In all these activities, capitalists will make every effort to use government economic intervention to their own advantage—both in domestic markets and in expanding capitalist hegemony into the world.

However, the efforts of individual capitalists—either on their own or aided by government—to expand profit produces, taking the system as a whole, a crisis in obtaining profits. For instance, the capitalist goals of keeping wages low and prices high must lead to situations where workers as consumers simply cannot clear the market of available goods. Accordingly, the aggregate economy deteriorates into periodic recession or depression, with rising unemployment among workers and falling profits for capitalists. With capitalist support, a variety of government monetary and fiscal efforts may be employed to offset these ups and downs in the capitalist business cycle—in particular to improve the profit and profit-rate situations of capitalist enterprises. However, so-called mixed capitalism (a mixture of private-sector and government planning of the economy) cannot overcome the fundamental contradictions of a dominantly private, production-for-profit economy. And, of course, with the expansion of capitalism throughout most of the world, the capitalist crisis takes on international proportions. Quite as Marx predicted, the general economic crises deepen and occur more frequently. The search for profit becomes more frantic and more destructive to the lives of ever greater numbers of people living under capitalist hegemony throughout the world.

From the Radical point of view, periodic crisis in capitalism is not the result of excessive tinkering with the market system, as Conservatives claim; nor will the tendency toward crisis be contained by Liberal interventionism. *Periodic and deepening crisis is capitalism.*

Radical analysis is, of course, more penetrating than this short résumé can indicate. One further point that should be examined briefly is Marx's view of the relationship between a society's organization for production and its social relations. To Marx, capitalism was more than an economic system. Private values, religion, the family, the educational system, and political structures were all shaped by capitalist class domination and by the goal of production for private profit. It is important to recognize this tenet in any discussion of how Marxists – or Radicals with a Marxist orientation – approach contemporary social and economic problems. Marxists do not separate economics from politics or private belief. For instance, racism cannot be abstracted to the level of an ethical question. Its roots are seen in the capitalist production process. Nor is the state ever viewed as a neutrality able to act without class bias. Bourgeois democracy as we know it is seen simply as a mask for class domination.

Marx, in his early writings before his great work, *Capital,* had emphasized the "qualitative" exploitation of capitalism. Modern Radicals have revitalized this early Marx in their "quality of life" assaults on the present order. In these they emphasize the problems of worker alienation, commodity fetishism, and the wasteful and useless production of modern capitalism. The human or social problems of modern life are seen as rooted in the way the whole society is geared to produce more and more profits.

In addition to their Marxist heritage, modern Radicals derive much of their impulse from what they see as the apparent failure of Liberalism. Liberal promises to pursue policies of general social improvement are perceived as actions to protect only *some* interest groups. In general, those benefiting under Liberal arrangements are those who have always gained. The corporation is not controlled. It is more powerful than ever. Rule by elites has not ended, nor have the elites changed. Moreover, the national goals of the Liberal ethic – to improve our overall national well-being – have stimulated the exploitation of poor nations, continued the cold war, and increased the militarization of the economy.

The Question of Relevance   Quite obviously, the Marxist prediction of capitalism's final collapse has not yet come to pass. In fact, Radicals—particularly those very closely associated with the Marxist tradition—are increasingly obliged to account for what many non-Radicals see as an historical turning away from all collectivist political economic alternatives with the rise of market economics in previously socialist states. Glasnost and perestroika in Gorbachev's Russia, the encouragement of entrepreneurialism in China (despite the Beijing Spring Riots of 1989), the political collapse of communism in Central Europe, and the drift toward market economics in Poland, East Germany, Hungary, Bulgaria, and Czechosolovakia are readily cited by critics as proof that Marxism and its practical political manifestation, communism, are dead. These trends, along with certain internal analytical problems of Marxist analysis, are quite sufficient for most non-Radicals to consign the whole Radical paradigm to the garbage heap of worthless, worn-out ideas.

A thoughtful observer may question whether this is an entirely enlightened conclusion to reach. First, the tendency to lump Marxism and real-world Communist systems together as one and the same, while long a habit in the non-Communist as well as the Communist world, rests on a grossly inaccurate understanding of Marx's philosophy. Second, Marxism—at least as American Radical scholars have developed and used it—is more a way of looking at how our economy works than a prophecy of things to come. It is the technique of analysis rather than the century-old "truth" of Marx's specific analysis that counts.

As noted before, not all Radicals subscribe to all Marxist doctrine, but Marxism in one form or another remains the central element of the Radical challenge. Marx's fundamental contention that the system of private production must be changed remains the badge of membership in the Radical ranks. This sets Radicals apart from mainstream Conservative and Liberal economists.

Critics of Radicalism usually point out that Radical analyses are hopelessly negativistic. Radicals, they say, describe the problems of capitalism without offering a solution other than the end of the whole system. While there is much truth to this charge, we shall see in the following sections that indeed some solutions are offered. But even if their program is vague, Radicals would argue that their greatest contribution is in revealing the truth of the capitalist system.

Despite lessened political influence, modern Radical economic thought still looms as a logically important alternative to the more broadly supported Conservative and Liberal paradigms. The force of an idea is not dependent on the number of true believers. Were that the case, Conservative economic doctrine would have disappeared thirty years ago.

Applying the Analysis to the Issues

We have identified representative paradigms; now we will put them to use. The following selected issues by no means exhaust the economic and political crises troubling the nation; nevertheless, they provide a good-sized sampling of the social agenda confronting us. The issues presented here were selected because of their immediacy and representativeness in illustrating the diverse ideological approaches of Conservative, Liberal, and Radical economic analyses.

In each of the following issues, the representative paradigms are presented in a *first-person advocacy approach*. The reader might do well to regard the arguments like those in a debate. As in a debate, one should be careful to distinguish between substantive differences and mere logical or debating strategies. Thus some points may be quite convincing whereas others seem shallow. However, the reader should remember that, shallow or profound, these are representative political economic arguments advanced by various economic schools.

The sequence in presenting the paradigms is consistent throughout the text: first Conservative, then Liberal, then Radical. In terms of the logical and historical development of contemporary economic ideologies, this sequence is most sensible; however, it is certainly not necessary to read the arguments in this order. Each one stands by itself. Nor is any ideological position intentionally set out as a straw man in any debate.

Readers should look at each position critically. They should test their own familiarity with economic concepts and their common sense against what they read in any representative case. Finally, of course, as students of economics and as citizens, they must make their own decisions. They determine who, if anyone, is the winner of the debate.

Because of space limitations, the representative arguments are brief, and some important ideas have been boiled down to a very few

Alternative Economic Philosophies: Applying the Analysis to the Issues   31

sentences. Also, within each of the three major positions there is a wide range of arguments, which may sometimes be at variance with one another. Conservatives, Liberals, and Radicals disagree among themselves on specific analyses and programs. For the sake of simplicity, we have chosen not to emphasize these differences but arbitrarily (although after much thought) have tried to select the most representative arguments. Each paradigm's discussion of an issue presents a critique of present public policy and, usually, a specific program proposal.

In all of the arguments, the factual and empirical evidence offered has been checked for accuracy. It is instructive in itself that, given the nature of economic "facts," they can be marshaled to "prove" a great variety of different ideological positions. Different or even similar evidence supports different truths, depending on the truth we wish to prove.

PROBLEMS IN THE MARKETPLACE

Part 2 focuses on issues generally accepted by economists as *micro-economic* in their analysis. Microeconomics examines specific economic units—households, firms, industries, labor groups—and the behavior of these individual units.

The focal point of formal microeconomic analysis since its nineteenth-century origins has been the market. Accordingly, Part 2 looks at selected problems in the marketplace. Topics include problems of agricultural supply and demand, consumer market behavior, environmental economics, firm size, government regulation, productivity, labor unions, and income distribution. Each topic presents some important dimension of market performance; each has been selected for its representative qualities in developing a broadened understanding of microeconomic problems within the contemporary American economy.

American Agriculture
Which Route: Competition or Protection?

Farmers should raise less corn and more Hell.
Mary E. Lease, Kansas, 1890s

Farmers are motivated by just old-fashioned greed.
Robert Berland, Secretary of Agriculture, 1979

You can't farm $1,500-an-acre land. It'll take all you can
produce to pay the interest.
Bandy Jacobs, Nebraska farmer, 1982

We produce too much food in this country.
Marty Strange, Farmer Advocacy Group, 1982

Because farmers are provided an incentive to make cropping
decisions according to program rules rather than market signals, the [farm] programs reduce the responsiveness of U.S.
agriculture to changes in world market conditions and reduce
its international competitiveness.
Economic Report of the President, 1990

THE PROBLEM

The teaching of economic reasoning usually begins with a general examination of the market model and, more particularly, with a consideration of how the market determines production, pricing, and resource allocation under conditions of pure competition. Such an introduction to economics presents the beginner almost immediately with a confusing irony. On the one hand, markets for agricultural goods would seem to be especially appropriate for illustrating the general conditions of competition because they are dominated by many small producers selling virtually identical products to a very broad range of consumers. Thus agriculture should be a marvelously useful example of the market forces of supply and demand at work, and introductory textbooks invariably use wheat, corn, or some other farm product when they begin constructing simple analytical models.

In the real world, on the other hand, agricultural markets illustrate a quite contrary tendency. Here we do not find competition and free-flowing market forces, but rather some of the most elaborate efforts ever devised to insulate an industry from the market and to employ government intervention to promote private objectives. Agricultural output and pricing decisions actually are directly affected by a price support program that has been in place in one form or another for almost sixty years. Meanwhile, a variety of government agencies provide emergency aid of staggering proportions. In fact, annual payments of emergency loans and other funds in excess of $25 billion or more per year were not uncommon in the middle of the 1980s, as net farm income (in real dollars) hovered near the levels it had been in the Great Depression decade.

The condition of American agriculture has not always been one of unrelenting crisis, but the "farm problem" has been around, on and off again, for most of the twentieth century. The rhythm of farm fortune and misfortune has been like this: First, World War I created an exceptional demand for American farm products to feed soldiers and starving civilians. With rising prices resulting, farmers increased their output, but, in the 1920s and 1930s, after production increased, foreign demand for American farm products declined and prices plummeted. The deepening depression after 1930 soon transformed the growing agricultural crisis into a full-blown catastrophe. With the coming of the New Deal in 1933, the federal government introduced numerous market interventions aimed at artificially raising or maintaining prices. These actions laid the

FIGURE 1.1 Net Income of Farm Operators from Farming, 1970–1988

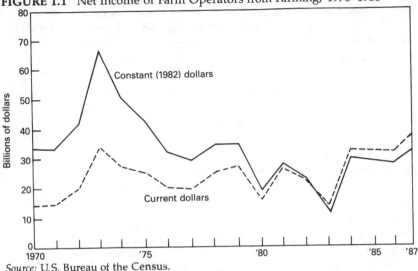

Source: U.S. Bureau of the Census.

economic and political foundations for what was to become a long-term, if not actually permanent, government intervention in agricultural markets. World War II pumped up demand and farm prices, but peace again brought tumbling prices and reliance on government support programs. Several Russian grain deals in the 1970s returned good times for a few years; however, farmers were soon caught up in new problems—a few of which were of their own making. Figure 1.1 illustrates the roller coaster ride that American farm income has taken since 1970.

As farm exports rose in the mid-1970s and farm prices and income followed, American farmers developed a false sense of newfound security. Planting "fencepost to fencepost" became common. Many farmers undertook considerable acquisitions of additional land and new equipment, swelling their mortgage and loan obligations. Farm debt tripled between 1973 and 1983. Few farmers paid much attention to the fact that interest rates on their new loans were high and rising during most of this period. The farm mood was upbeat, and many farmers thought they had finally escaped from the traditional boom-bust cycle of the agricultural economy.

What farmers failed to foresee, however, were the wrenching economic events of the late 1970s and early 1980s. The general rise in prices of the inflationary last half of the 1970s raised fuel, machinery, and interest costs. And agricultural prices failed to keep pace with costs. The world market that so many farmers had counted on failed to materialize. In 1980, in retaliation for the Soviet invasion of Afghanistan, President Carter placed an embargo on grain sales to the Soviet Union. Even after the embargo was lifted, sales did not improve. Worse still, although the inflationary period began to draw to a close in 1981, prices of American farm products remained high in world markets. With the American dollar strong among international currencies, prices of all American products remained relatively high compared to foreign goods. As a result, overseas sales for American farmers declined, and cheaper foreign agricultural goods began to penetrate American domestic markets.

Farmers were suddenly caught in a worsening price-cost squeeze. Burdened with large mortgages and loans with high interest rates, and with their credit (borrowing ability) shrinking as disinflation caused land values to tumble, many farmers watched their real income and ability to borrow deteriorate. Financial collapse was inevitable for many, and in some areas farm bankruptcy was followed by the collapse of local banks that held farm loans and mortgages.

And nature got its licks in too. The disastrous drought of 1988 reduced corn production 30 percent and soybean output by 20 percent. Similar declines were reported in livestock production. The drought had differential effects across American agriculture. Farmers already hard-pressed by debts, who lost most of their crops, were in worse shape. But others who were able to produce benefitted as reductions in agricultural product supply drove prices upward. In some cases the price gains more than offset the losses in output. However, the overall effect of the weather changed very little in American agriculture as the 1980s came to a close.

During this recent period of crisis, farmers attempted to use their political muscle by lobbying for government aid. In past bad times—the 1930s, 1950s, and 1960s, for instance—the government had responded with a variety of programs, some purely of an emergency nature and others that were built into the economic structure of American agriculture. These efforts included tariffs on imported farm products, marketing boards, subsidy payments, output quotas, and payments for letting land lie idle, among many others. Whether or not these interventions had actually relieved farm distress or only served to worsen the chronic farm problem had long been a matter of debate among economists of different ideological persuasions. That debate had cooled a bit after the Russian grain deals, when farm prices were up and government intervention was at a minimum, but the new agricultural crisis of the early 1980s reopened all the old arguments.

The debate over agricultural policy remains an important issue and a profoundly significant theoretical question, since it goes to the very foundation of American economic belief; namely, do free and competitive markets work, or do they need constant repair and support by means of government intervention? Exactly how divided economists are on this question becomes apparent when we look at the policy alternatives proposed by our three paradigms.

SYNOPSIS

The Conservative position holds that the free operation of supply and demand is the correct and most effective determinant of agricultural prices. Liberals most frequently argue that an agricultural market left to itself is subject to wild cyclical fluctuation; thus a variety of government interventions are necessary to maintain reasonable order. Radicals see the American farm problem as a case of government being manipulated by agribusiness, with the result that government intervention has harmed both small farmers and ordinary consumers.

Anticipating the Arguments

- Why do Conservatives believe that most government efforts to help farmers by "artificially" raising crop prices actually hurt both farmers and consumers?
- What is the historical and economic foundation to the Liberal argument that farmers can't "depend" on unregulated farm markets?
- Why do Radicals believe that most farmers have been losers under both regulated and unregulated agricultural production in the United States?

The Conservative Argument

Discussions of the "American farm problem" almost always begin with a mistaken identification of what the problem really is. Most agricultural observers, including many economists writing on farm issues, suggest that there is something inherently unstable about American agriculture. Somehow, agriculture is presented as "proof" that the market economy simply does not work, that the free market forces of supply and demand break down. Conservatives agree that there is indeed a farm problem; however, that problems begins and remains in Washington, D.C., not in the corn and wheat fields of the Midwest or the commodities markets in Chicago. In other words, the American farm problem is not the result of some basic failure of the market, but rather the failure of federal policy to allow the market forces to work.

POLICY FAILURE IN TIMES OF SURPLUS

Although many politicians and some economists may believe and act to the contrary, supply and demand remain the only effective determinants of prices and resource allocation. Of course, it is possible to contrive "desired" prices and output through a manipulated agricultural policy, but regardless of short-run success, such policies must produce serious misallocations and costs in the long run.

For a considerable period of time, at least since World War I, most economists have seen the American farm problem as a matter of rising productivity with comparatively stable or modestly increasing demand. The result in the marketplace was a general and persistent downward pressure on farm prices. The economic options under such conditions were either to let prices fall to whatever level they might reach or to maintain prices artificially. Due largely to political pressure from the farm lobby in the depressed 1930s, the government devised a potpourri of farm programs to keep prices up and supposedly guarantee a living income to the American farmer. Tariffs were slapped on foreign farm products. Certain "basic" farm products were guaranteed a government-paid "parity" price well above the going market price. Bureaucrats worked out production controls and acreage allotments, with the curious economic aim of paying producers not to produce.

These tinkerings with the market forces of demand and supply, however, did not produce order in agricultural markets. Each intervention, regardless of its noble intentions, increased agricultural dependence on government price-setting efforts and, at the same time, heightened market instability. For their own part, farmers paid less and less attention to production signals from the marketplace and relied increasingly on the government to bail them out whenever farm income showed signs of falling. With the government establishing minimum price levels (using either parity price or target price mechanisms) and standing ready either to buy surplus production (before the 1970s) or, more recently, to provide loans secured by surplus output, there has been little incentive to pay attention to market forces. Except for two brief interludes—during World War II, when America virtually fed the world, and after the early Russian grain deals in the 1970s—farm prices and the income of most farmers have been held up only by government manipulation of crop prices.

THE PRICE OF FAILURE

The Cost to Consumers   The benefits accruing to the farm lobby from government intervention have only recently become recognized as costs to the general public. Americans have paid for government subsidies, tariffs, and production controls in two ways: First, the price of food in general has been higher than it would otherwise have been in a "free" agricultural market. For most Americans over most of the past sixty years, this higher price presented few problems. With the steady rise in American standards of living, the artificially higher food prices seemed quite tolerable, and as food expenditures declined as a share of total consumer purchases during the post–World War II years, the farm lobby met little resistance in its efforts to expand market intervention. Not until the inflationary 1970s did Americans show signs of balking at rising farm prices, and even then most of their anger was aimed at grocery chains and other middlemen.

Second, Americans, in a sense, must pay for their food *twice*. Consumers are also taxpayers, and as such they are obliged to shoulder the cost of expensive government subsidies—direct payments and low-cost loans—to farmers. Moreover, they have had to pay for the maintenance of an elaborate bureaucracy developed to administer the various farm programs. As with the higher farm product prices, this hidden second price was for a very long time ignored by most taxpayers, a cost somehow obscurely buried in the federal budget. However, with pressure growing recently to reduce government spending and to reverse the growth of government debt, this previously concealed second charge for food became more obvious. By

1985, federal price support and other income programs for farmers were costing the average American family $250 per year—for an agricultural program aimed in the first place at keeping tabletop food prices artificially high.

Inability to Sell Overseas   Meanwhile, higher American farm prices closed off U.S. food products from world markets. Due to climate, soil, technology, and agricultural science, American agriculture had an enormous advantage over the rest of the world in food production. This advantage, and the export income it would have created, was frittered away by programs aimed at keeping domestic prices relatively high. Precisely at a time when the United States faced a worsening balance of international payments (after World War II), the government pursued an agricultural program that denied the nation earnings it could have been making by exporting food.

The Russian grain deals of the mid-1970s brought a dramatic but brief reversal in agricultural export habits. In 1972, the Russians negotiated the purchase of 19 million metric tons of grain. For a number of years, Soviet leadership had been yielding to consumer pressure to produce more meat protein. Of necessity, this meant providing greater amounts of grain for beef in feeding lots. When the 1971 and 1972 crops failed to reach expectations, the Soviet leaders decided not to slaughter their beef herds or tell their people to eat potatoes and beets. They chose instead to buy U.S. grain and to allow their "protein program" to continue.

The Russian purchase in 1972–1973 was not a one-shot affair. Some 8 million metric tons of grain were sold to the Soviet Union in 1974 and about 3 million tons the next year. The Russians experienced crop failures again in 1975 and negotiated another sale—for 13 millions tons—for 1976. Although this sale was suspended temporarily when worldwide prospects of underproduction caused world and domestic grain prices to skyrocket, it was reinstituted when the bumper 1975 harvest came in. Meanwhile, the Soviet Union and the United States concluded long-term agreements for Russian purchase of 6 to 8 million tons of corn and wheat each year, with the American government reserving the right to curtail sales if reserves or domestic output fell too sharply.*

*During the "Afghan crisis" in 1980, sales to the Russians were halted briefly.

To growers and sellers, the "discovery" of the Russian market was a critical new direction for American agriculture; putting an end to the long era of chronic excess production, depressed prices, and dependence on government subsidy programs. By selling the equivalent of one-quarter of the 1972 crop, the Russian grain deal literally emptied American storage bins and grain elevators. This additional demand drove the prices of wheat from $1.70 per bushel in mid-1972 to $5.00 in 1973.

The trouble was, however, that commitment to free agricultural markets was unfamiliar, and when net farm income began to tumble in 1977 as the combined result of increases in production (a natural reaction to the increase in worldwide sales), a deepening worldwide recession, and worsening domestic inflation, farmers returned to their old habits. When the Agricultural Act was renewed in 1977, the farm lobby succeeded in setting target prices (the prices government will guarantee farmers through subsidies regardless of the going market prices) at about 25 percent higher than the existing world prices for most key crops. The "free market" experiment was over.

Insofar as government agricultural policy continues to "aid" farmers by artificially raising farm prices, farmers will be unable to exploit their efficiency and natural advantages in world food markets. Indeed, American farm prices are high enough to invite threats of agricultural imports. In 1985, Cargill, Inc., a large American grain trading company, determined that it was cheaper to import Argentine wheat, even with the transport and tariff costs, than to buy American wheat.*

*A final note must be added with regard to farmers' recent difficulty in selling overseas. With the value of the dollar high and rising in comparison to other world currencies during the early 1980s, American goods were expensive in foreign markets (since more pesos, pounds, and marks were needed to buy a dollar's worth of goods) and foreign goods were cheaper in the United States (since a dollar bought more goods denominated in pesos, pounds, or marks). The origin of this problem—which confronts all American producers, not just farmers—is traceable to the same mentality that created an expanded and expensive government intervention in agriculture. Quite simply, the general growth of government debt in the years of interventionist Liberal ascendency contributed to the long inflation of the 1970s, which in turn created a long period of high interest rates. High and rising interest rates in the United States made foreign owning of American dollars attractive—in a sense bidding up the price of dollars in world currency markets and thus raising the price of American goods overseas (and lowering the price of foreign goods in the United States). The cure to this aspect of the farm problem is simple enough (we shall examine the problem and cure in Issue 15): reduce government deficits, which in turn will bring about lower interest rates and readjustment in international currencies, making U.S. exports, including our valuable farm exports, more attractive.

FIGURE 1.2   Changes in Farming, 1950–1988

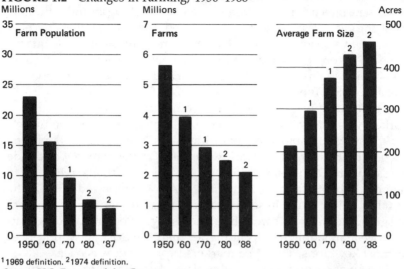

¹1969 definition. ²1974 definition.
Source: U.S. Bureau of the Census.

Maintaining Production Inefficiencies   Before taking up the question of production inefficiencies resulting from interventionist farm policies, we need first to square with reality the myth of the lonely and hardworking individual agriculturalist. The myth of the independent family farm is deeply ingrained in American popular belief and Liberal political posturing, and is the foundation of American farm policy. The irony is, however, that the small family farm has ceased to be an important supplier of foodstuffs. Figure 1.2 tells the story very quickly.

The farm population has fallen to about one-fifth of its 1950 level, while the number of farms has declined by more than half and average farm size has more than doubled over the same period. Figure 1.3 makes the point quite clearly: At present, 72 percent of the value of farm production is produced by just 13.5 percent of all operating farms. Moreover, less than 2 percent of all operating farms produce one-third of our food production.

The myth of the independent farmer is the basis for government subsidies — an effort to provide an income floor for the very poorest of farmers. The effect is to subsidize the least efficient farm producers at

FIGURE 1.3   Shares of Total Farm Sales by Farm Size, 1987

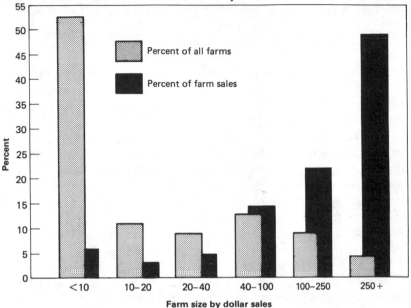

Source: Statistical Abstract of the United States, 1989.

the very bottom of the agricultural ladder (two-thirds of government payments go to small farms that produce only a quarter of the nation's output) and very large farms that do not need it. This expensive agricultural welfare system has discouraged the out-movement of marginal agricultural producers who might better shift their resources to other productive pursuits. Worse still, subsidies paid to large and efficient farm producers act as restraints on improving their existing efficiency and productivity.

So long as we approach the farmer as if we were protecting a rare bird from extinction, we will not benefit from the practical forces of the marketplace. We will sustain at great economic cost farmers who should stop farming and, at the same time, hold back the application of business management methods and technological advances among the farm enterprises most capable of exploiting new techniques. We must recognize that farming is a business and, mythology notwithstanding, should be open to the forces of a production-for-profit economy, just like the manufacture of automobiles or personal computers.*

TOWARD A NEW POLICY DIRECTION

A Conservative program for dealing with the nation's chronic agricultural problem is easily stated: *Let markets work.* This means ending all subsidies, special loan arrangements, crop control programs, target pricing, and other arrangements aimed at setting selling prices above free market prices. Falling agricultural prices (or at least a halt to their artificial rise) will have a number of salutary effects: First, it will be a direct benefit to American consumers. Second, it will expand American markets overseas. Lost revenues from lowered prices will be more than offset by expanded total sales. Third, the resulting emphasis on efficient and innovative use of productive resources in agriculture will create a strong, self-sufficient, and highly productive agricultural sector where the market actually directs resource inputs.

To be sure, reliance on the market will not be without some adjustment problems. Critics will be quick to point out the effect of short-term cycles in agriculture on production and prices: This year's high price causes next year's production to rise, increasing next year's supply faster than demand increases. The resultant lower prices lead to a reduction of supply in the next year and to a rise in prices, which in turn stimulate an increase in supply. According to many critics, this price instability perpetuates adverse effects alternately visited on consumers and then on farmers. The trouble with the argument is that no one has ever shown market-priced agricultural products to be more unstable than most other goods priced according to market forces of supply and demand. In fact, demand for agricultural goods is much more stable over time than demand for steel, automobiles, or even PCs. Moreover, a good deal of the volatility on the supply side is actually the result of government tinkering. There is a high probability that farm prices will fluctuate under a free market mechanism, but it is wrong to conclude that such fluctuations are undesirable. They are simply the market at work.

*Indeed, we should recognize the growing importance of business corporations in American agriculture. By 1987, 53,000 corporate farms, amounting to about 1 percent of all farms, produced more than a fifth of farm output in the United States.

Certainly price fluctuations will pose problems for farmers long accustomed to prices rigged by the government. The less efficient will find survival difficult. On the other hand, efficient family farms and farm corporations, applying the best production methods and determining output decisions on rational calculations of past *and* present market trends, should adjust quite nicely. Many small farm enterprises will fail, but this should be counted as no greater social loss than the disappearance of the corner butcher shop when supermarkets revolutionized food retailing. Nostalgia may have its virtues, but it can rarely be trusted for efficient allocation of resources and optimal pricing of outputs.

The Liberal Argument

Conservatives are quite right in stating that the American farm problem has been largely one of gains in production consistently outstripping increases in demand. Throughout most of this century, food demand was essentially a function of domestic population increase. Until recently the United States has exported large quantities of food abroad only in time of war. Meanwhile, steady advances in agricultural technology and science have produced greater output and reduced human labor needs. Table 1.1 puts these gains in perspective.

TABLE 1.1 U.S. Agricultural Productivity, 1800–1950

Crop	1800	1880	1920	1950
Wheat				
yield/acre (bu)	15	13	14	17
labor hours/100 bu	373	152	87	28
Corn				
yield/acre (bu)	25	26	28	39
labor hours/100 bu	344	180	113	39
Cotton				
yield/acre (bu)	147	179	160	283
labor hours/bale	601	318	269	126

Source: U.S. Bureau of the Census, *Historical Statistics of the United States*, Series K 83–97 (Washington, D.C., 1960).

RISING PRODUCTION AND GROWING CRISIS

Each unit of land has been producing greater yields as a result of new fertilizers and hybrid strains. At the same time, the application of greater capital has reduced substantially the number of worker-hours needed in production. By the 1930s, American farmers were the most productive in the world—and were going broke the fastest. It is easy enough for the Conservative devotee of the laws of supply and demand to say, "Leave things alone and let the devil take the hindmost." The fact is, excess agricultural production and falling prices affected people—a great number of people.

In 1930, about 44 percent of the U.S. population was classified as rural. About 57 million people still lived on farms or in small towns dependent on agriculture. At least 31 million were full-time farmers. To have adopted the Conservative proposal of letting these human resources "drop out" of farming if it didn't pay and find alternative employment would have been inhumane and stupid. In the Great Depression decade, there was no alternative employment. The exodus from farming (which did reduce the farm population to less than 10 million by 1972) would have been faster and would have created even greater employment problems for the general economy.

With this in mind, the New Deal policies of reducing farm migration through price supports, direct payments, and other subsidies (easy credit, electrification, and so on) were created. To be sure, these programs *did* artificially hold up farm prices and, in terms of subsidy costs *did* pass the cost of the farm program on to taxpayers at large. But they also brought a degree of order to the agricultural sector and improved the income distribution inequities between farmers and nonfarmers. For example, 1934 farm income was only about one-third that of nonfarm income ($163 per year per person compared to $469 per year per person, respectively). By 1964, after nearly thirty years of New Deal-type "tinkering," annual farm income per person stood at $1,405 and nonfarm income at $2,318. Moreover, the supposed costs of federal farm subsidy programs have been vastly overstated. For instance, subsidies and support payments paid to farmers in the 1980s amounted to less than 15 percent of all federally paid subsidies to the private sector.

It must be conceded that past American agricultural policy has had its failures. For instance, the improved income level of the farm sector, a noteworthy achievement, masks some other problems. The farm programs of the 1930s, 1940s, and 1950s could not halt the eventual decline of the family farm or the regional small farm in the Northeast. With greater application of technology and changes in farm production, farm employment (mostly family workers) fell from 7 million in 1960 to about 3 million in 1988. Although average farm income did improve relative to nonfarm income during the 1960s and 1970s, maldistribution of earnings within the farm sector increased. Large farms (those with annual sales of $100,000 or more) increased their share of agricultural markets from 17 percent in 1960 to 77 percent in 1988.

We easily can conclude, then, that the few big farms have been getting bigger, but that most remaining farmers still earn very modest incomes. In such a situation, it is quite likely that past farm subsidy programs and payments for nonproduction have provided the greatest gains for the large farm producer. However, even with these shortcomings, the earlier farm policies are defensible. They did raise and maintain average farm earnings above what a purely laissez-faire solution would have produced, thus strengthening agriculture in general. They mitigated the impact of the Depression on many farmers, and when farm out-migration did occur after World War II, the displaced farmers were more easily absorbed into a growing economy. The Conservatives' laissez-faire policy would have emptied rural America sooner, encouraged the growth of only the largest farms, and led to unacceptable human costs.

While past Liberal farm policies are historically defensible, it is apparent that America has moved into a new agricultural era demanding policy changes. The capital-intensive nature of agriculture is everywhere apparent, and the day of the small family farm is past. At the same time, the long-run future growth in world food demand is undeniable. These trends, however, are misunderstood by the free market advocates.

THE RECENT FAILURE OF
MARKET-BASED PROGRAMS

Between 1972 and 1975, agricultural prices generally rose and price supports and any effort to restrict output were unnecessary and ill-advised. However, as the Agriculture and Consumer Protection Act of

1973 anticipated, high prices paid to farmers would not hold permanently. The 1973 act introduced the concept of target pricing. Under this arrangement, government announces a target price on a specified list of commodities. If the market price is below the target price, the government pays the farmer the difference between what they would receive for selling their goods in the market and the targeted figure. According to such a plan, consumers would still enjoy the benefits of the lower market price, but farms would be guaranteed a reasonable return on their crops. To prevent the very large producers from tapping the public treasury for outrageous subsidy payments, the 1973 law specified that no farmer should receive more than $20,000 in payment for any crop.

Although subsequent agricultural acts (the Agricultural and Consumer Protection Act is renewed every four years) have raised this per-farmer ceiling, the ceiling never was a very significant restriction because the larger farmers learned early on to "divide" their holdings among their relatives with each smaller "farm" qualifying for the maximum payments. Meanwhile, very small farmers were virtually unaffected by the restriction on payments and they continued to fail in large numbers. However, the target pricing and payment program did provide an important cushion for the middle-sized farms that are still the backbone of American agriculture.

If such payment programs, along with various loan programs, had not been in place in the 1980s, the disaster that struck American farming regions would have been much greater. More "free market" would have meant more farm agony. The early 1970s' experiment with reliance on supply and demand had introduced "fencepost-to-fencepost" planting and encouraged farmers to expand debt and mortgage obligations to heighten production. Meanwhile, the collapse of demand for American farm products could only be partly blamed on high agricultural prices and the strong U.S. dollar. Quite simply, even in a hungry world, effective demand for food did not keep pace with the growth in world food supply. It should be remembered that the high interest rates and rising costs confronting farmers in the early 1980s were not the farmers' fault nor the fault of farm policy. They were the outcome of a number of "supply shocks" (e.g., rising oil prices) that generated inflationary pressures. It was the Reagan administration's decision to fight this inflation with a "tight money" policy that drove up interest rates and forced massive bank-ruptcies in American agriculture.

What the Market Can't Do Without standby government pay-ments and credit and loan programs, many more than the estimated one-third of American farmers would have been facing bankruptcy in the late 1980s. The Conservative focus on long-run trends in agricul-tural markets is misleading, and their argument for "free" agricultural markets is simple-minded. A long-run trend is nothing more than the average of a cycle of short-run highs and lows. If short-run fluctuations are extreme, especially the lows, the agricultural sector will be torn apart. Resources forced out of agriculture in bad periods will not return quickly when prices later rise. A farm is not an enterprise that can be worked for a few years and then briefly retired until the boom "natur-ally" reappears. The land "blows away" if it isn't cultivated, and the equipment rusts and becomes obsolete. Neither the farmer nor the con-sumer, who would face violently fluctuating prices, should be subjected to the severity of short-run market readjustments. The laws of supply and demand, in fact, can be regulated to improve market outcomes.

Price support programs provide stability at a minimum cost. This, however, is not all that is required. Establishment of a crop reserve program for certain storable crops in good years as a hedge against drastic price increases in bad times or times of excessive demand would lead to price stabilization and more rational production plan-ning. Various credit and loan programs must be available to finance planting and the purchase of farm equipment.

The object of such a farm policy should not be to sustain the mythical small farmer. Indeed, Conservatives are quite correct in pointing out the futility of such an objective. However, the Conserva-tive argument on behalf of reliance on market forces masks its real effect: The eventual domination of American agriculture by giant farm combines and corporations. The Liberal does not oppose that outcome because of some nostalgic attachment to a vanished past; rather, the Liberal opposes it because it could lead to the domination of American agriculture by a comparative handful of giant farm producers who can effectively raise prices by jointly controlling out-put. In the name of the free market, a monopolistically determined price system might indeed replace the mild interventions of govern-ment—to the considerable anguish of American consumers.

The Radical Argument

When conventional economics textbooks reach for an example in discussions of "how supply and demand sets prices" or "how competition works," agricultural markets are usually cited. In the idealized models, at least, there are many small producers and consumers of homogeneous products who haggle and bargain until a fair and equitable price is established. For anyone vaguely familiar with the real-world conditions of American agriculture, the irony is heavy; nothing could be further from the truth. Perhaps because we start with such subtle deceptions when we talk about agricultural markets, we continue to deceive ourselves when we look for solutions to real farm problems. American agricultural affairs are dominated by a comparatively small number of giant producers, not by many small equal-sized farms, and prices are more the result of market power or government intervention than of the free market at work. Agriculture, as much as any sector of the economy, reveals the conflict between the professed ideal of a modified, production-for-profit system and the reality that a few benefit at the losses of many. The losers, of course, are small farmers and consumers in general.

THE OLD POLICY: HELP THE BIG GUYS

While most farm programs between 1920 and 1973 were supposedly aimed at protecting the family farm and supporting the agricultural sector in general, they failed utterly to halt the concentration of agriculture into fewer and fewer hands. Programs of price supports and payments for nonproduction stimulated this concentration, since small farmers could not possibly reap many gains from them. Between 1930 and 1983, land under cultivation actually increased, but the number of farms declined from 6.5 to 2.2 million. Although Liberals reluctantly note this tendency, they do not understand that it has meant higher prices to consumers, with few, if any, benefits to most individually owned farms.

The market power of individual farmers, never very strong anyway, was eroded further during the 1950s and 1960s as marketing procedures were increasingly affected by the entrance of large business corporations into agriculture—*agribusiness*. Food chains bought orchards and feedlots and integrated their operations all the way from planting and slaughtering to the store checkout counter. Cereal producers, dairy products firms, baking companies, and other farm purchasers became more concentrated. At the same time, suppliers of farm machinery became increasingly integrated. As a result, farmers paid high, monopoly-established prices for equipment and had to sell their produce to comparatively few buyers. These buyers rarely had to pay more than the support price or "take it or leave it" prices for non-supported commodities. Contract production with big companies replaced the old market relationships. For instance, half of all fresh vegetables are grown under contract.

By the early 1970s, agriculture had been "discovered" by the large industrial conglomerates. Agribusiness grew and matured as ITT absorbed Wonder Bread and Smithfield Hams, Ling-Temco-Vought took control of Wilson Meats, Greyhound joined with Armour Packing, and other similar mergers took place. Basically, this phenomenon extended and accentuated the "price taker" situation of American farmers, even large farmers. Whether selling to the government, A&P, or General Foods, farmers had long been accustomed to dealing with buyers who set their own prices. The real power of this new and rejuvenated agribusiness, however, would be felt by the consumer as well. The new conglomerate middlemen in food production and distribution had the potential capacity to extract enormous profits. By 1972, the structure for increasing food prices and middlemen's profits had been established. The only restraint was that posed by general overproduction in American agriculture. And the Russian grain deal soon changed that. By eliminating both the fact and the psychology of overproduction and comparatively low prices in agricultural goods, the deal paved the way for agribusiness to assert its power over table food prices.

In 1972, the United States and the Soviet Union secretly negotiated the sale of 19 million metric tons of American grain. Ironically, this sale was completed precisely as the United States was mining Haiphong harbor in North Vietnam and bombing rail lines north of Hanoi in an effort to stop the flow of Russian goods into the war zone. Although critics were to attack the sale as the "Great Grain Robbery," Secretary of Agriculture Earl Butz defended it as a boon to the American farmer. When accused of being willing to trade with the devil if it meant a profit, Butz replied, "If he has dollars."

THE NEW POLICY: KEEP PRICES UP

The Russian grain deal actually reflected a highly calculated effort to create superprofits out of the anguish of farmers and the general public. Since the government itself lacked the legal authority to export goods, the grain sales had to be consummated by some half-dozen leading American grain-trading firms. The steps in the selling process were something like this: First, the harvest came in and could not be altered by farmer action. Second, the Department of Agriculture's Commodity Credit Corporation (CCC) granted the Russians exceptionally low credit arrangements. Third, the companies purchased the wheat owned and stored by the government in CCC bins and sold it to the Russians at a price significantly below the prevailing domestic price. Fourth, the companies, over and above their sales fees, received millions in subsidies from the government (the difference between the domestic price and the sale price).

The effects of the grain sales were injurious to practically all Americans except the grain companies and a few insiders who were able to make extraordinary profits by speculating on grain futures. Farmers were unable to take advantage of the resulting rise in wheat prices, since most had sold their grain to the government at the going market price. The American grain reserve was eliminated. Wheat prices and prices of substitute products went up, and so did the prices of beef and bread, both dependent on grain prices. Restive consumers were told it was just the law of supply and demand.

The Conservative prediction that growing world agricultural sales would eventually bring prosperity back to farming, although creating some hope in 1973 and 1974, had turned to ashes by 1978. Four years after Secretary Butz promised a new era for farming by opening American agriculture to the world, farmers had become dependent on world demand to get rid of two-thirds of their wheat, one-quarter of their corn, and half their soybeans. While American overseas grain sales remained fairly high, world grain prices (indeed, most world agricultural prices) tumbled.

And how did American consumers fare as agricultural prices fell? With large food corporations and agribusiness controlling the final goods prices for most U.S. food consumption, lowered per-unit farm prices meant higher profits, not lower prices at the grocery store. Food processors and distributors (who received on the average 65 cents of every food dollar) saw their revenues and profits soar as farmers groaned and consumers cursed. Consumers blamed farmers. Farmers blamed unions for rising equipment costs and Arabs for higher energy and fertilizer bills. Almost no one placed the responsibility where it really belonged—with the grain-trading companies and their agents at the Department of Agriculture and with agribusiness monopolies, which were well represented in Washington.

By the mid-1980s, a new farm crisis was building, and it too would support the older trends of "helping the big guys" and "keeping prices up." With the overextension of many individual farmers during the fencepost-to-fencepost 1970s, bankruptcy promised to decimate the numbers of working farmers and open new opportunities for the growth of agribusiness.

WHAT STRATEGY TO DEAL WITH THE PROBLEM?

From the Radical perspective, the farm problem has a number of different and troublesome dimensions. First of all, the chronic tendency toward overproduction and falling prices followed by underproduction and rising prices simply reflects the instability and irrationality of "free" markets. The vicious cycle that sometimes brings prosperity and sometimes crisis can be mitigated only by an effort to plan output and control prices. The trouble is that past control efforts have been biased toward helping the large farmer and agribusiness at the expense of the small farmer. As Table 1.2 indicates, the share of government support payments going to giant enterprises has been growing. Farms with sales over $40,000 per year received 54 percent of all government payments in 1975. By 1988, they received 82 percent.

Such a payment schedule encourages increased production among the large farms while at the same time pushes the small producer to the wall. By 1983, one-third of all farms, mostly small ones, were delinquent on their debts. Unsurprisingly, the Reagan administration made few efforts in 1985 to halt the increase in farm bankruptcies. By and large, it was the small and middle-sized farmers who were going broke, not the large farmers or farm corporations. In terms of our agricultural policy, that was precisely what was supposed to happen. Reversing the direction of payments would equalize income but encourage inefficient farm producers to continue operations. The Gordian knot can be untied only if we develop an output

TABLE 1.2   The Big Farmers Get More and More

Size and Distribution	1975	1988
$100,000 and over sales		
% of farms	10.7	13.3
% of government support payments	28.4	56.1
$40,000 to $100,000 sales		
% of farms	18.6	13.2
% of government support payments	25.9	25.5
$20,000 to $40,000 sales		
% of farms	14.5	9.0
% of government support payments	18.9	9.7
Less than $20,000 sales		
% of farms	56.1	63.5
% of government support payments	26.7	9.8

Source: U.S. Department of Agriculture, *Farm Income Statistics*, July 1985, and *Statistical Abstract of the United States*, 1989.

and pricing program that humanely moves inefficient agricultural producers out of production while curbing the ability of the giant farm enterprises to set output and prices for their own — but not the consumer's — advantage.

Also, the other half of giant farming's ability to "double dip" must cease. Presently, agribusiness gets *both* higher prices *and* transfers. The ordinary citizen pays twice. Often taxpayers pay a producer not to produce. Those who would argue that pricing and output controls proposed by Radicals create inefficiency should explain how payment for nonproduction is efficient.

Meanwhile, the development of policies regulating agribusiness and middleman processing profits is also essential. The tendency for food prices to remain high while farm prices fall can be explained only in terms of maintaining unjustified profits at the processing, transporting, or retail levels. Thus far, all farm policies — both Conservative market solutions and Liberal transfer payment systems — have avoided confronting a fact that every homemaker knows: There is precious little correlation between falling agricultural prices and the price of a market basket of food.

Such short-term strategies as boycotts of grocery chains have not been effective. Choosing not to eat simply doesn't work against food prices in the long run. As a tactic for mass political organization, it may be a useful educational experience, a lesson that can be applied later in more effective ways; however, the long-run solution requires a system of allocating and pricing that is totally inconsistent with our historical approach to agriculture and food production. The "unthinkable"— social control of production and prices—must be thought about. As we shall see, it is an approach that should not be limited simply to the farm problem.

Consumer Protection

Is the Consumer Sovereign or Exploited?

Consumption is the sole end and the purpose of all production; and the interest of the producer ought to be attended to, only in so far as it may be necessary for promoting that of the consumer.

Adam Smith, 1776

The upshot of consumer protection, when it succeeds, is simply to hold industry to higher standards of excellence, and I can't see why they should object to that kind of incentive.

Ralph Nader, 1967

Let me emphasize: competition does not protect the consumer because businessmen are more softhearted than bureaucrats or because they are more altruistic or because they are more generous, but only because it is in the self-interest of the entrepreneur to protect the consumer.

Milton Friedman, 1978

I believe that when you are dealing in questions related to human life, economic costs are irrelevant.

Congressman David Obey, 1985

THE PROBLEM

Our survey of American agricultural policies illustrated the outcome of efforts to "correct" the market on behalf of certain producers of goods. We now turn to an example of market intervention on behalf of consumers. Just as we found that there is "no free lunch" when government acts to protect and promote certain sellers of goods, we now find that protecting buyers also exacts costs. While the existence of costs associated with such intervention is not a matter of much disagreement among economists and economic observers, much debate centers on whether the costs are offset by direct benefits obtained.

According to the time-honored doctrine of *consumer sovereignty*, the final authority in determining production and prices is the consumer. In this view, consumers vote with their dollars in the marketplace. Their decisions are expressed by their final selection and willingness to pay for goods. In theory, at least, consumer sovereignty further presumes that buyers' tastes are given and unchanging, that buyers are expert and fully informed about products they are purchasing and the range of alternative products they might buy, and that prices are efficiently set in fully competitive markets. In the real world, however, such expectations, particularly those concerning buyer knowledge of the products they are purchasing, have long been viewed by many economists as unrealistic. As early as 1906, the federal government established the Pure Food and Drug Administration to protect consumers from adulterated food and unsafe drugs—two areas of consumer activity where acquiring the necessary knowledge to act "expertly" could in fact prove fatal. However, the development of a full-blown consumer protection movement is a comparatively recent phenomenon.

The consumerist movement was launched in 1965 with the publication of Ralph Nader's *Unsafe at Any Speed*, an effective muckraking attack on a popular General Motors car, the Corvair. Nader argued persuasively that the sporty rear-engined auto had a number of defects, among them a dangerous habit of flipping over when turning corners, even at low speeds. He also claimed that GM engineers and managers knew about the car's engineering deficiencies but had kept quiet about them. Corvair sales dropped after Nader's attack, although General Motors disputed his influence. The company made its last Corvair in 1969.

Spurred by Nader and his activists and by the sobering fact that auto fatalities had grown by about 1 percent each year since 1960, Congress enacted the National Traffic and Auto Safety Act in 1966. This legislation required that the auto industry begin to install certain specific safety features in all new cars. The first requirements (which went into effect in 1968) specified seat belts for all occupants, energy-absorbing steering columns, increased windshield resistance, dual braking systems, and padded instrument panels. Over the years, additional safety requirements have been mandated by the National Highway Safety and Traffic Safety Administration (also established in 1966).

Meanwhile, Nader's consumer advocate activities soon spread to other areas, and his popularity and political effectiveness grew. Within a few years, state and federal laws were introduced to give consumers greatly expanded power in product-liability and class-action suits. By 1975, over a million such suits were being initiated each year. More important, perhaps, has been the creation of new consumer protection agencies. The Federal Trade Commission now includes a Bureau of Consumer Protection and a Bureau of Deceptive Practices. The executive branch boasts a special Assistant for Consumer Affairs and a Consumer Advisory Council. By 1976, over 400 separate units in forty different government agencies were operating to advance consumer interests or protect consumer rights.

Although opinion surveys of American consumers report broad popular support for most consumer protection activities, the movement has run into trouble recently. Consumer protection, of course, costs money—in the form of higher costs for safer products and expanded government payrolls for consumer protectionists. After the Conservative Reagan victory in 1980, these cost elements came under increasing attack. Having pledged itself to roll back government regulation in all areas of economic life, the administration returned to the scene of the original "consumer protection crime"—automobiles. For the American auto industry, hard hit by a deep recession in 1981–1982 and by a flood of cheaper foreign imports, the Reagan administration provided a virtual freeze on pending speedometer, passive-restraint, bumper, windshield, and 35-mph crash-rating requirements. At the same time protectionist zeal at the Food and Drug Administration (FDA), the National Highway Safety Administration (NHSA), the Consumer Product Safety Commission (CPSC), and the Federal Trade Commission (FTC) was cooled substantially by tight budgets and politically appointed administrators who sought to move back from what many considered to be the excesses of consumer protectionism that had grown up in the 1970s. The focus on safety had reached what many thought were ludicrous extremes by the 1980s, with "warning labels" on stepladder rungs, power mower housings, and other useful goods that could be used foolishly. Meanwhile, the FTC's "protection" efforts not only focused on television commercials, but also on the content of some broadcasting (especially children's programming). Yet, in spite of such overzealous protection efforts, opinion surveys regularly show that most Americans still believe that an active consumer protection effort by government is a "right."

SYNOPSIS

Conservatives argue that consumers are best able to determine for themselves what they should buy and that efforts to "improve" on consumer rationality diminishes satisfaction, raises prices, and lowers economic efficiency. Liberals maintain that consumers do not have enough strength to protect themselves from the manipulative power of giant enterprises. Radicals go beyond mere "consumer protection," raising questions about the commitment of society to consume uncritically as an end in itself.

Anticipating the Arguments

- How do the Conservative, Liberal, and Radical views differ regarding the consumer's rationality and ability to choose freely and intelligently?
- In what ways do the Liberal and Conservative views of calculating the cost of goods differ?
- Why are Radicals suspicious of all efforts to "protect" consumers in a production-for-profit economic system?

The Conservative Argument

Consumer protection efforts exist in many guises. The earliest were at the turn of the century when a variety of state and federal laws aimed at maintaining the purity of food and drug products were passed. A second thrust developed in the 1930s with the passage of "disclosure legislation" that was intended to protect consumers from mislabeled or fraudulently labeled merchandise and false advertising. In the late 1960s and throughout the 1970s, consumer protectionism developed along a third line: specifying product standards for the alleged purpose of making all consumer products safer. Taken together, these three efforts, as they have developed over the past eighty years, constitute the contemporary American consumer protection movement.

Obviously, the consumer protection movement is neither a passing nor inconsequential attempt by social engineers to "correct and improve on" the workings of the market. In fact, few efforts at market intervention have been so assiduously nourished as the belief that government is better able to protect and advance the interests of the consumer than anyone else—naturally enough, better than business, but even better than consumers themselves. Indeed, this idea sounds so sensible to many citizens that the irony of the last sentence will be lost entirely on many readers. However, in the name of consumer protection, consumers have been abused to a much greater extent than is generally appreciated.

FREE MARKET AND THE FREEDOM TO CHOOSE

To understand the Conservative position in the consumer protection debate, recall that all Conservative arguments start from the presumption that each individual's economic and political freedoms must be preserved—that free men and women making their own rational choices in the production and consumption of goods in free markets is the ideal social condition. While the exercise of individual freedom of choice may not always produce perfect economic and social consequences, "free" market conditions are ultimately preferable to those that arise in "regulated" or "protected" markets. Consequently, the underlying logic of Liberal consumer protectionists must be rejected out of hand since it rests on the view that individuals are not capable of making free choices affecting their own lives, or that if they do make such choices, there will be disastrous results. Such a dim view of people's abilities to reason and to choose, of course, inevitably leads to the conclusion that "more thoughtful" individuals must act to protect the ignorant majority. It is on such a rock of authoritarianism that Liberals build their arguments on behalf of social tinkering of all types, whether in the area of consumer affairs or in other realms of economic behavior.

Having said this, however, we must qualify our position in the case of consumer protection. Conservatives believe that sellers of goods, "free" though they may be, do not have the "right" individually or collectively to undertake conscious actions intended to do harm to consumers. Indeed, fraudulent sellers of shoddy products may be held responsible for damages resulting from their products, and damaged individuals must be able to recover losses resulting from fraudulent activities of sellers. Conservatives also recognize that the complexities of products present the modern consumer with problems in rationally evaluating and choosing among goods offered for sale. Consumers will be well served if a hidden hazard is brought to their attention either by the government or private agencies, so they can make purchases based on rational risk calculation, such as in the case of potential side effects of certain medicines. As Milton Friedman has accurately observed: "Insofar as the government has information not generally available about the merits or demerits of the items we ingest or activities we engage in, let it give us the information. But let it leave us to choose what chances we want to take with our own lives." Such a two-pronged effort on behalf of consumer protection goes a long way toward redressing the possible market imperfections that adversely affect consumers without destroying the market in the process. The freedoms of individual consumers to choose from among a broad range of alternative goods will not be impaired, as they invariably are under a Liberal "protectionist" scenerio. The Conservative solution also avoids the peculiar "unfreedom" that excessive consumer protectionism ultimately produces. After all, it takes little imagination to see that government efforts to insulate us from all risks associated with goods we might voluntarily choose to consume must require the elimination of a wide range of useful or pleasurable goods—from stepladders to bicycles—that even in their ordinary use might cause us harm.

THE HIGH COST OF SAFETY

Simple and rational as the Conservative proposal is, it has not been the strategy we have adopted as a nation. Over the past eight decades or more, Americans have come to accept the philosophy and practices of an ever-growing body of consumer protection legislation, apparently on the premise that more protection will lead to fuller, more satisfied lives. The premise, however, fails on a number of grounds. The level of consumer protection we have been drifting toward imposes very heavy costs not fully appreciated by consumers. The costs of protection are levied in two ways. First, as taxpayers we must absorb the administrative overhead of operating numerous consumer protection agencies. In 1989, the budgets of the three most prominent product regulation agencies (the FDA, the NHSA, and the CPSC) totaled nearly three-quarters of a billion dollars. The Center for the Study of American Business estimates that all federal outlays for consumer safety and health exceeds $2.75 billion.

A second cost burden, and one of monumentally greater proportions, is the greater price of products, caused by the increased production costs that consumer protection efforts produce. For instance, the CPSC, with jurisdiction over 10,000 products, requires manufacturers to keep detailed records on the performance of all products and even more substantial records of testing and evaluation on any product that may be deemed to "create a substantial risk of injury"—a category that has come to include everything from power mowers and stepladders to bathrobes and infant back-carriers. The CPSC also has the power to recall products, demand their redesign, and, ultimately, to ban them altogether. All these costs are absorbed by the manufacturer. To these costs, arising in extreme but not uncommon cases, firms must add the ordinary costs of keeping abreast of the blizzard of CPSC paperwork and hiring professional "safety experts," recall managers, public relations specialists, and the like. Of course these business costs are then passed along to consumers. Incidentally, these costs may be spread among a whole array of a firm's products; consequently, certain products not directly affected by consumer protection activities nor made safer by protection, may actually bear some of the protection costs associated with other goods.

How large the final bill is for consumers is uncertain, but one study of auto safety requirements legislated between 1968 and 1982 placed direct costs at about $700 per car, or about 10 percent of manufacturers' total costs (and this does not count another $900 in environmental protection costs per car).

IS IT WORTH IT? THE COST-BENEFIT QUESTION

The conventional Liberal justification for the high and escalating costs of consumer protection rests on *cost-benefit analysis*. According to this method of accounting, protectionist endeavors can be undertaken as long as the net money amount of social gains or benefits, after subtracting all private and social costs resulting from such requirements, continues to grow. (Or, to put it in the stricter terms of economic jargon, up to the point where marginal social costs equal marginal social benefits.) Nowhere has this technique of calculating the gain from required safety been so extensively applied as in auto safety. Needless to say, the protectionist advocates have been able to prove to their own satisfaction that the money value of safety costs are but a small fraction of the money value of social gains obtained from safety requirements. Unless the calculating techniques are examined closely, cost-benefit arguments are impressive. For instance, a 16-to-1 benefit-to-cost ratio was reported by the National Highway Safety Administration for one improved standard for auto windshields. Sounds impressive, right?

The key, however, to any cost-benefit analysis is the calculation of benefits. Benefits, of course, are equal to private and social outlays that would have to be made if the degree of protection required *was not* required. Naturally, benefits look impressive when lost earnings, property damage, medical costs, and the like, attributable to a presumably preventable hazard, are estimated quite high and less impressive if lower estimates are applied. But here is the problem with calculating benefits. Benefit estimation is certainly not an exact science and the estimator's efforts are usually self-serving. Thus it is no surprise that the government agency, the U.S. Safety Administration, sets the overall cost of auto accidents three times higher than the cost calculated by the private National Safety Council. The higher estimate increases the justification for greater auto safety requirements since larger benefits (in terms of reduced personal and social losses) will accrue.

Calculation of benefits is not the only difficulty. Costs are a sticky issue too. Each mandated safety cost is an *opportunity cost* — dollars not spent in some other way. For instance, what if the $1 billion plus in safety costs spent by GM (and presumably passed on to auto buyers) in 1986 had been spent on driver education? Would the social benefits have been greater or less? No one really knows — most certainly not the Liberals who use cost-benefit analysis to justify, rather than to objectively evaluate, consumer safety actions.

For Conservatives, quite apart from the challenge of calculating social costs and benefits, cost-benefit analysis fails for more fundamental reasons. It simply defies the logic of the free market, replacing it with political value judgments. Accordingly, the cost-benefit method is inefficient and unfair. Individuals, rather than purchasing units of "safety" according to their preferences and willingness to pay, are obligated to pay for safety they do not want. Rational suburbanites who keep their fingers out of their lawn mowers must pay for protection devices they don't need. Although mental midgets who might, out of perverse curiosity, put a finger into the mower blades are protected (thus providing some alleged social gain), the thoughtful operator who gains nothing must pay more. In effect, efforts to obtain an uncertain, elusive degree of greater social benefits requires that private cost-benefit considerations—the very heart of free markets in operation—be disregarded.

The search for greater net social benefits may actually produce the opposite—people acting against their own interests. For instance, higher-priced but safer cars may force some consumers to drive older, unsafer ones. But, most important, such an approach toward consumers attacks the fundamental freedom of choice and therefore compromises the liberty—even the liberty to act foolishly—that Conservatives consider so essential to a free society and a free economy.

The Liberal Argument

The Classical economic assumption—that buyers and sellers bargain equally in the marketplace and that buyers, acting with restraint and wisdom, are sovereign—falls into the same intellectual category as belief that the world is flat. As in the case of the "flat worlders," a great many compelling reasons can be mustered to "prove" the argument, but they fly in the face of virtually all available evidence.

THE NEED FOR INTERVENTION

From the Liberal viewpoint, protectionist interference in the private production of goods is justifiable and necessary for several reasons. First and foremost is the fact that as products have become more complex, they present potential risks and hazards that consumers are simply unprepared to evaluate and act on rationally. Sometimes the effects are comparatively benign; for example, the consumer buys a product that fails to function as promised in its advertising and labeling, and the only loss is the purchase price. But sometimes the product is dangerous and the consumer has no way of knowing this. Without government intervention, how would we have learned about the dangers of thalidomide, red dye no. 2, tris, cyclamates, certain pesticides, and other commodities that have been removed from the market for health reasons?

Second is the matter of *external costs*—costs paid by society that may not be accounted for in the selling price of a good. Consider the case of the automobile. Conservatives would look at only the private cost of an automobile: How much an individual must pay in the marketplace for a minimally equipped transportation vehicle. Additional costs for safety features are seen as purely private purchasing decisions: Buy safety if *you* want it. This misses an important point in understanding real costs. Automobiles have a cost that goes beyond merely the production, assembly, and sales expenditures and the expected profits of the automaker. The private decision to drive an unsafe but cheaper car means that society pays an additional bill for the costs inflicted on others by automobile accidents. Auto accidents, however, effect more people than just those who are injured. They lead to higher insurance rates, greater court costs, and heavier expenditures on roads, accident prevention, and enforcement. Nor are injuries or deaths simply "personal" matters. These human losses mean the dollar loss of present wage earnings and the loss of productive workers (now and in the future) and thus a greatly expanded social cost to the whole society.

Thus the Conservatives' argument against automobile safety standards on the ground that they unfairly raise consumer costs is misguided. Higher-priced autos are necessary to cover all the costs involved in auto driving. As we shall see, it is still a good bargain.

RESTRAINING SELLERS

The extraordinary growth of giant enterprises over the past century, along with the development of huge advertising budgets and sophisticated selling techniques, has created immense power on the sellers' side of the market. Economic concentration has given producers great freedom in establishing and maintaining their own price and quality standards. Mass advertising, meanwhile, has moved well beyond an informational function to one of actually creating and manipulating consumer wants. In such a situation, it is essential that government intervene on behalf of consumers to protect them from false advertising and poorly made or dangerous merchandise.

Recent efforts in automobile safety demonstrate how govermentally supported consumer protection actions can improve the quality of an important consumer good. Besides a house, a car is usually the largest single purchase made by a consumer. Americans own about 150 million cars. Once considered a rich man's luxury (and, after the Model T, the poor man's luxury), today the auto has become everyone's necessity. The vast majority of citizens are dependent on the auto to get to work, school, stores, and many recreational activities.

However, just as consumers began to buy more and more cars after World War II, automakers began to shift consumer attention from a car's serviceability and economy to its size, horsepower, and styling. (This trend actually had begun with General Motors in the early 1930s, but depression, war, and poor highways did not allow it to blossom until the late 1940s and 1950s.) The "ideal" car became one with speed, internal comfort, and annual style changes that could quickly distinguish it from last year's model or from other manufacturers' offerings. While social critics sneered at Americans' fancies and fantasies in automobiles, very few paid much attention to safety hazards. Autos had probably never been very safe, but by 1965, about 55,000 Americans were dying each year on the roads. New highways, along with greater horsepower and more weight, had made automobiles lethal weapons. The auto industry, which had shrunk from ten producers to just four, paid no attention to safety standards. Their advertising and research emphasized speed and comfort, and the buying public had accepted these values. Until Ralph Nader and a few others focused attention on safety inadequacies, rarely did car dealers have to respond to queries about how safe their products were.

Since the 1970s, all this has changed. Government, working through Congress and protection agencies (such as the National Highway Safety Administration), created minimum safety requirements for all cars: safety belts, bumper improvements, window defrosters, stronger glass, and the like. Careful monitoring of autos has led to massive recalls to remedy specific safety deficiencies. And, of course, the CPSC's and FDA's monitoring in other product areas have similarly contributed to the improvement of product quality and consumer safety throughout the economy.

THE SAVINGS FROM SAFETY

Government safety requirements have no doubt added to the price of what we buy, although much less than Conservatives have argued. Safety belts, for instance, which (when used) have radically reduced serious injuries in collisions, add less than 1 percent to the price of a $15,000 automobile. The problem, of course, is to measure the increases in costs to consumers against the savings to society from reduced auto hazards. It would be inaccurate to stress only increased auto prices in a survey of auto safety costs and benefits.

Using the crudest kind of calculation, the dollar costs per year of automobile safety could be estimated as high as $4.5 billion. (This is based on GM's own 1982 calculation that the various safety mandates—not to be confused with environmental requirements—added $500 to each car's production cost and further assumes average sales to be 9 million cars.) The benefits are more difficult to calculate. We do know, though, that each life unnecessarily lost is also a loss to society in earned wages for the period of the victim's work life. We also know from available auto safety statistics that auto-related deaths have declined by about 10,000 per year since the first significant auto safety features were added in 1969. Using a recent U.S. Department of Transportation "interrupted earning stream" estimate of $500,000 per victim's life and calculating that at least three-quarters of the 10,000 reductions in fatalities is the direct or indirect result of improved safety standards, we can demonstrate at least $3.7 billion in social savings per year from reduced fatalities alone. Additional savings from reduced or less serious injuries and the psychological gratification of feeling safer in one's auto would more than cover the liberally estimated dollar cost of the safety equipment. In a more complicated and extensive benefits model, the U.S. Department of Transportation estimated that presently mandated auto requirements reduced fatalities by 24,000 by 1990, producing social savings of $9.5 billion. Doubtless other models could be constructed, but even the most conservative should prove easily that auto safety pays for itself. Consumer protection isn't free, but it is a bargain.

Meanwhile, manufacturers complain that enforced recalls of cars to remedy defects constitutes an assault on their profits, and there is probably some truth to this. The answer, however, is better workmanship and engineering on the industry's part, not relaxed consumer protection. The cost for shoddy construction must be borne by industry, not by society at large.

If there is any serious defect in the government's efforts to protect consumers, it is that not enough has been done. The Highway Safety Bureau, for instance, operates on a yearly budget of about $150 million and employs a staff of about 1,000. That is a very small bureaucracy indeed to watch over safety standards in the nation's largest consumer-oriented industry.

The recent trend toward deregulation and reducing government interference in business decision making will cost the nation dearly if it continues. Conservatives are right in saying that withdrawing safety and consumer protection standards (and environmental and job safety standards as well) could lead to lower-priced goods or, more realistically, greater industry profits. Conceivably such deregulation could give a sluggish economy a quick fix for a time. But these are cruel and false gains obtained only through "creative accounting"—by shifting the social or external cost of goods onto certain groups in the society. Greater efforts in consumer safety are essential. Consumer protection will not be attained until *caveat emptor* (let the buyer beware) is replaced by *caveat venditor* (let the seller beware) as the dominant motto of the marketplace.

The Radical Argument

The relevant issues in the controversy over improved consumer safety are rarely raised. Conservatives approach the question as a matter of maintaining free markets and free choice, and Liberals argue for the improvement of market conditions and the protection of buyers; but these are really evasions of what the consumer safety question highlights. Why, in an advanced and supposedly civilized society such as ours, is consumer safety a problem at all? Is it that we lack the resources and technology to manufacture safe products? On the contrary, we all know that technology has nothing to do with the problem. Unsafe autos, like unsafe food and dangerous drugs, are just "there." They are part of our economic and social systems—to be tolerated or, when things get bad enough, to be reformed. They are the necessary but unwanted effects of an irrational social order.

WHY "CONSUMER SOVEREIGNTY" DOESN'T EXIST

Capitalist economic systems are organized to make profits, not to make people happy or to make life safer. For a capitalist enterprise to make large profits, it has to sell in great quantity, and must obtain as great a surplus over costs as possible. Obviously that calculation nowhere contains any estimate of social costs and benefits. Insofar as the production-for-profit system is concerned, satisfaction is maximized simply if we have *more*. Irrespective of the time-honored tradition of consumer sovereignty, it is not really the consumers' power to choose among goods that is important. What is important is that they consume, period. Citizens in a capitalist society are taught from birth to accept uncritically that the object of life is to obtain goods; the more goods, the better their lives.

Looked at this way, it is easy to see why modern capitalism periodically becomes absorbed in such developments as the consumer protection issue. The social costs of the mass consumption of dangerous products as well as private concerns about safety have finally developed to such a point where reformist action must be taken. The recent auto safety movement, for instance, is merely another step in the long progression of product reform movements. It differs very little from the public outcry against adulterated food that created the Food and Drug Administration in 1906. The FDA certainly has improved food cleanliness, and probably the current consumer movement will make cars safer to drive (or at least we will believe so). However, the "success" of such reforms deflects us from questioning the reasonableness of an economic system that sells poisoned food or hazardous vehicles in the first place.

Conservatives and Liberals may bicker over whether consumer sovereignty is best expressed in free or regulated markets, but both are committed to encouraging high levels of essentially irrational consumption. No traditional economist has ever proposed that consumer sovereignty be defined as the rational, coordinated control of production by the users of goods. That, of course, would lead to the abolition of the capitalist system. However strongly Conservatives and Liberals seem to disagree on the extent of government interference with production, both hold firmly to the principle of maintaining high levels of output as well as the primary goal of production for profit.

THE SELF-SERVING USE OF THE SAFETY IDEA

Americans have been misled about the high costs of safety. Conservatives emphasize that safety features increase product prices. Liberals admit that price increases are an outcome but that the costs are worth it given the social benefits obtained. The thrust of both arguments is that safety costs money—and corporations have not missed their cue. With a public prepared by the media and the economics profession to accept higher prices as the cost of greater protection, business has used the safety argument to push prices even harder. In 1977, as extensive safety requirements were being built into American autos, General Motors reported a record-breaking net income of $4 billion on sales of $55 billion. At the same time, this firm, supposedly racked by the costs of expensive safety features, managed to rank thirty-seventh among the top 500 American corporations in income as a percentage of shareholder's equity. And paid earnings-per-share were two-thirds higher than stockholder earnings a decade earlier, in pre-consumerist 1966. Ford and Chrysler also ranked in 1977 in the top 200 firms in earnings ratio, with their earnings-per-share record better than a decade earlier (Ford's had increased almost 100 percent). Such evidence seems to suggest that, initially at least, the safety boom of the 1970s may have been a ploy for digging even deeper into consumers' pockets and, of course, hiding the action.

Only later, as the economy stagnated between 1979 and 1983, did corporate management begin to push energetically against many previously accepted safety mandates. Faced with declining domestic demand and rising imports of foreign-made products, it became expedient to use "safety costs" as a contributing factor in the profit squeeze felt by many American firms. In the auto industry especially, consumer, environmental, and job safety programs *and* workers' salaries were obvious targets. Automakers quickly mounted a highly successful public relations and political lobbying effort to "take back" on all these fronts. Once a boon to profit making, auto safety was now depicted as a threat to profits as well as to the continued strength of a basic American industry. In the new political and economic setting, many consumers even became convinced that we could no longer afford rigorous auto safety standards.

THE RADICAL DILEMMA

No doubt the Radical position seems hopelessly negativistic and irrelevant to the specific question of "protecting the consumer"; indeed it is, if Radicals are expected by conventional economists to offer long-run remedies that do not consider the underlying philosophy and social organization of consumption activities in a capitalist society. Radicals understand that capitalism is propelled by the private search for profit and that profits increase, *ceteris paribus*, either by increasing sales or by keeping costs down. Profits by themselves are not tied to intrinsic social concerns about safety—unless, of course, "safety" can be used as a gimmick to raise prices. Similarly, Radicals understand that Liberal efforts to improve safety, regardless of their posturing on behalf of consumers, cannot seriously assault the profit prerogatives or the rights of capitalists in a production-for-profit economy. Liberal actions on behalf of the abused in a production-for-profit system can never be so massive that they damage the basic system.

Given the constraints of a system that depends on private profit making on the one hand, and, on the other, requires the political pretense of repairing the more egregious functional shortcomings and social atrocities resulting from such a system, Radicals are inclined to ask a broader philosophical question: Why don't we have a more rational approach toward the production and use of goods? Conservatives adroitly avoid raising the issue of how demand may be manipulated by advertising, and Liberals pay little more than lip service to this problem. Both fail to understand how a "consumer society" may become locked into thoroughly irrational patterns of consumption. However, if we see that most purchases are made because the goods are merely being sold, rather than because we have received cerebral messages that we *need* the particular commodities, it will become easier to unravel the dilemma of wasteful consumption as well as the consumption of unsafe products.

Of course, people shouldn't have to drive unsafe cars, nor should they have to own unsafe "pet rocks" or any other item sold in a capitalist society. Neither should automakers (or even pet rock sellers) be able to profit from selling "safe" automobiles (or "safe" pet rocks). For Radicals, however, the issue is really whether the goods themselves are socially useful. It is not a matter of making socially wasteful goods "safe." The Radical, then, approaches the question of consumer welfare by questioning the very goods that are offered for sale. For instance, in the case of the privately owned automobile and the enormously expensive system of roads and ancillary services needed to make auto ownership feasible, most Radicals see an incredibly irrational and wasteful transportation mode. Accordingly, Radicals view the debate over private automobile safety and the virtual absence of any discussion about devising an efficient system of mass transportation as a good example of how we never address the basic questions in our analysis of consumer behavior.

However, recognizing that the broader questions of "what and why we consume" are not part of the present economic agenda, Radicals, in addressing the current consumer protection problem concretely, embrace most protectionist objectives: the maintenance of quality and purity in product manufacture, the accurate dissemination of information about a product's uses and limits, the recall of dangerous products, and the ability of the consumer to gain redress for damages and defrauding. *Caveat venditor* is an acceptable short-term strategy, but it scarcely goes to the root of our problems as long as production-for-profit drives the nation's economic and political engine.

The Acid Rain Crisis
How Shall We Deal with Spillover Costs?

These pollutants originate in the Midwest, eastern Canada, and western New York State; rain and snow wash them out of air passing over the state to fall on our forests, lakes, and cities. Because some of these air pollutants become sulphuric acid, nitric acid, and other acids when dissolved in the precipitation carrying them to earth, this whole process has been dubbed "acid rain."

John Hawley, The Conservationist, 1977

Are we going to have to count bodies before we determine that the time has come to reduce sulfur emissions throughout the whole country to ensure there is no impact on human health? . . . We don't need more evidence to conclude that action needs to be taken.

Dr. David Axelrod, New York State Health Commissioner, 1984

When we calculate all the costs to everyone, on balance, we will save money when we pass this [the Clean Air] bill.

Senator George Mitchell, 1990

THE PROBLEM

They began to notice the problem in the Adirondack Mountains of upstate New York over two decades ago. Plant and aquatic life in many of the region's lakes began to undergo a significant change reflecting a general degradation of lake water quality. Within a few years the problem rapidly worsened as dozens of lakes became "dead"—virtually void of fish and plants. The cause, at least as far as New Yorkers were concerned, was "acid rain." Precipitation containing high levels of sulfuric and other acids was altering nature's balance, not only killing lakes but showing signs of damaging the trees and ground cover as well. The source of the acid rain was, to most scientists, easily explained: The burning of fossil fuels unleashed sulfur dioxide, nitrogen dioxide, and other chemicals and particulates into the atmosphere. These returned to earth with falling rain and snow and, combined with water, became highly acidic. Since northern New York had no significant fossil fuel burning, the source of the problem was determined to be the industrial Midwest. There, manufacturing plants and electric generating facilities belched large quantities of chemicals into the air from high smokestacks, to be carried northeastward and deposited by the prevailing wind and weather systems.

In general terms at least, economic theory offers both a theoretical explanation and a potential remedy to the problems posed by acid rain and other types of environmental pollution. The theoretical tool employed is the concept of "externalities." The analysis runs like this: Under free market conditions, the interaction of all individual sellers (supply) and all individual buyers (demand) establishes a market price for a product. Yet the market price may not reflect all the incidental costs or benefits associated with the good. For instance, a student may value (in terms of his or her estimated private benefits) a college education at around $40,000 or $50,000, but society in general may derive benefits of much greater value from individuals who obtain college educations. A better-educated public may be more creative, more efficient, and harder-working, thus producing a larger economic pie for everyone, not just the solitary student. These additional gains are spillover or external *benefits* (sometimes called *external economies*) beyond the actual market price paid for the commodity.

In the case of acid rain or pollution, however, we are talking about spillover or external *costs* (also known as *external diseconomies*). In a market economy, output decisions are based on calculations of direct production costs. Air, water, and even the land space itself may be viewed as "free goods" in the production process. Insofar as the atmosphere and the earth are "free" sewers and dumping grounds, the producer enjoys a private benefit by polluting. Society, living in a dirtier world, however, accumulates social costs. The market price of the good is obtained by not internalizing the social costs into the costs of manufacturing the good. Obviously, to be efficient in its production and pricing decisions, an economy needs to calculate all costs, both private direct production costs and social costs, in setting a price for a good. The objective of an efficient economic policy, then, is to internalize the social costs of pollution in the price of the good so that preventive or remedial action may be paid for.

However, the step from theory to practice is a big one. From the viewpoint of New Yorkers (and New Englanders and Canadians, too, who have been living with acid rain for some time), it is essential to attack acid rain at its source by restricting midwestern industrial emissions. At the same time, naturally enough, midwesterners have an interest in keeping their industries operating at low costs and in obtaining cheap steam-electric energy.

Maintaining environmental quality has been a highly popular social priority with Americans for more than two decades, but acid rain has been a tough problem. Unlike most pollution, which affects the immediate surroundings of the polluter and usually inspires community pressure on the polluter, acid rain's apparent source and its effects are a thousand miles and many state lines separated from one another. Given conflicting regional interests, it is difficult to comprehend any solution to the acid rain problem below the federal level. Moreover, any resolution at that level would require, both in scope and application, a much broader application of the Environmental Protection Agency's powers than has been exercised to date. But beyond the politics of maintaining environmental safeguards, there remain important economic questions. How, precisely, does one determine the social cost of acid rain? How is its source to be pinpointed? And even if the cost and the specific polluters are identified, what means should be undertaken to internalize the social cost?

Conservatives, Liberals, and Radicals come to quite different policy conclusions in answering these three questions, even when they start from an agreement about acid rain's existence, its threat, and its source. The issue, of course, is not simply acid rain but a strategy that will be effective in dealing with all environmental problems.

SYNOPSIS

Conservatives recognize the "neighborhood effects" of pollution and advocate a cost-benefit technique in determining the amount of environmental cleanup outlays. They favor use of emissions taxes, operating through the market mechanism itself, as the best way to allocate cleanup costs. Liberals place less trust in market-based tax schemes and favor direct government controls or even the use of a subsidy policy to clean up the environment. Radicals argue that most efforts to protect the environment are doomed to failure since actual environmental damage is always underestimated. Production-for-profit systems simply do not find it to their advantage to undertake truly effective actions to protect the environment.

Anticipating the Arguments

- On what grounds do Conservatives favor emissions taxes over direct government controls in eliminating pollution?
- On what grounds do Liberals believe that emissions taxes are insufficient in dealing with pollution problems?
- Why do Radicals believe that conventional market-directed or government-directed efforts are likely to be insufficient in protecting the environment?

The Conservative Argument

The debate over pollution and acid rain raises a somewhat different set of economic and theoretical questions from those considered in our earlier discussion of automobile safety. Owning and wearing seat belts is, after all, a purely voluntary matter directly affecting no one but the party involved. Pollution, on the other hand, focuses directly on third-party effects – damage done to individuals who have no economic stake in the polluting action and who can exercise no voluntary control over the effects of pollution.

According to Milton Friedman and most others who have looked at the pollution issue, there is a "neighborhood effect" that must be calculated and accounted for. According to Friedman:

> A ... general class of cases in which strictly voluntary exchanges is impossible arises when actions of individuals have effects on other

individuals for which it is not feasible to charge or recompense them. This is the problem of "neighborhood effects." An obvious example is the pollution of a stream. The man who pollutes a stream is in effect forcing others to exchange good water for bad. These others might be willing to make the exchange at a price. But it is not feasible for them, acting individually, to avoid the exchange or to enforce appropriate compensation.*

NEIGHBORHOOD EFFECTS AND THE ROLE OF GOVERNMENT

Clearly in this situation, it is appropriate to expect the community to establish some technique for determining the costs that one individual imposes on another and to develop a mechanism for allocating the costs. Admitting to such occasional needs to remedy market failures, however, should not be construed as a total condemnation of the market or as license to introduce all manner of "benevolent" tinkering with the market. Indeed, it becomes quite important that the community action chosen to deal with neighborhood effects be as neutral and nonbureaucratic as possible. Quite simply, the object is to develop a policy that makes a firm internalize all of its costs (social as well as private) in its production decisions.

In our time, magnificent government structures have been created in the name of protecting the innocent from the polluters. Yet society's gains from expensive and creative antipollution efforts have been few — and often obtained only at an unacceptable burden to everyone's voluntary rights and to economic well-being and efficiency in general. Consider the ruthless application of antipollution standards in the 1970s. With the creation of the Environmental Protection Agency (EPA) in 1970 and the passage of the Clean Air Act in the same year, the EPA was given authority to (1) determine national air quality standards; (2) set emission levels for old and new plants; (3) set motor vehicle emission standards; (4) establish which fuel substances may be burned in motor vehicles; and (5) establish standards in emergency situations (including the power to close down industrial polluters presenting an "immediate danger" to public health).

*Milton Friedman, *Capitalism and Freedom* (Chicago: University of Chicago Press, 1962), p. 30.

FIGURE 3.1 Estimated Effects of Air Pollution Controls

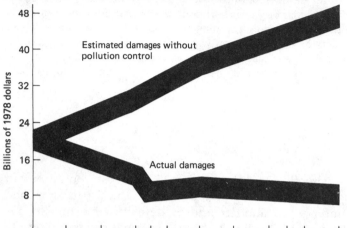

Source: Thomas E. Waddell, *Preliminary Update and Projections of Selected Categories of Damage Cost Estimates*, prepared for the Council on Environmental Quality, May 1978, with updated estimates by the author.

With great zeal and little contemplation of the consequences, the EPA wrote standards and enforced them vigorously. Murray Weidenbaum of the Center for the Study of American Business has estimated that between 1979 and 1986, public agencies and private firms spent nearly three-quarters of a trillion dollars in efforts to meet the EPA requirements. Looking at the data another way, Weidenbaum estimates that meeting EPA direct control standards absorbed 14 percent of the paper industry's capital outlays and 20 percent of the steel industry's new investment. Before the Reagan administration began to relax EPA direct pollution controls in the early 1980s, nearly 200 plants employing over 200,000 workers had closed as the direct result of imposed pollution abatement costs.

Did such antipollution costs produce benefits? The answer is a qualified yes. National urban air quality has improved fairly steadily since 1974. The Great Lakes and the Far West have experienced significant environmental improvements. As Figure 3.1 shows, the expected rate of environmental damage without pollution controls has slowed, with actual damages falling in recent years. However, it is a matter of some debate whether the benefits, in dollar terms, came anywhere close to the dollar costs imposed by the EPA.

The problem in dealing with acid rain and other pollution problems lies in establishing a method for bringing costs of control and benefits into balance. It is patent nonsense to argue as Radicals and some Liberals do that an absolutely clean environment is essential *whatever its cost*. To begin with, there is no technically feasible way to return the environment to its unspoiled, pre-fossil fuel era standards regardless of the cleanup outlays we might undertake. We shall be left always with some level of environmental damage. Given this fact, we must establish reasonable cleanup expectations that are based on (1) the value of real benefits actually attainable and (2) the community's willingness to pay the cost of obtaining such benefits. Government-imposed cleanup costs vastly in excess of antipollution benefits that the community deems reasonable lead to a serious misallocation of resources, resulting in closed plants, inadequate new capital investment, failing world competitiveness, lost jobs, and other consequences.

The techniques available for determining reasonable cleanup objectives and bringing the costs into balance with the benefits are various. From a Conservative perspective, the most useful techniques employ the minimum of social tinkering and the greatest reliance on forces of the market to bring social and private benefits into line with social and private costs.

THE POSSIBILITY OF PRIVATE APPROACHES

Although reliance on the market to deal with neighborhood effects has its limitations, two private (nongovernment) means of assigning the costs of pollution to polluters are possible: negotiation among affected parties and setting specific liability rules. Although their effectiveness is limited, they deserve mention.

Negotiation of pollution costs between polluters and damaged parties is feasible where one person's property rights are clearly damaged by a second party's polluting—for instance, a city's loss of its water supply or added costs in preparing its drinking water because of a single identifiable upstream polluter. Given recourse to the courts, the damaged party may sue for damages, which gives an incentive to the polluter to clean up its emissions. In fact, the polluter and the damaged party may sit down and bargain rather than go to court. Presumably, the pollution fee or the extent of cleanup agreed to reflects both parties' balancing of benefits and costs.

Failing negotiation, liability rules depend on use of the courts to establish private costs resulting from pollution. Once the court sets particular damages for polluting actions, the firm must calculate such damages as a fairly certain cost of any production having polluting side effects. If the firm pollutes more, it pays more; if it pollutes less, it pays less. The incentive — without any government directives — is on the side of reducing pollution.

The obvious difficulty with relying on negotiations and liability rules is that they don't work well when the specific effects of a specific polluter are uncertain or where specifically damaged parties are either hard to determine or have difficulty establishing clear property rights. How, in fact, does a New York fisherman establish the level of personal damage from acid rain and determine who actually caused the acidity in the first place?

COLLECTIVE ACTION

Given the shortcomings of purely private approaches to environmental issues, we are left with collective action as the only alternative. Collective action comes in only three general forms: direct controls, emissions taxes or permits, and subsidies.

Conservative opposition to direct controls was already noted. When government sets specific emissions standards backed with the force of fines or the power to close plants, government wields a dangerous degree of power. Even if used cautiously, there is no certainty that this power will produce the desired effect of balancing cleanup costs and benefits. As a matter of practice, government has tended to overvalue the benefits of halting or slowing pollution while underestimating the costs of attainment. To a considerable degree, direct controls reflect imperfect pollution measuring standards that vary widely from firm to firm, industry to industry, and region to region.

Most important, however, direct controls provide little monetary incentive for the marginal polluter (at or just below the accepted emission standard) to reduce pollution at all. Direct controls can, at best, establish only an acceptable minimum; they have no effect in bringing about a generally improving environmental quality as a function of a market economy's constant drive to lower costs.

Subsidies paid to firms as inducements to installing antipollution devices may sound attractive but are hopelessly inefficient. Like direct emissions controls, there is a strong element of imposed government problem solving that looks better than it really is. Subsidies provide no market-based inducement for firms to take antipollution actions; they do not cause firms to internalize the social costs of polluting. Ironically, they simply lower polluters' costs, possibly increasing levels of pollution in the long run. If government installed "scrubbers" in the smokestacks of midwestern coal-burning plants, which are allegedly the source of acid rain, the effect would be to lower production costs (in terms of the alternative of the firm internalizing its own pollution costs). This might encourage more coal burning, wholly offsetting the initial clean air gains.

A more acceptable method for repairing the neighborhood effects of pollution is levying an emissions tax. The tax is essentially a levy on the firm equal to the amount of damage the particular firm is causing. Relying on the firm's desire to maximize profit, cleaning up its production emissions will lead to reductions in its pollution tax burden. Firms most able to adapt to antipollution requirements will respond most quickly, thus benefiting from the resultant tax reduction. Essentially inefficient or poorly managed enterprises that do not act to reduce emissions will find their profits adversely affected by the emissions tax.

Technical problems remain in metering the amount of an individual firm's emissions and translating this into a dollar value of social damages that will be the basis for estimating the tax. Nevertheless, the emissions tax concept is attractive because of its lack of direct intervention and its reliance on the firm's own profit-maximizing desires to make environmental protection work. Emissions taxes, and a related idea—selling emissions permits (whereby the environmental authority determines the permissible level of emissions and then sells permits in the marketplace up to that level)—rely on market signals rather than on social control to direct resources toward a cleaner environment. They avoid the inefficiency and inequity of direct controls.

PITFALLS NEVERTHELESS

Though a feasible economic solution can be developed to deal with the problem of acid rain or pollution in general, technical problems should not be minimized. Metering emissions is still an imprecise science. Connecting emissions levels to specific damages (coal burning in Ohio to a dead lake in New York State) is still a matter of scientific debate. And determining the reasonable social valuation of a dead lake or stream (or revitalizing these bodies of water) on which any tax levy or penalty will be based is also a matter of much argument. We cannot return to the distant pristine past under any conditions, and determining the degree to which we want a "clean environment" must be done with the understanding that there is no such thing as a free lunch. Environmental quality improvements can come about only at a price.

The Liberal Argument

Although Conservatives may seem reasonable enough in their concession that pollution involves neighborhood effects that the community has the right to regulate, their actual track record with regard to environmental protection is a poor one. Their less-than-enthusiastic embrace of federal government action to control pollution stems from their blind commitment to a "free market." Moreover, the pollution problem goes a long way toward demonstrating that free markets may not in fact assure society's well-being.

THE FAILURE OF THE MARKET TO ALLOCATE EXTERNALITIES

As noted earlier, externalities arise when, beyond the market price of a good, there is either a calculable external cost (detrimental externality) or gain (beneficial externality) to the individuals consuming the good or to society as a whole. Externalities are not, as Conservatives might suggest, merely interesting exceptions to the theory of markets in which the free play of supply and demand establishes prices and allocates resources accordingly. Instead, they reflect a serious market failure and are ample justification for the Liberal assertion that "the market can very often be improved upon."

Externalities reveal two types of problems in allocating resources purely according to market dictates. First, there is the problem of external benefits or economies. A firm that perhaps inadvertently supplies substantial benefits to a community—say, by laying out attractive parklike playgrounds around its production site—has little monetary incentive to continue such investment in this site because it receives no gains in sales from such activity. Although the community derives esthetic and health benefits, there is no market incentive for the firm to allocate resources to such objectives (hence it is not surprising that most places of production are so drab). Second, whereas there is little incentive to invest in the "good things" that produce no private market gains, there is considerable incentive to spin certain costs off onto the community rather than internalize them as part of the firm's own production costs. Thus the rivers and the air have been viewed as free sewers by firms spewing chemicals out into the community, therefore not requiring the firm to invest in antipollution controls. Left to its own devices, a free market allocation of resources can be counted on to produce few beneficial externalities and many detrimental externalities.

In developing a useful economic policy, this logic of the market requires modification and redirection. In terms of our discussion of environmental problems posed by acid rain, we are addressing a specific problem that can only be dealt with through government action.

THE NEED FOR A NATIONAL ENVIRONMENTAL POLICY

As a general rule, Conservatives oppose collective action, and in particular they oppose collective action at the federal level, preferring to support state and municipal intervention as more "democratically" responsive to local needs. Clearly, the case of acid rain demolishes such an argument. Ohio simply has no incentive to lower the acidity of New York's lakes. Hence Conservatives' first consideration for "voluntary" agreement between polluters and damaged parties is a flawed argument. Since New Yorkers possess few powers to persuade Ohioans to voluntarily reduce emissions, and since there is no economic advantage for the polluters to comply, negotiation between these distant and differently motivated parties is most unlikely.

Nor does the prospect of enforcing property rights and liability rules in the courts seem more probable. While class action suits against the polluters are technically possible, the courts offer infinite delaying tactics. Moreover, individually damaged parties have no realistic possibility of financing these long legal battles with well-staffed and well-financed midwestern corporations.

Given the shortcomings of voluntarism and the interstate nature of the acid rain problem, it becomes quickly evident that only strong federal intervention provides a possible solution. Even the Conservative argument, despite basic opposition to broad collective action, concedes this point—at least theoretically. The Conservative political record in the 1980s nevertheless demonstrates a different view in practice. When it came to office in 1981, the Reagan administration, among its many efforts to reduce American society's commitment to providing collective goods and to offsetting externalities, undertook the destruction of the EPA (as it similarly began to erode the power of the Department of Education, the Department of Health and Social Services, and other government agencies). Administrators sympathetic to business (read: "polluters") needs began to wind down pollution control programs developed during the 1970s. "Superfund" cleanup programs ground to a halt, and no new efforts to exert federal leadership in cleaning up the environment emerged. Whatever their arguments to the contrary, Conservatives have shown themselves markedly less concerned about neighborhood effects than maintaining corporate profits.

DIRECT INTERVENTION VERSUS EMISSIONS TAXES

Lately, emissions taxes have become the rage among many economists. Supposedly by metering a firm's discharges and then taxing the firm on the basis of its measured pollution, a neutral tax mechanism develops that internalizes the external costs or diseconomies. The tax becomes another cost of production that the profit-maximizing firm will seek to lower by introducing emission controls. However, in the real world, things need not work this way at all. Technologically speaking, we are nowhere near the point where we can install pollution-measuring meters. Such methods simply do not exist. Thus we are not presently able to develop an effective pollution tax. And even with a tax in place, there is no certainty that firms will opt for less pollution rather than paying the tax. In many cases, paying the tax might be a less costly short-term strategy than undertaking the expense of removing pollutants from the air or water. Even in the most ideal scenario—efficient taxes and rational firms operating in competitive markets—emissions taxes are a slow process for forcing change in pollution habits.

Direct intervention, if seriously undertaken, promises a quicker short-run solution. By setting emission standards and enforcing them with stiff fines or the threat of plant closure, a firm has an immediate incentive to introduce emission controls. Should a carrot rather than a stick be preferred in inducing industry compliance with environmental standards, direct subsidies, either to pay for the cost of pollution control or as cash incentives to firms that voluntarily reduce emissions, could be paid.

The Conservative argument against direct controls and subsidies maintains that they are inefficient, creating greater total social and private costs than the value of the benefits obtained. This supposedly results from compelling too much antipollution activity too fast. Northeasterners, whose recreational areas are quickly deteriorating and whose water and forest resources face immediate danger from acid rain, are not likely to be impressed by such logic. While we may not be able to restore the environment to pre-Industrial era conditions, excessive cost consciousness may produce a "rational" pro-environment strategy that does nothing at all for the environment.

The Radical Argument

Over the past three decades, a noteworthy social awareness has developed about various market failures and their effect on the quality of life under a capitalist system of production. With fairly substantial popular support in the 1970s, a number of collective efforts were launched to deal with such issues as consumer protection, occupational safety, developing new sources for energy and other scarce resources, and, of course, environmental protection. Yet two points are worth remembering: First, it was erroneously believed that more government intervention to correct any market failure was all that was needed. Second, the few timid gestures undertaken produced very limited benefits, and, in fact, we have recently marched away from the minor victories of the mid-1970s. The problem is that we have not seen "market failures" for what they really are: the market working precisely as it is supposed to work under a production-for-profit system.

CAPITALISM AND THE ENVIRONMENT

Profits, of course, are merely the revenues obtained by the capitalist after all production and distribution costs have been subtracted. To maximize profits, the rational capitalist must minimize costs. Insofar as it is cheaper (more profitable) to emit sulfur and other particulates into the atmosphere rather than invest in antipollution devices or nonpolluting production, acid rain and other environmental horrors are a quite "rational" and expected by-product of a production-for-profit system. Viewed this way, it becomes apparent that whatever the advantages to people in general from a clean environment, there are no advantages to a firm to undertake antipollution activities voluntarily. And so it is also true of other socially directed objectives such as consumer protection and occupational safety.

The record of capitalist destruction of the earth, its atmosphere, and ultimately its inhabitants is obvious enough. The degradation of the land through clear-cutting hardwood timber in the nineteenth century to obtain nothing but tannic acid for bootmaking; the mid-twentieth-century practice of stripmining coal; the modern crises of acid rain and of nuclear fallout from the Three Mile Island disaster illustrate that the search for private profits stands in open opposition to environmental, and hence human, concerns.

THE FAILURE OF PAST
ENVIRONMENTAL EFFORTS

Liberals and Conservatives (who, after all, cannot deny the evidence of environmental decline) concede the need for some pro-environmental activity. Liberals tend to favor direct control mechanisms implemented by a benevolent and all-seeing state, whereas Conservatives prefer the use of neutral emissions taxes that "induce" firms to reduce their polluting. Will either approach work?

The Liberal reliance on government direct controls or subsidies presumes, of course, that government is neutral—that government can determine environmental targets and develop and enforce rules that might directly threaten business enterprises' profits or continued operations. Yet the supposed neutrality of government in the marketplace has proved an illusive notion in practice. Even under Liberal administrations, the Environmental Protection Agency has shown a softness in forcing business to pay cleanup costs. Effectively using their lobbying power, firms have successfully pointed out that cleanup efforts that are too energetic can lead to lost profits, diminished ability to compete abroad, and finally to the loss of workers' jobs. In fact, even the unions have joined private enterprise in "going slow" on acid rain and other pollution problems. Accordingly, in the last years of the Carter administration, the EPA introduced "pollution offset" programs in which new firms and new plants could emit pollution so long as they could induce (pay) other firms to reduce emissions or within their own company reduce emissions elsewhere by an equal amount. Meanwhile, using a "bubble concept," old firms were given general permissible emissions limits over each plant, with the firm choosing where and how it cared to cut total pollution within the plant to meet the limits — more in the water and less in the air, or vice versa, if it made profitable sense. Such actions reflected concerns that too strenuous an antipollution policy could damage firm profitability. At best they slowed the rate of pollution buildup without recognizing the need to undo the crimes of the past as well as the present.

Conservatives showed their practical lack of concern for pollution problems during the Reagan years. While talk of emissions taxes and the sale of emission permits characterized the writings of Conservative economists when they actually addressed the pollution problem, no national emissions tax program has been put in place. In fact, the EPA has even been pulled back from the limited level of effectiveness that characterized the Carter years.

To be perfectly blunt, even though surveys show that most Americans believe the environment must be protected "whatever the cost" and even though the public's environmental awareness is now well over two decades old, no effective national environmental program has emerged yet nor seems likely to emerge soon.

THE NEED TO GET BEYOND "COST-BENEFIT"

For some, the Radicals' discounting of Liberal and Conservative environmental proposals will be interpreted as silly obstructionism. As in the case of consumer protection, the Radical opposition at first seems contradictory—that Radicals somehow oppose "serious" efforts to make safer products or to clean up the atmosphere. Such an inaccurate perception stems from a failure to grasp the basis of the Radical argument.

From a Radical perspective, failure to deal with environmental issues is not merely a capitalist oversight or some accidental consequence of a market-dominated society; it is directly traceable to capitalism's dominant feature—*the drive for profits*. Furthermore, it is not possible for capitalism to be itself (searching for profits) and to be better than itself (taking actions that reduce profits) at the same time. Capitalist (Conservative or Liberal) discussions about halting acid rain or cleaning up pollution in general are therefore nothing more than seductive deceptions.

The point becomes obvious when we peel back the Conservative and Liberal arguments to examine their real content. Both rely on a cost-benefit measurement of the extent of pollution as a problem and as an indicator of how much antipollution activity should be undertaken. The ultimate determinant of the extent of antipollution activity is, according to conventional theory, established by the point at which marginal social costs equal marginal social benefits (in other words, where the last dollar spent on cleaning up the environment is at least equal to a dollar's worth of gain from the actual cleanup). On the surface, this seems rational enough until we consider how costs and benefits are calculated. "Social costs" are seen as the sum of all private costs plus any governmental outlays for reducing pollution as determined by market-established prices. "Social benefits" are the sum of dollar benefits accruing to all individuals affected by the reduction of pollution. The bias of such an approach is always to overestimate costs and underestimate benefits, since costs are comparatively easily calculated in market terms while only a portion of benefits can be assigned a particular market value. A $10 million outlay for a steam electricity plant scrubber (whether paid for by the firm or by tax dollars) is easily perceived as a cost. However, what is the benefit of not killing a lake? A lake is only partly a commodity to which a market value can be assigned as a piece of real estate lost to its owners for personal or business use. A lake, a stream, or, more pointedly, a sunset has certain intrinsic values that are not calculable in current market terms.

Cost-benefit discussions under capitalism are always limited to property and commodity relationships. The "neighborhood effect" of Conservative theoreticians (and used also by Liberals) rests on calculating damages to individuals' property rights as the beginning point for offsetting spillover costs. Hence the estimated value of "social benefits"—which in discussions of external diseconomies are nothing more than the sum of estimable private property or market value gains—will always be stated lower than the real benefits to society of ending pollution.

In our previous discussion of consumer safety, we saw that once the issue was stripped to its basics, the conventional debate over consumer protection was off target and avoided the real issue of socially irrational production and consumption choices being the natural outcome of a production-for-profit system. As we found no remedy there to irrationality within even a modified capitalist system, we find no remedy forthcoming from efforts alleged to "offset" the market failure of external diseconomies resulting in acid rain or other pollution. Remedial antipollution actions of any consequence will take place only when social policies reflect real human needs, not the requirements and values of a commodity-dominated society. Ending pollution and maintaining a safe and humane environment, now and for the future, is a social goal that must be understood as having no ultimate "cost" limits with regard to what must be paid for its attainment. From a Radical perspective, society is more than the sum of each of its individual members. Society, or humankind, also has a historical dimension. We in the twentieth century have no right to limit the rights and blight the lives of human beings in the twenty-first century and beyond any more than midwesterners presently have the right to brew acid rain for northeasterners.

The Giant Corporation and Government

What Should Be Our Strategy toward Bigness in Business?

People of the same trade seldom meet together, even for merriment and diversion, but the conversation ends in a conspiracy against the public, or in some contrivance to raise prices.
Adam Smith, 1776

Every contract, combination in the form of trust or otherwise, or conspiracy, in restraint of trade or commerce ... is hereby declared to be illegal.... Every person who shall monopolize, or attempt to monopolize, or combine or conspire ... to monopolize ... shall be deemed guilty of a misdemeanor.
Sherman Anti-Trust Act, 1890

The problem in America is not that the top 100 corporation presidents are violating the laws, though God knows they are; the problem is they're writing the laws.
Nicholas Johnson, Federal Communications Commissioner, 1972

[The current proposal to relax antitrust prosecution] would be mainly to allow ... companies ... severely affected by foreign competition to have a better opportunity to merge.
Larry Speakes, White House spokesperson, 1986

THE PROBLEM

The economic theory of markets distinguishes between competitive market structures and numerous imperfectly competitive alternatives (monopolistic competition, oligopoly, and monopoly). Moreover, conventional theory demonstrates that society reaps greater benefits under pure competition: Maximum output is assured, prices are lower, and excessive profit making is avoided with all firms reacting to the dictates of a free market as "price takers." Under imperfectly competitive conditions, firms are able to exercise some degree of "price making," controlling prices and output for their own profitable advantage. In a textbook situation, there is little disagreement among economists about such generalizations. The trouble develops when we move from textbook examples to the real world.

A seemingly paradoxical situation appears when we examine the existing structure and organization of American business enterprise. On the one hand, the official ideology of American capitalism espouses a competitive ideal of many smallish producers, no one of which can materially affect price or output. On the other hand, everyday experience tells us that most markets are dominated by a comparative handful of very large firms. Exactly how much "bigness" might alter or eliminate desired competitive conditions has long been a concern in American capitalism. Since the passage of the Sherman Anti-Trust Act in 1890, a considerable body of law has been enacted "to protect competition." The essence of these accumulated laws may be summarized as follows.

1. It is illegal to enter into a contract, combination, or conspiracy in restraint of trade or to monopolize, attempt to monopolize, or combine or conspire to monopolize trade.
2. When the effect is to lessen competition or create a monopoly, it is illegal to acquire the stock or assets of competing companies, to discriminate among purchasers other than what can be justified by actual costs, or to enter into exclusive or tying contracts.
3. Under all cases, whether the effect is to monopolize or not, it is illegal to serve in the directorships of competing corporations, to use unfair methods of competition, or to employ unfair or deceptive acts or practices.

Despite the thrust of law and prevailing economic theory, the tendency toward larger and larger market structures has persisted since the

closing decades of the nineteenth century. Although bigness has sometimes been occasioned by a firm's own individual production and sales
efforts, by far the most popular route to increasing corporate size is
through merger and combination. The earliest merger efforts of the late
nineteenth century were largely *horizontal mergers*, which combined
side-by-side competitors in the same industry. Very shortly, there followed *vertical mergers*, combining suppliers and purchasers of goods
involved in the same chain of production. United States Steel, General
Motors, and the American Tobacco Company came into existence following the former path. National Biscuit Company and Standard Oil
(which also used horizontal combination) grew in size and influence
using the latter strategy.

Three eras of horizontal and vertical mergers are easily identifiable:
the 1890s, the 1920s, and the period immediately following World War
II. In recent years, horizontal and vertical merger activity has slowed, in
part because the really "juicy" combinations had already taken place and
in part because antitrust law impeded greater concentration and growth
of market power by existing giants. Merging, however, did not cease.
Beginning in the 1960s and continuing to the present, firms have increasingly undertaken *conglomerate mergers*, uniting enterprises where no
horizontal or vertical market advantages are present.

How significant has the recent conglomerate merger trend been?
As Figure 4.1 illustrates, there were as many mergers in the period from
1960 to 1980 as had taken place in the first sixty years of the century.
Moreover, there have been more major mergers in the past decade than in
any comparable period in our history. Of these most recent mergers, more
than 75 percent were conglomerate combinations. The obvious effect
of such consolidation activity has been to concentrate more and more
of the nation's productive capacity into fewer corporations. For instance,
in 1945 the nation's 200 largest manufacturing firms owned 45 percent of all assets of U.S. industry. Today they own over 60 percent. Looking at the data somewhat differently, we find that 94 percent of all U.S.
corporate assets are owned by just 12 percent of the nation's corporations.*

---

*In 1986, The Reagan administration proposed changing American antitrust law so
as to permit greater horizontal and vertical merger activity. To those who argued that
this would diminish domestic competition, the secretary of commerce replied that it
was because of competition—foreign competition for American markets—that relaxation of antitrust restraints on mergers was required. This approach has continued during the Bush years.

FIGURE 4.1   Major Mergers and Acquisitions by Decade, 1900–1988

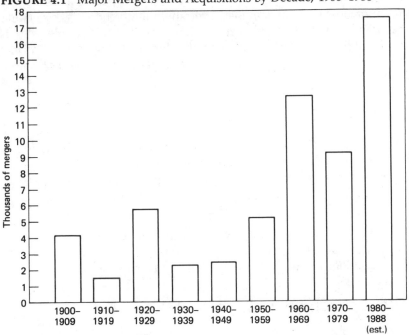

Source: Statistical Abstract of the United States, 1989.

What is the significance of this growing business concentration? To what extent are large firms able to act as price makers, setting excessive prices, restricting output, and creating market inefficiency? To what degree do antitrust law, foreign competition, and other economic developments offset or negate the trend toward bigness?

While no economist, regardless of ideological preference, denies the existence of big business, there is widespread disagreement as to whether modern corporate size and increased merger activity represent a serious monopoly threat to the economic and social organization of American society.

SYNOPSIS

The Conservative argument asserts that there are sufficient market and legal checks to make certain that big business does not act in an exploitative way but actually improves our economic well-being. Liberals accept the fact of bigness but maintain that government intervention is essential to control potential monopoly exploitation. The Radical argument holds that monopoly is the logical historical development of capitalism and that there is no way to halt this tendency without abolishing the production-for-profit system.

Anticipating the Arguments

- How do Conservatives argue that bigness in business is not proof of growing monopolistic power?
- What role do Liberals propose for government in dealing with the rise of giant enterprises, and how does their view differ from the Conservative approach?
- How do Radicals support their claim that the growth of alleged monopolistic business behavior in the United States is "merely the logical progression of capitalist development"?

The Conservative Argument

The rash of giant mergers over the past few decades has stimulated, largely unjustifiably, public concern over the so-called monopoly problem in the United States. In general, this concern rests on gross misunderstandings of the structure and performance of American business. Foremost among these is the confusion of bigness with monopoly, and the resulting corollary that big is bad. The anti-big-business attitude that emerges from these views is a serious threat to the American economic system. Far from leading to the rebirth of a competitive business society, most antimonopoly efforts erode free enterprise itself. Ironically, an attack on big business boils down to an attack on business of all kinds. More than they realize, the owners of mom-and-pop grocery stores and the like are themselves threatened by assaults on A&P, IBM, GM, and other business giants.

BIGNESS DOES NOT EQUAL MONOPOLY

Bigness in and of itself is not proof of monopoly power. Of course, there is no denying the existence of "dominant firms" in certain

American industries and of the concentration of market share and capital in the hands of a few firms in others. However, a variety of *real world* market forces come into play which negate or significantly diminish the "price making" powers economic theory suggests these business giants might possess. The point here is to get beyond "monopoly theory" and look at the world as it is. For instance, there are many cases of interindustry competition among different "concentrated" industries. Glass, aluminum, steel, paper, and plastic producers, for example, all battle each other for the food-container market. Nor should international competition be forgotten. While tariffs and shipping costs do offer some protection to American firms, the protection is not absolute—witness the 20 percent share of the auto market seized by foreign car makers. The point is simple. Big business, far from ending competition, has heightened it. The solitary village blacksmith, barrel maker, or flour miller of a century ago had far greater monopoly power over price, quality, and output than does his present-day big business counterpart.

Those who worry about excessive monopoly power should consider one further point. In a market society, the great check against price gouging, by IBM or by a barrel maker, is consumer demand. If prices go too high, sellers simply cannot sell their products—or enough of them to make a profit—and prices will come down.

If we can get beyond the silly but appealing logic of the "big is bad" argument, we might truly understand that the opposite is much more nearly correct: Big business has been good for America.

IN DEFENSE OF BIGNESS

The primary reason for merger and combination among enterprises in the past has been to obtain technical economies that lower production costs. To be sure, there have been examples of firms attempting to exploit their market power as monopolistic price makers; however, such mergers are rare indeed, and when detected (as they easily are), antitrust and civil law provide ample protections to society at large. In the meantime, *big* business has been the major vehicle for economic and technical advance in the United States. Few can deny that product progress and relatively falling prices for most consumer and producer goods during the twentieth century have been the result of expensive technological advancements; these could only have resulted from the great capital concentration and large-scale market-ing strategies of big enterprise. Would those who want to abolish GM also want to abolish the assembly-line production technique with its efficiencies and savings?

Recently, Liberal and Radical critics of business enterprise have directed their wrath against the newer conglomerate mergers. Such attacks are also threats to business growth, since conglomerate mergers presently account for about 90 percent of all combinations. This strategy is an extension of the "big is bad" argument; however, it fails to consider that conglomerate mergers may also provide con-sumer benefits. By strengthening inefficient and costly businesses through improved management techniques and by providing badly needed capital, prices will be lowered. Moreover, the conglomerate merger often increases competition by resuscitating firms that other-wise would fail. And strong firms are strengthened by acquiring many diverse operations that permit the firm to avoid "putting all its eggs in one basket." In this era of immense and swift technological and product change, diversification is an important insurance policy for a large enterprise.

The size and scale of the truly large American firms become a bit less threatening if two factors are considered: (1) the threat posed by giant foreign manufacturing enterprises and (2) the health and abun-dance of small enterprises in the United States.

A policy aimed at weakening large firms simply because they are large will not protect the American consumer—and certainly not the American worker. A host of foreign giants stands ready to flood Ameri-can markets with goods should large American firms fail to maintain their vitality and profitability. Indeed, the relative slippage of American producers in world competition is an important argument on behalf of reducing constraints on the size of American business.

In any case, bigness is vastly overemphasized. Of America's 11 million businesses, 10.8 million qualify as small businesses according to the Small Business Administration. Regardless of the size of the giant enterprises, no other economy can boast this proportion of small, independent enterprises to the entire population. Small busi-ness employs more than 60 percent of the total work force. The smallest of the small, those employing twenty or fewer workers, the fastest-growing segment of the business economy, hires two out of every three current entrants into the labor market. Given these characteristics of American business enterprise, it becomes obvious that big business, even if it were a problem, gets undue attention from Liberals and Radicals. Smallness and competition remain the dominant characteristics of American enterprise.

Singling out big business is unfair and misleading. Even if business bigness were demonstrably bad, why isn't the same logic applied to big government or big labor unions? Those who cry "monopoly" in the business sector rarely apply that argument against the United Auto Workers or the Teamsters, nor do they see the bureaucratic state management of pricing—from hospital rooms to agricultural products—as analogous to the imagined monopoly power of big enterprise.

THE PROMISE OF A NEW APPROACH BY GOVERNMENT

The record of government enforcement of antitrust law has, since the beginning of the century, been inconsistent and contradictory, tending always to reflect the political ideology of the current occupant of the White House. Naturally enough, the intensity of antitrust action heightens with Liberal occupancy. However, even under Conservative administrations, there remained a troublesome ambivalence about how to deal with giant enterprises. Frequently actions were initiated by both Conservative and Liberal administrations against firms purely on the grounds that they were big or that they were too profitable. Such an approach works against the development of dynamic and thriving firms. It is rather like punishing the winning runner in a race because she ran too fast. The profitable business is not the only loser, however; so is the society that has benefitted in jobs and lower product prices from the large firm's efficiency. However, two landmark antitrust cases of the 1980s seem to restore some reason to our public policy toward big business.

In the 1982 dismissal of a government action against IBM for monopolizing the mainframe computer industry, the Justice Department agreed that despite IBM's size and its share of the market, there was no proof that the firm has acted monopolistically. The decision should stand as an important legal landmark against those who would penalize a firm thoughtlessly simply because it has been successful. In the AT&T case, decided at the same time as the IBM case, the Justice Department affirmed the doctrine of competition. AT&T's monopoly

100 Problems in the Marketplace

power in the buying and selling of communications equipment and services was ended. AT&T was proved guilty of using its power (provided by government as a regulated monopoly) to exclude competitors from the data and electronic transmission market. AT&T was compelled to divest itself of its purely "public utility" local phone operations and join battle fairly with the other "big boys" (including IBM) in the information systems market. For the foreseeable future, a useful antitrust policy is in place: *Bigness itself does not prove collusion or unfair price setting, but when such activities are proved, they will be halted.*

Paralleling and complementing the IBM and AT&T cases has been a relaxation at the Justice Department of vigorous opposition to large corporate mergers. This, of course, has sparked criticism from some Liberal critics who fail to see the advantages obtained from most of these mergers. Far from being a submission to business pressure, the more passive approach toward mergers and "bigness" in its many forms is a recognition of the economic gains from size that provide important benefits to the entire society, not the least of which is an improvement of American firms' ability to compete with foreign giants. However, Conservatives are not unmindful that bigness *can* lead to abuses.

Conservatives do not deny the existence of monopoly abuse when it is real. Very clearly, monopoly power is unjustifiable and injurious to individuals. It prevents efficient allocation of resources. However, aside from those cases of monopoly initiated or encouraged by the government and occasional conspiratorial endeavors by individual enterprises (and even here government tax or purchase policies often stimulate criminal activity), the "monopoly problem" is mostly a phony issue. Liberals use it as a pretext for urging massive social or governmental interference with the market, while Radicals find it convenient as an excuse for their revolutionary assault on the entire system. Both groups would use the issue in a self-serving fashion to extinguish individualism and private property rights.

The Liberal Argument

Traditional economic analysis since Adam Smith has argued that the "great regulator" for business activity is the market. Here, small, competitive firms struggle against each other to sell goods and gain customers. Prices and the possibility of exploitation are always regulated by the "invisible hand" of supply and demand. Although we may nit-pick over whether this type of pure competition ever existed outside of economists' minds, it certainly does not exist in the United States today. Just 2,000 businesses in all areas of the economy produce about half of our GNP; the "invisible hand" has largely been replaced by the highly visible fist of corporate power.

THE PROBLEM OF POLICY SELECTION

While most modern-day Conservatives equivocate on the issue of big business, preferring not to see any monopoly problems except in the rarest of cases, Liberals face the problem directly. *Business concentration does exist in the United States.* As Figure 4.1 showed, the scale and intensity of efforts to increase concentration through merger is grow-ing. Nor are all merger efforts "safe" conglomerate combinations. The policy issue, then, is not a matter of recognizing the obvious but of determining how to deal with it.

The most rudimentary analysis of monopoly behavior tells us that, all things being equal, monopolistic firms tend to charge higher prices and produce less than might otherwise be expected under competitive conditions. They employ fewer workers at lower wages and generally foster resource misallocation. Moreover, the greater the degree of monopoly power, the greater the consumer exploitation.

The implications of this line of economic analysis are clear. The return of competition is apparently the only way to return to eco-nomic virtue. In a policy sense, this must mean the enforcement of a vigorous antimonopoly policy, leading to the restructuring of indus-try into greater numbers of similar-sized units of production. Liberals are not in total agreement on this point, but most would oppose a grand breaking up of giant enterprises. First of all, the practical appli-cation of a literal "break them up" policy is not politically or legally feasible. We long ago passed the point of being able to return to some romantic eighteenth-century concept of the marketplace. This is not to say that stimulation of competition in certain industries might not be desirable or possible through the application of antitrust laws. In fact, the Justice Department must always be prepared to initiate antimonopoly legal action, but this could not be carried out on a broad scale without weakening our legal and economic structures. Second, there is no solid evidence that pure competition, enforced

TABLE 4.1   Percent of Domestic Production Share Accounted for by the Largest Four Firms and the Largest Twenty Firms in Selected Industries

Industrial Category	Number of Firms	Four-Firm Concentration	Twenty-Firm Concentration
Motor vehicles, car bodies	284	.92	.99+
Cereal breakfast foods	32	.86	.99+
Tires and inner tubes	108	.66	.98
Aluminum production	15	.64	1.00
Soap and detergents	642	.60	.83
Petroleum refining	282	.28	.76

Source: U.S. Department of Commerce, *Concentration Ratios in Manufacturing, 1982 Census of Manufacturing,* 1986, Table 5; and adapted from H. Craig Petersen, *Business and Government,* 3rd ed., 1989, p. 51.

indiscriminately, would be beneficial, even if it could be attained without seriously wrenching society.

What these observations mean in a practical context is that Liberals approach the question of "bigness in American business" quite pragmatically. As Table 4.1 indicates, the degree of concentration varies from industry to industry, and concentration alone does not tell the whole story about abuses of market power. Accordingly, concentration in the oil industry might be approached differently from concentration in the auto industry. Domestic automobile production is limited to just three firms, with General Motors alone producing between 50 and 60 percent of American output. Charges that GM has worked effectively in the past as a price leader are difficult to question. However, price leadership does not necessarily mean consumer exploitation. Nor would breaking up GM necessarily lead to social improvement. Even though GM's size has probably pushed it well beyond what is necessary for attaining efficiency from economies of scale, there is no assurance that forty or even a dozen smaller GMs could produce a product of similar price and quality and hire the work force that the present monster does. And, at any rate, the once-dominant position of GM has been severely eroded by the extensive penetration of the American auto market by foreign car makers. In this case at least, most Liberals will agree with Conservatives that concern over national concentration ratios and domestic firm size must be weighed against the realities of world competition.

On the other hand, the oil industry, with less actual concentration than the auto industry, conspired during the 1970s energy crises to force up the prices of gasoline and natural gas by withholding supplies.

The point is that there are different types of giant enterprises, some highly predatory and exploitative and others reasonably responsible to the public interest. Concentration alone is no justification for applying a vigorous antitrust action against members of the American auto industry. But the behavior of the oil industry in the 1970s is the worst kind of monopolistic activity. There are no easy "monopoly tests." Each case must be taken on its own merits.

Having rejected the rigid competitive argument, we are left to accept the reality of modern corporate concentration. However, though Liberals realize that bigness itself need not be proof of monopoly abuse, they do not subscribe to the policy advanced by Conservatives. The quest for greater market power is not always enlightened; it may, in fact, destroy business itself, as large firms act consciously or unconsciously to protect and expand their influence. Certainly, the current preoccupation of American business with "merger mania" has had a negative effect because it diverts funds into takeovers rather than capital investment and it absorbs the brightest business minds in short-run profit objectives rather than long-run production planning. Meanwhile, unrestrained business power may lead to the domination of government by narrow business interests and the subversion of the rights of the many for the benefit of a few. Thus Liberals believe the creation of a clear public policy toward mergers and bigness in business is essential to protect the balance of pluralistic interests in an open society. An equitable balance of labor, consumer, and capital interests must be the philosophical cornerstone of any intelligent policy toward business.

Through fair and calculated government intervention, big business can be made compatible with the social objectives of economic order, reasonable prices and high quality, and technological advancement. Government actions, depending on the situation, must go beyond mere antitrust enforcement. They may take the form of selective tax and subsidy manipulation; more extensive direct controls over pricing, hiring, and capital policies; and direct regulation of such developments as multinational business activity. Monopoly policy, moreover, must not be separated from general public policy objectives directed at inflation control, maintaining full employment, and encouraging economic growth. Some people will argue that this external imposition of social objectives on the private sector is pure socialism, but they miss the point.

SOCIAL CONTROL IS NOT SOCIALISM

Pragmatic social control of big business is not the same as social ownership. Corporate ownership today is widely dispersed and far removed from the day-to-day management decisions of American business. Excessive concern over *who* owns the productive property only clouds the important business and public issues at stake. *How* the privately owned property is performing is the really important question. Even though privately owned, most large businesses are already "social institutions" with "social responsibilities." To put the point simply, GM—with its sales of around $100 billion and its 600,000 employees—does not have the right to fail any more than it has the right to conspire against the public. To demand social responsibility is perfectly consistent with the real-world structure of business and the economy, and it does not challenge private ownership in any serious way.

Businesses, moreover, are more responsive in the area of social responsibility than is generally understood. Social concern on their part is not purely altruism but good business. Flagrant monopolistic behavior invites government scrutiny and public outrage. The old era of "the public be damned" is past. Few firms, whatever their size and market power, want long and costly antitrust litigation. Even consumer boycotts and public pressure for legislative intervention are sizeable threats and induce thoughtful constraint. Moreover, there is significant pressure within the business community to police itself. Abuse of economic power disrupts markets and creates economic instability; this situation, while perhaps favorable to one or a few firms, interferes with general business activity. Social responsibility, finally, is not an ethical question but a matter of profit and loss.

These points should not be misunderstood. The Liberal fully understands that big business may indeed be a threat—in its pricing, labor, international, and other policies. But big business does not *have* to be a threat to the economic system. It can be brought under social control.

Public policy toward big business, then, remains a matter of directing private enterprise toward social objectives that include reasonable prices, efficiency, high employment, and adequate profit return while also taking into consideration such broad concerns as ecology, resource conservation, and the overall performance of the economy. The creation of such a policy must be the responsibility of an enlightened federal government. Government must act as an unbiased umpire, attempting always to balance the diverse economic and social interests of the nation. Such intervention need not abridge basic property rights (which is what Radicals want). But it would set social priorities above the pursuit of selfish individualistic goals (so feverishly defended by Conservatives).

The Radical Argument

To some, "monopoly power" may seem to be a nonissue. Who, after all, will defend a monopolistic organization of markets? Yet although Conservatives and Liberals oppose monopoly power, neither group understands monopoly's place in capitalist development. Neither Conservatives nor Liberals appreciate the current scale and political and economic impact of monopoly organization in the United States, nor do they understand that this phenomenon has not been accidental.

Among the capitalist strategies to enlarge profits, monopolistic price making is certainly the most effective. Monopolistic arrangements, either through the dominance of a single firm or through formal and informal agreements of otherwise competing firms, allow for the maximum possible extraction of profits, as the gap between sale prices and costs expands. Thus the Radical position can be distinguished easily by its interpretation of monopoly as being the centerpiece of modern capitalism and the logical progression of capitalist development. Monopoly power is not merely *a* problem; it is, in the broadest sense, *the* problem of our time. Accordingly, this issue looms much larger for Radicals than for Conservatives or Liberals.

THE ORIGINS AND SCALE OF
MONOPOLY DEVELOPMENT

In the early formative stages of capitalist development, competition among many enterprises of relatively similar size and power is the dominant economic characteristic. This is only a temporary and transitional stage, however, not the perfect, unchanging economic state of affairs idealized by Conservatives and even some Liberals. The reason that this stage comes to an end is not difficult to explain. Competition over expands the productive base and cheapens the price of commodities. With falling prices come falling profits. Many competitive capitalists, faced with the frequent periods of general economic crisis that grip a capitalist economy, cannot survive. At first, "gentlemen's agreements" to maintain prices, divide profits, or allocate sales territories may be tried, but these strategies break down as the larger enterprises violate agreements and drive out the smaller producers. These small firms are eliminated either through bankruptcy or through merger, but the effect is the same: concentration of production among fewer and fewer producers and centralization of wealth in fewer and fewer hands.

In the process of concentration and centralization, merger remains the favored technique. In the United States, merger activity has occurred in four great waves: 1897–1900, 1924–1930, 1945–1947, and the current stage, which dates from about 1960. During the first three periods, mergers were usually horizontal (among producers of similar products) or vertical (among buyers and sellers in different stages of the production process). Most American industrial giants evolved during these periods of horizontal and vertical merger activity. Meanwhile, once size was established, greater size was generated as the dominant firms were able to control prices, technological introductions, and, most significant, profits to their own growth advantage.

Nowhere is the historical increase of concentration more evident than in the automobile industry. The number of independently owned automobile producers fell from 181 in 1900 to 44 in 1927 to just 4 by the 1960s. Today, GM alone accounts for about 60 percent of American-made auto and truck sales. Evidence of industry concentration and one-firm dominance is easily apparent in even a cursory survey of modern American business: steel (United States Steel), aluminum (Alcoa), mainframe computers (IBM), and so on. The top four firms in such diverse industries as aircraft, machine tools and instruments, dairy products, baking, industrial chemicals, petroleum refining, rubber, cigarettes, soaps, photographic equipment, and office equipment account for more than half of all output, employment, and profits in that industry.

Since the 1960s, practically all mergers have taken a conglomerate form (combining enterprises in wholly unrelated lines of production).

While Conservative and Liberal apologists are quick to point out that with the decline of horizontal and vertical mergers, industrial concentration in particular industries has slowed down, they scarcely recognize the enormous centralization potential of conglomerate mergers. Practically every giant enterprise has diversified into unrelated markets. This, of course, means that a giant such as GM, which is involved in autos, aircraft engines, household consumer products, banking, and much more, can bring its awesome power to bear in more than one market.

The reality of increasing concentration and centralization is obvious. The number and dollar volume of large corporate mergers has been high and basically rising for nearly twenty five years. Indeed, any future slowdown in the merger mania will most likely be a reflection of the fact that there is simply less left to merge rather than a change in corporate or government strategy. In 1950, the top 200 industrial firms owned about 48 percent of all industrial assets. By 1960, this share had grown to 53 percent; by 1989, 63 percent. Looking at corporate concentration another way, less than 1 percent of all corporations now own more than 60 percent of all corporate assets.

THE EFFECTS OF MONOPOLY

As every veteran of introductory economics knows, traditional theory holds monopoly power to be disruptive to the economy and society. While conventional economists commonly hold to such theoretical views of monopoly power, few are able to recognize the real thing when they see it. Somehow the present concentration and centralization of economic power is not associated with the monopoly model. Consequently, the real effects of monopoly power on American workers and consumers are overlooked. These adverse effects appear in various forms, from higher pricers to fewer jobs to greater political and personal manipulation.

The ability of a firm to earn profits clearly depends on its size. Billion-dollar enterprises earn profits at rates about three times larger than those of million-dollar firms. It may be argued with some truth that larger size allows for some economies of scale in production and therefore larger profit margins, but the phenomenal profit rates of the giants are mainly the result of monopolistic pricing abilities rather than greater efficiencies. In fact, in some industries (autos, for example), the habit of setting monopolistic prices first and tending to efficiency questions last is well known and easily demonstrated.

Automobile producers long ago exceeded the economies-of-scale benefits of bigness. Indeed, American business leaders have tacitly admitted this. George Romney, then president of American Motors, told a Senate subcommittee in 1958 that in auto production, cost economies are a "negligible thing" after 400,000 units per year. The inefficiency of the giant auto producers became evident in the 1970s and 1980s as foreign competitors grabbed more than a quarter of the American market. As the domestic auto industry slumped through the recession of 1981–1982 and struggled to keep itself afloat among a flood of foreign imports, workers were furloughed by the tens of thousands.

Whereas the auto industry's difficulties reflect the natural tendencies toward inefficiency in an established monopolistic enterprise, the recent merger movement has produced a special kind of inefficiency. With corporate capital being absorbed in grand merger schemes, little has been made available to expand output and improve production techniques. Again, the worker pays as American products lose ground to foreign competition. (More on this in Issue 7.)

While some workers are squeezed from jobs due to giant firms' productive inefficiency, others are forced into unemployment as concentration and centralization produce a variety of "labor-saving" schemes. In some cases, growth and merger lead directly to more capital-intensive output techniques. (Of course, capital intensiveness is not to be confused with greater efficiency.) In other cases, the giant may merely close what it considers duplicating operations or relocate them overseas or elsewhere in the United States where wages are lower.

In the old industrial heartland of the Northeast and the Midwest, joblessness resulting from the latter type of monopolistic behavior is well known. The scenario goes like this: First, a small- or medium-sized manufacturing operation is picked up by a growing multinational conglomerate. Second, after acquiring the local firm's good name, market, patents, and anything else of value, the conglomerate announces that current operations will be "relocated." Third, the plant "runs away" to a new location—often overseas but frequently to safe nonunion American sites. Although it is possible that some jobs are created elsewhere, the runaway plant leaves massive joblessness and devastated communities in its wake.

Whether jobs have been lost to new production methods, to closing redundant facilities, or to production inefficiencies, the relative stagnation of employment in the big business sector is easily shown. Between 1964 and 1988, the nation's 500 largest industrial firms increased the real value of their capital assets by more than 150 percent; yet this growth increased their employment (and much of this took place overseas) by only about 30 percent. Looking at the trends another way, the 500 largest industrials increased their share of the nation's output by about 50 percent, but their share of the nation's employment actually fell. The trend is obvious: As fewer and fewer firms control more and more of American output, they employ relatively fewer workers. More workers are pushed downward into the lower-paying, less secure bottom rungs of American business, and many slip into permanent unemployment.

Meanwhile, the giant enterprises exercise their power beyond the marketplace. Education, from the public school to the university, is organized to fill the labor and consumer needs of big business at several levels. Through such "charitable" foundations as Ford, Rockefeller, Carnegie, and Exxon, acceptable educational and cultural values are subsidized. Such actions, far from being examples of the "social responsibility of big business" so applauded by some Liberals, are but self-serving attempts to gain respectability for monopoly power. This fact is blatantly apparent at Exxon, for instance, whose educational foundation is organized as a sub-bureau of the public relations department.

As ITT's attempt in the early 1970s to grab the American Broadcasting Company showed, giant corporations also seek to control the media. Even when such control is not direct, it may be exercised indirectly because of the financial dependence of radio, television, newspapers, and magazines on advertising revenues from big business. When such societal controls by monopolistic enterprises are added to the exploitative economic domination of monopoly power, it is evident that almost every aspect of our lives—on the job or at leisure—is molded by the needs of giant corporations.

Nor is the influence of monopoly capitalism limited to the national boundaries of capitalist nations. The growth and expansion of the

United States as an imperialist power almost exactly paralleled the centralization and concentration of capital. The same ceaseless drive to accumulate surplus and profits that led to monopoly development soon forced American entrepreneurs outside their borders in search of markets, cheap labor, or raw materials. The burden of monopoly is felt around the world.

THE FAILURE OF GOVERNMENT

Given this grim picture of the giants' domination, can we construct a policy to alleviate the problem? If by a policy we mean some enlarged form of government antitrust enforcement, the answer is no. The tail does not wag the dog. Corporate domination of government is perhaps the most obvious example of naked monopoly power. It is hoped that this fact is becoming more widely appreciated by the mass of citizens. As Marx said, "The state is the form in which individuals of a ruling class assert their common interests." The power of business interests to dominate government dates back to the writing of the Constitution; however, it has been most obvious since the rise of the trusts and modern corporations. Business was able to create regulatory agencies in its own interest (the Interstate Commerce Commission, for instance) and to have antitrust laws used as antilabor devices. Even after antitrust law finally was directed against business, it was used to halt concentrations of business power in only the most flagrant cases of malignant monopoly. The 1982 Justice Department decision that IBM's 65 percent share of the mainframe computer business did not violate antitrust law and the Reagan and Bush administrations' efforts to ease restrictions on mergers should serve to prove that big business has little to fear from trust-busting.

We already have discussed in earlier issues how manufacturers have used and manipulated consumer protection laws, how agribusiness has created governmental farm policy, and how the polluters control environmental policy. As we shall continue to see, the manipulation of government by monopolistic business enterprise is natural to our economic organization. Neutrality is simply not possible for a government that depends on business support to elect its officials and that is formally committed to the production-for-profit system. Liberals may argue that social control and accountability are their goals, but this is nonsense if the maintenance of capitalism as a system is a prior and overriding objective.

The solution to the monopoly problem does not lie within the framework of conventional economic analysis and policy. The only humane solution is some degree of social ownership and operation of the means of production at least in the heavily concentrated industrial sectors of the economy. This entails the participation of individual workers and citizens in determining such basic economic questions as what goods shall be produced, how, and for whom. In terms of immediate Radical strategy, this means support for all efforts leading to greater worker control over production, profits, and wages. Citizen planning, not corporate planning, is the final objective; however, such planning must be coordinated with the needs of the entire society. For those who sneer at such proposals as "pie in the sky," it should be pointed out that the "social democracies" of Western Europe have followed this course for some time with considerable success. Meanwhile, despite the much-vaunted rise of "market economics" in Eastern Europe and the Soviet Union, the shift of their economies away from "ideological central planning" has not ended experiments in broader citizen control over production decisions, but has actually enhanced such developments.

Government Regulation of Business

Has Deregulation Worked?

The committee has found among the leading representatives of the railroad interests an increasing readiness to accept the aid of Congress in working out the solution of the railroad problem which has obstinately baffled all their efforts, and not a few of the ablest railroad men of the country seem disposed to look to the intervention of Congress as promising to afford the best means of ultimately securing a more equitable and satisfactory adjustment of the relations of the transportation interests to the community than they themselves have been able to bring about.

U.S. Senate Select Committee on Interstate Commerce, 1886

Railroads were totally regulated for almost a century. Obviously it will take time for railroads to learn all of the things that can be done in a freer climate. It will also take shippers time to learn this as well. But already it is apparent that both can use deregulation to their respective advantages.

Association of American Railroads, 1982

The headlong descent into ideological and haphazard deregulation is over as far as Congress is concerned.

Congressman Charles E. Schumer, 1987

THE PROBLEM

The objective of antitrust law and its enforcement, as discussed in Issue 4, is to maintain an acceptable degree of competition in most markets. A second type of government intervention in the structure and performance of markets rests on the assumption that certain markets perform best under less-than-competitive conditions that are strictly regulated by government agencies. In these regulated industries, a kind of "monopoly bargain" is struck whereby one firm, or at most a few, is granted various protections from competition in return for surrendering to a regulatory agency power over pricing, output, and other production, financing, and marketing decisions.

The most common example of a regulated industry and a regulatory agency is a regional public utility (a gas and electric company or a regional phone company), which is regulated by a state "public service commission." However, the concept of public regulation has been applied much more broadly than in the so-called public utility sector. The first federal venture into direct regulation came with the Interstate Commerce Commission (ICC) in 1887 (a full three years before federal antitrust law was laid down in the Sherman Act). The ICC was charged with restoring order to the nation's ailing railroads, an industry long characterized on the one hand by periodic episodes of financial collapse resulting from vicious rate wars and on the other by the very worst type of monopolistic practices. Over the next century, more than a dozen independent federal agencies and commissions were erected to bring a measure of government regulation to everything from banking to the airwaves to nuclear power.

Initially, the logic of insulating certain industries from the forces of the market rested on two economic considerations: (1) that there existed the economic advantages of lower costs (*economies of scale*) resulting from a single producer or a limited number of producers and (2) that a discernible *public interest* would be served by exempting the industry from competition and by establishing government regulation of price, service, and output. As the years passed, however, these two criteria were stretched, modified, and sometimes neglected altogether as the extent of government regulation expanded in many directions. The idea of regulating "in the public interest" was a peculiarly American experiment. As Figure 5.1 illustrates, most European nations either nationalized or operated as public enterprises the industries that Americans put under regulation.

FIGURE 5.1   Which Industrial Sectors Are Nationalized? A Comparison between the United States and Selected European Nations

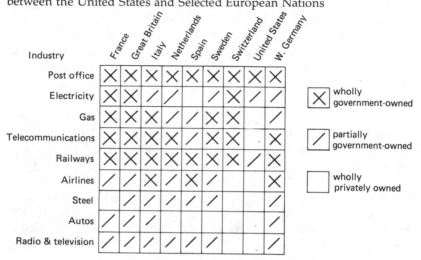

For most of the past century, industrial regulation enjoyed a high degree of public support, with most practicing economists nodding their approval at the work of regulatory agencies. The regulatory high-water mark was reached in the early 1970s. However, in the economy of the late 1970s, troubled by inflation, recession, unemployment, energy crises, and growing federal budgetary problems, regulatory activity was placed under greater scrutiny. What a closer examination showed pretty much reflected what one wanted to see. Most Liberals, who had long been supporters of the regulation "in the public interest" philosophy, defended the practice. Conservatives, sensing the direction of a new ideological wind that was blowing up, were quick to attack federal regulation of industry. Never strong supporters of regulatory efforts anyway, most Conservatives felt that the regulatory link was among the weakest in the chain of Liberal interventionism in the economy. Their attack was direct enough: Regulation produces greater costs to society through creating and maintaining market inefficiency than any benefits it might provide for the public interest. By the mid-1970s, a new buzzword had entered academic and political discussions of the regulatory process: *deregulation.*

Between 1978 and 1985, the deregulators (that now included a fair number of Liberals as well as most Conservatives) had succeeded in eliminating most regulation of airlines, buses, trucking, radio broadcasting, and natural gas production and distribution. Considerable relaxation occurred in the regulation of railroads, television and cable broadcasting, and banking and financial services. Meanwhile, the splitting up of the Bell Telephone System in 1984 as the result of federal antitrust action opened much of the previously highly regulated phone system to market competition. The deregulatory mood spread during the Reagan years to a variety of government agencies charged with overseeing broad areas of social regulation such as the Department of Consumer Affairs and the Federal Trade Commission.

By the late 1980s, however, the deregulation movement seemed to be running out of steam. The financial shock of a 500-point decline in the stock market on October 19, 1987, brought forth calls for greater regulation of the securities market by the federal government. This shock was followed quickly by a monumental solvency crisis in the savings and loan industry that seemed to be the direct outcome of "excessive deregulation" of banking institutions. In the airlines industry, formerly hailed by antiregulation advocates as the model for successful deregulation, the initial consumer benefits of increased competition and lower fares seemed to be ebbing in favor of greater monopoly power and higher prices. At the same time, deregulation of the television industry seemed to be pointing toward a decline of over-the-air-waves television and the potential loss of a long-held American "right," that of free television programming. Such developments began to generate second thoughts about deregulation as well as serious political and economic pressure to make another 180-degree turn in public policy toward business—*reregulation*.

SYNOPSIS

Conservatives argue that regulation is counterproductive, producing more costs than benefits to both the regulated industries and the public. Accordingly, they support the drift to deregulation and advocate more deregulation. The Liberal argument defends the general performance record of most regulated industries and maintains that many recent experiments in deregulation are dangerous to the economy. Radicals see the historical development of regulation as essentially a prop to monopoly privilege and recent deregulation efforts as merely a smokescreen for doing away with what business now considers the less attractive aspects of serving the public interest.

Anticipating the Arguments

- What are some of the counterproductive results of regulation that Conservatives see, and how would their plan for deregulation end such problems?
- On what grounds do Liberals defend at least limited regulation over complete deregulation?
- Why do Radicals reject regulation and instead call for public ownership and operation of previously regulated industries?

The Conservative Argument

The Conservative position on regulation is based on two sturdy and now-familiar principles. First, regulation—or any interference with the market—tends to create resource misallocation, inefficiency, and, ultimately, greater costs to the community. Second, left alone, the market is capable of more rational decisions about the success or survival of a firm or industry than is the voting public or its representatives and bureaucrats.

THE FAILURE OF REGULATION

Except for the very limited and infrequent situations where a "natural monopoly" exists, there are no justifiable conditions for regulating industry. A natural monopolist, such as a local power and lighting company, enjoys the advantages of large-scale production techniques that can provide all of a market's output at lower unit costs than could exist if there were a number of producers. In such a situation, the community can obtain the lower costs only if it restrains the monopolists' natural propensity to maximize profits by setting prices at whatever the market will bear. The problem with the American application of this regulation principle, however, is that regulation has mostly been applied in situations where some degree of competition actually exists or where competition should be encouraged. The result has been that the community gets a regulated monopoly or a tight oligopoly when it would have been better served by creating and maintaining competitive conditions. Even the regulation of so-called natural monopolies has had its problems because of inefficient rulings on pricing and service by the regulatory agency, usually in the name of protecting the "public interest."

To get the point directly, let's examine our first effort at using an independent regulatory agency to supervise an industry: the ICC. As the oldest U.S. regulatory agency, the ICC has the longest list of "classic" regulatory errors and is a good example of all the debilitating effects age brings to commission activity. The original intent of the ICC was to bring order to the chaotic and excessively competitive rate-making practices of the railroads. Its goal was to protect the public from railroad price collusion and to protect the railroads from one another. By the mid-1930s, ICC power extended to all surface commercial transportation in the country. Specific ICC controls covered rate setting, mergers, financial issues, abandonment, and service discontinuance, as well as carrier layoffs of labor. There was virtually nothing that a rail carrier or any other carrier regulated by the Interstate Commerce Commission could do without first obtaining commission approval.

Before attempts at rail and trucking deregulation were introduced in the 1970s, the ICC followed a narrow, two-sided strategy: first, to maintain a "competitive balance" between and among the different modes (trucks and railroads) of surface transportation that provided each carrier with an adequate return on its investment, and second, to provide service at a cost and to the extent broad public interest objectives were served.

In misguided efforts to "maintain competition among different modes," the ICC long followed the strategy of "umbrella rate making," a practice of setting a rate high enough to allow less efficient modes of transport to earn a profit on specific services. This provided a special handicap to railroads, which lost traffic to other modes simply because they were not allowed to set lower rates (prices) and use their greater efficiency in the movement of certain goods. In protecting trucks and water carriers, the ICC directed business away from the more efficient railroads. At the same time, shippers and consumers absorbed higher-than-necessary transport charges in their purchases.

Similar anticompetitive outcomes resulted from the ICC's opposition to rail mergers. This led to costly "balkanization." The line-haul railroads were unable to combine to increase freight exchange and coordination and to strengthen their financial structures. By denying the industry access to these economies of scale, service remained expensive and inefficient. The ICC also prohibited intermodal mergers. Railroads were not allowed to consolidate with trucks and other carriers to improve their overall efficiency.

Meanwhile, in search of the will-o'-the-wisp "public interest," the ICC also acted to raise transport costs and reduce rail efficiency by maintaining redundant routes and little-used spurs. Permission for abandonments of low-density or loss-producing operations was difficult to obtain from the commission, and railroads were compelled to pour millions of dollars into expensive routes that generated only a few dollars in traffic.

By prohibiting railroads from setting their rates freely, denying them the right to develop joint rail-truck transportation companies, and demanding that they continue to operate costly and inefficient services and schedules, the ICC rendered the railroads' competitive situation virtually hopeless. ICC decisions on rates, abandonments, and mergers were presented as proof of the agency's commitment to the public interest. In point of fact, its action harmed rather than protected the nation's welfare.

The general ICC strategy was applied by other regulatory agencies with not much better success. Whether we look at railroads, airlines, long-distance telecommunications, broadcasting, trucking, or banking, we see the same dismal results from the era of public regulation. First, regulation encouraged cartel pricing. This usually meant setting a price floor that was high enough to allow the least efficient member of the cartel to survive. The industry price was usually higher than the price that would have existed under competitive conditions. Second, in the absence of any effective price competition in the industry, competition could only emerge in nonprice areas. Banks emphasized "special services." Airlines promoted themselves as "friendlier" or as offering more sumptuous in-flight meals. Few regulated firms were likely to introduce new services that produced real benefits or savings to customers. New ways of doing business were always seen as posing elements of risk and instability that neither the regulated industry nor the regulators wanted. Meanwhile, new investment and modernization lagged in regulated industries. Third, industries in a regulated cartel developed a special inertia at the management level. In fact, as deregulation became an increasingly popular idea in the 1970s and 1980s, many of its strongest opponents were the very industries that were to be deregulated.

THE MARKET ALTERNATIVE

Efforts to introduce a market alternative to regulation have posed and will continue to pose special problems. Not only are government bureaucrats unwilling to destroy their own jobs, but a number of regulated firms and many of their customers have also shown some fear of living in a free marketplace. What, in fact, can unregulated markets do better than regulated ones?

The first advantage the consuming public enjoys is falling prices. Except in cases where certain consumers experienced benefits from price discrimination, competitive market prices will be lower than those established for regulated cartels. Airline passengers, for instance, have learned to enjoy these benefits on long-distance routes since the start of the 1980s, but, of course, some short-distance (and very high cost) flights have gone up in price to reflect real rather than administered pricing conditions. Meanwhile, the downward pressure on prices caused by competition among existing firms and the entry of new firms into the market (limited if not impossible under regulated conditions) will compel enterprises to improve operating efficiency. This will spark new investment among firms that are vital and capable enough to undertake the outlays; it will also act as euthanasia for firms and industries that are inherently inefficient or historically outmoded. With market profitability now directing resource usage, the application of labor and capital in production operations will require efficient resource allocation. The artificial wages and job protections unions possessed in certain industries such as railroads and airlines will, of course, come to an end.

Meanwhile, bad business habits and indefensibly uneconomical managerial activities will cease under competitive operations. The old regulated industry mentality of avoiding anything that smacks of newness will have to be replaced by a more innovative and entrepreneurial managerial philosophy. The habit of counting on the regulatory agency or the government to bail out financially troubled firms through rate increases or direct subsidies, such as the rail industry long enjoyed, will end.

Under regulation, price discrimination was common. Usually referred to as "cross subsidization," it appeared whenever certain customers were, with regulatory encouragement, charged considerably in excess of costs for the same service that other customers received at less than cost. In the telephone industry, before the AT&T breakup, cross subsidies existed when long-distance charges were artificially inflated to underwrite losses on local service. The result was to discriminate against business customers primarily and in favor of most residential phone users. In this case, deregulation has meant higher prices for residential phone users (but lower prices for all long-distance users). As with airline pricing, ending cross subsidies produces winners and losers. Only the shortsighted will oppose ending official price discrimination, for unless actual costs are the major determinant of rates and prices, we are employing a pricing system that is inefficient *and* unfair.

Finally, of course, a market-directed system explodes the fiction of the public interest. The notion that some bureaucratic authority can determine a transcendent public interest and then act to implement it belongs more to the realm of metaphysics than sensible economic reasoning. To return to our earlier discussion of the ICC and America's railroads, we might speculate that left to the dictates of a free market—and without an ICC—a national transportation mix might have emerged that would have allowed each transport mode to develop its inherent strengths. Instead of the artificial competition created "in the public interest" that pitted trucks and railroads against each other but provided no way of determining their relative efficiency, each form of transportation could have exploited its own advantages, dropping out of markets where it had none. The market is indeed the best determinant of the public's best interests.

EVALUATING DEREGULATION TO DATE

The final test for the effectiveness of deregulation is not logic but actual performance, and here deregulation has proved an important spur to the American economy. A look at the record should be convincing enough.

The Airline Deregulation Acts of 1977 and 1978 were the first important efforts to dismantle a regulated cartel and return it to competition. Under these laws, air carriers were granted greater rate-making freedom and greater freedom of entry and exit from airline markets. Accordingly, the Civil Aeronautics Board (which went out of business in early 1985, the first major regulatory agency so abolished) allowed airlines to fly on a "first come, first served" basis to most

American cities. The action ended the old, inefficient practice of granting virtual monopoly power to certain carriers over certain routes. As a result, dozens of old companies altered their routes (both expanding and contracting service on specific routes). At the same time, more than a score of brand-new long-distance carriers suddenly appeared. Meanwhile, the market, rather than the CAB, was allowed to determine most airline rates. The new approach brought most long-distance airfares down. Loss-producing routes were abandoned to new specialized commuter lines or fares were adjusted upward by the larger carriers to reflect real operating costs. The new market freedom allowed the airlines to price and operate according to actual supply-and-demand conditions and permitted passengers to enjoy the price benefits of competition.

Two years after the deregulation of the airlines, the Motor Carrier Act of 1980 brought gradual deregulation to the trucking industry (regulated by the ICC since 1930). Again the approach was the same: to allow greater freedom in rate making by individual truckers and the easing of entry restrictions into long-haul, interstate trucking. The benefits to the public came quickly. More than 5,200 new trucking firms entered the industry in the first eighteen months of deregulation; 20,000 new route applications were filed with the ICC; and average freight bills went down 10 to 20 percent.

In 1980, railroads were also given some relief from ICC control. In particular, they were freed to make most rate changes without prior ICC approval and were given permission to contract directly with shippers at less-than-market rates for long-term, bulk shipments. Previously, approval for rate changes had cost the railroads up to $1 billion a year as the ICC delayed adjusting rates for inflation, and special shipper-railroad contracts had been held to be an illegal form of rebating.

The gains from deregulation have not been limited to transportation. The deregulation of long-distance telecommunications has produced consumer savings and a more vibrant industry. In banking and finance, some restrictions have been lifted on branch banking, bank mergers, and overseas banking operations. There is more freedom to offer greater variety of financial options to customers. The elimination of artificial limits on the operations and functions of banks and other financial institutions (although more needs to be done here) has promoted increased competition among commercial banks, thrifts, credit unions, brokerage firms, and insurance companies in funds markets, raising investor earnings possibilities and lowering customer charges.

While "reregulators" will doubtless cite the recent savings and loan (or thrifts) crisis as proof that deregulation doesn't work, their criticism misses the target. The thrifts' difficulties are really due to the fact that they had been regulated (protected) for too long. The inability of some thrifts to adjust to a freer market is not the fault of the market. For the most part, the savings and loan crisis was the result of clearly fraudulent activities of some bankers who abrogated their fiduciary responsibilities. Indeed, these illegal actions were directly traceable to the government. Federal intervention since the 1930s on behalf of protecting depositers through deposit insurance has made it very easy for numerous bankers to shirk their own responsibility to protect their customers' funds. Appropriate legal action against fraudulent behavior—not more detailed regulation—is the remedy for theft.

Those who now see certain "shortcomings" with deregulation forget that the gains of market-directed economic activities are not possible without occasional risks. Avoiding such risks through regulation may produce a desired orderliness, but only at an exceptionally high cost. Overall, the economic costs of regulation impose a much greater burden on society than any risks associated with market competition.

The Liberal Argument

Regulatory agencies are the logical outcome of the need to improve market conditions in certain industries. Direct regulation is not essential to all markets, but in certain cases—mainly where natural monopolies tend to develop or should be encouraged—regulation by government agencies can maximize the benefits to both the consumer and the affected industry. Antitrust action, as we have discussed is employed in cases of conspiracy to attain a socially undesirable monopoly advantage in the márket, but direct regulation is a ratification of monopoly power. In exchange for this recognized monopoly position, a firm submits itself to close political and economic supervision.

THE "RULES" OF REGULATION

Under regulation, business firms are guaranteed certain rights. For example, their property rights are legally protected, and confiscation is not a serious possibility. They are entitled to receive reasonable prices and a fair rate of return on their capital. In the specific geographic area in which it operates, a regulated firm is given partial or total protection from competition. A firm can challenge in the courts any regulating decision made by the relevant commission.

Regulated firms also have certain obligations. Their prices and profits must not be excessive. Prices should be established that offer the greatest possible service without compelling a company to forfeit its capital through continuous losses. Moreover, the regulated firm must meet all demand at the established prices. Any change in the quantity or quality of service must be approved in advance by the regulatory agency. The final decision in such cases as petitions for abandonment of service must balance two conflicting objectives: the firm's operational benefits and the public interest. Finally, all regulated industries must be committed to high levels of performance with the highest possible standards of safety to the public. The key to regulation philosophy, developed over nine decades of experience and through sixteen independent agencies, is this: a balance of public and private (corporate) interests.

THE PUBLIC INTEREST REVISITED

The deafening roar of the Conservative crowd cheering on the recent drift toward deregulation has drowned out reason. While theoretical arguments are developed with considerable elegance to "prove" that regulation doesn't work and that a return to market competition for previously regulated industries would improve economic efficiency and well-being, the real issue has been papered over. What we have forgotten in our rush toward deregulation is to ask ourselves why Americans introduced the regulatory experiment in the first place. Surely regulation did not just happen accidentally. What, then, were its antecedents? It began with the long-held view that certain "public interest" objectives could never be well served in unregulated markets.

In the current rewriting of American economic history, Conservatives fail to recall that most ventures into regulation by independent regulatory commissions were not simply unconscious evasions of a market-dominated economy. A survey of previously or presently regulated industries shows that regulation evolved only after consistent evidence of market failure under conditions of competition.

The creation of the ICC in 1887 and its development of real regulatory power over the next twenty years came only after the excessive and irrational building of the American railroad network had brought about a cutthroat competition that destabilized the industry.

Periodically, bloody rate wars would break out among the giants as each tried to gain a larger share of the restricted transportation market. Consequently, there were frequent bankruptcies and breakdowns in service. Because of their critical place in the economy, as railroads went, so went the nation. Every major financial panic and recession after the Civil War—in 1873, 1884, and 1893—started with railroad bankruptcies. Attempts at private rate fixing and cartels, even before their unconstitutionality was established by the Sherman Anti-Trust Act, almost always failed. Even so, these expedients harmed farmers and other shippers. This, then, was the situation when the ICC was created in 1887. The free market operation of the rail industry could no longer be tolerated. This view was held widely by bankers, farmers, shippers, and railroad management.

Space does not permit a detailed description of the gradual elaboration of the ICC authority. It is sufficient to say that the initial limited powers of the commission over rate setting were enlarged to cover nearly all operations of railroads engaged in interstate commerce. Eventually all commercial surface transport enterprises came under ICC jurisdiction. The accretions of power in every case were responses to the failure of competitive market operations in the transport industry.

The story was similar elsewhere as public regulation was employed to offset a variety of problems rooted in an overly competitive economic system. The regulation of the airwaves in the 1920s by the FCC made it possible for radio listeners to interpret the chatter coming from radios. Competitive stations had operated without license or assigned frequencies and the public was ill-served. The building of the Federal Reserve System in 1914 came after a hundred years of unregulated and chaotic competition. Banks, usually operating with the skimpiest of reserves, showed a dangerous tendency to fall off into periods of panic, which in turn drove the nation into episodes of economic depression. The SEC was created in the 1930s after the overzealous actions of securities firms and banks had played a central role in the financial collapse of 1929.

The list of regulatory responses to the market failures of a purely free and competitive economy goes on and on. Regulation does not reflect a situation where the nation has not tried competition, but rather where it has been tried and found wanting, where the disadvantages of competition have shown themselves to be greater than the community wishes to shoulder. Conservatives attack the concept of "regulation in the public interest" without admitting that the public was badly served by an unreliable and frequently bankrupt transportation system, by dangerous if not fraudulent banking practices, by unscrupulous investment bankers and brokers, and by an unregulated use of the airwaves. When railroads fail and banks close or when unregulated energy prices close industries and chill homes, the nation is not simply faced with some "readjustment of markets" but with a threat to its very survival. Accordingly, it has been understood that certain basic sectors of the economy have responsibilities that go beyond private interest, that in fact serve a broader public interest even if they are privately owned. Europeans generally chose to deal with this conflict of interests by nationalizing or operating as public enterprises industries with board public interest responsibilities. Public regulation was a less extreme response to this problem.

Another dimension of the "public interest" approach is the commitment to maintaining "universal service." Under this philosophy, regulatory agencies frequently employ cross subsidization to assure that certain customers who might not otherwise obtain service if charges were based solely on costs do in fact have reasonable service. Essentially, an ability-to-pay principle is applied, with those with greater carrying capacity subsidizing those whose costs are high but capacity to pay is low. So it was that rural rail and trucking services were subsidized by long-distance shippers and that elderly, fixed-income phone users had part of their costs paid for by large corporations. To Conservatives, this is price discrimination, pure and simple; however, they make no attempt to explain how society's interests would be better served if small communities atrophy for lack of reasonably priced transportation or if low-income families are left without phone service.

Finally, on behalf of the public interest, it is appropriate for the government to act as an allocator of scarce resources. For instance, regulating prices and limiting exploitation of natural resources, with a view toward rationing their use, are appropriate public policy objectives that transcend any narrow profit interests.

To be sure, regulation in the public interest is not without its costs. The costs, however, are not really the alleged costs of inefficiency so frequently cited by Conservatives. They are the costs of creating market stability and equity that would not otherwise exist. Supplying reasonably priced phone service to all users may mean higher costs for some users. A safer banking system costs more to operate than a dangerously weak and speculative one. These costs are more than offset, however, by the long-run gains achieved for the entire society. Deregulation, meanwhile, stresses only the benefit of short-run savings (profits, really) from relaxing our concern for the public interest.

THE DEREGULATION BALANCE SHEET

Deregulation as an effective economic policy is now over a decade old. Evidence is abundant enough to make an evaluation, and, contrary to the cheery Conservative assessment, it is not all that supporting.

In the transportation industries, the results are at best mixed. Railroads generally have benefitted at the expense of the less efficient trucking competitors and of hundreds of communities that have lost rail service. Accordingly, some shippers—those able to use railroads—have gained, while others have lost. In the airlines industry, the early pricing benefits obtained under greater competition were quite temporary. Very quickly the opening of new routes and markets was followed by a wave of mergers that reduced the number of competing air carriers and consequently increased monopolistic control over passenger traffic at each of the major hub cities. Characteristically, airfares began to rise and passengers noticed a steady deterioration of service.

Although not the specific result of dismantling a regulatory agency but certainly the outcome of other public policies running in that direction, the breakup of AT&T stands out as a case of deregulatory failure (for specifics on this case, refer to Issue 4). The ending of cross subsidization translated directly into high and rising phone bills for virtually all residential customers. Meanwhile, the alleged benefits of competitive long-distance service seem lost in the confusion of phone bills and the selecting of one's long-distance carrier. Most average users of the telephone regularly report in opinion surveys that they feel costs have risen and service has declined since the breakup of Ma Bell.

The extent to which deregulation can produce truly catastrophic costs for society is best illustrated by the banking and finance industry. With thrifts freed in 1982 to compete with commercial banks and other financial intermediaries, they found themselves compelled to pay fairly high interest rates to attract funds. Indeed, the exceptionally high interest rates of the time would have caused problems regardless of deregulation. However, now freed of earlier restraints that confined the savings and loan activities almost exclusively to mortgage markets, thrifts ventured into high return—and high risk—lending. Loans to speculative real estate ventures, solar energy companies, windmill farms, and the like had very high failure rates in the early 1980s. Accordingly, many banks drifted toward and finally into bankruptcy.

With depositers' savings insured, government has been obliged to "socialize" the costs of savings and loan zeal in seeking high return investments—perhaps eventually having to pick up a $200 to $300 billion tab to keep the industry solvent. Some will argue that this is a unique situation, largely the result of government insulating financial institutions from market discipline by insuring their fiduciary responsibilities. However, it does not take an overactive imagination to consider that socialization of deregulatory costs are not necessarily limited to financial markets. Should conditions resulting from deregulation demand it, government bailouts of airlines, telecommunication companies, and the like are not unthinkable.

Naturally enough, true believers in deregulation do not argue that it is government's responsibility to save failed enterprises, even if the failure is directly traceable to deregulation. The market, they will argue, does not assure protection for inefficient firms, just as it does not assure that everyone will get the service or the goods they want at the price they would *like* to pay. The apparent logic and detached fairness of free market arguments is always impressive in the abstract, when no particular firm or no particular service or consumer is in mind.

Of course, some criticisms of regulatory agencies—especially regarding their inflexibility in the face of changed economic and technological conditions and their habit of becoming too cozy with the very firms they regulate—are quite valid. However, these deficiencies are correctable and are not causes for abandoning regulation altogether. At best, a reasoned and longer view of deregulation and its effects indicates that dismantling regulation machinery will provide us with an opportunity to reexperience old problems. Liberals see little benefit from having to learn again that unregulated capitalism produces serious market failures and imperfections that must sooner or later be offset by government intervention.

The Radical Argument

History readily shows that the natural inclination of production-for-profit enterprises is to acquire as much price-making power as possible. Therefore, the long-term outcome of competition is invariably the development of some degree of monopoly power. Yet, monopolistic power is not always easily attained. It often requires enlisting the apparatus of the state in its behalf to be effective. Accordingly, public regulatory commissions were organized in the United States to ratify the existence of monopoly. Regardless of the intention of reformers who championed their development, regulatory agencies worked primarily on behalf of the industries they regulated. The creation of independent regulatory agencies and their performance do not support the Liberal claim that "public interest" is a major element in regulatory action. Neither do they support the Conservative charge that regulation has been "antibusiness."

Curiously, however, the deregulation movement of the 1980s also advanced the objective of creating monopoly—but, of course, not in an obvious way. From a Radical perspective, the free market regulation to deregulation (and recently) to "reregulation" oscillations in public policy toward business are not a cycle at all, as conventional economists suggest, but are variations on the same monopoly capitalist theme. Such an argument will be unfamiliar to many non-Radicals and may initially appear to be contradictory. To make the Radical position a bit clearer, we will examine one regulatory case in considerable detail rather than undertake a broad survey of American regulatory activities. The Interstate Commerce Commission's regulation of surface transportation in the United States is an excellent representative example.

REGULATION AS A CREATURE OF INDUSTRY: THE CASE OF THE ICC

Progressive Era legislative and regulatory actions, rather than being single-minded efforts to "compromise" the differences of parties on either side of a particular market (as the then-current political rhetoric maintained), were really efforts to bring order to highly disrupted and overly competitive markets. But "order" was achieved on terms that supported the principles of private property and corporate profit seeking, terms that replaced competition with official recognition of limited monopolistic power and cartelization.

The ICC from its very beginning was an attempt to create an official cartel in rail transportation. This policy was steadily enlarged and elaborated on by the industry. Eventually, it also was applied to other modes of public transportation (buses, trucks, water carriers, and pipelines under the ICC and air carriers under the Civil Aeronautics Board). The development of the ICC was not a haphazard abandonment of high principles; it was the unfolding of a planned and rational policy. (It was rational at least in the sense that it consistently pursued clear ends, even though these goals might ultimately result in economic and social loss to the nation.)

Although many economic interests favored the creation of a federal railroad regulatory agency in the late 1880s, one of the most influential groups consisted of railroad leaders themselves. The closing decades of the nineteenth century had witnessed costly rate wars and other competitive difficulties, resulting largely from the enormous excess capacity built into the industry. These conflicts could not be handled through private efforts at cartelization, partly because these efforts usually collapsed of their own enforcement weaknesses and partly because other economic groups challenged such blatant attempts to build monopoly power. The railroads, therefore, turned to the federal government for official sanction of cartel creation. Progress toward this end began with passage of the Commerce Act of 1887; over the next twenty years, in the ICC and in Congress, railroads obtained important recognition as a cartel. Indeed, the Elkins Act (1903), which ended the hated competitive practice of paying rebates to certain shippers, was written in the legal offices of the Pennsylvania Railroad. The Hepburn Act (1906), which enlarged the ICC's power, supposedly at the expense of the rail monopolies, had considerable management endorsement.

"Community of interest" (informal domination of all rail operations in a region by a few large roads) and other plans formulated to integrate rail properties for the purpose of gaining greater monopoly power were frustrated for a time, but railroads emerged from World War I, after their ignominious operational collapse and more than two years of government control, with the Esch-Cummins Act of 1920. This law, as interpreted by the ICC and the courts, firmly established the principle of railroad cartelization. The old competitive situation within the industry no longer existed and the rail network was reduced to a limited number of essentially noncompetitive systems. Most state regulatory powers over finance and operations were abolished. The old ambition of industry pooling and rate bureaus was nourished during the Depression. Throughout the disastrous 1930s, the government, at Franklin Roosevelt's insistence, officially recognized the Association of American Railroads as the industrywide policy-making body. It was a powerful lobby and a tool for encouraging collusion within the industry. At the behest of rail leaders, the government moved in 1935 to control competition from the hated trucks and buses by placing them under ICC regulatory control. Finally, with the passage of the Transportation Act of 1940, the federal government officially declared an end to any pretense of maintaining "costly competition," either between railroads or among competing transport modes.

None of these regulatory and legislative successes by the railroads could, however, insulate the industry from competition or the structural and demand dislocations that persistently wreaked havoc with railroad balance sheets through the 1950s and 1960s. The decline was not halted even by the hastily drawn Transportation Act of 1958, which took away the last effective regulatory power of the states over passenger trains, nor by the ICC's growing willingness to approve almost any kind of merger or abandonment. The railroads had succeeded in getting themselves established as a protected cartel. Though they were not totally free to undertake whatever was in their interest, the official commitment to maintaining railroads as a privately owned industry meant that railroad legislation and regulation were loaded in their favor. The industry had to be kept going—on its own terms. For society, this translated into the reduction of rail service and the steady deterioration of service that remained.

THE "DEREGULATION" PHENOMENON

In many respects, the emergency legislation efforts to deal with the rail crisis in the Northeast corridor reveal the actual content, past and present, of our transportation and regulatory policy. Under the 1976

Regulatory Act, the six bankrupt northeastern railroads were organized into Conrail. Two points are noteworthy in this development. First, Conrail, although federally organized, was to become a private production-for-profit corporation after it had been reconditioned by a massive infusion of government funds and by a ruthless reduction in its trackage. Second, Conrail was devised to rescue the funds of the bankrupt railroads' investors. Although the initial government estimate of the scrap value of the bankrupt roads was set at $621 million, the owners claimed their deteriorated rolling stock and rusting rails to be worth at least $7 billion. Under pressure from banks, insurance companies, and other holders of railroad securities, Conrail was initially granted $2.1 billion in federal funds to acquire the nearly worthless financial paper of these roads. As of this writing, individual stockholder and bondholder suits promise to vastly increase this figure. The prospects of monetary gain from Conrail were evident to the investors in the bankrupt lines, many of whom spoke glowingly of government ownership. There was little talk of such actions being "socialistic," but John Kenneth Galbraith has correctly called it "socialism for the rich."

The Motor Carrier Act of 1980 and the Staggers Rail Act of the same year put the finishing touches on what had been started four years earlier. The former deregulated trucking, and the latter gave broad rate-making and other freedoms to railroads. Deregulating surface transportation can only help the railroads, just as regulation helped in an earlier stage. With rising energy costs and limited government funds to maintain the highway system, deregulation gives railroads a major cost advantage over trucks. Regulation previously protected railroads from competition between themselves and the highly subsidized truckers. Now, with the railroad industry highly concentrated (and few new railroads likely to be built), intermodal competition will create rail domination of trucking. The less concentrated trucking industry is already feeling the effects as its profits fall and rail profits rise. In the railroad–truck competition, giant transportation firms will be built on the railroad stem as railroads add their own trucking facilities at either end of their rail routes. For a while there may be an illusion of competition (more truckers, more rate freedom, and so on), but the competition only masks the development of new monopoly power in the transportation industry.

The surface transportation industry scenario, which we have examined in detail, reflects the case of other industries undergoing deregulation. Among the deregulated airlines, despite the early appearance of new entrants in the market, recent mergers are increasing the likelihood of greater concentration among long-distance carriers. Caught up in the deregulation mood of the times, the Federal Communications Commission has permitted several giant mergers and a very large number of small ones in the radio and television industries. These mergers have narrowed the number of independently owned radio and television stations and created several absolute giants in broadcasting. Deregulation in banking has meant the building of giant "financial service" enterprises that combine banking and nonbanking functions as well as the enlargement of already huge banks by reducing restrictions on branch banking and interstate banking.

Such developments in no way support the Conservative claim that deregulation is restoring competition. Deregulation only continues the cartelizing of certain industries that commenced in the now discredited era of regulation.

Deregulation, whatever its immediate short-term gains to particular industries, can never be a long-term strategy. The destablizing effects of excessive monopoly power—the direct result of deregulation—must be corrected to maintain economic and social order. The potential for abuse by deregulated but monopolistic railroads and air carriers provokes pressure for reregulation from the public and from commercial shippers. Similarly, the destablizing of American banking and finance cannot be permitted. The banking industry requires reregulation to provide "orderly" financial markets. The recent appeal of controlling and cartelizing deregulated industries, while appearing to be a new public policy direction, is merely a return to the old strategy of creating officially protected cartels.

As deregulation pressures wind down and give way to calls for "reregulation," we should learn this lesson: *Social ownership and control of predominantly "public interest" industries offers the only viable alternative.* Public ownership and operation of transportation, banking, telecommunications, and the like is a means of establishing the collective control that regulation initially promised but could not achieve and that deregulation directly opposes.

Labor Problems
Is the Union Era Over?

We, the members of the National Association of Manufacturers of the United States of America, ... do hereby declare
the following principles ... (1) that fair dealing is the fundamental and basic principle on which relations between
employees and employers should rest.... (6) Employers must
be unmolested and unhampered in the management of their
business, in determining the amount and quality of their
product, and in the use of any methods or systems of pay
which are just and equitable.

Statement of Principles, N.A.M., 1903

In the profit sharing scheme, we're trying to find a rational
means by which free labor and free management, sitting at
the bargaining table, can attempt to work out in their relationship practical means by which you can equate the competing
equities—in workers, stockholders, and consumers.

Walter Reuther, United Auto Workers, CIO, 1958

TIME TABLE OF THE HOLYOKE MILLS
(to take effect on or after Jan. 3d, 1853)

Morning Bells ... first bell at 4:40 A.M.
    yard gates open at ringing of bells for ten minutes
Breakfast Bells ... ring out at 7 A.M.; ring in at 7:30 A.M.
Dinner Bells ... ring out at 12:30 P.M.; ring in at 1 P.M.
Evening Bells ... ring out at 6:30 P.M.*
*excepting on Saturdays when the sun sets previous to 6:30.
    At such times ring out at sunset. (in all cases the first
    stroke of the bell is considered as the marking time)

Posted hours of a Massachusetts Mill, 1853

THE PROBLEM

Although the labor union movement can be traced back to colonial times, the development of unions as a political and economic force is comparatively new. As recently as seventy years ago, unions were fought in the courts and, failing that, the streets, by employers who were unwilling to relinquish their traditional power over the work force. The bloody conflicts between union organizers and strikebreakers hired by stubborn business owners remain an unpleasant page in American history. Not until the 1930s did labor unions receive a feeble mandate from government (under the Wagner Act of 1935) to organize and collectively bargain with management. However, as Figure 6.1 shows, the New Deal years were a golden period for American unions, with membership growing by more than 300 percent—from 4 million members in 1934 to over 15 million by 1942.

By the end of World War II, unions were firmly established in all basic American industries—steel, autos, petrochemicals, construction, and transportation. Moreover, the unions' political clout was a formidable force in American politics. Working closely with the Democratic party in the postwar years, the AFL-CIO and a number of large independent unions helped to shape government policy toward unions and other social programs affecting labor. Welfare, social security, job training, and minimum-wage legislation all bear the imprint of organized labor.

The 1970s, however, saw the end of more than three decades of union expansion, and the 1980s were an uncomfortable and unaccustomed period of continuous decline. The earlier victories had not erased a deep-felt opposition to organized labor among many Conservatives. While few opponents contested a union's legal right to organize, many believed that the courts and legislation had gone too far, creating an imbalance in labor-management negotiations that greatly favored labor. Conservative attacks on organized labor became louder and more persuasive in the stagnating economy of the 1970s and early 1980s. With profits low, prices rising, and unemployment levels challenging Great Depression levels, many non-union Americans came to agree with the charge that unions were significant contributors to the nation's economic woes. Union workers found themselves at odds with nonunion fellow workers, who no longer considered organized labor the champion of all working persons, but an obstacle to their own employment. Increasingly, unions lost jurisdictional votes,

FIGURE 6.1   Union Membership, 1900–1988

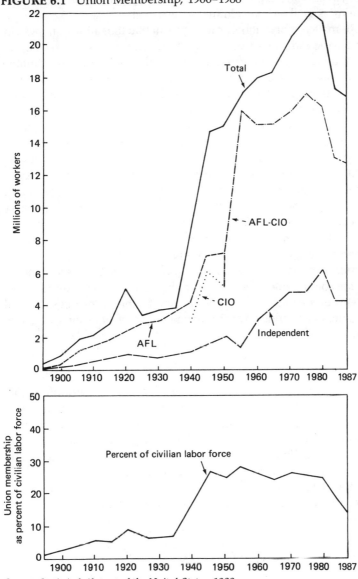

Source: *Statistical Abstract of the United States, 1989.*

failing to organize some targeted firms and actually resulting in decertification of unions as workers' bargaining agents in other cases.

To make matters worse, it became apparent that the unions' strength in the nation's basic industries was not the bulwark it was supposed to be. Indeed, this strength soon appeared to be a weakness. These "basic industries" had ceased to grow, and as their place in the American economy declined, so did union influence and power. From a peak of more than 22 million members in the early 1970s, union membership fell by a quarter to less than 17 million members in 1988. Only about 14 percent of American workers claimed any union affiliation, about the same proportion as in 1939.

Throughout the high-unemployment 1980s, unions faced growing intractability from management at the bargaining table. With the threat of plant closure, movement overseas, or even bankruptcy (a common and plausible management strategy), unions were compelled to negotiate contracts in autos, transportation, construction, steel, and other industries that amounted to abandoning previous union gains. A new word, *givebacks*, entered the vocabulary of labor-management bargaining.

In the new economic setting, the old question—*Are unions too powerful?*—was transformed into a question that had once seemed affirmatively resolved—*Are unions necessary?* The answer to this latter question will have a considerable bearing on labor-management relations for a long time to come.

SYNOPSIS

The Conservative argument presents unions as true monopolists that exact higher wages at the cost of higher prices to consumers, reduction of business profits, and interference with the labor market. The Liberal position maintains that unions are a necessary balance to corporate power and that they have improved the general well-being of all workers. Radicals, while agreeing that the union movement has aided workers, hold that it has not played a sufficiently active political role and that many of organized labor's gains have come at a cost to nonunion workers.

Anticipating the Arguments

- According to Conservatives, how have unions worked against the interests of workers in general?

- How do Liberals justify their claims that unions have redressed the balance of power between capital and labor?
- On what grounds do many Radicals argue that labor unions have been an essentially conservatizing force in the past?

The Conservative Argument

Whereas union members have always represented only a small proportion of American workers, unions have exercised inordinate power. Concentrated in the past in critical industries and trades, they were able to use extraordinary leverage to obtain wage gains and other benefits. To a very considerable extent, unions' power was simple blackmail. If government or business failed to agree to union demands, the result would be devastating strikes in key industries, with spillover effects involving the entire economy. Only a few years ago, a protracted labor struggle in the steel industry could throw millions of other Americans out of work and create a national recession. A truckers' strike could keep food off thousands of tables. Although still theoretically possible, such adverse effects from the overzealous exercise of union power seem less likely today. The American union movement has peaked and has entered a period of decline—not only in the size and power of its membership but, more important, in its popular appeal to American workers. The trend is desirable, and lest it be only a trend, it is important to remember the awful consequences when unions are able to exercise extraordinary political and economic influence.

WHO PAYS THE BILL?

Liberal dogma tells us that the growth of union power was beneficial to all Americans. Does this argument stand the test of the most obvious economic analysis? How have unions produced more and more for everybody with nobody the loser? The answer is that they haven't. Union progress has had a very high price tag for the American people.

First and foremost, unions adversely affect the price and total output of goods and services. Gains in wages and fringe benefits, won through union pressure, add to the costs of any firm's output. The firm's only options are either to absorb the costs through lower profits or pass them on in the form of higher prices. The first alternative reduces a firm's competitive strength and lessens its ability to acquire capital and make needed investments. The second alternative penalizes consumers by forcing them to pay prices that are higher than necessary. High prices, of course, tend to stimulate even higher prices, since everyone has to run a bit faster to catch up.

The problem is not that unions don't know about the effects of unreasonable wage gains. It is that they don't care. I. W. Abel, former head of the United Steelworkers of America, was asked in 1977 whether he felt that his union's current contract demands for a guaranteed life income might not be a heavy burden for the steel industry and, ultimately, the consumer. With the unionist's typical indifference to the cost of union victories, Abel replied, "We're not concerned with that side of the question. We must look out for our members." Such an attitude contributed mightily to the decline of the American steel industry, which, by late 1982, had furloughed indefinitely more than 40 percent of its workers.

Even more burdensome than the direct wage costs of unionism are union efforts to usurp ownership and management powers. Unions force on firms contracts that interfere with efficient labor hiring and use (railroad full-crew, or "featherbedding," arrangements are an example) and that often specify maximum daily or hourly output. Industrial inefficiency and reduced productivity are the result. Such violations of employers' rights to their own capital and property and their freedom to hire and fire also add to production costs and, finally, to consumer prices.

Furthermore, the excessive power of labor unions disrupts the operation of supply and demand in the labor market. Since unionized industries must pay higher wages, they lower their demand for labor as they shift toward greater, and cheaper, capital use. Moreover, as individuals are forced out of, or prevented from entering, jobs "protected" by unions, they drive down wage rates in other areas. With a greater supply of available labor, all things being equal, wages are lowered in nonunion jobs. The overall effect of these shifts has been an increased imbalance in national income distribution. The gulf between the labor union elite and the disadvantaged bottom grows; union gains have to come from someplace, and they come mostly from other workers, especially the poorest workers.

Another undesirable effect of unionism is the aggressive advocacy of "union shop" or "agency shop" conditions for employment. Under these arrangements, a company-recognized union can compel union membership (union shop) or at least dues payment (agency shop) as a requirement for employment. Such specifications obviously deny individual workers the free choice of joining or rejecting a union. Perhaps of equal importance, this forced dues collection vastly increases a union's economic (read: "strike-making") power. To halt this trend, Conservatives have fought hard in recent years for "right-to-work" laws that would end enforced union membership and union appropriation of part of each worker's pay.

One further example of excessive union influence is the use of "union-made" power. By forcing industries to purchase from and sell to unionized firms only and by pressuring fellow unionists to buy only union-made products, industrial unions can effectively lower the demand for the goods of certain nonunion firms. While this practice is a direct interference with property rights and should be opposed as such, it also creates inefficiency, destroys jobs, and causes needlessly high prices.

Ironically, all these strategies have imposed costs on union members *as well as* the general population. Higher wages, for instance, have certainly accelerated the substitution of capital for labor. The proof is that despite the continued growth of output in most union industries, employment gains in these areas have been slight. Moreover, union wage gains have led to the export of American jobs. Competition from lower-paid workers overseas has often been the price of labor's domestic victories.

UNIONS AND GOVERNMENT

Aside from these direct effects on the marketplace, others—equally undesirable—have resulted from union efforts to develop so-called progressive legislation. A couple of examples should suffice. First, let's take the union's longtime support of a national minimum wage. Superficially, this stand is justified as an attempt to improve the lot of the nonunion worker. In fact, unions favor the minimum-wage concept because it lays an ever-rising legal floor on which they can build ever-higher union wage ceilings. The true result is not to help the poor but to increase union wages and lower the average non-union worker's income. This happens because hikes in the minimum wage destroy jobs, especially marginal jobs; if an employer must pay more than a worker creates in value, the employer will lay off the worker.

A second example of unions and "progressive" legislation was their practice, in the 1930s, of supporting social legislation to "protect" female workers. Protection actually became discrimination, as laws and union contracts denied women access to certain jobs and kept them locked in low-paying "female" occupations. Feminists who charge business with sex discrimination should start looking in the right places—among the labor unions and social-rights advocates of several decades past.

Apart from unions' ability to use their political clout to manipulate favorable legislation, unions have been highly successful in organizing government workers. Twice the proportion of public-sector workers are unionized (36 percent) compared to the private sector (15 percent), and only public-sector unionism has failed to report membership declines over the past decade. The unionization of the public sector poses special problems: One is that public-sector unionism leads to unionist activity directly in opposition to the interest and welfare of society at large. Strikes by police officers, fire-fighters, and teachers have become common, and the monopoly power of public-sector unions over these critical functions has led to the extortion of unjustifiably high wage increases and expensive fringe benefits (for example, pensions).

A second problem is that the unionizing of public employees creates a special-interest group committed to ever-expanding state bureaucracy. For instance, the 1 million members of AFSCME (American Federation of Federal, State, County and Municipal Employees) have a vested interest in protecting and expanding public-sector expenditures and areas of public intervention in the economy. The reason is obvious enough. Their jobs depend on it. Thus public unions, through the strength of their numbers and their place in the economy, can exert enormous political leverage in subverting the market system. At the same time, their "gains" represent a heavy cost to the taxpayer.

DEALING WITH THE UNIONS

By the 1980s, such excesses of union power had gained a broad, popular recognition, and, with a Conservative administration in the White House, efforts were made to restrict union power. The signal ·'went out in 1982 when the air traffic controllers — public employees — struck. Quickly and summarily, President Reagan fired all striking members of PATCO, their union, stating that they did not have the right to threaten the safety of millions of American air passengers. The president's action, practically unthinkable a decade earlier, was generally applauded by the public.

Partly because of inspiration provided by Washington and partly because there seemed to be no other choice, increasing numbers of firms determined that it was time to fight back against unions' insatiable demands. Largely supported by a public that understood unions' contributory role in the past decade of high unemployment, rising prices, and comparatively poor profits by American business, management confronted union power directly. Increasingly — and surprisingly, to many managers who had assumed that unions were unbeatable — major union-management contracts written after 1982 contained a variety of "givebacks" (concessions by the union on past contract victories). The monopoly power of unions in many critical industries was now being challenged successfully.

While Conservatives are hopeful that the power of the union movement has peaked, it is inaccurate to label the Conservative position as mindless antiunionism. Conservatives are committed to protecting workers' rights, even unionists' rights, so long as those rights do not infringe on the rights of others.

A Conservative program for dealing with the union problem could be reduced to the slogan "Don't outlaw the unions, outlaw their power." Workers, like everyone else, should have the right of free association. Much can be said in favor of fraternal workplace or skill organizations. Indeed, these groups should have the democratic right to lobby for their ideas and programs. However, union strength should be curtailed by a three-pronged attack on their monopoly power.

First, unions' special exemption from antitrust laws should be terminated. Second, compulsory unionism should be ended; right-to-work protection should be given all workers, whatever their feelings about joining a union. No worker should be compelled, as is the case with a "closed shop," to join a union as a prerequisite to getting and holding a job. Third, the right to strike should be defined and limited to specific lawful ends. While workers should have the right to withhold their labor, they should not be allowed to do so if (1) the national welfare is endangered; (2) the purpose is purely political; (3) the union has made no effort to negotiate—in other words, no wildcat strikes; or (4) there is violence.

Such a program would go a long way toward restoring the balance of power between unions and management. With some exceptions, organized labor has marched down a one-way street for most of the past sixty years. Happily, that era of union domination is now ending.

The Liberal Argument

The Liberal position with regard to the place of unions in the economy is very simple: Unions are necessary in order for labor to have an equitable balance with management in establishing wages, hours, and conditions of work. Without a balance of power in bargaining, one side soon dominates the other, and the very essence of pluralist democratic capitalism is endangered. From the Liberal standpoint, commitment to governmental intervention to redress imbalances is essential, for history shows that working out labor-management issues in a "free market" leads to chaos.

THE FAILURE OF FREE LABOR BARGAINING

Contrary to the fantasies of its Conservative defenders, a free labor market is not free at all, but controlled by the purchasers of labor. To attack unions as disrupters of the economy may be defensible within free market logic, but it shows no understanding of economic conditions in the real world. Without the protection of unions, workers have always been price takers, forced by the necessity of survival to accept whatever wage rate is offered. To be sure, as the free market advocate may point out, a worker is free to turn down a wage he or she considers inadequate. However, this is somewhat like saying that a person has the choice of death by poison or execution by a firing squad. Freedom there is, but the choices are equally dismal.

Perhaps in an idyllic Adam Smith world of many buyers and sellers, no one of whom had excessive economic or political power, the society might depend reasonably on the "laws of the market." But this was not the actual condition as industrial capitalism began to emerge in the last century. The few who hired had excessive power over those who worked, and unionism was a natural, humane, and necessary development. Any other view simply ignores American history.

Necessary as it was, unionism did not emerge without a long struggle. Efforts to unionize in the late nineteenth century were opposed in the courts, which upheld entrepreneurs' property rights and treated unions either as criminal conspiracies or, after the Sherman Anti-Trust Act of 1890, as monopolistic efforts to restrain trade. Management ruthlessly attempted to weed out union organizers and members. Under threat of being discharged or blacklisted, workers were compelled to sign yellow-dog contracts—promises never to join or support a union. When these efforts at intimidation were not sufficient, management simply staged lockouts—they closed down, so that laborers, without savings or strike funds, were driven back to work by the reality of starvation. When all else failed and it was faced with a full-fledged strike, management could hire strikebreakers and, finally, use police and bullets.

These struggles between capital and labor were creating irreversible class divisions and bloody social disorder. Haymarket, Homestead, Pullman, and Ludlow (classic labor struggles between 1880 and 1910) were names synonymous with industrial warfare and harbingers of what might happen on a grander scale unless labor-management relations were improved. Largely under the pressure of Liberals, first in the Progressive Era and then during the New Deal period, a new strategy for dealing with labor-business conflicts evolved. In its simplest form, the strategy had two parts. One was legalizing and protecting the rights of workers to organize; the other was establishing the principle of collective bargaining between labor and management in order to determine wages and work conditions in all unionized businesses. With the passage of the Wagner Act in 1935, labor received its "Magna Carta." This law forbade employer interference with workers' rights to organize unions, outlawed company unions, prohibited discriminatory antiunion action by employers, compelled employers to bargain "in good faith," and established a National Labor Relations Board to oversee labor-management affairs. Unions had finally arrived, and membership grew from 4 million in 1935 to 18 million over the next twenty years. Collective bargaining had replaced industrial violence as the basis for industry-worker relations.

It is doubtful today that many businesses would like to return to the wild "free market" era of labor relations. Collective bargaining is as much a part of business as it is of labor. As business has grown larger and more complex, uncertainties of all kinds are less desirable. Collective bargaining and long-term labor contracts have tended to stabilize labor situations, to business's distinct pleasure. Nevertheless, criticism of unions continues. Here we must deal with several of the more inaccurate and obnoxious arguments.

CORRECTING THE EVIDENCE

Many critics of unions argue that they have caused economic inefficiency and suffering in our society. The record does not bear this out at all. Before the union movement succeeded in forcing higher wages, improved working conditions, and greater concern for the rights of labor, suffering was the common plight of *all* workers. The history books are replete with examples of the abominable working conditions during the early industrial period in England, the United States, and all developing capitalist economies. Even in the more "enlightened" modern period, union political pressures are virtually the only check to assure safe working conditions and adequate rates of pay for all workers.

Meanwhile, union-sponsored social programs in the areas of improved education, compensation for illness or disability, and security against unemployment and old age have become accepted facts of life. Without union political agitation in these areas, state and federal action simply would not have happened.

What about the charge that unions cause inefficiency, higher prices, and even joblessness? There is no hard evidence to support this claim. Although American labor struggles date back to colonial times, the great advances made by unions have come in this century, mostly in the last sixty years. During this period, the United States has become the preeminent industrial power in the world. The standard of living for all Americans has advanced continually. To argue that union gains have been won at a cost to other members of society is not true. As union wages and benefits have increased, they have pulled up those of nonunion workers. While unemployment and unfair income distribution remain serious problems, the modern union era—that is, 1914 to the present—has actually seen a doubling of the income share (percentage of national income) of the lowest fifth of the population. Such evidence disputes the Conservative logic that the poor pay for unionism.

With regard to the Conservative charge that union shops and agency shops deny some workers their rights and their wages by compelling them to pay union dues, Liberals see this as a smoke screen. Right-to-work laws aimed at ending this long-established practice are in reality efforts at union busting. Required union dues are designed to prevent "free riders," workers who enjoy union-gained wage and job benefits but wouldn't otherwise pay to support union expenses. Most important, though, they wouldn't have these benefits and their salaries would be much lower if the comparatively small contributions to the union were not paid. It is not the worker's free choice that right-to-work advocates have in mind but the employer's. By dividing the workers against each other on the issue of union dues, worker solidarity—the first requisite for effective unionism—is destroyed. Breaking the union is the next step.

As to the charge that unions are a source for cost-push inflationary pressure that falls heavily on the whole society, evidence does not support this Conservative claim. Granted, on a few occasions in the superinflationary years of the 1970s, annual union wage gains did outstrip increases in labor productivity and general price increases. However, these instances of cost-push inflation were few and must be looked at over the longer run. Many of the negotiated wage increases in the 1970s were merely efforts to catch up with past inflationary erosion of workers' paychecks. More important, the insignificance of unions' alleged "excessive" wage gains becomes obvious when we look at the relevant wage data. The fact is that between 1969 and 1989, the average real wages of American workers—both union and nonunion—declined in most industries.

WHAT ABOUT UNIONISM'S FUTURE?

There can be little denying that antiunion sentiment in the United States is fairly strong, even among those who have much to gain from unionization or who directly benefit from unions' past and present legislative efforts. Regrettably, this reflects a common belief—widely nurtured by Conservatives—that unions have cost Americans jobs. Indeed, in the high-unemployment 1970s and 1980s, such a belief was reasonably easy to hold. Nor could it be refuted very effectively by the union movement. Faced with high national unemployment rates and employers who threatened to move their businesses to nonunionist locales, union bargaining power eroded. "Givebacks" entered the collective bargaining vocabulary as new contracts cut out old union gains. Fringe benefits were the first to fall, followed by horizontal wage slashes. Some unions were compelled to accept two-tiered wage systems in which there was one wage structure for presently employed workers and another, leaner, structure for future hires. The 1985 General Motors–United Auto Workers pact, which paid old workers as much as $20 per hour while new workers earned $9 for basically the same job, was representative of this trend. Such contracts, of course, did little to enhance the image of unions with younger workers or with nonunionized Americans. Yet, at a time of labor surplus, unions had few other alternatives.

   Although some will conclude on the basis of the past two decades that unionism will soon disappear as an economic and political force in the United States, that conclusion would be premature. First of all, demographic trends now indicate that we are beginning to experience a serious labor shortage that will continue into the foreseeable future. Experience has shown that tight labor markets invariably increase unions' bargaining power (certainly a well-known fact to Conservatives who would like to bury unions *now*). Second, unions may benefit from a gradual change taking place in labor-management relations. As we note in the next issue, modern management methods increasingly stress the importance of worker input in production operations. This necessarily requires partnership, not an adversarial relationship, between labor and management. To this end, the Japanese model of "shared responsibility" between labor and management is attractive. Worker-management committees in *different* parts of a firm may set work rules, wages, and plans for dealing with technological changes, compromises, and other critical labor issues rather than depending on the old strategy of companywide, sometimes industrywide, negotiation of a single contract.

In such a work setting, unions, as a collective instrument for coordinating worker input, could become revitalized. However, shared responsibility will also require that unions be more adaptive and creative than they have often been in the past. With regard to worker compensation, the old union strategy of *more* will have to be tempered by a recognition of the connection between compensation and productivity and perhaps connecting compensation to company profitability (for example, accepting some type of profit-sharing plan). There is much evidence to suggest that some American executives, who are well aware of the success of the Japanese in shared responsibility efforts, are indeed willing to experiment with a variety of "labor participation" programs.

Meanwhile, organized labor must come to terms with its own image and its own potential constituencies. Closer connection between labor leaders and rank-and-file members is required. Labor must begin to win new members in the emerging high-tech and service industries and even among such professionals as doctors, lawyers, and accountants.* With a revitalized approach toward collective bargaining strategies as well as immediate economic goals and with a fresh view of its potential membership, a new labor union era can commence.

The Radical Argument

Without much doubt, unions have brought workers protection and advantages that could not have been obtained in the "free market."

*With membership declining in the old union strongholds of the United Auto Workers and the United Steelworkers by as much as a third to a half from peak years, it is absolutely critical that labor find new constituencies.

By organizing together, many workers have obtained job security, higher wages, better working conditions, and a host of fringe benefits (paid vacations, retirement and health plans, and the like). These would not have been possible if they had stood, hat in hand, waiting for their capitalist employers to humanize work conditions and better their incomes.

THE FAILURES OF AMERICAN UNIONISM

There are, however, basic defects in the American system of trade unionism. With the exception of the Industrial Workers of the World (known as Wobblies) in the early twentieth century and a few communist and socialist unions of the 1930s and 1940s, American unionism has usually lacked a radical political direction. In fact, political organization or agitation of any kind has never been important in the big unions. While one thinks of the AFL-CIO and the Democratic party as almost synonymous, the union's support for this traditional party is not political activism in any radical sense. To the founding father of modern unionism, Samuel Gompers of the AFL, labor struggles were motivated basically by bread-and-butter issues. Gompers, who was interested only in organizing along craft lines, believed that unions should avoid political involvement and support the social order of capitalist society. Neither the broadening of the union movement to industrywide organizing under the CIO in the 1930s nor the AFL-CIO merger in 1955 changed this outlook. In World War I, in the New Deal of the 1930s, and in World War II, establishment unionism was rewarded handsomely by both government and business as they came to appreciate the politically nonmilitant nature of American unions. Contrary to the views of Conservatives and some Liberals, American corporate leaders came to see unions as more beneficial than detrimental. As industry, especially heavy industry, became more technically complex and economically concentrated, unions served as useful organizers of the labor supply. They provided stability in hiring and employment that more than compensated for the enforced recognition of unions and the legalization of such labor tactics as the strike, the boycott, and exclusive jurisdiction.

This is not to say that all businesses agreed with unions all the time. Some remained implacable and were willing to resort to violence to destroy "bolshevik" unionism. The Republic Steel massacre on Memorial Day 1937 is a bitter example.* Such business attitudes, however, are pretty much past history, as is labor militancy. Today, few businesses oppose unions in principle, and most unions support the capitalist system in practice. Union leaders worked with the FBI and CIA in the 1950s to purge radicals from their ranks and to help eliminate radical elements in the unions of friendly foreign nations. Most union leadership vigorously supported the Vietnam War and continues to support a strong-military foreign policy for the United States. In time of domestic economic crisis, union leaders have shown a willingness to collaborate with business to hold down wages and prices, as when President Nixon introduced wage and price controls in the early 1970s. The point is that in our time, the corporate attack on unions has been mostly rhetoric; practice indicates mutual acceptance and collaboration.

On labor's side, the growth of the collaboration between unions and management has been facilitated by the domination of a distant and bureaucratic leadership. The "professional" leaders and managers of the unions have usually found themselves more at home speaking with their management counterparts than with their own members. Not infrequently, they have negotiated "sweetheart" contracts that sold out their members very cheaply.

While the overall record of union collaboration with management objectives is fairly clear in American capitalism, there are occasions when capitalism, being what it is, turns against unions. In the conservative 1980s, unions have been successfully squeezed to give up past gains and have been isolated so that organizing new and growing sectors of the economy has been quite difficult. The effect has been to increase capitalist profits by holding down wages—of both union and nonunion workers. However, the current pattern of givebacks, two-tiered wage structures, and occasionally militant antiunionism by

---

*Ten strikers were killed outside Chicago's Republic Steel plant on Memorial Day 1937. They were demonstrating peacefully for recognition of their union when they were fired on and beaten by city and plant police. No police were convicted, but a number of strikers went to jail for disturbing the peace.

business should not be overestimated. Excessive exploitation of workers will trigger worker militancy, which is the last thing any thoughtful capitalist really wants. Not even in the deep 1982 recession did management push organized labor to the wall as it well could have. Givebacks were obtained at the bargaining table, but no large firm turned to outright union busting.

Although the growth of public-sector unionism is often viewed with alarm by believers in the traditional economic and political faith, it too has proved to be a blank cartridge among the weapons of working-class struggle in the United States. Very much as private-sector unions serve to organize and discipline workers in private industry, public-sector unions serve the same function in government employment. The level of militancy among public-sector workers has never proved to be very strong. Although public employment remains extremely vulnerable during this contractionary stage in American capitalism, it should be expected that unions in this sector will react no differently from other unions. They will try to protect their more senior members, even collaborating with management efforts at payroll and employment reductions if this must be the price.

RADICALS DISAGREE ON TACTICS

Up to this point, most Radicals would agree: Labor unions have been more of a Conservative than a Radical force in American history, and current labor leadership is hopelessly detached from the real interests and needs of workers. But what does this mean for the future and for developing a Radical program for labor unions?

The working class must finally be the political vehicle for progressive social change. Without working-class support and, ultimately, working-class leadership, a radical reordering of society remains only the dream of intellectuals. Labor unions are a critical institution in approaching the working class, but should unions be opposed on the basis of past evidence, or should they be utilized? Radicals are divided on this question, and the division must be explained.

The antiunion position, which sometimes sounds surprisingly similar to Conservative logic, holds that unions are elitist, both at the top and among their members. Union membership is comparatively small (and even smaller than official figures indicate if we recognize that many unionists are inactive). Thus the old socialist idea of seeing the unions as a means to reach most workers is wrong today. Moreover, because of their wage and job security advantage over other workers, union members are the least politically developed of American workers. In fact, many of their wage gains have come as the result of relative wage losses (through inflation) and greater job insecurity for nonunion labor. Union workers are at the top of the hierarchy of American labor, and they would have little to gain from a Radical program aimed at greater worker control of jobs and a fairer distribution of income. Arguing from these premises, some Radicals see unions as an enemy, an element that increases internal working-class warfare and division. They argue, however, that the heyday of powerful unions is over; more and more of the work force now occupies less secure and less remunerative jobs. Unions thus become unnecessary and even insignificant as labor organizes directly against capital.

The other, and preponderant, Radical view argues that labor unions are essential in developing working-class consciousness about the system. To be sure, unionism is not a substitute for militant efforts to increase popular participation in the economy and the development of some variety of democratic socialism in the United States. However, if the present conservative leadership of unions is replaced, there is a real possibility that unions could become a progressive force toward these ends. Moreover, the rank and file are increasingly willing to challenge the "rights" of management that the union leadership takes for granted. Increasingly, workers will move beyond mere bread-and-butter issues to deal with such questions as labor control over the introduction and use of capital equipment and labor's sharing directly in corporate earnings. Such progressive ideas and increased militancy, the prounion argument holds, will carry over into nonunion labor. This view sees some virtue in the Liberal proposal for "labor-management partnership" discussed earlier.

While this division among Radicals on the position of unions should not be underestimated, it is only a tactical disagreement. Organization of the working class into a self-consciously progressive force is still a common objective. That requires the bringing together of all workers, union and nonunion, in a common struggle and the support of all efforts to enlarge worker power, whether through existing union offices or other types of organizations. Thus the Radical position is to go beyond the "union question" as it is posed by either

Conservatives or Liberals. Radicals may differ dramatically in their evaluations of the progressive possibilities of the existing union structure, but they agree on the necessity of organizing labor against capital by whatever means possible. Moreover, Radicals do not believe that the "Union Era" is over, at least not in the way Conservatives do. Workers' struggle for control of their lives and their labor will continue as long as capitalism exists.

The Productivity Problem
How Can We Increase Output?

The opening up of new markets, foreign or domestic, and the organizational development from craft shop and factory to such concerns as U.S. Steel illustrate the same process of industrial mutation . . . that instantly revolutionizes the economic structure from within, instantly destroying the old one, instantly creating the new one. This process of Creative Destruction is the essential fact about capitalism. It is what capitalism consists in and what every capitalist concern has got to live with.

Joseph Schumpeter, Capitalism, Socialism and Democracy, *1942*

Government has got to wake up to the fact that it is abusing the industrial base of this nation.

Robert E. Coleman, Riegel Textile Company, 1980

The American auto industry is a perfect example of short-term strategic planning by American business.

Donald W. Mitchell, business consultant, 1981

The United States needs an industrial restructuring board. . . . Without it industries that could be partially saved will not be saved.

Lester C. Thurow, economist, 1985

THE PROBLEM

A popular business buzzword of the last half of the 1980s that promises to be around for a while in the 1990s is *competitiveness*. The term, of course, refers to the ability or inability of the United States to hold its own in the battle for world markets. It reflected the growing concern in the 1980s that American producers were increasingly unable to meet the challenges laid down by foreign sellers—whether in distant markets we had once dominated or in our own domestic markets. The evidence of our difficulties was abundant. First, there was the shift of trade balances. U.S. trade deficits steadily increased as our export growth sagged precisely as we turned to importing more. Second, there was growing criticism of a whole range of alleged management malpractices by American firms. Once the pacesetter in management style as well as in new product development and new production technologies, American business was increasingly seen as lagging well behind its Japanese and German counterparts and in some cases behind Italy, South Korea, and other countries that until recently had not been considered forward-looking manufacturing nations.

Competitiveness is merely another way of looking at the problem of productivity: the ratio of outputs achieved for a given set of inputs. Simply put, the higher the level of outputs per inputs, the greater the economic efficiency of a nation. With greater productive efficiency, a country enjoys a faster-growing level of output as well as lower relative prices for what it produces. Throughout the closing decades of the nineteenth century and the first six decades of the twentieth century, high and generally rising levels of American productivity translated into an economic growth rate unequaled anywhere in the world. Of course, such growth translated into a steadily rising standard of living for Americans.

Beginning in the 1970s, however, American productivity started to slacken. As Figure 7.1 indicates, other non-Communist industrial nations have generally reported greater annual increases in productivity (changes in output per hour of labor). Although the American productivity record has brightened since 1980, we still lag well behind the Japanese, our principal international trading competitor. Meanwhile, we have much ground to make up against the French, the Germans, and other European nations. With greater output in comparison to similar inputs, these nations are successfully challenging American industry in world markets, as well as in our own backyard. And, naturally, the lowered levels of economic

FIGURE 7.1 Comparative Annual Changes in Manufacturing Output per Hour in the United States, France, West Germany, and Japan, 1970–1987

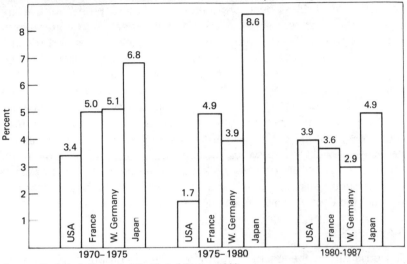

Source: Statistical Abstract of the United States, 1989.

performance have caused American economic growth to slow, adversely affecting our living standards.

Although output per hour of labor is the usual basis for measuring productivity, it is obvious that the American productivity dilemma goes much deeper than the question of how hard the individual American works. After all, workers can be more or less productive if they have more or fewer capital goods (machinery) with which to work. An hour of work done by a person with a pick and shovel will not challenge the output of an individual with a backhoe. All of this leads to another dimension of the problem: Is the capital being used, even if it is of great quantity, at the highest level of available technology? Then we might ask: Is the available technology the best we are capable of producing? Overarching all these components of productivity is the question of management skill: Is American industry managed in an intelligent and efficient way so as to assure the best decisions about what is produced, how much is produced, and under what production arrangements?

The evidence, of course, suggests that somewhere, perhaps everywhere, in the labyrinth of economic forces that determine productivity, something is wrong. Depending on ideological viewpoint, there is a long list of possible culprits: government intervention, excessively powerful unions, poor business decision making, the "quick profit" motive, too much business dependence on government, a decline in entrepreneurship, and so on. The differing assessments of the causes and possible cures for flagging American productivity go to the very roots of the ideological differences among our economic paradigms. Yet there is something each can agree on: *America faces a serious productivity problem that must be resolved.* Whereas each ideological view may follow a different path, all could agree (for different reasons, of course) with the *Business Week* editors' conclusion that "to rebuild America's productive capacity . . . will require sweeping changes in basic institutions, in the framework of economic policy making, and in the way the major actors on the scene—business, labor, and government—think about what they put into the economy and what they get out."*

SYNOPSIS

To Conservatives, the recent tumbling of American productivity is directly traceable to government intervention in business decision making and the growing American desire to receive more for less work. Liberals see the productivity problem as basically resulting from inadequate business policies, in particular the short-term profit focus of most enterprises. Radicals argue that worker productivity has in fact remained quite high among most American industries and that it is not really productivity but profits that concern most business leaders.

Anticipating the Arguments

* In what specific ways do Conservatives see government economic activity retarding the growth of American productivity?
* What particular elements of recent business activity or inactivity do Liberals see as major contributors to the declining rate of American output?
* How do Radicals prove their contention that profit making, not productivity, is the real driving force in private enterprise?

*"Revitalizing the American Economy," *Business Week*, June 30, 1980, p. 56.

The Conservative Argument

Frequently, the decline in American productivity is approached as if it were the root of our economic problems. Such a perspective is mistaken; falling productivity is the *result* of our economic problems, many of which we have addressed already in these pages. To be blunt and direct, low productivity is the price an economic or social system must pay when its utilization of the factors of production ceases to be directed by market forces. In our time, the two principal forces interfering with business's efficient application of the productive factors of the nation have been labor unions and government.

THE GENERAL IMPACT OF LABOR UNIONS AND GOVERNMENT ON PRODUCTIVITY

In a somewhat different context, we reviewed in the last issue the problems of inefficiency and misallocation that result from labor unions exercising inordinate power. The monopoly position of unions (provided over time by sympathetic Liberal government) impedes increasing productive efficiency in two ways: First, insofar as unions have been able to impose "featherbedding" (artificial efforts to increase the demand for union labor), they have restrained firms' abilities to increase worker output. Featherbedding, of course, refers not only to an unused and unneeded worker that must be hired according to the union contract (the railroad fireman or coal shoveler on diesel engines is the classic example), but to specific worker output limits – small shovels for construction workers and daily limitations on bricks laid by bricklayers or tons of freight lifted by forklift truck operators, for instance. Second, unions have lowered productivity by squeezing firm profits through excessive wage payments. The profit squeeze directly reduces the enterprise's internal funds available for capital improvement and indirectly has the same effect on external funds since low profit rates discourage investors. The failure to modernize plant and equipment, a charge leveled against many companies by Liberals, has usually been the result of high wages squeezing out needed capital investment rather than management oversight. However, as we noted in the last issue, organized labor's ability to impose such production inefficiencies seems to be waning. This is not yet true of government.

Government's role in reducing productivity can be categorized into at least two general areas of incorrect actions: (1) the actual physical expansion of the government's claim on the nation's output and (2) the various interventions of government into resource markets, social policy-making, and pricing decisions that affect the activities of what remains of the private sector.

THE ROLE OF GOVERNMENT TAX AND SPENDING POLICIES

The growth of government's share of the gross national product from a mere 7 percent in 1902 to more than one-third today is not simply a matter of cutting up the total economic pie in different proportions. To follow the analogy, the aggregate growth of government activities has altered the recipe of the pie and interfered with the cook's ability to bake it. The growth of a government's budget has two sides — revenues and expenditures. Each must be examined separately to see how government interferes in microeconomic decision making.

Revenues The immense taxation necessary to sustain the government sector interferes directly with the individual production and allocation decisions of enterprises. A purely neutral tax policy has yet to be developed. Worse still, even if some tax policies were less biased than others, American tax programs of the past sixty years have been constructed purposely by Liberal social engineers *not* to have unbiased effects. Taxes have been used for many other things than just collecting revenues to finance bloated budgets. In particular, taxes have been used as tools to redistribute income, converting the earnings of the more productive members of society into outright gifts to the least productive. Although we will explore this problem in the next issue, it should be noted here that such penalizing of the productive elements of a nation and rewarding the nonproductive gives precisely the wrong signals in a society worried about improving productivity.

The long-standing Liberal strategy of laying heavy tax burdens on upper-income groups has been a particularly objectionable policy. The usual economic justification for higher taxes on upper incomes is that they are relatively "painless," falling on individuals who have a diminishing value (marginal utility) for each additional dollar received. However, the national economic effects are not painless. Such taxation reduces the nation's fund of savings, which is supplied

FIGURE 7.2   Savings as a Percentage of Disposable Income, 1974–1988

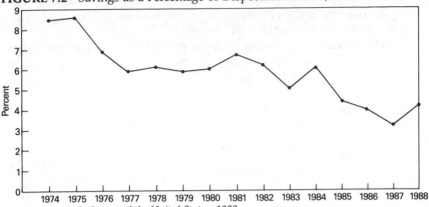

Source: Statistical Abstract of the United States, 1989.

mostly by the well-to-do. Savings are, of course, the source for investment funds; therefore, reductions in the nation's savings limits the
ability of business to expand and ultimately lowers productivity.
Under the Reagan administration, some headway was made in moving away from "soak the rich" taxation. The Revenue and Reform Act
of 1981 provided an across-the-board 25 percent reduction in income
tax liability. In addition, the "flat tax" revisions of 1988 have brought
the heavy personal taxation of middle- and upper-income savers to
even lower effective rates.

Nevertheless, the changes in tax law have not been enough to
arrest the general decline of American savings rates. As Figure 7.2
shows, American savings rates have continued to plummet since the
1970s. By 1989, American personal savings as a percentage of disposable income was less than half that reported in West Germany, about
a quarter of that in Japan, and a fifth of Italian savings rates. Saving
less than a nickel of every dollar received, Americans reported the
lowest savings rate of any industrialized nation.

Given the importance of savings to facilitating capital formation
and, thereby, improving American competitiveness, it is essential to
have progrowth tax policies. For instance, following the Japanese example, we might reduce or eliminate taxation on earned income that is
saved. Or, we could abandon our longtime strategy of subjecting all
income to the same taxation rate, regardless of whether the income is

earned from work or from savings and personal investments. In particular, relief from high capital-gains taxes would stimulate the supply of funds for venture-capital purposes.

The tax dilemma, however, is not limited to personal taxes alone. Long ago, Liberals, in their search for "painless" taxes, focused on the corporate-profits tax. What could be better, after all, than levying a tax on an entity that doesn't vote? In fact, corporate-profits taxes amount to a double-dip of taxation on those that provide the savings to finance investment. First, the corporation's profits are taxed before stockholders are payed, and then recipients of dividends are taxed again on what they have received. Admittedly, the top tax rate on corporate profits has fallen substantially in recent years—from about 50 percent to about 34 percent—and, with the adoption of extensive tax credits and depreciation allowances, the actual tax burdens on business have been reduced. (In 1951, business paid a third of the nation's total tax bill; by 1988 it paid about 10 percent.) However, our corporate tax policy is such a crazy-quilt of rules and exceptions that tax policy tends to "drive" investment decisions in ways that may not produce the most efficient and useful outcomes.

Although Liberals often complain about the "inequitable" effects of reducing tax burdens on savers, on those seeking capital-gains earnings, and on corporations—arguing that the rich pay less—they miss the point that tax equity (and certainly "soak the rich" taxes) may not be as *fair* or *painless* as such proposals sound. In the absence of higher levels of savings, which "pro-savings" tax policies might encourage, economic growth will remain low. Many who would prefer the wealthy to pay more will actually end up paying an even heavier "tax" in the form of lowered wages and unemployment that will result from economic stagnation.

Not all tax policies have unintended negative effects on productivity. Some policies are created consciously to discourage efficient business decision making. The best example is the longtime AFL-CIO/Liberal effort to contain the investment of American firms within the United States by placing prohibitive taxes on multinational businesses. Reformers argue that productivity and employment are falling in the United States because some American firms are able to obtain better returns on their capital overseas. So-called runaway firms are supposedly starving their domestic production facilities on purpose. Never mind that unions, through outrageous labor agreements, have priced American workers out of world labor markets and have placed important restrictions on the ability of business to innovate and introduce new capital-intensive production methods. Never mind that practically the only American corporations to show steady improvement in earnings and productivity are the very ones that have exploited multinational investment, production, and sales. We are asked to disregard all this and to tax the efficient firm so it will stay home and remain inefficient.

To recapitulate, under current government tax policies, capital and technology sources for productivity growth are made scarce. At the same time, corporations are discouraged by tax policy from acting wisely as profit managers. Instead of heeding the market command to close down unproductive operations, tax policies soften and hide the market signals.

Expenditures   On the expenditures side of government operations, the shift of resources from productive to unproductive agents is even stronger. Social expenditures made in the name of a better life for "working Americans"— everything from welfare to unemployment insurance to social security—have the ironic effect of discouraging work altogether (more on this in the next issue). With greater numbers of the labor force artificially insulated from the market forces of supply and demand, the desire to work, and especially the desire to work very hard, is deeply eroded. Nonwork, after all, is to be rewarded, and no one can slip through the social "safety net," no matter how hard one tries.

From the point of view of productivity, this situation, along with the excessive power of labor unions to write their own work rules, means that labor inputs in production are vastly changed from earlier pre-safety net and preunion days. Quite simply, we all have become accustomed to working less diligently. The decline of the "work ethic" is, of course, not all bad. Few Conservatives will defend the seventy-two-hour work week and the intolerable working conditions of a century ago. But we cannot have it both ways. Increased productivity has made possible better hours and better wages; however, better hours and better wages are not possible in the future unless our output increases. If we choose to work less while at the same time we are producing less, we must accept living on less. There is no free lunch.

Lowered worker productivity is not the only outcome of government spending programs. Transfers to undeserving corporations and subsidies to nonproducers are also methods of taxing the productive sectors of the economy to benefit the unproductive. They are not "free rides"; they entail a cost we all must pay.

THE ROLE OF GOVERNMENT SOCIAL POLICY

Apart from budgetary actions, government has also reduced productivity by its direct intervention in business affairs through misguided social policies. The list of such offenses against market efficiency is virtually limitless, and we have discussed several in earlier issues, so a few cases must suffice.

Environmental protection remains very high among Americans' priorities. As social objectives, clean air, water, and earth and conservation of resources for future generations are certainly noble concerns. Indeed, environmental protection can be had without abandoning the market system—if we understand it is not a free good and are willing to pay the price. Accordingly, capital investment required to meet EPA emissions controls reduces the amount of capital available for new investment and research and development. Some production operations have closed altogether when business enterprises determined that cleanup costs exceeded profit possibilities. The air got cleaner in many American industrial cities during the 1970s precisely as the lines at the unemployment office grew longer. While actual job losses are difficult to estimate, *Forbes* magazine calculated that meeting government environmental standards during the highwater period of antipollution regulation in the 1970s caused from 500 to 1,000 plant closings and lowered productivity by 1.3 percent. To be sure, environmental protection *is* important but an excessively protective program can have very undesirable consequences.

Similarly, the struggle to end racial and sex discrimination through certain economic contrivances has not uplifted many minorities or female workers, but it has raised the cost of government administration and created at the upper levels of employment a "reverse discrimination" hiring effect. Those who condemn a free economy's inability to absorb minorities and women quickly into mainstream employment fail to understand the problem. Most workers who are allegedly "discriminated against" do not in a real economic sense deserve, here and now, to be in the mainstream. Only in the simple-minded thinking of Liberals and Radicals does it make economic sense to promote unqualified and inexperienced workers and upper-level managers over more productive "mainstream" employees. While many white males may rejoice at such an observation, they should not misunderstand it. Claims to jobs or to promotions depend solely on one's efficiency and diligence. If any other criteria are used, both reason and order cease to exist in labor markets; and as labor market disorder grows, output shrinks.

It should be obvious that the list of recent social engineering efforts that lower output and raise costs goes on and on. It also should be obvious that none of these efforts, however well intended, will succeed if the nation is unable to increase productivity.

THE PROBLEM OF CHOICES AND EXPECTATIONS

The productivity enigma points up a fundamental economic principle (really *the* fundamental economic principle) that is always taught rigorously in economics courses but is forgotten so easily in ordinary life: *opportunity cost*. Everything, absolutely everything this side of the land of the tooth fairy, costs something. The decline of American productivity is not the result of some twist of fate. It is not caused by the Japanese or the Germans or even the Russians. It is not, as too many believe, unexplainable. Our lowered productivity is the result of our decisions, collectively and individually, to opt for more nonoutput. Rarely does the decision present itself this way, but that is exactly what we are choosing when we choose clean air over industrial smoke, affirmative action over free labor markets, subsidized early retirement over work, keeping failing corporations alive rather than letting them fall into bankruptcy, taxing the rich heavily to sustain the nonrich, and so on.

From a Conservative point of view, many of the nonoutput decisions are defensible, as long as everyone agrees to the objectives and understands that the result will be a lowered standard of living. However, most of our nonoutput decisions are imposed by the few on the many. That is pure tyranny—not democratically defensible on any grounds. Philosophically, it is wrong. Economically, it is disastrous. Unless we realize soon that our unrealistic expectations about the "good life" for everyone (deserving or not) and our reliance on government to painlessly fulfill these expectations only produce the opposite of the intended effects, productivity declines will continue.

The Conservative scenario for improving productivity should by now be self-evident: Rely on the market forces to organize and direct production. Artificial interventions by Liberal social tinkerers, by manipulative labor unions, and by well-organized minority-issue groups prohibit market efficiency. They shift investment and rewards to the unproductive elements and activities of society. The market cannot resolve instantaneously all of the social problems, real and alleged, that exist. But in the long run, as the illustrious past record of American productivity and growth shows, the market will decide the *what*, *how*, and *for whom* questions much more efficiently than can government or some weird mixture of government and the market.

Declining productivity is the result of a failure of the market, produced by the failure of government. The continued decline of productivity will produce the failure of everything that we hold of value. Without continued growth, we all must have less, which we are not prepared by our natures to accept. This paradox is the central economic and political fact of our time. It will be solved one way or another, for better or ill.

The Liberal Argument

While Conservatives blame falling American productivity and declining international competitiveness on "big government" and "big labor," it is notable that few American business leaders agree with this perspective. Instead, most business spokespersons have admitted, privately and publicly, that the fundamental causes for the recent decline in American productivity and competitiveness are to be found in decisions made (or not made) in the boardrooms of American corporations. The significance of these admissions—which have been frequently stated in books and speeches by corporate leaders over the past decade—should not be underestimated. They reveal much about the challenges facing America as it enters an era of heightened international competition.

THE PROBLEMS OF FALTERING
CORPORATE STRATEGIES

In *The New Industrial State*, John Kenneth Galbraith argued in the 1960s that planning had taken on a central role in the modern giant corporation. Not to plan, to leave business decisions to the short-term whims of the market, was simply too irresponsible a strategy to contemplate. Galbraith was doubtless correct in his observation, but his timing was wrong, for American enterprise had not yet reached the level of mature corporate planning. Now confronted with falling productivity, tumbling profits, and dwindling shares of both domestic and world markets, long-term corporate planning may be coming of age.

Looking back over the recent decline in American productivity, the shallowness of business strategy becomes apparent. In the first place, preoccupation by most firms with short-term profits led to neglecting long-term trends. Nowhere was this more obvious than in the auto industry. After the energy shortage of 1973, the market (even as Conservatives understand "market") gave clear signals that the era of the 300-hp "dinosaur eights" was over. However, as buyers began to sample Japanese and German "world cars" in greater numbers, Detroit continued to follow the old tried-and-true strategy of the auto industry: Make them big and fast! As a result, American auto dealers' lots continued to fill up in the middle and late 1970s with unsold giant machines, while the roads became cluttered with more Volkswagens, Datsuns, Toyotas, and Hondas. Within five years of the energy crisis, Detroit lost 20 percent of the American car market to foreigners. Worse still, the auto giants were slow to use their enormous capital resources to design and build the kinds of cars that energy prices forced Americans to buy. When the changes finally came in the late 1970s, they were done too swiftly, creating serious design, production, and marketing problems.

Corporate policy through the 1970s and 1980s also reflected a short-term profit bias in the decision to follow an essentially foolish merger strategy. The popular corporate myth that sheer size was a measure of strength led to thousands of ill-conceived combinations. In the 1970s, established and efficient giants squandered their cash and credit acquiring enterprises in wholly unrelated industries. In the 1980s, "hostile takeovers," "stock unbundling," "leveraged buy-outs," and other schemes absorbed capital and the talents of management. While the amounts of capital paid for acquisitions grew, there was a corresponding decline in what was spent on research and development. None of the acquisitions created new value—they only reorganized the corporate ownership landscape. Meanwhile, firms grew larger but weaker as capital resources were overextended and management and marketing problems developed in the new, unfamiliar operations that had been acquired.

The short-term strategy of quick growth through takeover was paced by another trend in dangerous short-run planning: multinational growth. From most firms' perspectives, multinational operations made sense; and looked at solely from the firm's balance sheet, they still do. The lure of cheaper overseas labor markets and the possibility of tapping enormous foreign final-goods markets was irresistible. By 1980, firms like IBM were earning 50 percent of their profits in overseas operations. Of course, much of this flight of capital overseas was helped along by government tax policy, which left foreign earnings virtually untaxed. However, the short-term and even the long-term profitability of overseas operations often added up to declining profits at home. Each investment dollar going overseas was a dollar not invested in improving domestic production facilities. Plants in the United States grew old and obsolete as new structures went up in France, Italy, Brazil, Taiwan, and Germany. Steel, once the backbone of American industry, limped along in the United States, using turn-of-the-century plants and production methods. The effects, of course, were low productivity and high costs.

As American business squandered its technological, management, and production leadership through short-term profit strategies, other industrial nations, particularly Japan and Germany, took a long-run view. Through coordinated capital planning, along with supportive government actions, their productivity soon surpassed that of the United States. By the early 1980s, both Japan and Germany had almost caught up to the United States in output per worker. Meanwhile, the United States, once the world leader in living standards, had fallen to tenth in the world.

Far form the Conservative scenario of a shrinking economic pie caused by workers opting for less labor and more leisure and a government hamstringing industry with taxes and social legislation requirements, we find that the American economic pie has been getting smaller because the corporate cook has been skimping on capital and management skills, two key ingredients of growth.

THE NECESSITY FOR DEVELOPING
AN INDUSTRIAL POLICY

As the economy and business profits began to pick up after 1983, the urgency of the debate over American productivity subsided. Yet, few close observers of American business seriously believed that we had done anything fundamental to solve the underlying problems or that the crisis would not surface again. The "reindustrialization" agenda of the early 1980s still exists even though it has not been attracting attention recently.

Among the agenda items was a call for the establishment of a national "Industrial Policy"—the active intervention of government to stimulate investment, to modernize American industry, and to coordinate capital planning. Industrial Policy would also attempt to salvage many industries, such as steel and machine tools, which now seem about to be overwhelmed by foreign competition. The argument, very simply, is that the nation cannot afford to sit quietly by, in the name of the free market, and watch its industrial base collapse—a collapse that is, after all, largely the outcome of flawed business decision making, not inexorable economic laws. One of the best known Industrial Policy advocates is Felix Rohatyn, a former ITT executive and a partner of the Lazard Fréres investment house (hardly a man of Radical background). One of Rohatyn's pet projects—and an idea having considerable Liberal support—is the establishment of a federal investment fund, patterned after the old Reconstruction Finance Corporation of the Great Depression years. The object of the fund would be to make low-interest, long-term loans to financially troubled corporations—firms that otherwise might not secure needed funds in private markets and thereby might fail.

Another assistance project, widely supported by business but opposed by Conservatives, is to increase investment in human capital. By developing job training programs and paying subsidies to businesses that hire the poorly skilled, this type of government outlay would work in two ways to increase national output: Welfare (nonproductive) payments would be reduced *and* worker productivity would be raised. Although studies indicate that human capital investments in education have higher productivity and growth paybacks than direct capital investments, it is precisely the educational and training programs that were most vulnerable to Conservative budget cutters in the 1980s.

To halt the squandering of capital funds in productively pointless and wasteful mergers and to shift such monies toward actual reinvestment in capital facilities, a new corporate tax policy must be considered. By using a mix of tax reductions on new productive investment and tax penalties on mergers that do not demonstrate possible economics of scale, an effective "carrot and stick" approach to better investment strategy would emerge. Similarly, such a tax policy could be employed to slow down the rate of capital flight into multinational corporations' overseas operations. Presently many firms find that their overseas tax payments are deductible against their U.S. tax liabilities; thus tax policy tends to encourage migration of capital. By removing such privileges and by placing other tax restraints on the firm, tax policy could be used to encourage corporate "deepening" of investment in the United States. Meanwhile, the careful, selective use of tariffs and import quotas can provide breathing space for industries presently hard-pressed by foreign competition. The "free trade" argument of Conservatives, however convincing the logic, will not give American enterprise the time it needs to reindustrialize.

Of course, there remains the broader question of just what we should be investing our national capital in. Obviously, a scattershot approach that provides a little capital for everyone will not be as effective as directing large amounts of resources to areas in which we have a special advantage. Moreover, our investment needs are far greater in the area of capital-goods production than in quality-of-life improvements. To be direct, it is a lot more important that the American steel industry be redeveloped than that McDonald's be able to renovate its golden arches. Necessarily, this involves choices—*indicative planning*—by government or a quasi-governmental agency.

Another essential line of government policy is stimulating savings and reducing consumption. Despite Conservative arguments that voluntary savings-consumption decisions work best, the evidence does not support the claim. Americans of all income levels have become accustomed to high mass consumption. Savings at all levels of income have fallen. Nor was this trend stopped, as Conservatives argued it would be, by the Reagan tax cuts of the early 1980s. Forced savings through consumption taxes, such as value-added taxes, offer the only short-term means to reverse this trend.

Such programs as we have outlined here will increase the availability of capital resources. By broadening and deepening our capital base, we can start to reverse the productivity decline. But capital shortage and wasteful investment are not the only problems.

A NEW PARTNERSHIP BETWEEN
BUSINESS AND LABOR

Regardless of our capital strength, labor remains the chief component in all productivity questions. In this area, reindustrialization requires new approaches to labor-management relations. In particular, the traditional adversary relationship between workers and employers must end. Neither the old capitalist mentality of complete control over workers nor the unionist approach of "more, more, more" can be continued if reindustrialization is to succeed. Both capital and labor can learn much from the Japanese model. In Japan, earnings (wages and shared profits) are tied to increased productivity. Workers as well as management have a shared interest in the outcome of the firm's operations; however, labor is not a passive element, simply accepting management decisions and sharing in their effects. On the contrary, labor, right down to the least significant employee on the plant floor, participates in a variety of management decisions. Labor input is not limited to such matters as wages and hours, but is involved in how goods are manufactured, how jobs are defined, where responsibility lies, and so on.

Such a change in industrial relations is not merely a cosmetic change. Effectively, it redefines the power balance between labor and capital. It admits that the modern corporation is not manageable from remote corporate offices. Only by shared management and labor decision making will corporations be able to adapt to the new production requirements. Conservatives who hold out for the traditional powers of corporate leadership and a passive, dominated role for labor are still living in the era of Adam Smith's pin factory. They fail to understand that the complexity and interconnectedness of production today require more than division of labor. There must be shared responsibility. Conservatives also fail to comprehend that we are at the end of the era of individual, atomistic workers and capitalists, each pursuing selfish, materialist goals. Probably no aspect of the process of redeveloping American competitiveness is so potentially revolutionary in changing economic and social relations in modern mixed capitalism as the changes that must take place in the workplace. Economics as it is known and taught in the United States has yet to absorb these trends into conventional theory.

A SUMMING UP

Closing the productivity gap, quite as Conservatives argue, is essential for the nation to survive and for the production-for-profit system to continue. However, by maintaining and defending a no-government, no-labor-union, no-social-policy approach to all output decisions, Conservatives, even if they succeeded in generating greater productivity and economic growth, would limit the benefits to a very few in society. For most of us, growth or no growth would make little difference. Unless everyone shares in rising productivity, the social and political foundations of our society will collapse and the productivity question itself will become as irrelevant as debating how many angels are able to dance on the head of a pin.

The Radical Argument

Conservative and Liberal handwringing over U.S. competitiveness is deceptive. Discussion tends to focus on only one aspect of the problem. While productivity may indeed measure the relative output capacity of a nation, it is not, in a capitalist society, the guiding measure of economic performance Conservatives and Liberals suggest it is. Profit, not productivity, is the guide for capitalist decision making, and only in the obscurantist models of advanced microeconomics do the two become the same thing. In the real world, businesspeople know the difference—and they always follow profit. As Thorstein Veblen argued long ago, the businessperson's desire for profitable buying and selling very often leads to wasteful production. However, business "makes up for its wastefulness by the added strain which it throws upon those engaged in the production work." In our time, the search for profits has meant declining national productivity *and* increased worker exploitation and anguish.

UNRAVELING THE DECLINING-
PRODUCTIVITY PARADOX

The problem of declining national productivity needs to be clarified. Both the Conservative and Liberal scenarios somehow suggest that for one reason or another (too much government interference or too little management initiative) capitalists have stopped acting like capitalists. That is, business has stopped introducing labor-saving devices. However, the evidence is quite to the contrary. Productivity—output per worker—remains high and is rising in many sectors of the economy. In the manufacturing sector it has become spectacular. To take some representative firms as examples, between 1964 and 1980, precisely as the United States was reporting significant overall productivity declines, the real value of each worker's output increased 40 percent at General Motors, 45 percent at IBM, and 90 percent at U.S. Steel. In fact, in 1980 U.S. Steel produced almost twice the 1964 output with 40,000 fewer workers.

The low overall productivity rates develop when we add in the labor that has been squeezed from high-productivity sectors of the economy, such as manufacturing, and forced into less productive (and less rewarded) service industry and government work or into unwanted idleness. Even in the highly productive manufacturing sector, output-per-worker averages are reduced artificially by adding in the employment of growing numbers of nonproductive managerial, promotional, and office personnel. It must be remembered that the national productivity rate is a ratio of the entire labor force to the levels of national output. In America, there has been a steady growth of marginally productive and nonproductive labor since the late 1950s. This development is not accidental, nor is it evidence that capitalists have forgotten how to use labor to their advantage. Rather, it simply reflects a new stage in our economic development.

The decline in overall productivity has not produced the corporate profit declines that might be expected; indeed, before-tax profit rates have stayed very steady (except in recession years) over the past several decades. The reason for this is that productivity is only one element affecting profits. The other major constraint on profit making is the labor wage rate. Wage rates are an industrial firm's real guide to how "productive" labor is. After all, what does management care about "output per hour"? The firm isn't spending hours. Firms spend dollars to obtain hours. Thus output-per-wage dollar is the "productivity" measure that really counts.

In the earlier epochs of industrial development, productivity gains allowed for the advance of profits and the gradual improvement of real wages. In recent years, a new trend has developed. Looking at the whole economy, maintaining stable profit rates has entailed both limiting productivity advances (at least in the leading industrial sectors) and holding down real wage rates where possible (usually in the least productive sectors). In other words, with average productivity gains falling for the entire economy, profits were increasingly obtained by reducing average real wages. In some industries, wages fell even when productivity increased.

In terms of specific corporate strategies used to force wages down and profits up, two developments are illustrative of the problem facing American workers: capital flight overseas and "runaway" firms at home.

THE INTERNATIONALIZATION OF CAPITAL

American productivity began to decline at almost precisely the same time that American enterprises began to discover the advantages of multinational operations and investment. The increasing shift of American capital to overseas production, beginning in the mid-1950s, accelerated the already evident trend of a growing labor surplus in the U.S. economy. Just when American firms expanded overseas, unemployment began rising and real wages stagnating. Only the war economy of the Vietnam era masked the seriousness of this exporting of employment.

The newest and best American technology rushed overseas to fill the new European markets for electronics, machine tools, and consumer goods. Cheap foreign skilled labor attracted other investment to the Far East, where goods were produced for sale in the United States. The effect of both moves was virtually to halt the growth of skilled jobs in the United States. At the same time, labor-intensive firms discovered the unskilled labor markets of Korea, Taiwan, and the Philippines, where workers were paid the equivalent of 20 cents an hour. This discovery had adverse effects on unskilled American labor. Only the domestic growth of low-wage jobs in the service sector and the expansion of government war and social spending mitigated the dramatic export of employment. It does not demand mastery of Marx's *Capital* to realize that an economy based on fast-food drive-ins, war, and government bureaucracies is in deep trouble.

The reported profits of multinational corporations (MNCs), which are certainly much lower than their real profits, expanded precisely as the well-being of most Americans declined. Income inequality was increased, government fiscal problems worsened, and labor's bargaining power diminished. The MNC export of domestic capital (past American labor) was producing a tremendous economic contraction in America. By the mid-1970s, Americans everywhere were being urged to lower their expectations as workers and consumers. Corporations, however, were not lowering their profit targets. From an American point of view, the MNC was an effective new tool of capitalist exploitation at home.

RUNAWAY FIRMS AT HOME

As we have discussed, the flight of capital overseas did not prevent some important productivity gains in domestic industry, but one can only speculate on what these gains might have been had the cheaper overseas wage rates not drawn off billions of investment dollars. Nevertheless, overseas investment began to trigger a "disinvestment" process at home. With many firms putting their best resources overseas, their domestic plants began to decay. At the same time, labor surpluses started to grow. This encouraged the new domestic strategy of "runaway" plants—running not always overseas but often to new, lower-cost (read: "lower-wage") areas within the United States. In particular, industry found the unorganized labor markets of the southern states to their liking. During the 1970s, the Frostbelt lost 111 jobs for every 100 that were created, while the Sunbelt lost 80 for every 100 new jobs. The result was industrial devastation across the Northeast and Midwest and a miniboom in the South. Whereas many of the new plants used the best and newest technology, some smaller industries found the labor-wage differential so attractive that they avoided capital-intensive production methods, choosing instead inefficient but profitable labor-intensive techniques.

The domestic runaway firm leaves more than its own wreckage in its wake. The effect on the local community is not merely the jobs lost by the initial closing. There follows a "multiplier" contraction effect as services and businesses supported by the industry or the paychecks of its workers shrivel up after the closing. Indeed, other businesses, especially small enterprises, may then also be candidates for failure. With an ever-growing reduction of production and jobs, the community is hit by declining revenues on one side of its budget and rising social expenditures to support unemployed workers on the other. Taxes rise and costs for other firms rise, encouraging additional closings. Meanwhile, the local pool of unemployed grows, reducing union bargaining power as well as nonunion wage rates.

TOWARD THE SOCIAL PLANNING OF PRODUCTION

Viewing the so-called productivity crisis this way, we see that efforts to lower output costs and increase profits have a paradoxical result. While the individual enterprise acts rationally to ensure its own survival, the entire society is decimated. Individual firms may prosper, but only by driving down the general level of the nation's standard of living. Obviously, Conservative attempts to end the few existing restraints on business behavior and to free up the profit effort can lead only to an acceleration of these tendencies. Despite the present popularity of Conservative ideology, the unspeakable social and private anguish that would result from applying their programs is appreciated by most business and political leaders. Many people correctly understand that that kind of business freedom would quickly destroy social and political order and the production-for-profit system altogether.

Consequently, the Liberal program for shared business-government planning through industrial policy reflects a much more realistic effort by capitalists, at least temporarily, to save themselves and their system. From a Radical perspective, it is easy to point out the contradictions of such a strategy—for instance, building up capitalist power on the one hand while sharing its authority with workers on the other. Yet, over the short run, such a strategy is indeed a likely alternative; and from a Radical perspective it is not totally objectionable—*in the short run*. The Liberal recognition of the need to restrain and redirect individual corporate behavior and to create a new relationship between capital and labor could mean the beginning of social control over capital. Workers and consumers, of course, will soon learn to expect and then to demand more control than businesses are willing to give. But it is probable that the modern reformers of the production-for-profit system will not be able to withstand this pressure, and greater social control will result.

Whether or not this scenario develops very quickly remains to be seen. What is obvious in the current productivity decline, however, is that one era of American business expansion, in which both business profits and workers' earnings advanced, has now ended. Real corporate growth presently means greater real losses to people. The need for social control over the basic economic questions of what is produced, how, and for whom becomes more evident as the capitalist answers to these questions becomes increasingly unacceptable in human terms.

Issue 8 _____

Income Distribution and Public Policy
Can We Ever Eliminate Poverty?

Like all other contracts, wages should be left to the fair and free competition of the market, and should never be controlled by the interference of the legislature.

The clear and direct tendency of the poor laws is in direct opposition to those obvious principles: it is not as the legislature benevolently intended, to amend the condition of the poor, but to deteriorate the condition of both poor and rich; instead of making the poor rich, they are calculated to make the rich poor.

David Ricardo, 1821

It is not to die, or even to die of hunger, that makes a man wretched; many men have died, all men must die.... But it is to live miserable we know not why; to work sore and yet gain nothing; to be heart-worn, weary yet isolated, unrelated, girt in with a cold, universal Laissez Faire.

Thomas Carlyle, 1853

A very substantial portion of poverty and unemployment is chronic, beyond the control of individuals or the influence of rising aggregate demand.

The President's Commission on Income Maintenance Programs, 1969

THE PROBLEM

Government's proper role in income distribution through tax policies and transfers to individuals is, naturally enough, a matter of much disagreement among our ideological paradigms. For the most part though, general discussions of income distribution tend to be rather broad, unfocused, and philosophical. Therefore, the income distribution debate is a bit slippery and difficult to grasp unless we turn to a specific distributional issue. Of all such issues, none has been as enduring as "poverty in America." For more than twenty-five years, since President Lyndon Johnson inaugurated the "War on Poverty" in 1964 as the centerpiece of his Great Society programs, intense ethical, political, and economic arguments have characterized American discussions of its poor, maintaining "poverty" as the central income distribution question on the nation's agenda. To ask what, if anything, we should be doing about poverty goes to the very heart of American beliefs on the matter of income distribution.

As the United States enters the last decade of the twentieth century, approximately 35 million citizens are officially classified by the government as "living in poverty."* Statistical evidence on the extent of official poverty is not a matter of much dispute, but attempts to fathom the meaning of the data are quite another matter. Does the extent of American poverty reveal basic shortcomings in our political-economic system? Or, is the poverty problem overstated both in terms of its relative importance and in terms of long-run national trends in income distribution? Is poverty a problem of such dimensions that it requires a special national commitment to facilitate its eradication? Or, in fact, have our past efforts in this direction caused more grief than gain?

At this point in our survey of contemporary economic issues, the reflexive responses of our ideological paradigms to these questions should produce no surprises. However, before proceeding to a survey of Conservative, Liberal, and Radical analyses, an objective observer is well served by looking a bit closer at the facts. The reader should be forewarned: The evidence, although providing important insights on poverty

---

*The "Poverty Income Threshold" is, according to federal government definitions, attained when an individual's income is "lower than three times the annual cost of a diet that is minimally acceptable." Obviously, the exact dollar threshold will change from year to year as general price levels vary. In 1981, the poverty threshold for a family of four was $8,410; by 1991, it was about $13,400.

FIGURE 8.1   Poverty Rates in America, 1959–1988

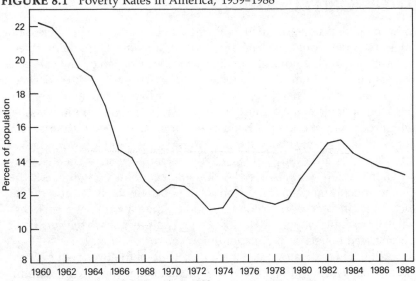

Source: *Economic Report of the President,* 1989.

and income distribution problems in the United States, is not one-sided and still requires interpretation before reaching a final conclusion.

With regard to the question of how well we have been doing in eliminating poverty, the answer depends on the time frame used in measuring its extent. In the early 1960s, before the War on Poverty commenced, poverty rates were significantly higher then the current 15 percent. Moreover, if we were to use the same *real income* measures used to set the poverty line in 1960 ($3,000 in 1954 dollars for a family of four), we find that the 22 percent of the population living below this level in 1960 was still a vast improvement over the pre–Great Depression, 1929 figure of 59.2 percent. Simply put, most Americans lived at or below an impoverished standard of living only a few decades ago, while just a small proportion fall in this category today. However, if we shorten our time frame, there is cause for concern. As Figure 8.1 shows, Johnson's War on Poverty and other economic forces had driven poverty rates to as low as 12 percent by the early 1970s but over the last two decades the poverty rate has been steadily increasing. Thus it can be concluded that poverty

TABLE 8.1 The Incidence of Poverty among Specific Groups

National Average	13.6%
White	11.0%
Black	31.1%
Hispanic	27.3%
Over Age 65	12.4%
Families Headed by Women	38.3%
More than 1 year of College	5.0%

Source: U.S. Bureau of the Census, *Money Income and Poverty Status of Families and Persons in the United States, 1986.*

in America, while not the overwhelming problem it was in the more distant past, is currently a greater problem than in the recent past.

Beyond the question of the *extent* of poverty, there is the matter of just who the poor are. In other words, do the demographics of poverty support the argument that the American poor possess special characteristics that require special attention? As Table 8.1 shows, the incidence of poverty falls unevenly across the nation's population. African-Americans, Hispanics, children, women, families headed by women, and individuals with comparatively low educational levels all have significantly higher poverty rates than the national average. Not surprisingly, such a statistical picture suggests to some observers that present-day poverty in America is basically a problem of identifiable groups. Accordingly, the argument is made that this demonstrates the necessity of "special" antipoverty measures. Others, however, are not persuaded that the unique demographic characteristics justify compensatory programs that might impose excessive burdens on the nonpoor.

Finally, there is the issue of how many of the poor are actually able to escape their impoverishment. Recent data suggest a mixed picture. For those who consider poverty an overblown problem, one that is best left to solve itself, there is the comforting fact, statistically speaking, that one-half to two-thirds of the presently poor will eventually escape this status largely through their own efforts (though many of them will return—usually temporarily—to poverty at some time in the future). However, the remainder—and we are talking about 10 to 15 million people—

constitute the *hard-core* poor, those who never have nor ever will escape poverty.

Considering the available evidence and the varying interpretations, it is not surprising that economists and policymakers are not of one mind on whether poverty is or is not a major economic problem confronting the nation. And even if there was agreement that poverty is a serious problem, there would not automatically be agreement on how to deal with it.

SYNOPSIS
The Conservative argument holds that income inequality is natural and that efforts to change it through taxes and transfers will diminish the entire society's well-being. According to the Liberal argument, a more egalitarian distribution of income is humane and necessary. The Radical argument contends that income disparity is normal and even needed in capitalism, but at the same time it undermines the capitalist system.

Anticipating the Arguments

- Why do Conservatives believe that public charitable efforts are essentially self-defeating and harmful to the poor themselves?
- What are the basic philosophical differences between Conservatives and Liberals on the "ideal" distribution of income?
- How do you account for the Radicals' argument that our past income redistributional efforts have at best failed and have perhaps made the income gap widen?

The Conservative Argument

For the past twenty-five years or more, the question of poverty in the United States has been a central agenda item for Liberals and Radicals. Indeed, this issue, as it has been presented in political debate, in the press, and in economics textbooks, has been defined along the lines of an essentially Liberal–Radical argument: Poverty is morally evil, poverty is a measure of our economic system's failure, and poverty must be cured whatever the cost. Anyone doubting this observation need only turn on the television to watch the evening news' "objective" reporting on homelessness and other symbolic representations of poverty. Conservatives, however, see poverty and antipoverty efforts in a larger context that can only be understood in relation to the bigger issue of income distribution in general and its connection to the workings of the whole society. Thus Conservatives prefer to address the entire system of rewards in a free society before turning to the emotionally charged topic of "poverty."

TOWARD A JUST SYSTEM OF REWARDS

A unifying feature of all Liberal and Radical programs for the past hundred years has been the call for egalitarianism in income. The "Robin Hood" illusion is the very beginning of any collectivist's social dream. In the United States, income redistribution efforts in this century have appeared in two general forms: (1) a highly progressive income tax structure aimed at piling the expense of social spending on the upper-income elements of society, and (2) a vast giveaway of these appropriations to the poor and the nonproductive groups within the nation. Both schemes rest on serious errors of economic and social thinking that we explored in the last issue on productivity, but that deserve fuller elaboration and criticism.

Distribution of income should be governed by the simple and equitable principle that all members of a society should receive according to what they, or whatever they own, are able to produce. The abilities, tastes, and occupational interests of individuals vary. People value work and leisure differently. Some individuals are willing to forgo an assured lower income in favor of taking a risk and possibly earning more. Enforced equality of income utterly fails to consider these possibilities. It presumes that greater social satisfaction is attained by income parity than by letting people make their own valuations of what money means to them.

Consider, for instance, a person who is quite content to live on $100 a week. From this person's point of view, needs are satisfied and the right balance between leisure and work has been achieved. To transfer to this person one-quarter of the wages of another person who makes $200 a week will hardly increase the first person's welfare or happiness. At the same time, it subtracts much satisfaction from the second person, who is willing to work hard enough to earn the $200 wage. If we now added up the relative satisfactions of the two·

workers, it would be lower after redistribution than before. In other words, proof is lacking that a more equal income distribution actually maximizes community satisfaction.

At another level, egalitarianism leads to more serious troubles. Enforcing equal distribution of income penalizes the industrious and inventive and subsidizes those with less initiative. If the industrious fail to obtain rewards for their talents and work, they will naturally slacken their efforts. As a result, the total productiveness of society is lessened. In the subsequent egalitarian redistribution, everyone gets less than before. Just how far the detrimental effects of income equalization can go in destroying a society is evident in Great Britain. Subsidy for nonproduction and confiscation of earned income have lowered British output and put the nation at a disadvantage in world trade. The best minds and the nation's capital have fled to other countries. At home there is a shabby equality as well as mediocrity.

While the discussion so far has been mostly concerned with individual labor, it also applies to individuals' command over capital and wealth. Appropriating the wealth of one person to support another denies the individual's right to property and will lead to inefficiency and economic contraction in the whole society. (Whether the wealth is inherited or has been earned by the individual is irrelevant.) This is not just an economic matter. Seizures of wages and property are violations of freedom. It is not such a big step from telling people what their income will be to telling them what work to do or what ideas to think.

Of course, we must move from the realm of abstract theory justifying existing income inequality and protecting property rights into the real world. Here, taxes must be collected to carry on the business of government (even if that business is excessive). And to help those who are not able to take care of themselves, transfer payments are necessary. However, taxes and transfers should express the principles just summarized.

Since tax policies have long been the principal redistributive tool for social engineers committed to egalitarianism, we shall turn to this topic before discussing antipoverty transfer measures.

REFORMING THE TAX STRUCTURE

The Robin Hood strategy of taking from the rich and giving to the poor rests on a simple set of assumptions: The rich will scarcely miss their losses since they have so much in the first place, whereas the poor will benefit very greatly from the small amounts they receive. The idea is attractive, perhaps even appealing as children's fiction, but when elevated to public policy, it is an invitation to economic disaster (as we pointed out in the last issue). Nevertheless, Liberals have continuously advocated "soak the rich" tax schemes, defending heavily progressive income taxes, high inheritance taxes, and corporate-profits taxes (that amount to a kind of double taxation on investors).

Theoretically, such tax efforts have been justified with the so-called ability-to-pay principle. The greater-than-proportional taxes levied on the well-to-do were seen as *fair* because the well-to-do were less likely to be harmed by heavy taxes than were the nonwealthy. Liberal politicians over the years were quite aware that "soak the rich" tax programs were always politically attractive, appealing as they did to that greater proportion of the voters who were not rich.

The Conservative response to Liberal attempts to build and maintain an unfairly progressive tax structure has been a matter of consistent opposition. Philosophically, progressive taxation, whatever its form, is a discriminatory confiscation of certain people's property and a limiting of their rights and freedom. Economically, however, it makes even less sense. If successively higher tax rates are to be applied to increases in income, working to acquire more income provides less real reward. The diminished reward reduces the desire to work and, as we saw in our study of the productivity problem, also reduces the entire society's savings, investments, and growth rate. Moreover, as Arthur Laffer and others have pointed out, the higher tax rates yield less and less in receipts as they discourage additional earnings. Thus the progressive income tax approach, apart from its unfairness and adverse economic effects, is also self-defeating.

Some people, of course, will not accept these arguments. But there is more evidence of folly in our past efforts to maintain a progressive tax structure. Rather than having the intended Robin Hood effect, it encouraged legal tax evasion by creating numerous tax loopholes: tax-free status for state and municipal bonds, unfair "effective" rates (lower for single taxpayers), expense account deductions, and so on. Therefore, for many taxpayers the actual rates paid on their incomes were much lower than the published rates. Since not everyone enjoys the same loophole privileges, tax collection has been uneven and unfair. Make no mistake, true Conservatives are not heartened to learn that several hundred millionaires legally avoid tax payments every year.

Quite apart from these inequities, our tax structure encourages individuals to take actions that may save them taxes but are economically foolish in terms of the larger society. They may decide to buy tax-free municipal bonds rather than corporate bonds. Thus urban debt is traded off against corporate expansion.

By the 1980s, the nation was ripe for tax reform. The Liberal case for high progressive taxation collapsed as the inflationary 1970s drove up the *nominal income* of most Americans, who now found themselves in higher tax brackets, paying ever-higher rates on the less valuable dollars they were earning. With an across-the-board tax cut of 25 percent phased in over three years after 1981, and with a flattening of all tax rates in 1986, American tax policy began to move away from the disastrous irrationality of "soak the rich" taxation. (By 1988, maximum marginal tax rates, which had once been as high as 91 percent and were 50 percent in 1985, had been capped at 28 percent.) As we noted in the last issue, this is only a modest beginning. Much more must be done if American tax policy is to accomplish its two basic objectives: (1) fairness to all citizens and (2) stimulation of the market forces that drive the economy.

THE WELFARE PROGRAM

While taxes are one way of equalizing income, a second and more disruptive method for doing so is the welfare system. Broadly speaking, welfare includes a wide range of subsidies paid to individuals to offset low incomes. These include direct support transfers (as in the Aid to Families with Dependent Children program), public housing, minimum-wage laws, unemployment insurance, Medicaid, and social security.

Table 8.2 illustrates the recent enormous growth of federal social spending to provide a so-called safety net for low-income Americans. Even though the Reagan administration carried on a steady effort to bring down most social spending, the growth of such outlays since the early 1970s far exceeded the rate of growth of the nation's gross national product or federal budget outlays in general. Looking at the data somewhat differently, "human resource" expenses account for

TABLE 8.2   The Growth of Social Benefits, 1970–1989 (in billions of dollars)

	1970	1989	Percent Change
Gross national product	992.7	5,233.2	427
Federal budget outlays	195.7	1,140.6	483
Human resources outlays	75.3	589.5	683
Income security	15.6	136.3	774
Health	5.9	48.9	729
Veterans' benefits	8.7	30.1	246
Education and Training	8.6	36.7	327
Social security and Medicare	36.5	337.5	825

Source: *Statistical Abstract of the United States, 1985* and *Economic Report of the President*, 1990.

about 13 percent of the nation's GNP today. In still-depressionary 1940, such outlays accounted for only 6 percent. The rate of growth in welfare programs and spending is particularly dangerous because it means that ever-greater tax sacrifices must be demanded of working citizens. For many workers, after-tax income is less than welfare grants paid to nonworkers.

Apart from their cost, however, have the welfare programs and other plans to assist low-income Americans attained their goals? Whatever their intentions, most of these programs fail to deliver what they promise. Indeed, they often do more harm than good. Aid to Families with Dependent Children (AFDC), given only to mothers and children in the absence of a working father, has broken up families. Public housing programs, which involve tearing down old neighborhoods and building new housing complexes, have actually caused a shortage of low-income rentals and forced rents upward. Minimum-wage laws, rather than assuring a desired wage, have destroyed marginal jobs. Unemployment insurance induces people not to work. Medicaid has forced health costs up. Virtually all cash-granting welfare programs encourage fraud and, as a result, our welfare system is not only excessively expensive, but it fosters criminality. The list of tragedies ensuing from well-intended social tinkering is endless. On top of all that, we are burdened with a vast bureaucracy at all levels of government to administer these programs.

Beyond their more obvious defects, welfare endeavors are particularly lamentable because they create a strong disincentive to work and discourage people from improving themselves. People have to be poor in order to qualify for welfare protection; they have to stay poor to keep getting it. Thus our welfare system has created a vast, permanent subculture of the disadvantaged. Meanwhile, the rest of society must pay support costs.

The ideal situation would be to end such a system of transfers, but realistically we must face the fact that some people are indeed unable to care for themselves or will be the victims of lags and "stickiness" in the economy. We shall have to pay some welfare support. That support, however, should not reduce the incentives to work or for self-improvement, and it should be administered as simply as possible.

As with proportional, no-exemptions income tax, welfare payments should follow simple and unalterable rules. First, we should determine a minimum subsistence level of income for a family. Once determined, this minimum income can be guaranteed through a *negative income tax* payment that subsidizes private earnings up to a predetermined minimum level of legal taxability. At this point, the recipient becomes just another taxpayer. These transfer arrangements, however, should be tied to a "workfare" system for all able-bodied recipients. The obligation to be ready and willing to accept work is a fair one. At a minimum, this would probably require registration at employment offices and active job searching. Obviously, there are a number of possible ways to set up a negative income tax program, but Conservatives should support those that encourage work incentives, lead to the dismantling of most present subsidy efforts, demand the least administrative overhead, and are subject to rules, not discretion. All cash (particularly unemployment compensation) and noncash support payments should, from a tax liability perspective, be treated as ordinary income, subject to taxation after the guaranteed minimum level of income from all sources is achieved.

The Conservative, while recognizing the adverse effects of taxes and transfers, also understands the need for them. However, taxes and transfers must be based on economic reason and fairness and not the collectivist obsession with creating greater income equality. The market distributes income. When politicians do, economic order is lost.

The Liberal Argument

Conservatives are on the right track when they attack past tax and transfer redistributive efforts but not for the reasons they propose. The "failure" of public policy endeavors is not due, as Conservatives

TABLE 8.3 Money Income Received from All Sources by Each Income Quintile, 1929–1987

Income Quintile	1929	1936	1947	1960	1970	1980	1987
Lowest	12.5	4.1	5.0	4.9	5.5	5.1	4.6
Second		9.2	11.8	12.0	12.0	11.6	10.8
Third	13.8	14.1	17.0	17.6	17.4	17.5	16.9
Fourth	19.3	20.9	23.9	23.6	23.5	24.3	24.1
Highest	54.4	51.7	43.0	42.0	41.6	41.6	43.7

Source: Statistical Abstract of the United States, 1989.

believe, to some collectivist utopia in which a massive Robin Hood program takes from the rich and gives to the poor, simultaneously trampling on property rights, reducing work incentives, and lowering overall economic efficiency and national economic growth. Liberals maintain public policy *has* failed in its professed efforts to close the chronic income gap between those at the very bottom of the income ladder and those at the top. This fairer, more equitable distribution of income appropriate for a rich and humane nation has not yet been achieved. Before delineating the real income distribution problem as Liberals see it, we must first dispose of the errors of fact and logic in the Conservative perspective.

THE FACTS OF INCOME DISTRIBUTION AND TAXATION AND TRANSFERS POLICY

As Table 8.3 illustrates, shares of money income received by various American income groups showed some movement toward greater equality fifty years ago during the New Deal era, but have basically held steady since the late 1940s. Looking at the 1980s, however, we can detect a recent trend toward increased income inequality as those at the bottom experienced declining shares while those at the top got larger slices. Clearly, such evidence does not support the Conservative suggestion that we have been on a long and dangerous slide toward egalitarianism.

So much for the receipt of income (earned or cash transfers), but what about tax liability on this income? Although we do have a mildly

188   Problems in the Marketplace

TABLE 8.4   1988 Federal Income Taxes for a Family of Four

Adjusted Gross Income	Tax Liability	Marginal Tax Rate	Average Tax Rate
5,000	−700	−14.0%	−14.0%
10,000	−800	14.0%	−8.0%
20,000	1,080	15.0%	5.4%
50,000	5,148	28.0%	10.3%
100,000	16,348	33.0%	16.3%
150,000	29,563	33.0%	19.7%
200,000	42,763	28.0%	21.4%
1,000,000	221,816	28.0%	22.2%
10,000,000	2,237,816	28.0%	22.4%

Source: United States Internal Revenue Service.

progressive income tax structure, as shown in Table 8.4, it clearly was not enacted by Robin Hoods or would-be Robin Hoods. In fact, the top marginal rate, about half of what it was in the mid-1980s, is one of the lowest of all industrial nations.* Indeed, these same "overtaxed" nations have for the most part reported greater efficiency and growth than the United States, thus disposing of the Conservative charge that our "soak the rich" tax strategy is a major cause of our recent sluggish economic performance. We should also remember that we pay taxes other than federal income taxes; for instance, state and local sales, income, property, and use taxes. And, of course, corporate income and other business taxes are to some extent pushed forward onto consumers. When the effects of all of these taxes (many of which are highly regressive) are considered, the alleged progressiveness of our system of taxation simply does not materialize.

During the 1980s, federal taxation turned sharply regressive, a kind of "Robin Hood in reverse" effect taking place as low- and middle-income citizens experienced increases in tax burdens as the well-to-do enjoyed declining obligations. The top income tax rates fell

*The U.S. top marginal tax rate of 28 percent was lower than Canada (34 percent); Denmark (40 percent); Sweden (44 percent); Germany (56 percent); United Kingdom (60 percent); France (65 percent); and Japan (75 percent).

TABLE 8.5 Income Distribution before and after Taxes, Cash Transfers, and In-Kind Transfers

	Percent of income received, 1986	
Quintile	Before taxes and transfers	After taxes and transfers
Lowest 20 percent	1.0	4.7
Second 20 percent	7.6	10.6
Third 20 percent	15.0	16.1
Fourth 20 percent	24.1	23.0
Highest 20 percent	52.4	45.7

Source: U.S. Bureau of the Census.

from 70 percent to 28 percent in the 1980s, but individual worker payroll taxes (levied only on wages and not on interest, dividends, capital gains, rent, and the like) grew from 6.13 percent on the first $29,700 earned to 7.65 percent on the first $51,300. These payroll taxes were, of course, matched dollar for dollar by employer contributions and, as a business expense, would partly be passed on to consumers in the prices charged for goods. This regressive shift in the 1980s is evident in that personal income taxes' share of federal revenue fell by 6 percent and corporate income taxes' share fell by 23 percent, while social security taxes' share rose by 23 percent.

Finally, when we look at the combined effect of taxes, cash transfers, and in-kind transfers (Medicaid, Medicare, housing assistance, food stamps, and the like), as shown in Table 8.5, it is apparent that the overall redistributive impact of government is very modest indeed.

As the record amply indicates, the Conservative premise is fraudulent. In fact, the real Conservative agenda rests on two objectives that Conservatives would prefer to mask behind other arguments: (1) Keep the taxes on the well-to-do as low as possible and (2) keep income claims distributed as inequitably as possible to force a work discipline on the less well-to-do and especially on the poor. Such an approach may be represented as a "fairer system," but few thoughtful observers are likely to be convinced. But even if by some strange logic it was *fairer*, is it a humane and civilized system?

"LOSING GROUND" IN AMERICA

The Liberal view on income distribution holds that there is a real need for revitalized public policy that is civilized. More particularly, it should be a policy that addresses the unpleasant facts of contemporary economic life: that real income disparities are increasing and that for large numbers of Americans upward movement has ended.

The proposition becomes a bit clearer if we ask a simple question: Why is it that the boom of the 1980s, the longest peacetime expansion in American history, was accompanied by no reduction in the percentage of poverty-stricken individuals? Whereas past economic expansions invariably produced economic improvement for the poor, there were no significant gains in the 1980s. In fact, the very lowest income groups as well as some just over the poverty line actually experienced falling real income. When we look only at average American income, which did in fact rise, a misleading illusion of prosperity is created. While some gained a great deal in the 1980s boom, enjoying vastly expanded standards of living, many Americans have been "losing ground" (to use a phrase coined by Charles Murray in his recent book).

Losing ground has been the result of many forces—demographic, social, and economic. Significant among the economic trends that must be considered by an enlightened public policy are two: (1) the diminishing of economic opportunity in the private sector that might allow individuals to help themselves and (2) the reduction of publicly supplied resources that would assist those who cannot yet help themselves. The shrinking of private-sector opportunities to move up the income ladder is, of course, the result of various structural changes in the American economy. Most prominent among these have been the general stagnation and decline of basic manufacturing industries and the rise of a service-dominated economy. We have earlier lamented these trends and argued for policies to arrest them (see Issues 6 and 7). For purposes of our discussion here, however, the decline in private-sector employment opportunities is important because it places an increasing number of Americans who heretofore were sharing in the American dream in jeopardy of falling backwards into some degree of relative impoverishment. At the same time, this decline means that many already at the bottom of the income-employment ladder have no place to move up to.

FIGURE 8.2   Real Family Income Relative to 1948 Levels

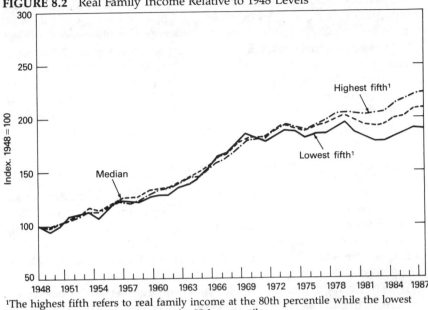

[1]The highest fifth refers to real family income at the 80th percentile while the lowest fifth refers to real family income at the 20th percentile.
Note: Fixed-weighted price index for personal consumption expenditures used as deflator.
Source: Department of Commerce.

The dwindling of public-sector resources to deal with the truly poor not only has further reduced the prospects of this group developing the skills needed to advance but has made their impoverished conditions even worse, as shown in Figure 8.2. Reductions in spending for education, Head Start, and job training combined with similar curtailments in health, housing, food stamps, and other programs add hopelessness to misery, producing a sense of destitution unlike that confronted by most of the poor in the past.

The decrease in public-sector resources is the result of two developments, both very difficult to counteract. First, the Conservative ideological position of the 1980s that directed popular attention away from poverty and toward "making it" in America (even though "making it" in any legal occupation was never an option for the truly poor), sapped the nation's will to face up to the problem of poverty. Second, the fiscal crisis triggered by excessive Conservative tax cutting and military spending drained resources away from antipoverty efforts.

As our discussion about "losing ground" in America should indicate, not only the presently poor are at risk. The prospect of other Americans steadily sliding down is real and demonstrates that poverty and income inequality are inseparable from broader trends in the economy. Whether or not we soon devise policies aimed at these trends remains to be seen. But poverty here and now can't wait.

STOPPING THE ASSAULT ON WELFARE

Probably the most enduring Conservative misinformation about the dimensions and cost of our welfare system stems from their assumption that most social spending goes only to the undeserving poor. In fact, only about one-sixth of all so-called social spending (less than one-twelfth of the federal budget) is allocated specifically to the needy.

The nonpoor are the chief recipients of federal transfer payments. Even if the Conservatives succeeded in completely sacrificing the truly poor to the requirements of maintaining work incentives for the well-to-do, it would hardly make a dent in federal spending and the federal tax bill. Ultimately, their budgetary adversary is not the poor, but middle-income Americans. As the old comic-strip character Pogo once observed, "We have found the enemy and it is us." The genuinely needy are only a scapegoat for Conservative attacks.

The attack on the principle of maintaining minimum levels of social welfare has not been limited merely to questioning the public spending levels. The long, bitter struggle to create a single federally administered welfare system, which has proceeded ever so slowly since the New Deal era, was challenged directly in 1982 by President Reagan. Under his New Federalism plan, the president urged the gradual return of social welfare budgets to the individual states. Each state in its own wisdom would decide what its poor would need to survive. Never mind that this would return us to the old "local" welfare system of Herbert Hoover's time and that it would dismantle over half a century of efforts to create a national program; the New Federalism fitted perfectly into the Conservatives' antigovernment scheme of things.

Aside from the fact that such an approach is a dangerous and questionable exercise in creative accounting — making federal spending appear to decline by shifting it to the individual states — it will certainly worsen the problems of the poor. Inequities will certainly grow if each state arbitrarily establishes its "social minimum." In the 1930s, some states denied voting rights to those on public assistance. In the 1950s, "welfare" in some Mississippi townships consisted of $75 and a one-way bus ticket to Detroit. Even in the "socially concerned" 1970s, Mississippi's AFDC payments, which are based on a formula of federal, state, and local sharing of costs, paid benefits only one-tenth those paid in Massachusetts.

THE NEED FOR A NATIONAL WELFARE SYSTEM

The first step in improving the welfare system is to place it totally under federal jurisdiction. A nationwide minimum must be established and must be paid for federally, not locally, to equalize the cost burden.

There has been much talk in recent years about a federally guaranteed annual income (GAI) or negative income tax (NIT). These methods of providing a national social minimum deserve policy attention, and even Conservatives like Milton Friedman have advanced some support for the idea. However, the basic problem with GAI and NIT proposals is how to determine and administer a minimum that helps only the genuinely poor and does not at the same time destroy work incentives. While the GAI or NIT problem may be resolved and such a plan adopted in the future, the federalizing and redesigning of existing programs is a more plausible current solution.

Let us assume that the nation adopted a minimum guarantee of two-thirds of the poverty-level income for the 35 million Americans who live below it and that the federal government took over the present state and local welfare contributions up to that level. Such a proposal has been studied by the Committee for Economic Development, a prestigious policy group of business leaders. Applying their estimates of additional costs to present outlays would amount to about a 5 percent increase in the federal budget. While not modest, this would be a small outlay in a federal budget of about $1 trillion. Moreover, such a guaranteed income approach would reduce the need for the present multiplicity of federal programs and effect savings by shrinking the overblown federal welfare bureaucracy. It also would reduce state and municipal welfare costs, although local government units would, of course, be free to add to their welfare minimum if they saw fit.

Whereas reasonable minimum welfare payments are essential (and should be higher than those now administered under our present patchwork programs), welfare is not the real solution to eliminating poverty or income inequality. Welfare programs designed merely to pacify the poor create a permanent poor. A useful federal program aimed at greater income equalization must attack the roots of the problem. This means that welfare measures must concentrate on education and job creation.

Liberals, admittedly, have not always supported "workfare" as an alternative to unrestricted grants to the poor. But most have come to embrace this approach as the only long-run strategy for eliminating chronic poverty. Congress's action in 1988 to tie welfare payments to job training and entry-level, on-the-job training for recipients is generally a step in the right direction. Of course, its long-term effects depend on the continued commitment of funds to facilitate "escapes" from poverty *and* sufficient growth in the private sector to ensure available jobs to escape to.

The Liberal program, then, requires devoting additional resources for the elimination of poverty. Liberals must plead guilty to the Conservative charge that they would indulge in social engineering, *but there is no other way*. Eliminating poverty and improving economic opportunities has a very substantial price tag. It will be expensive not only to fund specific antipoverty programs, but also to undertake public policy efforts that stimulate the private economy so that lower-income groups stop losing ground. And how should such endeavors be paid for? For sure, a growing national economy would help to finance the programs. But—with growth or without it—Liberals believe a simple "ability-to-pay" principle justifies that the well-to-do pay more. Indeed, there is no one else. If those who are able to pay more balk, they must be reminded that they will pay one way or another—either more for education and training or more for police protection, courts, and prisons. At roughly $25,000 per year for a prisoner and $35,000 per year for a person hospitalized for addiction or other health problems, paying to eradicate poverty is the less expensive alternative.

The Radical Argument

Although they may appear miles apart on the question of income distribution policy, Conservatives and Liberals share a common perspective: Poverty is poor people's fault. To the Conservative, low incomes or no earned income at all reflect the market-determined value of an individual's talents and initiative. Defects of character and skill of the poor themselves are the roots of their poverty. To the Liberal, poverty is also the result of a person's circumstances—race, sex, insufficient education, or some other characteristic of the individual. Conservatives, of course, are content to let the poor struggle out of their condition by themselves, whereas Liberals are quick to apply moderately redistributive tax and transfer programs and other social policy bandaids for the economically "disadvantaged." By looking only at the characteristics of the poor, albeit in different ways, neither Conservatives nor Liberals recognize that poverty is the system's fault, that extreme income inequality, with its attendant suffering, is essential to the capitalist order.

THE DUAL LABOR MARKET AND ENDURING POVERTY

Contrary to general impressions, very few of America's poor are poor because they don't work. At least two-thirds of the families with income below the poverty line have one or more members working at a job of some sort.

In a capitalist society, work is the primary determinant of income. The work a person does and the wages paid for the work set absolute limits on that person's participation in the American dream. Skipping for a minute the situation of the very few who through inherited wealth and privileged position need not work at all, the rest of us are required to work or to accept the handouts of those who do. Yet those of us who work do not encounter the same equal opportunities.

Clearly, two different and discernible sectors exist in American labor markets. In one, which we might call the *primary* sector and which is familiar to most persons reading these pages, work involves reasonable wages, fairly pleasant working conditions, job security and stability, recognition for industriousness and initiative, and a real chance for improving one's economic lot. This is not to say that the work is always stimulating, but it is at least dependable and monetarily rewarding enough to build a reasonably secure and stable life. It includes the world of the white-collar manager and professional as well as the upper end of the blue-collar elements of society. The primary sector is the work world of what is commonly called "middle-class America."

The *secondary* sector of our labor markets, though everywhere visible and constantly growing, hardly receives our attention. There, jobs are less attractive. They pay less (never much more than the minimum wage) and have little security. Working conditions are poor, and experience teaches workers that there is little likelihood of promotion or upward movement, however hard they work. Work itself is usually only occasional, with frequent lengthy periods of unemployment. The secondary sector is the work world of the poor. It is the sweatshop, the fast-food restaurant, the discount retail outlet.

The obvious Conservative response at this point might be, "Leave the secondary labor market for the primary market if you don't like it!" Such advice utterly fails to recognize these facts about secondary labor: (1) The secondary labor market, unstable as it is for individuals, is a source of considerable profit to entrepreneurs; (2) the secondary labor market is growing much faster than the primary market; and (3) the scarring effects of being caught in the secondary market make upward movement virtually impossible. In other words, a segment of the population caught in the chronic poverty of secondary labor markets cannot break out because their low-paid labor is profitable, because opportunities of entrance into better-paid positions are limited by the production-for-profit system, and because the poor are, in a sense, trained to be poor.

The self-sustaining nature of secondary labor markets is helped along by the fact that its members are easily identifiable. They are African-American, Hispanic, female, young, or possessed of some other characteristic usually identified by employers with "marginal" labor. Thus stereotyped, few are ever able to obtain an equal opportunity with primary-market workers in vying for primary-sector employment. A self-perpetuating discrimination tends always to hold them back.

At this juncture the Liberal usually appears, arguing that education and enforcement of "equal opportunity" laws will break the poverty cycle. However, the facts simply don't support such a conclusion. In the early 1990s, African-Americans continue to earn only about 60 percent of white income—about the same as three decades earlier, before the passage of extensive antidiscrimination legislation. Meanwhile, African-American unemployment continues to be about twice as high as the national average. For women the evidence is pretty much the same; women's average income is also about 60 percent of men's, although their unemployment rate is only slightly higher. To be sure, at the very top, among the few women and African-Americans who attained higher educational levels, the black-white and female-male income gaps have closed somewhat. However, rather than proving that education will raise earnings, as Liberals claim, this more accurately reflects the "tokenism" of the past three decades—a little space at the top to placate civil rights and women's movement advocates.

TAXES AND WELFARE TRANSFERS FROM THE NONRICH TO THE RICH

In terms of understanding the role of taxes and welfare in capitalist society, Conservatives and Liberals are correct on two different points. First, as Conservatives argue, the combined income effects of our tax and transfer policies are not supposed to destroy work incentives. Second, as Liberals argue, tax and welfare policies also are intended to ameliorate the most glaring inequalities in income, or at least hide them. In American capitalism, maldistribution of income is essential to support the work ethic, but too big a gap erodes the credibility of American political and economic institutions. Thus taxes and transfers walk a tightrope, maintaining yet hiding the income gap.

Our national tax system does not close the income gap but, in fact, tends to widen it. While the well-known tax loopholes of the rich allow legal evasion, we forget the heavily regressive effect of certain taxes on the poor and the middle class.

Take property taxes, for example. These account for about two-thirds of collections by local governments. Most studies indicate that property taxes, whether paid directly by homeowners or indirectly by renters are regressive. Those in the lower 40 percent of wage earners pay, as a proportion of their income, two to three times the rate paid by the top 20 percent of income earners.

Sales taxes, the other important source of state and local revenue, are also regressive. As these taxes have been extended to cover necessities, they fall more and more heavily on those with little discretionary income. Obviously, the taxes on a wealthy person's electricity are much less of a burden than are sales taxes for a low-income worker, regardless of the number of rooms in the wealthy person's estate.

The result in absolute terms is that lower-income and middle-income groups pay for most city and state governmental expenditures, but they receive fewer of the social benefits. The poor have less police and fire protection, poorer roads and schools, and inadequate sanitation services. Thus a serious effort to develop a fair—let alone progressive—income redistribution must start at the level of local tax inequality.

At the federal level—quite as Conservatives and Liberals agree—a progressive tax system has been made regressive in the past by the implementation of legal tax evasions. However, the Conservative argument that a "flat-rate tax" will produce fairness evades two facts. First, it fails to recognize that the well-to-do receive disproportionately larger benefits from the social system and ought to pay disproportionately higher taxes. Second, Conservatives neglect to point out that in the Reagan "flat tax" proposals of 1985, the powerful interests were very easily able to modify the original proposals to protect a wide range of investment income sources from taxation. There is little reason to believe that any "tax reform" likely to be inaugurated very soon will, in the long run, avoid the tendency to write special tax exemptions and privileges into law. Although politicians speak out against tax loopholes and legal tax evasion, their public stand on behalf of "fairness' is unconvincing. For one thing, loopholes are the result of political power and lobbying—something that is not likely to end very soon. And many loopholes are seen as economically necessary. For instance, the mortgage and property tax credits of middle- and upper-income taxpayers serve as a stimulus to the construction industry. Business investment tax credits are intended to encourage business expansion. Therefore, the discretionary use of tax policies for fiscal manipulation or to keep interest groups happy will always create loopholes that benefit the few greatly and the masses slightly.

Equalization of income through taxation cannot be a serious objective in a capitalist system as long as the powerful control government. Under capitalism, the tax structure will remain merely another device to transfer income and wealth ("surplus" in Marxist terms) from the nonrich to the rich.

Meanwhile, the primary function of welfare measures is not humanitarianism but legitimation. The problems of the poor are always a social threat. This has been especially obvious in the recent history of African-Americans. Although the deteriorating condition of the ghettos was well known before the urban riots of 1964 and 1965, there was no expansion of welfare programs or benefits. Only in the wake of the riots were AFDC payments tripled and other welfare programs enlarged.

The welfare system is as much an economic benefit to the well-to-do as it is to the needy. Welfare dollars buy the goods of corporate America. They assure doctors, dentists, and drug companies of payment (usually excessive) for health services. Poor people, in fact, get a very small amount of the public dole. In 1990, federal spending for the truly needy (where income eligibility tests are required) amounted to only 8 percent of the federal budget. Meanwhile, cash and in-kind transfers to the nonpoor amounted to about 40 percent of all federal outlays. Exactly how vulnerable the truly needy are and how weak our commitment to maintaining social welfare is became obvious in the Reagan years, when ruthless budget cutting increased the agony of the poor.* However, while the poor's safety net was being removed, business tax cuts, an enlarged military budget (taking about a third of all federal expenditures), and a variety of corporate subsidies provided a comfortable cushion for the undeserving. The Revenue Reform Bill of 1981, for instance, provided deductions and exemptions to individuals (practically all of whom were in the top 20 percent income bracket) worth $173 billion. Investors, business owners, and corporations got another $100 billion in special tax reductions. There was little concern that the recipients of these "corporate welfare" transfers might lose their incentive because of "living off the dole." As someone aptly observed, "In America, we have free enterprise for the poor and welfare for the wealthy."

*Exactly how "ruthless" became evident in the spring of 1986 when President Reagan submitted a budget calling for $2 billion in cuts for AFDC, legal services to the poor, food stamps, and child nutrition. Subsidized housing programs were to be cut 20 percent and job training by 15 percent. The cuts were defended as "required" by the Gramm-Rudman-Hollings Act (passed in 1985), which mandated expenditure cuts to meet a 1991 budget-balancing deadline. Past Conservative indifference to poverty now seemed to be shaping up as an active effort to balance the budget on the backs of the poor.

A RADICAL PROGRAM TO END INEQUALITY

It is obvious that the combined effect of our tax and transfer system is to maintain income inequality. It serves the system well. The welfare poor act as a potential labor pool to be tapped as needed and to be used as a check on excessive labor demands by those who work.

With large numbers of people held in a "poverty reserve," unions cannot push too strongly against capital's power. Inequality also serves the purpose of disciplining labor. Maintaining the bottom layers of society at bare subsistence levels does provide a work "incentive." Given the oppressive and alienating nature of most work in America, wages and the hope for better wages are practically the only device to keep labor in the market and keep it producing. Inequality also serves an important social purpose of dividing the working class. The overtaxed and underpaid worker frequently turns against the welfare-supported nonworker. Nonworkers often hate themselves as well as those above them who have comparatively slight income advantages. The source of income inequality is thus ignored.

From a Radical view, some degree of income equalization is crucial. In terms of short-run socialist reforms, this means a total renovation of the tax structure—elimination of taxes on incomes below a certain level, along with the guarantee of a *reasonable* minimum income for everyone, working or not. The elimination of all tax loopholes, adoption of high and steeply progressive income taxes, and virtually confiscatory taxes on accumulated wealth would be desirable. At the same time, the extent and content of social welfare programs should be altered to fit human needs.

All of these steps, even though they fall short of actual long-run social ownership of capital, would be unacceptable to defenders of the capitalist system. However, the system's failure, indeed its inability, to achieve some equitable measure of income distribution, along with its chronic problems of joblessness, inflation, and lagging economic growth, must eventually erode popular acceptance of existing realities. To be sure, the American dream of equal and unlimited opportunity for everyone has remained a powerful myth, always constraining the emergence of a truly Radical political and social movement in the United States. However, as the conflict between the dream and everyday reality sharpens, Radical alternatives to conventional social and economic measures will become matters of public debate and discussion. Just as America has used the promise of equal opportunity as the social glue to hold the nation together, the actual drift toward greater inequality becomes the device that undoes the entire production-for-profit economic system.

PROBLEMS OF AGGREGATE ECONOMIC POLICY

Part 3 focuses on issues that are primarily *macroeconomic* in origin. In other words, our attention will be directed to issues affecting the economy as a whole and to variables affecting its aggregate economic performance. Specifically, we shall examine such problem areas as business cycle behavior, stabilization policy, the federal deficit, unemployment, the military and social budgets, international trade and money policy, and centralized economic planning. Part 2 examined problems of specific economic units—households, firms, industries, labor groups, and the like. As one economist described the difference between microeconomics and macroeconomics, the former examines the trees, while the latter studies the forest.

Macroeconomic Instability

Are We Depression-proof?

We have nothing to fear but fear itself.

Franklin Roosevelt, 1933

The predictors of doom were dead wrong. This administration has replaced the gloomy talk of recession with an economy that is strong and getting stronger every day.

Donald Regan, presidential adviser, 1985

Reagan is putting up a notable effort to have another Great Depression. But the important structural and psychological safeguards built up since 1929 are still in place.

John Kenneth Galbraith, Harvard University, 1982

The United States enters the 1990s as a prosperous nation with a healthy and dynamic economy. . . . Since 1982, American firms and workers have produced the longest peacetime expansion on record.

President George Bush, 1990

In world market crisis, the contradictions and antagonisms of bourgeois production break through to the surface. But instead of investigating the nature of the . . . catastrophe, the apologists content themselves with denying the catastrophe itself.

Karl Marx, 1867

THE PROBLEM

Fluctuations in the general level of economic activity have long been one of the more prominent features of the macroeconomy. Through the nineteenth century and the first third of the twentieth, the cyclical pattern of national economic performance was more or less accepted as the normal state of affairs: first a period of boom and expansion, then a stage of general contraction (until the 1930s usually called a "panic"), followed by a recovery that culminated in yet another boom, and, sooner or later, another contraction. Always a matter of some interest to economists, public interest in the business cycle varied inversely with the ebb and flow of business conditions. Not until the long contraction of the 1930s did the business cycle become a matter of serious and enduring discussion among ordinary citizens. The dreary decade after the stock market crash in 1929 directed almost everyone's attention to efforts to understand the causes of economic fluctuations. This was especially true because the Great Depression was, by most past standards of cyclical behavior, exceptionally deep and protracted.

Although the Great Depression is no longer a part of "recent American history," and is remembered only dimly by a comparative handful of living Americans, its impact on our economic thinking and reflexes remains extraordinarily strong. This was borne out on Black Monday, October 19, 1987, and again on Friday, October 13, 1989, when sudden and very significant declines in the stock market immediately evoked comparisons with Black Tuesday, October 29, 1929, and all that followed that event.

That Americans might have a special concern about severe business downturns is not surprising when the severity of the "Great Rupture" in American history is recalled. Between 1929 and 1933, the gross national product (the nation's annual output of goods and services) was sliced almost in half. Unemployment, which had averaged about 3.2 percent in 1929, soared to 24.9 percent by 1933. Unemployment for 1933 totaled 13 million men and women, but this figure was deceiving because several times that amount, perhaps 65 percent of the labor force, suffered some unemployment or could obtain only part-time work. On the business side, before-tax corporate profits fell from a record $11 billion in 1929 to an operating loss of $1.2 billion four years later, and industrial production declined by more than 45 percent.

Historians have documented the wrenching effect of the Depression on institutions and values. However great the changes in modes of American thought and behavior, none were more profound than those in economic thinking and practice. Before Black Tuesday's stock market collapse on October 29, 1929, and the crisis that followed, conventional economic wisdom unashamedly espoused the virtues of laissez-faire. The economy was to operate freely. Although this meant the periodic toleration of bad times as business activity occasionally slowed, these downturns were offset by succeeding periods of expansion and prosperity. Left alone, economic analysis held, the economy would right itself and, over time, move upward to new, higher levels of output, employment, and real income.

But recovery was not spontaneous, and for good or ill, the orthodox belief in the self-regulating business cycle fell from favor. Ruminating in England on the worldwide depression, John Maynard Keynes concluded it was time to clear the intellectual stage of all the old furniture of economic orthodoxy. In 1936, his *General Theory of Employment, Interest, and Money* proclaimed that capitalist economic institutions were not self-balancing mechanisms but instead tended toward chronic stagnation. This situation required action by governments through fiscal and monetary policy to forestall collapse. The solution: Raise aggregate demand for goods through massive government spending, thereby putting to work unemployed people and closed plants. Not given to modesty, Keynes correctly warned his readers that his ideas would change the way people thought about modern capitalist economies. And they did, as Keynes's "New Economics" became the new dominant wisdom in economic matters.

For most of the first three decades after World War II, Keynesian orthodoxy reigned. The Keynesian view that periodic slumps in the economy could and should be offset by government efforts to stimulate the demand for goods went virtually unquestioned, and many economists began to think and act as though fluctuations in business activity were only a feature of the past, pre-Keynesian era. With the new economic logic maintaining that depressions were unnecessary and could always be headed off by appropriate use of public policy, a good many Americans came to believe in the 1960s that we were now "depression-proof." However, events in the mid-1970s prompted a reexamination of the New Economics. Although no "Great Depression" developed, the economy did stagger through a "Great Stagflation" as economic growth slowed, unemployment rates rose, and price inflation gnawed deep into the economy's innards.

The ungluing of Keynesian doctrine, with its confident assertion that cyclical economic behavior could be controlled by appropriate government policies, had a number of effects. First of all, it reopened the entire question of whether another Great Depression was possible, and rekindled a wariness about the future of the economy. Even the return of some expansion after 1982, during the modest Reagan boom, did not allay basic fears. Through the 1980s, numerous "doomsday" economics books acquired a large popular audience. One, *The Great Depression of 1990*, enjoyed more than half a year on the *New York Times* nonfiction best-seller list.

The American public's fear and fascination with depression scenarios was not, as we shall see in this and subsequent issues, without empirical foundation. Irrespective of the continued expansion, one did not have to look very far to find fundamental weaknesses in the economy—in particular, a growing mountain of public and private debt and a chronic erosion of the nation's trade and financial position with regard to the rest of the world.

Meanwhile, the general economic uncertainty that prevailed during and after the 1970s, had reopened old debates among contending economic philosophies on what were the appropriate and most effective strategies for dealing with business fluctuations or any impending depression. Liberals had to reexamine their earlier claims that the business cycle had indeed been brought under control through demand-management policies. While not abandoning their views on the inherent instability of production-for-profit economies, modern Keynesian Liberals have accepted more modest countercyclical targets, no longer arguing so vigorously that the economy can be sustained on a permanent expansionary course by simply "fine-tuning" levels of aggregate demand. For Conservatives, the stagflationary epoch provided, first, visibility (which had all but disappeared during the era of "High Keynesianism") and, then, a high degree of respectability. In the new economic setting, it was appropriate to challenge the Keynesian explanation of the Great Depression as well as Keynesian policy-making in general. For Radicals, meanwhile, the stagflationary crises of the 1970s and early 1980s were seen, at least in the short run, as a vindication. They had always viewed the 1930s as proof that unregulated capitalist economies were inherently self-destructive, and the economic problems of the 1970s had shown that regulated capitalism didn't work either.

As to whether or not another Great Depression was *possible*, most economists would answer in the affirmative. *Unnecessary perhaps, but possible.* It all depended on the strategies we would undertake in dealing with the macroeconomy. And, of course, the strategies varied with the ideological predilections of the economic reasoner.

SYNOPSIS

The Conservative position maintains that depression and protracted economic stagnation are not central to capitalist economic systems and that the business cycle downturn after 1929 was worsened, not moderated, by government intervention in the economy. Liberals argue that only through vigorous, active countercyclical policies by government can the economy's natural propensity toward recession and depression be controlled. To Radicals, crisis and depression are quite natural to production-for-profit systems, and although crises may be delayed by governmental actions, they cannot be eliminated in the long run.

Anticipating the Arguments

- On what grounds do Conservatives argue that Liberals and Radicals have failed to prove their case that capitalism "naturally" tends toward protracted periods of economic stagnation? How do they account for economic downturns?
- In what ways did the Keynesian critique depart from the "conventional wisdom" of the 1930s?
- How does the Radical scenario of capitalism's "chronic tendency toward crisis" differ from the Liberal Keynesian view?

The Conservative Argument

The Classical economic tradition from which most Conservatives draw their analytical perspectives and their strength of purpose, holds to a simple proposition: *When free human beings operate freely in free markets, this necessarily will lead to optimal economic and social outcomes.* This view is not limited to microeconomic (individual market) operations, but extends to an aggregate or macroeconomic analysis of economic activities. Left to operate freely, the aggregate economy, like an individual market, will be self-correcting over time, setting optimal output, price, and employment conditions to avoid excessive long-term swings in business activity.* Business fluctuations over the short term are, of course, not surprising since an economy must from time to time adjust to changing conditions. But long-run or violent contractions are essentially the result of unwarranted interventions by government or others seeking to "improve on" market outcomes.

For a long period of time this point of view did not enjoy extensive currency among economic reasoners nor much practice by Western political leaders. The long depression of the 1930s signaled a decline in Classical economic modes of thought that was not reversed until the late 1970s. Given the long economic boom of the 1980s, however, it is easy to forget the economic past. Yet, two important points need to be recalled lest we repeat, in our forgetfulness, our past errors. First, we need to understand the real causes and effects of economic events in the era that came to be known as the Great Depression. Second, we must comprehend how our errors in understanding these events led to the development of economic doctrines and policies that produced the near catastrophic economic crises of the 1970s. Much mythology surrounds these questions, but also much danger if we are not historically and factually accurate in our understanding of the past six decades of economic history.

To put matters directly, most of what is believed about the causes of the Great Depression is wrong. More important, the body of economic policy developed to make us depression-proof was dangerously irrelevant, constructed to deal with a problem that never existed. Alas, the cumbersome structure of government intervention in the economy through countercyclical fiscal and monetary policy has been unnecessary. Indeed, government intervention has been more of a threat to stability than a bulwark.

ON MISREADING THE SIGNIFICANCE OF CAUSES OF THE GREAT DEPRESSION

Contrary to popular economic beliefs, the initial business downturn between 1929 and 1930 was not in itself a unique event. As most economists know but sometimes overlook, the general economic

---

*This principle, sometimes called Say's Law after the French economist Jean Baptiste Say, who formulated it in 1803, is, of course, directly challenged by Liberals and Radicals.

performance of the United States, both before the Great Depression and after (even with the tools of the new economists), has followed a cyclical course. Indeed, the expansion-contraction rhythm of economic affairs had fascinated many students of business cycles long before the Depression of the 1930s. Business contractions had appeared at intervals of about eight to twelve years, each eventually succeeded by a counteracting stage of growth and prosperity. Economists offered a variety of explanations for such cyclical behavior, including new inventions, changes in investment or consumer behavior, and even sunspot activity. But before the 1930s, few, except perhaps the Marxists committed to the destruction of the system, held that business contraction could become a permanent state of affairs. Just as surely as the business cycle turned downward, it would sooner or later turn upward.

This pattern, however, did not occur in 1929–1930. To obtain a clearer understanding of modern-day economic tendencies, we must ask why. According to the zealots who quickly snatched up John Maynard Keynes's ideas and perverted them to their own uses, the Depression of the 1930s was not merely a periodic movement within the business cycle. Instead, it was a problem of chronic "stagnation," a situation in which the economy could no longer maintain high levels of employment and output because of the inadequacy of business investment. In short, depression had become a permanent state of affairs.

Such a situation, according to Keynes's followers, demanded firm action. First, the economy would have to be managed by government since Treasury and monetary authorities could no longer count on the natural bottoming out of a depression. Second, government would have to act to "stimulate demand" to increase consumer spending and business investment. Third, this demand stimulation would probably have to come from enlarged state expenditures, purposely unbalanced budgets and deficit spending for public goods, and transfer payments to business and individuals.

Thus began the "modern" period of economic thought. The epoch of laissez-faire was to be closed, with government replacing private accumulation and private instincts as the driving force of the economic system. Never mind the past spectacular performance of the private and open economy in building the nation. Never mind the implied assaults on individual economic freedom and choice that were the underpinnings of political freedom in the United States. Lord Keynes and his followers had determined that these now were outmoded beliefs and that only through massive government intervention in the economy could survival be assured.

A BETTER INTERPRETATION

Ordinarily, the best test for a hypothesis that interprets a set of events is to ask whether the hypothesis adequately explains the situation and is the best explanation possible. Applying this rule to the Keynesian critique, we find it wanting.

There is no evidence to support the idea that the Great Depression was, at its beginning in 1929, exceptional or that it differed markedly from past business downturns. Therefore, there is nothing to support the Keynesian belief that depression had become a permanent, congenital economic condition by the 1930s. What we do know, however, is that the depressed business conditions were worsened by the money policy actions of the Federal Reserve Board, the government authority charged with maintenance of the nation's money and banking system. The Fed succeeded in transforming the difficulties of an excessively careless epoch of stock market speculation, coupled with an ordinary downturn in the business cycle, into an economic catastrophe of the first magnitude.

Lowering interest rates had always served to bring forth new investment and stimulate recovery in past downturns. However, reacting to the speculative bull market, the Fed had pursued a tight money policy even when it was apparent in early 1929 that a business downturn was forming. With high interest rates discouraging new business borrowing and reducing the stock of money (the money supply), business investment and consumer buying sagged even before the stock market collapsed. This was the Fed's first mistake. Its second came in December 1930 when the Bank of the United States in New York City closed its doors. Although it was an ordinary commercial bank, many people believed it to be an official government bank, and panic set in. Depositors in New York City and elsewhere rushed to withdraw their savings. Bank after bank faced liquidity crises. Unable to meet depositors' demands, banks began to fall like a line of dominoes. Meanwhile, the Fed, created in 1914 for just such an emergency, failed to take any action to improve bank liquidity. In fact, its next action was simply disastrous. In September 1931, as economic and financial problems spread worldwide and more and more gold was drained from the United States, the Fed raised interest rates in an attempt to stop the flow of gold overseas. Banks, now unable to borrow from the Fed (because of the high interest rates), had insufficient funds to meet their customers' demands and had to fold. Fourteen hundred closed their doors in three months, and the nation's money supply (consisting largely of demand deposits) fell by 12 percent. Meanwhile, on the business side, high interest rates discouraged new investment, and consumer spending fell as the money supply contracted. An ordinary depression had been transformed into an unprecedented financial crisis and, in turn, a near-complete prostration of business.

One other misguided economic action deserves special note: passage in 1930 of the protectionist Smoot-Hawley Tariff. Under pressure from businesses seeking to protect domestic markets from foreign competition, the Hoover administration, caught up in the anxiety following the market crash, encouraged Congress to pass a tariff that established the highest duties on imported goods in American history. Predictably, our protectionism was quickly matched by similar actions by our trading partners, and while we were protected from imports, we soon found it impossible to sell our products overseas.

The foregoing analysis differs sharply from the Keynesian stagnationist approach. While the Keynesians are partially correct that the Depression did finally become a matter of insufficient aggregate demand, that happened only after and as a result of the failure of the Federal Reserve System and the passage of Smoot-Hawley. Rather than the economy manifesting some sinister and fatal stagnationist flaw, the evidence suggests that the Great Depression was largely accidental. That being the case, there is no proven analytical foundation for the Keynesian prescription that only through massive government intervention can a free enterprise economy be kept afloat. Ironically, when we focus on the critical failures of monetary and tariff policies between 1929 and 1933, we find the reverse of the Keynesian analysis to be true: that government actions (through the Fed and Smoot-Hawley) in fact caused the Great Depression.

The worsening and deepening of the Depression after 1933 was also the result of government activity. Liberal defenders of Franklin Roosevelt like to depict the New Deal as an experimental, pragmatic program to "prime" the economy. Not yet convinced by the Keynesian arguments, FDR is usually presented as doing too little with counter-cyclical policy to get things going (until the government spending boom of World War II). This interpretation of the New Deal period of the Great Depression is guilty of a serious error of omission.

FDR's antidepression strategy, Keynesian or not, was antibusiness and antibanker. The president's public addresses identified these two groups as both the cause of the Depression and the reason why his own policies had not turned the economic tide. FDR's attempts to increase regulatory agency power, to insert government in the pricing mechanism, to reform the banking community, and especially to reform the Supreme Court when it threw out key pieces of his interventionist legislation created considerable business uncertainty. Within such a charged political atmosphere, business expectations, key to the undertaking of new investment and critical to recovery, remained essentially negative. Thus the interventionist policies of the New Deal tended to deepen and broaden the already critical business depression.

THE PAINFUL LEGACY OF THE DEPRESSION

The passing of the Depression did not signal the passing of Keynesian ideas; indeed, it only marked the beginning of a long era of wrong-headed economic thought and policy. The victory of the Keynesian analysis led to the building of ever more elaborate theories to justify the enlargement of the government sector. The size of federal spending grew, and the extent of fiscal and monetary manipulation of business activity was expanded. For decades, beginning students of economics were taught, as if it were received religious truth, that deficits do not matter, that the growth of the public sector is healthy, and that the macro performance of the economy can be insulated from depression and "fine-tuned" to produce desired levels of output, employment, and price stability instantaneously as well as in the long run.

By the 1970s, however, the basic flaws of such an analysis were becoming uncomfortably evident as the nation slipped into a decade of inflation, unemployment, and disappointing growth. The Keynesian emphasis on "maintaining demand" meant neglecting and even restricting the production or supply side of the economy. As we shall see in subsequent issues, it led by the 1970s to an explosion of the

THE COLLAPSE OF ORTHODOX IDEAS
IN THE 1930s

The prevailing economic view in 1929 was that the economy was a "natural," self-adjusting mechanism. Wages, interest, and rents were paid to individuals according to the value of their contributions to national output. Such payments were, over time, equitable and just rewards for work and risk. The general mode of economic activity was pure competition. Interferences in the economy, whether by government, labor unions, or collusive business practice, were condemned. The "economy" was thus described and analyzed theoretically in terms of an open laissez-faire system. To be sure, periodic downturns in the national economy were possible, just as periodic stickiness in wages, savings, and business investment were possible. However, the focus was on the long haul, and, over time, such deviations were thought to be self-correcting.

Within this general economic structure, traditional economists based their analysis of the national economy on a four-cornered foundation. First, there would be no long-run overproduction of goods (or, to look at it from the other side, no long-run underconsumption). This was true because payments to the producers, labor, business, and so forth, were always equal to the value of the goods produced. As the nineteenth-century French economist Jean Baptiste Say put it in what has since come to be known as Say's Law, "Supply creates its own demand."

Second, and following from the first point, there could be, again in the long run, no such thing as involuntary unemployment. With flexible wages and prices, there would always be sufficient work at any given wage level to employ all those willing to work at that wage. Individuals who chose not to work at a particular wage (supposedly because they valued leisure more) were not "unemployed" at all.

Third, through free and flexible interest rates, private savings would be just enough to meet the investment (or borrowing) needs of businesses. If business sought greater investment, interest rates would rise, people would choose to save more, and funds would become available for business expansion. This, in turn, would create jobs, raise wages, and stimulate balanced economic growth.

Fourth, the level of prices in the society were determined by the rate of growth of the money supply. An increase in money would stimulate spending and demand for goods, which would raise market prices. A decrease in money would lower prices.

To the orthodox, these theories offered policy solutions to the periodic downturns in the economy. If business output exceeded consumer demand, just wait! Prices would fall to clear the market of goods. Wages would fall, and the number of workers seeking employment would be reduced until an equilibrium wage was reached. Interest rates would fall, and individuals would shift savings to consumption. With lower interest rates and increasing consumption, business would again invest. Public policy within such a self-balancing economic order could be described quite easily: Do nothing!

As the international economy continued to inch downward after 1929, John Maynard Keynes began to rethink the orthodox analysis and reach his own conclusion on the evidence at hand. First of all, he observed that the automaticity of Say's Law was unfounded. Indeed, it was possible for overproduction or underconsumption to develop if individuals held money rather than saved it (lent it to borrowers). Second, wages were not, in the real world, freely flexible. Business could and did keep prices up and laid off workers while awaiting the sale of inventories. The alternatives available to workers were not lower wages or leisure but simply increased unemployment. Third, lowered interest rates did not induce business investment at a time of overproduction. Business, with goods on hand, would be unlikely to produce more goods even if the cost of borrowing were near zero.

Thus in Keynesian analysis, the "short-run" business fluctuations of the economy could become very long indeed. The self-correcting nature of the economy was an incorrect premise. And squaring with the real evidence that continued to build after the early 1930s, it was possible to have a continuing low level of output that left large numbers of workers and factories idle. Indeed, it was not only possible, it was quite natural in an unregulated economic system.

THE KEYNESIAN SOLUTION

Keynes's objective in his *General Theory* was to lay out the path to a high-employment economy. His approach emphasized aggregate rather than microeconomic aspects, as orthodox analysts did. First, aggregate levels of employment depended on the total demand for goods, including consumer purchase of goods and business investment as well as government spending. Second, the primary culprit in the cyclical downturn of an economy was the activity of investors, since it is through changes in investment outlays that changes in total demand for goods and services are affected most directly. Consumer spending was a fairly constant function of total income, with consumer outlays rising and falling directly as national income fluctuated. Government spending was small, and, in depression conditions, tended to get smaller as governments tried to live within the orthodox doctrine of annually balanced budgets.

Keynes's position was that only through artificially induced higher levels of aggregate demand would it be possible to attain full employment and full utilization of plants and equipment. The course was clear: Business investment had to be stimulated, government spending had to be inflated, or, more likely, some combination of both had to be tried. The combined effects of expansionary fiscal policy (greater government spending and/or tax cuts usually accompanied by a budget deficit) and expansionary monetary policy (lower interest rates and easier money) were to produce enlarged aggregate demand and diminished unemployment.

THE VICTORY OF THE NEW ECONOMICS

Although Keynes quickly gained academic adherents for his ideas, he made little headway in Washington during the Depression. For all his alleged fiscal profligacy, Franklin Roosevelt, with his "pump priming" and "ABC" government agencies, never grasped the Keynesian analysis and never embraced massive federal spending until he was forced to—during World War II.

There was enormous federal spending during the war (with government spending in 1944 nearly twice the GNP of 1933), which produced a rapid growth of demand that was restrained only by rationing and price controls. Simultaneously, there was an equally rapid growth in the federal debt. When the war ended, many economists still feared the economy would drop back into depression. Instead, the stored-up wartime demand became the engine for a long postwar boom. Even before the inadvertent Keynesianism of World War II proved to be effective, however, the United States had rung down the curtain on the laissez-faire era. On February 20, 1946, President Truman signed Public Law 340, better known as the Employment Act of

1946. This act committed the federal government to the three objectives of (1) providing high levels of employment, (2) maintaining stable prices, and (3) encouraging economic growth. The groundwork had been laid for countercyclical fiscal and monetary policy.

The lessons of World War II fiscal expansion and the license for government fiscal and monetary intervention in the economy granted by the act of 1946 opened American economic thinking to the "New Economics." Although Presidents Truman and Eisenhower showed only passing interest in the new doctrines and the new possibilities for public policy, university economists were quickly won over.

With the election of John Kennedy in 1960, Keynesian theory became policy. Coming to office during the third Eisenhower recession (1960-1961), Kennedy introduced a fiscally experimental program. With an investment tax credit worth $2.5 billion to business in 1962 and a proposal for an $11 billion general tax cut in 1963, the Kennedy agenda offered sound Keynesian medicine. Lyndon Johnson continued and elaborated on the Kennedy theme. For almost eight years the economy moved forward, and Americans learned (although they were soon to forget) that economic crisis, whether periodic or congenital, need not be the nature of the economy.

IS THE KEYNESIAN ANALYSIS STILL RELEVANT?

There is little denying that the simultaneous appearance in the 1970s of high unemployment, slow growth, and raging inflation was very unkind to Keynesians. Displaying a propensity "to throw out the baby with the bath water," many economists (including some previously ardent Keynesians), politicians, and ordinary citizens incorrectly identified Keynesian thinking and policy-making as the cause of the stagflationary crisis. True, the Keynesian focus had not prepared the nation for all economic crises—it had not anticipated the severe "supply shocks" of the 1970s (more on this in the next issue). Moreover, Keynes's original critique had emphasized an economy caught up in severe and pervading depression. It accounted for this chronic contraction as the result of insufficient private spending and argued correction required massive offsetting government spending. While, as we have seen, the events of the depression and war seemed to prove Keynes correct, it was discovered by the late 1960s that Keynesian demand-management efforts did not work well when the focus of policy attention was on a nearly fully employed economy or under conditions of overly full employment. Although some of Keynes's followers argued for fine-tuning—simply turning on or off the demand spigot as conditions dictated—events soon showed that closing the spigot demanded painful and thus unpopular remedies when such anti-inflationary actions were called for. The short-run benefits of expansionary economic policies were quickly perceived by politicians, as were the politically suicidal effects of contractionary policies that required raising taxes and reducing government spending. Indeed, as much as anything else, it was this politicization of Keynesianism that transformed what was mostly a technical shortcoming into a near catastrophic deficiency.

Keynesian ideas, however, did not disappear even though the limitations of fine-tuning and anti-inflationary policy were exposed. Based simply on a survey of the content of the average college introductory economics text, as well as the op-ed pages of the *Wall Street Journal*, it becomes obvious that most economists still use the Keynesian identities and causalities in setting up the framework of macroeconomic analysis. Most texts retain the Keynesian view that production-for-profit economies still tend "naturally" toward periodic stagnations. They still outline the potential uses of government policy to remedy such situations, although these exercises are decidedly more theoretical than policy oriented, reflecting the constraints imposed by the experiences of the 1970s. However, those accepting the Keynesian framework (whether they actually use the label or not) pay a great deal more attention now than in the past to the role played by private investment in the long-run maintenance of high levels of employment.

While Conservative economists like to claim credit for ending inflation, their cures were little more than an application of Keynesian principles. How was inflation halted in the 1980s? The Federal Reserve closed off investment and consumer spending by raising interest rates and bringing on the worst recession since the 1930s. How was the longest period of peacetime growth after 1982 achieved? The tax cut of 1981 and enormous defense outlays produced a tripling of the national debt—to $3 trillion by 1990—that provided sufficient demand stimulation to keep the boom going (although the "boom" was quite moderate by past standards).

In a perverse and economically dangerous way, Conservatives were applying Keynes's aggregate demand analysis without giving appropriate credit or understanding the long-term consequences. As a result (as we shall see in the following issues), the economy remains plagued by serious fundamental problems. The events of Black Monday, October 19, 1987, pointed up the basic weaknesses of a nation burdened under a mountain of federal debt and suffering from acute problems in its financial and trading relations with the rest of the world. The specter of another Great Depression looms real enough for many observers. Our ability to head it off or to deal with it when it arrives will depend upon our willingness to remember the last great economic rupture in our history. Indeed, Liberals may not possess *all* the answers, but at least they understand the question when asked: Are we depression-proof?

The Radical Argument

For both Conservatives and Liberals, albeit for different reasons, the imminent or future collapse of the American economy is not an inevitable event. Their views, of course, are not very startling. That defenders of varieties of capitalism believe the system has a future should be expected; however, the evidence, if looked at closely, points to a different conclusion. Contrary to the cheery Conservative view that free enterprise economies suffer only periodic and inconsequential business downturns, it is apparent from an historical as well as a recent perspective that crisis is part of the nature of production-for-profit economies. The Liberal contention that the countercyclical use of fiscal and monetary policy can insulate us from depression enormously understates the systemic roots of economic crisis and fails to comprehend the costs and effects of the tools of countercyclical policy.

THE CHRONIC TENDENCY TOWARD CRISIS

Economic crisis and instability are not peculiar to capitalist societies alone. However, with the dawn and maturity of capitalism, crisis (or what we presently might call depression) took on a new dimension. In precapitalist societies, economic contraction resulted largely from wars, plagues, crop failures, or other natural disasters. The granaries were empty, people starved, and there were shortages of goods of all kinds. Crisis was associated with underproduction. Paradoxically, in the capitalist era of crisis, this situation has been reversed. Capitalist contraction usually appears after an era of growth in the productive forces of a society. With excess goods on hand and no market, producers reduce current output, unemployment rises, and wages and prices fall. In short, capitalist crises usually begin when the granaries are full.

To be sure, the periodic panics and depressions that strike capitalism have usually been followed by recoveries. For many years, before the appearance of Keynes's work, the periodicity of boom and bust (especially boom) allowed Conservatives to describe economic contractions as "mere disturbances" that would go away and therefore did not merit very serious analytical study. No effort was made to see stagnation as fundamental to the capitalist order. Nor has this view changed much among modern Conservative economists. Keynesian Liberals, meanwhile, have accepted the fact that underconsumption generally leads to depressions in modern capitalism, but they hold that the tendency is easily manageable through the tools of modern public policy.

From the Radical perspective, however, economic crises are both fundamental to capitalism and beyond the capitalists' capacity to resolve. As capitalist economies grow and mature, crises become ever more frequent and progressively deeper, each succeeded by a less satisfactory recovery.

The crises are inherent in the capitalist system of production. In their perpetual search for expanded profits, capitalists must create surplus value—that is, they forever attempt to maximize the difference between the higher price for which goods sell and the lower price of the labor involved in production. To acquire greater profits, the capitalist must enlarge surplus value through the introduction of greater amounts of capital equipment, through the direct exploitation of labor, or through some combination of the two. The object is to produce greater output per unit of wage labor paid. As capitalists endeavor to produce more and more at greater profit, the capacity of the workers (consumers) to purchase this output declines. Although the people may "need" the goods, they do not have the "effective demand" to obtain them. Overproduction and underconsumption create periodic gluts of goods, which in turn cause crises wherein production ceases, capital is destroyed or left idle, and human beings starve.

As capitalism progresses, its productive capacity constantly enlarges. The possible depths and duration of production-consumption crises are heightened, and the ultimate end of the system is brought that much closer. Nineteenth-century Marxists observed the growing incidence of capitalist crises and predicted early collapse as profits fell, unemployment grew, real wages declined, and the system became discredited before the masses.

In point of fact, all this has not happened, but that is not proof that the underlying Radical analysis was wrong. Rather, it must be adjusted to take certain events into account.

First, the capitalists' persistent need for markets to dispose of their surplus production and to realize surplus value and profits was partially attained through overseas exploitation—imperialism. One case might illustrate. In the latter half of the nineteenth century, the depressed British textile industry experienced a significant boom after the British colonial rulers of India systematically destroyed the Indian weaving industry. British machines, and even British workers, went back to work precisely as Indians were forced from old occupations and compelled to buy imported British textiles.

Second, capitalist enterprise, which Marx had depicted as largely competitive, began to respond to the periodic crises by developing monopolistic characteristics. Industries became more integrated and dominated by a few firms. Possessing the power to set and control prices, output, and quality, monopoly capitalism was able to avoid the internecine struggles that had wiped out enterprises in the earlier competitive era.

Third, the growth of the state in the economy provided additional insulation from crisis. The state could foster or sanction monopoly behavior, mitigate the effects of labor exploitation and unemployment, and act directly to absorb the surplus production through government purchases (especially during war) and transfer payments.

THE COLLAPSE OF 1929

The expansion of overseas markets and sources of cheap labor and resources, the increasingly monopolistic behavior of business enterprises, and the enlargement of government protective actions held back the breaking of the dike before 1929. It did not, however, stop serious leaks.

In the case of the United States, seven major business cycles can be identified between the panic of 1893 and the beginning of World

War I. Each downturn lasted longer and became more pronounced. As the United States entered World War I and a wartime business boom, unemployment stood at about 10 percent. The "roaring twenties" were not much better. Probably the worst depression in U.S. history to that point occurred in 1921–1922, and throughout most of the decade unemployment was higher than 4 percent. Meanwhile, real wages moved upward only slightly. Only the phenomenal expansion of consumer debt buoyed the economy. For those who wished to see the evidence or could at least understand it, it was apparent that the dike would soon collapse.

The crisis after 1929 was a near-classic example of Marx's overproduction-underconsumption scenario. Moreover, it precipitated a general international collapse. The mature capitalist economies had exhausted markets for their goods. Overseas, the underdeveloped economies had little capacity to absorb output. At home, warehouses bulged because consumers lacked effective demand. As the first signs of crisis appeared, the banking and financial system, which itself rested on the capitalists' ability to realize their surplus, tottered and collapsed: first the Wall Street crash, then New York bank failures, then European bank failures. Full-scale industrial contraction followed.

THE OLD ECONOMICS IN A NEW PACKAGE

The Keynesian response to the deepening Depression was to accept the essential outline of the older Marxist critique of capitalism: Overproduction and crisis were endemic to the system. However, the Keynesians neatly evaded the Marxian conclusion. According to their analysis, insufficient business and consumer demand could be either manipulated by fiscal and monetary policy or supplemented by government spending that would raise the level of aggregate demand. In Marxian terms, government now became the vehicle to "realize surplus value."

Much has been made of this new thinking on the problem of the capitalist system. The "Keynesian Revolution" came to describe dominant economic opinion; however, it was no revolution at all. Keynes and his followers have not sought to end capitalism, but to save it. The central features of capitalism—private property, production for profit, wage labor, the business system, and all the rest—were retained. Indeed, as business leaders came to appreciate the profit (surplus value) possibilities of increased government spending during World War II and the trial-and-error Keynesian years after the war, corporate America enthusiastically accepted the "New Economics." The frequent Liberal posturing against big business should be recognized as pure political rhetoric. In the 1964 Johnson-Goldwater electoral contest, big business showed its colors by rejecting the Conservative, laissez-faire Republican in favor of the big-spending Democrat from Texas. Giant corporations poured millions of dollars into LBJ's campaign.

THE KEYNESIAN MIRAGE AND BACK TO REALITY

Through the 1960s and most of the 1970s (remember that even Richard Nixon had proclaimed himself a Keynesian), the New Economics seemed to be just what capitalism needed. The old capitalist business cycle of roller-coaster ups and downs simply disappeared as the economy underwent continuous expansion. In silly self-congratulation, economists wrote and talked of "no more depressions" while they enjoyed a place never before reserved for them in the public's esteem.

With the Vietnam War and other government spending growing and an easy monetary policy usually operating to encourage private borrowing, high levels of demand kept factories operating at near-peak utilization rates and kept unemployment rates low. Yet these signs of success through the 1960s were actually danger signals, for in capitalism success invariably sows the seeds of doom. The basic problem, as with all expansionary phases of the capitalist business cycle, was that expanding demand put serious pressures on business by causing rising costs, which in turn squeezed profits. With unemployment at very low levels, workers—unionized and nonunionized alike—enjoyed a seller's market for their labor. Real wages rose as businesses bid against each other for needed employees. Between 1960 and 1973, real (adjusted for inflation) after-tax weekly earnings rose by 35 percent. Since this exceeded productivity (output per worker-hour) growth, it translated into rising per-unit costs for producers. To make matters worse, resource costs worldwide began rising, the principal source being rising energy costs resulting from the Arabs' opting to challenge their former colonial and neocolonial masters.

At any rate, after-tax corporate profits peaked in 1965 (at about 10.5 percent on investment) and fell thereafter (to about 4.5 percent in 1974). With profits falling, businesses continued to reduce their investment outlays through the late 1960s and into the 1970s. At first the decline was scarcely felt as demand remained high for a time, but in the late 1960s, unemployment began to edge upward. By the early 1970s, regardless of expansionary fiscal policy efforts to offset the trend, unemployment grew as profits fell. Prices, meanwhile, began to rise, producing the new phenomenon of *stagflation* (rising unemployment *and* rising prices). Inflation took hold simply because demand, fueled by government and private borrowing, remained high. Without an expansion of business production facilities and with productive efficiency falling as the investment base got older and more outmoded, the high levels of demand caused price increases rather than output expansion. Meanwhile, the high levels of demand had few salutary effects on employment since profits remained low and business actually reduced its rate of investment. The outer limits of runaway Keynesianism had been reached.

There remained only one solution—the old solution: recession. Through the mid- and late 1970s, under enormous pressure from rising prices, government fiscal policy turned less expansionary. Predictably, unemployment crept upward. Inflation, however, was not significantly slowed until Conservative Ronald Reagan slew the dragon with a bone-chilling tight money policy that shut off private borrowing. The immediate result was the recession of 1981–1983, which produced Great Depression levels of unemployment.

Although Conservatives crowed about their victory over inflation and enjoyed pointing out that Keynesianism had proved itself a failure, they, as we shall see in the next issue, understood little about what had happened. They offered no new "solution" to the capitalist system. However, as we shall see in subsequent issues, the Conservatives have enjoyed a measure of success during their present tenure in the White House and in key economic policy-making positions. The mild "boom" of the 1980s was a pleasant respite from the events of the 1970s. Yet, as Black Monday (October 19, 1987) pointed out, neither the boom nor the nation's sense of economic well-being ran very deep. In fact, the recent resurgence of Conservative antigovernment, pro-business ideology, after a generation of Liberal ascendancy, is profoundly ironic. Marx, commenting on the ironies of history, once remarked that when history repeats itself, it first appears as tragedy and then as farce. However, to the more thoughtful, the idea of America returning to the "good old days" of Calvin Coolidge and Herbert Hoover is both farcical *and* tragic.

Yet, in a sense, that is precisely where we are. Indeed, production-for-profit capitalism, in any substantial sense, has never really passed much beyond the era immediately preceding the Great Depression. Is another Great Depression possible? *Very definitely.*

Stabilization and Growth Policy
Supply Side or Demand Side?

We must recognize that only experience can show how far the common will, embodied in the policy of the state, ought to be directed to increasing and supplementing the inducement to invest.

John Maynard Keynes, 1935

Is fiscal policy being oversold? Is monetary policy being oversold? ... My answer is yes to both of those questions. ... What I believe is that fine tuning has been oversold.

Milton Friedman, 1968

Originating in a liberal effort to respond to the popular will and relieve the pressures of poverty, demand-oriented politics ends in promoting unemployment and dependency.

George Gilder, 1981

The tax and spending policies that the U.S. government has pursued throughout Ronald Reagan's presidency have rendered every citizen a borrower and every industry a liquidator of assets.

Benjamin Friedman, 1988

THE PROBLEM

As we saw in the last issue, Conservative, Liberal, and Radical paradigms are strikingly divided on the matter of long-run economic stability within a capitalist economy and on the macroeconomic role to be played by government within an essentially production-for-profit system. While these larger and more spectacular questions of whether or not the economy is ultimately depression-proof always loom in the background, the problems of short-run economic performance attract greater attention from economists and public officials. In other words, more day-to-day concern is placed on the trim of the economic ship than on what might be done if it actually capsized. Obviously the two concerns are not unrelated; however, we shall look more closely at specific policy measures aimed at maintaining our short-run economic stability and growth.

Since the passage of the Employment Act of 1946, the federal government has had the responsibility

> to use all practicable means consistent with its needs and obligations and other essential considerations of national policy, with assistance and cooperation of industry, agriculture, labor and State and local governments, to coordinate and utilize all its plans, functions, and resources for the purpose of creating and maintaining, in a manner calculated to foster and promote free competitive enterprise and general welfare, conditions under which there will be afforded useful employment opportunities, including self-employment, for those able, willing and seeking to work and to promote maximum employment, production and purchasing power.

This careful legal jargon has been simplified over the years to three basic public policy objectives: providing high levels of employment, maintaining stable prices, and encouraging economic growth. Although presidential comprehension of and adherence to the public policy objectives of the act have varied with intellect and ideology since 1946, these goals have, for most mainstream economists, been the essence of government economic policy for the past four decades. They are the great trinity of modern macro policy thought and analysis.

At the time of this writing, the economy is well into its seventh year of economic expansion and, regardless of whether or not this expansion will be maintained much longer, the very length of the boom is impressive. The recent period has also been impressive when compared with the dismal stagflationary years that immediately preceded it. Not surprisingly,

among most Conservative economic and political thinkers, the boom of
the 1980s has been held up as proof of the errors of the earlier Keynesian
heresy and evidence that a policy relying predominantly on market-
directed forces *is capable* of maintaining both economic stability and
growth.

With the accession of Ronald Reagan to the White House in 1981,
Conservatives had an opportunity to reconstruct macroeconomic policy-
making to their liking; principal among their theoretical and practical
efforts was *supply-side* economics. Rejecting the demand-management
strategies of the Keynesians as the primary cause of the economic crisis of
the 1970s, supply-siders argued that the productive base of the economy
should occupy the attention of policymakers.* Accordingly, they advocated tax cuts aimed at increasing savings—which in turn would be a

---

*The supply-siders' analytical critique of Keynesian theory can be fairly easily
demonstrated. For supply-siders the inflationary episode of the 1970s was directly
traceable to the Keynesian error of believing that demand increases had only a salutary
effect on output and employment and no impact on prices. The supply-side argument
is illustrated in Panel 1. With aggregate demand (AD) and aggregate supply (AS),
respectively, illustrating the total demand and total supply of goods at all possible combinations of GNP and price level, the economy is in equilibrium in panel 1, where
AD=AS. It can be noted that at a low level of equilibrium output (Q), an increase in
total demand from AD to AD_1 has a far greater impact in increasing GNP than in raising
the price level. However, the shift from AD_1 to AD_2 has a far greater impact on prices.
The reason is obvious: As the aggregate supply curve approaches full employment, it
slopes upward more swiftly, since increased competition among buyers of increasingly
scarce resources bids up prices. The solution to the problem is demonstrated in panel
2. Actions should be taken that shift AS (increase aggregate supply) to the right. This
will facilitate, *ceteris paribus*, an increase in GNP and a decrease in prices.

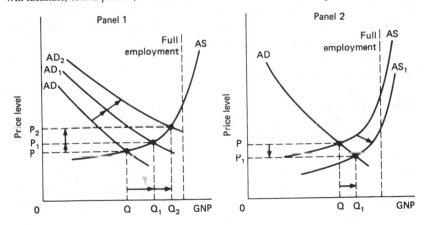

source for investment funds needed for the stimulation of the production, or supply side, of the economy. Along with tax cutting, they called for reduced government spending and a general pullback of government interference in business affairs.

Most supply-siders believe that the economic record speaks for itself. Through the combined effort of a 25 percent across-the-board tax cut (phased in over three years beginning in 1981) and a tight money policy (through 1981 and 1982) inflation was brought under control (falling from 13.5 percent in 1980 to 1.9 percent by 1986) *and* the economy was launched on a long expansion. The supply-side measures, as well as other Conservative programs during the Reagan-Bush years, are not without a large number of detractors, however. Opponents are quick to argue that the economic expansion of the 1980s masked many fundamental problems in the economy that were actually worsening during the decade. For instance, there was the near-tripling of the federal debt and the continued weakening of America's economic status in the world. Also, as critics point out, the 1980s boom, long as it may have been, was quite pallid compared to past expansionary epochs. Quite simply, the three principal measures of economic performance—GNP growth, price stability, and levels of employment—lagged well behind pre-1970s experience. Maybe modern-day booms just aren't what they used to be, but as Table 10.1 shows, the 1980s did compare poorly with the Keynesian 1960s.

Of course, criticizing the 1980s boom has been a lot easier than proposing a strategy that might have worked better than the Reagan-Bush actions. If the Conservative supply-side approach had problems, that in no way proved that an active demand-side management effort would necessarily be better. As we noted in the last issue, the efforts of Liberal Keynesians to fine-tune the economy in the late 1960s and early 1970s failed, or at least were perceived by most economists and ordinary citizens as having failed. Perhaps the demand-side approach was not entirely dead, but it had fallen from favor, and without major modifications or a thoughtful reappraisal by politicians and economists, it remains essentially irrelevant to practical policy-making at the present time.

Despite the tattered condition of demand-side strategies and the many doubts that exist about the *real* effectiveness of supply-side economics, we are, alas, left with only these two analytic alternatives, or a combination of both, in any attempt to develop appropriate macroeconomic policies. A more detailed examination of both arguments, therefore, must be the beginning point of any discussion of public policies aimed at maintaining growth and stability.

TABLE 10.1 Economic Growth, Unemployment, and Inflation Rates, 1960–1989

Year	Annual % Change in Real GNP	Annual % Unemployed	Annual % of Price Increase
1950	8.5	5.3	1.0
1951	10.3	3.3	7.9
1952	3.9	3.0	2.2
1953	4.0	2.9	.8
1954	−1.3	5.5	.5
1955	5.6	4.4	−.4
1956	2.1	4.1	1.5
1957	1.7	4.3	3.6
1958	−.8	6.8	2.7
1959	5.8	5.5	.8
1960	2.2	5.5	1.6
1961	2.6	6.7	1.0
1962	5.3	5.5	1.1
1963	4.1	5.7	1.2
1964	5.3	5.2	1.3
1965	5.8	4.5	1.7
1966	5.8	3.8	2.9
1967	2.9	3.8	2.9
1968	4.1	3.6	4.2
1969	2.4	3.5	5.4
1970	−.3	4.9	5.9
1971	2.8	5.9	4.3
1972	5.0	5.6	3.3
1973	5.2	4.9	6.2
1974	−.5	5.6	11.0
1975	−1.3	8.5	9.1
1976	4.9	7.7	5.8
1977	4.7	7.1	6.5
1978	5.3	6.1	7.7
1979	2.5	5.8	11.3
1980	−.2	7.1	13.5
1981	1.9	7.6	10.4
1982	−2.5	9.7	6.1
1983	3.6	9.6	3.2
1984	6.8	7.5	4.3
1985	3.4	7.2	3.6
1986	2.8	7.0	1.9
1987	3.4	6.2	3.7
1988	2.9	5.5	4.2
1989	2.5	5.3	4.8

Source: Economic Report of the President, 1990.

SYNOPSIS

Conservatives argue that past efforts at stabilization policy have not only failed to fine-tune the economy but were also instrumental in creating the economic stagnation of the 1970s. They argue instead for an approach to stabilization and growth that emphasizes tax and spending reductions and balancing the federal budget. Liberals interpret the stabilization record of the past quite differently, pointing out that "random shocks" over which economists had little or no control were the primary cause for the crises of the 1970s. They still argue on behalf of an active fiscal policy in bringing and keeping the economy under control. Radicals see the past efforts of Liberal stabilization policy as an attempt to intervene in the economy on behalf of business and ruling-class interests. The recent attempts to dismantle the old stabilization policies are a passing aberration, a measure of capitalism's modern crisis.

Anticipating the Arguments

- What are the basic components of a supply-side economic policy?
- In the face of recent economic difficulties, how do Liberals defend demand management?
- On what grounds do Radicals reject both supply-side and demand-side approaches?

The Conservative Argument

The Conservative program for stabilization and growth requires going back and reassessing what we knew before Keynes and adding what we have learned since Keynes. It is composed of three basic elements: (1) Redirect fiscal and monetary policy attention from the demand or consumption side of economic activity to the supply or production side; (2) oppose public policy actions that would return us to the awful demand inflation of the Keynesian years; and (3) restrain the disruptive effects of government spending by developing and maintaining a balanced federal budget. In this issue we shall examine the first two points. The third element will be examined in the following issue.

THE ERRORS OF DEMAND-MANAGEMENT ECONOMICS

Until recently, conventional macroeconomics was taught only one-dimensionally. Following the Keynesian critique of an economy in deep depression, with great quantities of labor unemployed and much of the nation's plants and equipment sitting idle, majority economic reasoning saw the economic dilemma as simply a problem of inadequate demand: Increase the demand for goods, and men, women, and machines would go back to work. In such a view, the supply side was taken for granted. Whatever amount of output might be demanded — right up to the point at which people and machines were fully employed — would be supplied virtually instantaneously. End of the Keynesian story.

The Keynesian remedy for the prostrate economies of the 1930s had been seductively simple and painless: *Spend your way out of depression*. Moreover, it had even seemed to work during the late 1930s and during World War II when massive government outlays did rejuvenate the economy. As an antidepressionary strategy, Conservatives will admit that Keynesian policies were — in the short term at least — a politically attractive alternative to simply allowing the business cycle to undergo a natural correction. However, its political appeal in no way made it sound economic policy. Worse still, its superficial "success" led to the eventual institutionalization of demand-management fiscal and monetary policies, not simply as antidepressionary devices but for persistently "fine-tuning" the economy.

Although the 1990s seem safely distant from the 1970s, that awful decade is worth looking at from time to time, if for no other reason than to avoid the economic policy errors of the past. What is to be recalled is that the demand-side management excesses of the late sixties and early seventies triggered a decade of stagflation in which price inflation soared precisely as the general economy stagnated, sending unemployment rates chasing upward after price increases. In particular, the Keynesian preoccupation with unemployment (a hangover from its Depression roots) led first to massive efforts to pump up the economy and then to grand expenditure programs (during President Johnson's Great Society) to either create jobs directly or to sustain the unemployed. The expansionary fiscal efforts and the expensive social engineering programs, along with the expanding

FIGURE 10.1   Inflation and Unemployment Rates, 1960–1989

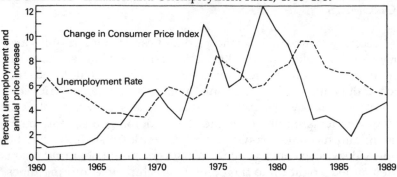

Source: *Economic Report of the President, 1990.*

military outlays for the Vietnam War, unleashed an all-consuming inflation as "too many dollars chased too few goods." As Figure 10.1 indicates, annual price increases in the 1970s approached and then surpassed double-digit percentages.

Keynesians, for the most part, kept their eyes on unemployment rates that stubbornly moved upward despite all the New Economists' efforts to use the appropriate antiunemployment tools that John Maynard Keynes had bequeathed to them. Their problem, of course, was twofold. First, they did not understand the source of the price inflation and the mischief that inflation could cause. Second, their preoccupation with the demand side of the economy and economic policy-making blinded them to the fact that their supposedly "stimulative" efforts were actually decimating the supply side, or productive base, of the economy and thereby worsening the unemployment problem with each effort to eliminate it.

To see the problem clearer, we need to focus a bit closer on inflation and the supply side. Not only does inflation gnaw at purchasing power and lower real demand, but it also interferes with business investment decisions, foreign trade, and financial and securities markets. The results are lowered business expectations and production levels that throw millions of people out of work. No one has ever argued the case that unemployment causes inflation; usually it is assumed to have some depressing effect on prices. But evidence from all the great inflationary spirals of the past shows that inflation *does* eventually depress employment. Meanwhile, a minimal mastery of macroeconomics should permit us to see that any public policy efforts to heat up the economy for the purpose of creating jobs can only add to existing inflationary pressures.

Some will say that this is a hardhearted position. They will argue that Conservatives care little about people who are unemployed. That is not true. Solving the inflation problem is a Conservative answer to the unemployment problem. A privately oriented economy with low interest rates, reasonably assured business expectations, and a slow but steady rate of money expansion to support higher levels of demand will be a growing economy. That means more jobs. An economic system dominated by government, where either monetary policy or fiscal policy (or both) is used recklessly to create jobs, will limit the freedom of the private sector, interfere with business investment, and sooner or later worsen the unemployment problem.

The deterioration of the supply side of the economy was deeply connected to the inflationary outcome of demand-management policies. Rising prices necessarily produced rising interest rates that quickly began to choke off new investment. Firms had little choice but to let their plants and machines age since they could not afford financing new equipment outlays. Meanwhile, saving, which after all is the source for business borrowing, was discouraged as price increases reduced real income and lowered savings rates. However, not all the battering of the nation's productive base was attributable to inflation alone. The social engineering measures of the early 1970s, particularly those aimed at consumer, environmental, and worker protection, got in their whacks too. The heightening of government regulation meant added business costs precisely as general economic conditions were forcing business profits downward. And coupled to the demand-management excesses of a rampant Keynesianism, was a "soak the rich and business" taxation mentality. To the degree that taxes were raised—either to cover the increased spending or as a fiscal policy management effort to cool an overheating economy, the tax burden fell disproportionately on the savers and investors of the nation.

Taking together the inflationary fiscal and monetary policies, the overeager efforts at social regulation, and the retrograde taxation strategies, it becomes obvious that social engineering demand managers were doing just about everything possible to sink the economy in the 1970s. The simple fact was that, in the period of "high

Keynesianism," economic policy was unwittingly working to slow the growth of the nation's productive base—to kill the goose that laid the golden eggs.

PAYING ATTENTION TO THE SUPPLY SIDE

Before turning to the Conservative strategy for maintaining stability and growth, it is important to understand how the production, or supply, side of the economy works.

To begin with, the aggregate supply of goods reflects cost considerations. Perhaps adding additional workers or using previously idled production facilities in deeply recessionary or depressionary general economic conditions has little effect on unit production costs. However, that is not the case when an economy approaches full employment. In fact, well before full employment is encountered, production costs may be rising. Additional workers and raw materials are, after all, obtained in competition with other firms seeking workers and materials; wages and prices are accordingly bid upwards. In other words, while output may be increased in response to an increase in demand all the way up to full employment levels, after some point, usually well short of full employment, output increases reflect greatly increasing production costs and rising prices. Thus the impact of increasing the demand for goods may be mostly to raise prices rather than to increase output. Given this theoretical situation, we can begin to see some of the problems demand-side managers were encountering in the 1960s and 1970s. Expansionary fiscal and monetary policies were bumping up against rising supply costs, with the result that prices were going up and few increases in real output were obtained. And as we shall see later, the inflationary pressures were counterproductive—lowering real output and creating more unemployment. We had encountered stagflation.

The second point to note about aggregate supply is that it reflects the existing productive base of an economy. The more efficient and productive a society is, the lower the unit production costs are and the less likely they are to rise for any given increase in demand. Through the 1960s and 1970s, the productive base of the American economy was allowed to weaken as public policy concentrated only on the demand side.

Before the ascendancy of Keynesian ideas, conventional economic wisdom held that "supply creates its own demand." The emphasis of economic doctrine and policy was on the supply side. Quite inaccurately, and with disastrous results, the old wisdom became rewritten to read: "Demand creates its own supply." Nothing could be further from the truth.

THE SUPPLY-SIDE "MENU"

By shifting our attention over the past fifty years from basic problems of production to the demand side of the market, we have shackled the basic productive structure of the economy and weakened our own capacity to produce. Once the model of industrial output, productivity by American workers and industry is near the bottom among industrial nations, and the trend can be broken only by developing new supply-side growth policies.

First, *savings must be encouraged*. Modern Keynesians incorrectly view savings as a reduction of total demand. However, without savings, funds are not available for the business investment required to reinvigorate American industry and make it once again competitive with foreign producers. Tired and old capital equipment and procedures are basic causes of our current inefficiency. Over the past several decades, our tax policies, with heavy progressive taxes on upper-income groups (who are most likely to be the savers) and our high corporate-profit taxes, have diminished our investment potential. Though called income taxes, these revenues have really been "savings taxes." As Arthur Laffer has pointed out, the irony of our tax approach in the past is that higher tax rates have the effect of producing lower tax collections. As work and savings incentives are lowered by rising rates, there is less output to tax. Thus lower tax rates, not higher ones, should produce more output and, ironically, more tax revenues.

The supply-sider objective of enhancing savings was implemented into policy during the Reagan years. The 1981 tax changes lowered all tax rates by 25 percent and the 1986 Tax Reform Act flattened taxes, lowering the top rate from 50 to 28 percent. Such actions have gone a long way to lay the foundation for a tax system that encourages rather than discourages savings.

Second, *the "tax wedge" must be reduced*. Apart from the disincentives of high tax rates on savings and corporate profits, taxes also have the effect of creating a "cost-push" effect on prices. That is, rising sales, excise, payroll, and other corporate taxes become added onto the final prices of goods. With taxes raising the relative price of goods, total demand for good falls. This in turn reduces corporate sales and induces layoffs and plant closings. Holding down various business taxes, including corporate income taxes that may in part be pushed forward as part of a firm's costs, are a virtual necessity.

Third, *restrictions on business investment and risk taking must be reduced*. New business undertakings, both in producing new goods and in producing old goods in new ways, will expand national employment and economic growth faster than any other approach. Yet a maze of government regulations over marketing and production activities hampers business enterprise. As a result, business adjusts downward to lower levels of output and lagging growth performance. To stimulate risk taking, we must reduce the regulatory overkill that exists in our economy. The Liberal "interventions" in consumer, environmental, and job safety areas are not free. They raise business costs just as the tax wedge does, and the results are rising prices, rising unemployment, and plant closings.

Fourth, *greater labor force participation and mobility should be encouraged*. Liberals have not faced up to the realities of American labor markets. Expensive welfare programs, which account for the bulk of federal spending growth since the 1960s, have been designed to cushion the effects of unemployment. In fact, they have nurtured unemployment. With lavish benefits for not working, there is little economic incentive for workers to improve skills, to relocate where jobs do exist, or to view work itself in a positive way. Transfers of funds to the unemployed may pump up their spending, but these increases in aggregate demand are more than offset by supply reductions resulting from a combination of high wages (to induce workers to work) and high taxes (to support workers who won't work).

THE SUCCESS OF THE SUPPLY-SIDE PROGRAM

Having made our case against demand-management economics and laid out the theoretical underpinnings of a supply-side analysis, we now turn to the record. How well did the supply-side approach work when it was tried in the 1980s?

On taking office in 1981, the Reagan administration faced two immediate problems: (1) Bring inflation under control and (2) stimulate economic growth. The first objective was undertaken via a tight money policy (which had actually been commenced in 1979 during the Carter presidency). In an effort to kick the inflationary habit "cold turkey," the Federal Reserve continued through 1982 a painful policy restricting the money supply and holding interest rates at very high levels. Painful as the resulting disinflation and recession was, it brought prices under control, as Table 10.1 and Figure 10.1 illustrated. Annual price increases, running at 13.5 percent in 1980, were down to an acceptable 3.2 percent by 1983. At the same time, the groundwork was being laid for a supply-side stimulation of the economy. With a 25 percent across-the-board tax cut phased in between 1981 and 1983, the economy commenced in late 1982 the longest peacetime economic expansion in its history. Through the rest of the decade, price increases stayed within an acceptable range, unemployment rates continued to fall, and real GNP growth—while not as great as in the 1960s (and happily so)—was sufficient to produce a noticeable improvement in national well-being.

Liberal critics of supply-side efforts, while grudgingly acknowledging a few gains in the leveling off of inflation and the decline of unemployment rates, point that no "miracle" has swept the American economy. They fail to realize, however, that the supply-side focus is over the medium to long run. Quick, up-front paybacks from adopting supply-side policies were never promised. Even after the distortions of five decades of Liberal Keynesian mismanagement are overcome, time is needed for the production side of the economy to adjust to new economic conditions. The quick fix—indeed, one quick fix after another—was the hallmark of Liberal policy-making. Conservative supply-oriented policies presuppose the gradual creation of market conditions that return economic order. Both pain and time are costs that must be incurred as we adjust to a new manner of economic thought.

The Liberal Argument

In the last issue, we laid out the case for fiscal and monetary policy to counter depressions. In brief, the argument held that since the Great Depression and the appearance of the Keynesian critique, we do possess adequate analytic and policy tools to manage the general level of economic activity. However, possessing the tools and using them correctly are different matters. In the case of fiscal policy, how effective have we really been and what should we presently be doing?

Conservatives, who do not believe in the efficacy of fiscal policy, are in fact long on theory and short on evidence. What evidence they do offer begs proper interpretation. Far from being "proven" ineffective in the past and the "cause" of the stagflationary problems of the 1970s, fiscal management of the general level of economic activity had a good record during the 1960s. To understand the 1970s crisis of the macroeconomy, we need to look at a number of developments unconnected to the theory and practice of Keynesian stabilization policy. There was the outright misuse of countercyclical policy during most of the 1970s. More important, however, were the series of unpredictable random shocks that hit the economy during this period, along with certain subtle structural shifts within the economy.

THE FISCAL POLICY RECORD EXAMINED

The general framework of antidepressionary policy-making was in place by the beginning of the post–World War II period. Steps to end the Depression, wartime spending, and the legal commitment of the Employment Act of 1946 helped to end the traditional government commitment to a balanced budget. Nevertheless, between 1946 and the early 1960s, the political leadership of the nation showed little mastery of the new policy possibilities. Fiscal policy, as it was practiced, was unplanned and ill-timed. Deficits or surpluses appeared at the wrong times or quite accidentally at the right time. Manipulative monetary policy was not practiced at all.

With John Kennedy's election in 1960, as we noted in the last issue, countercyclical fiscal policy was to get its chance. The Kennedy tax cuts of 1962–1963 and increased presidential awareness of how the aggregate economy could be manipulated by stabilizing fiscal and monetary policy meant the coming of the age of macro policy-making. There followed several years of economic growth, falling unemployment rates, and steady prices – precisely what the Employment Act of 1946 called for and Keynesian economists promised they could deliver.

The experiment in stabilization, however, was to be short-lived. The expanded war in Vietnam, coupled with Johnson's adamant

TABLE 10.2 Average Annual Changes in Per Capita Income, Average Annual Unemployment, and Average Annual Changes in the Consumer Price Index for Selected Periods

Year	Change in Real Per Capita Income (%)	Unemployment Rate	Change in Consumer Price Index (%)
1954–1961	1.6	5.4	1.1
1962–1969	3.1	4.5	2.4
1970–1977	2.0	6.3	8.2
1978–1985	2.1	7.6	7.4
1986–1990	2.6	5.8	3.9

Source: Economic Report of the President, 1990, and author's estimates.

stance that the economy could produce guns *and* butter, began to pump up excess demand. Richard Nixon's continuation of the war after 1969 and his own timidity in dealing with growing excess demand brought the short era of stabilization policy to an end.

The failure of fiscal policy in the late 1960s, however, was not a defeat for theory. If Johnson had shared his war intentions with his economic advisors and also shown more political courage, a tax increase in 1966 or 1967 could have cooled the economy down. Nixon, too, failed to utilize the fiscal brakes, fearing political reaction to a tax increase. Instead he sought to deal with the inflationary push by instituting an ineffective program of wage and price controls and by having the monetary authorities put a squeeze on demand through tight money. When excess demand inflation should have been halted according to elementary Keynesian analysis, it was not done.

As a consequence of these political developments, we have only a comparatively short period, roughly from 1962 to 1969, to evaluate countercyclical fiscal policy. However, these years stand out boldly in attaining the objectives of the Employment Act of 1946. Table 10.2 compares three important indicators—changes in per capita income, unemployment levels, and the consumer price index—over the eight years of Keynesian ascendancy with comparable periods before and since. As the data indicate, per capita income growth and unemployment levels had their most desirable showing between 1962 and 1969, and only the recessed Eisenhower years posted a slower increase in the consumer

price index. Alas, Camelot was all too brief, but it did provide proof of
the effectiveness of modern fiscal policy management.

RANDOM SHOCKS AND
STRUCTURAL CHANGES

Contrary to the Conservative view that Keynesian stabilization policy
caused the general price increases of the 1970s and 1980s, the real
cause was a series of random events that built an inflationary bias into
the economy. In the period between 1971 and 1973, the Nixon
administration attempted to devalue the dollar to ease worsening U.S.
balance-of-payments problems (which were caused mostly by our
Vietnam War spending). While American goods were more attractive
in foreign markets as a result of devaluation, foreign goods became
expensive in the United States. *Result*: Domestic prices of imported
goods went up. In October 1973, the United States exported 19 million metric tons of wheat to the Soviet Union, reducing American
supplies of grain to practically nothing. *Result*: Prices for finished
goods went up. In late 1973, OPEC (Organization of Petroleum
Exporting Countries) began a long series of petroleum price increases
that raised crude oil charges from less than $2 per barrel to nearly $40
by 1981. *Result*: All prices were forced upward.

These inflationary shocks created a general inflationary psychology. Each event seemed to support the view that prices would continue to go up. These expectations of future inflation induced both
labor unions and businesses to act to protect themselves from future
inflationary shocks. Wages and prices began to go up even faster than
the rise caused by the random inflationary events. The effect of this
general inflationary increase, which saw the consumer price index
more than double between 1970 and 1980, was to lower consumers'
real buying power. The inflation "tax" reduced the spendable income
of ordinary consumers and businesses, and aggregate demand fell.
With falling demand and slowing economic growth, there was an
accompanying rise in unemployment.

To many Liberals, the situation called for capping inflationary
increases by some use of price controls while maintaining employment and growth through appropriate fiscal policy. This was not to be
the case. President Carter's first efforts in 1978 and 1979 at voluntary
wage-price guidelines were a complete failure. At the same time,

expansionary efforts to reduce unemployment were blocked by Conservatives who decided that inflation was the biggest problem and who wrongly concluded that inflation was the result of past fiscal policy excesses.

EVALUATING THE SUPPLY-SIDE ARGUMENT

Despite the initially innovative appearance of Conservative supply-side theory, time has shown that its originality is negligible and its effectiveness marginal. To be sure, the rampant inflation of the late 1970s slowed down, but this was not the demonstrated result of supply-side policies or new economic thinking of any kind. Pursuing a tight-money, high-interest-rate monetary policy, the Conservative Reagan administration succeeded in applying what everyone had always known was a possible cure to inflation: *They created a deep recession in 1981–1982.* Construction, business investment, and new factory orders came to a standstill, and unemployment rose to Great Depression levels. To no one's surprise, prices fell — not because of any action on the supply side but simply because demand dried up.

The economy did begin to improve, however, in late 1982, and a miniboom continued through the rest of the decade. Was this perhaps the effect of supply-side policy? Supply-siders point to the 25 percent personal income tax reduction (over three years) and a variety of "enhancements" in business taxes enacted in 1981 as the source of economic improvement. There is not much doubt that the tax cuts did stimulate a boom, but the cuts had their effect from the demand side, not the supply side. Consumer spending went up, but changes in business investment were scarcely noticeable. Moreover, the boom was greatly inspired by vast increases in government spending for military goods and an exploding federal deficit. What the supply-siders were calling a victory looked exactly like the defeats they alleged to a demand-oriented policy.

To be sure, prices increased only very slowly during the mid-1980s. Was this necessarily evidence that a supply-side focus to stabilization policy worked? In fact, prices were low for a number of other reasons. First, the very depth of the 1982 recession meant that the economy could climb upward without exerting many price pressures. Second, world energy prices fell during this period. Third, a world economic slump followed our recession and also tended to have a downward effect on prices. Fourth, a strengthening American dollar (see Issue 15) invited a flood of foreign competition into American markets, holding down domestic price increases.

The sought-after increase in savings that was supposed to provide the source of new investment never materialized. Savings rates of Americans went down, not up, after the 1981 tax cut. Meanwhile, real harm resulted from other supply-side programs. Unemployment remained high, falling only 3 percent to 7 percent between 1982 and 1986. At the same time, low-income Americans suffered as Conservatives chiseled away at social welfare programs that were singled out as both the cause of federal deficits and a troublesome source of "stickiness" in labor markets. The persistent unemployment, the healthy tax cuts for the well-to-do and for business, and the dismantling of much of the social safety net that supported lower-income citizens had not brought a new opportunity for most Americans. Instead, the gap was widened between those at the top and those at the bottom of the economic ladder.

Supply-side stabilization policy stands revealed as either a very "meanhearted" policy or no policy at all. The crowning objective of the supply-siders—the constitutional enforcement of a balanced federal budget—will absorb our attention in the next issue. Suffice it for now to point out a legally required budget balance would make supply-side policy even meaner because social programs would be sacrificed to obtain balance: Ultimately, with tax increases off limits as a balancing alternative and military spending a "sacred cow," only social spending is left as the balancing item. However, an even bigger problem develops because budget balance means the effective end of any activist fiscal policy. The result would be to leave the nation disarmed in any war against short-term business cycle changes.

Supply-side Conservatives are correct, and Liberals have never really disputed the point, that a nation's productive base is the ultimate determinant of its capacity to produce. However, the condition of a nation's production facilities is not the only factor determining output. The level of demand also plays its role. By focusing on the supply side, Conservatives show understanding of only half the economic problem. And half a solution is really no solution at all.

FISCAL POLICY AND BEYOND

From the foregoing argument, the Liberal position should be clear: First, the fiscal tools of government taxing and spending are useful devices by which we can manage the general performance of the economy, whether it be dealing with inflation or unemployment. Second, although assigned a lesser role, monetary policy should be coordinated with and "lean" in the same direction as fiscal policy. Third, fiscal and monetary policies should be developed so as to have desirable and humane social effects, spreading the tax burden and the spending to close the economic gap between those at the bottom and those at the top of the economic ladder. Finally, unemployment should always be seen as the most important economic problem, and it must receive our attention in fiscal policy-making *first*. Any other approach will tear the fabric of our society. Faced with the problem of the Great Depression, Herbert Hoover, a president deeply committed to a Conservative fiscal outlook, once lectured a visiting delegation of mayors on the evils of deficits and enlarged government spending. "Gentlemen," he asked, "can you think of anything worse than an unbalanced budget?" James Curley of Boston, thinking of the bread lines, ugly social disorders, and misery in his city, raised his hand. "Well, Mr. President," he said, "how about a revolution?" Radicals advocate revolution. Conservatives, in their ignorant rejection of several decades of proven fiscal policy effectiveness, would unwittingly bring it about by their insensitivity to the problems of the economically disenfranchised.

Yet fiscal policy is only a partial solution to our economic problems. The decline of American output and productivity over the past two decades requires much more than an effective fiscal policy, and it also requires much more than the Conservative supply-sider's tax-cutting, budget-balancing, and deregulating efforts to "free up" investment and then let growth "trickle down." As we shall see in later issues, expanded governmental policy-making in the areas of unemployment, inflation, and investment is needed, not a retreat from policy. We must face the hard facts that not all employment is responsive to fiscal and monetary policy solutions, that not all inflation may be controlled by monetary authorities, and that not all businesses will make proper investment decisions.

The Radical Argument

The debate between Liberal demand managers and Conservative supply-siders has produced considerable confusion among thoughtful Americans. The arguments have usually been framed in either-

or terms. Either you intervene to manage the aggregate economy or you don't. Either an unregulated economy works better than a managed one or it does not. Given the record of the past sixty years of American economic history, there is little evidence to make either side's claims very convincing. Thus it is not surprising that modern macro policy debate produces more heat than light. In both actual policy-making and the classroom teaching of economics, the result has been "a little of this and a little of that." From a Radical perspective, however, there is no confusion about the issues: both Liberals and Conservatives, albeit for different reasons, are *wrong*.

WHY NEITHER DEMAND-SIDE NOR SUPPLY-SIDE EFFORTS WORK

The fundamental flaw of both Liberal and Conservative approaches begins from the same error: Neither truly understands what powers a capitalist economy. Although both agree that investment is the driving force, each sees investment as depending on different determinants.

Conservatives understand investment as being determined by the level of savings in the society. As savings grow, interest rates (the cost of borrowing) declines, and investors step forward in greater numbers to obtain funds. In turn, their investment actions propel the economy, providing growth and jobs. Accordingly, Conservative policy focuses on actions that will enhance savings. The Reagan tax cut of 1981 was called a supply-side tax cut (although it differed little from earlier demand-side cuts) because it was aimed at giving very large tax reductions to the very rich, who were expected to save their windfall, and to corporations, who were expected to translate aftertax profits directly into investment.* Similarly, Conservatives oppose government deficits that are financed in capital markets in competition with private seekers of funds. Government borrowing is supposed to "crowd out" private investment by raising interest rates (see the Conservative argument in Issue 11). In monetary policy matters, although low interest rates are attractive to investors, too-low rates are

*Although the 1981 tax cut reduced everyone's tax liabilities by 25 percent over three years, the progressive nature of the tax system meant, of course, that the upper-income group paid or was expected to pay a larger share in income taxes. A fixed-percentage reduction on a larger tax liability necessarily meant that the well-to-do received a very substantial portion of the total tax cut.

opposed because they might discourage saving and encourage consumer borrowing. Therefore, an expansionary money policy is discounted as having no useful effects on investment. In focusing on savings and the interest rate, along with their views on the excessive power of labor unions to raise wage rates, it is apparent that Conservatives take a *cost-based* approach to explaining how investment occurs and capitalism supposedly flourishes.

Liberals, meanwhile, see the chief determinant of investment as the actual level of aggregate demand. Abundant savings and low interest rates, they argue, will not induce a firm to invest if, as a result of an economic slump, it has a great deal of unused plants and equipment. As demand rises, utilization rates grow, and new investment becomes attractive as the firm actually seeks to expand output. Faced with an underemployed economy, Liberals are accordingly biased toward tax cuts that raise consumption, toward increases in government spending, and under some circumstances, toward very low interest rates (which, in their view, encourage borrowing). Their built-in bias focuses on *demand* conditions. Increase demand to stimulate the economy; decrease it to slow economic activity down.

To be sure, Liberals and Conservatives view the economy in its "natural state" in two different ways. Conservatives assume that left to itself and without government tinkering, an economy runs at full employment and near capacity utilization. Liberals view the natural state as being less than full employment but believe that full employment may be reached by means of adroit policy actions. In many other respects, Conservatives and Liberals are quite alike. Both zero in on business investment as the key that unlocks the economy; they differ, however, on their *cost* versus *demand* explanations of why investment takes place. *The difference is a very crucial one.*

To see this issue more clearly and to understand why Liberals and Conservatives are both wrong, we must first see that each is "a little bit right" in understanding how capitalism works. *Profit, not savings or aggregate demand, is the real determinant of investment.* Although few Liberals or Conservatives would disagree with the assertion that profit drives capitalism, they fail to recognize that profit has both a *cost* side and a *demand* side. Remember: *Profit equals sales minus expenditures.* Thus lower costs increase profits and increased sales raise profits, *ceteris paribus.* The trouble, of course, is with *ceteris paribus.*

The very actions aimed at lowering costs (the supply-side menu of cutting the taxes of only the rich, keeping government spending in check, balancing the budget, and so on) lower demand and thus business sales. Meanwhile, actions intended to increase demand (increased government spending, tax cuts to stimulate consumption, budget imbalance, and the like) raise costs as resource prices are bid upward in an expanding economy. This was precisely the dilemma of the 1970s, as we saw in the last issue.

Ironically, *either* a demand-based *or* a supply-based stabilization policy scenario is doomed to fail in the long run. The problem lies deep in a production-for-profit system. As the last issue demonstrated, the normal search for profits produces overproduction and underconsumption crises and *falling profits*. Efforts to remedy overproduction and underconsumption lead to rising costs and *falling profits*. In either case, profits, the driving force of the system, are perpetually threatened.

Over the past half century, stabilization policy has been simply a matter of trying now one and now the other of these bankrupt approaches. Although many economists have tried to reconcile the Liberal and Conservative extremes and build an eclectic system, that is bound to fail too. Invariably, cost-based and demand-based approaches come into conflict. The result is that they either negate each other or one comes to dominate the other.

THE CLASS BIAS AND IRRATIONALITY OF CONVENTIONAL STABILIZATION POLICY EFFORTS

Regardless of its failure, stabilization policy efforts in our time have had one permanent effect: They have erected government as a central feature of the modern capitalist economy. In turn, the modern capitalist state has become a vehicle for class domination and increasing productive irrationality.

Liberals and Conservatives both hold that government policy is capable of being "neutral"; that is, tax cuts or money policy actions, regardless of the particular kind of action, are viewed as having only economic effects. The social and political biases of any of these policies are never put up front for examination. This misses an important aspect of public policy-making, namely, that it is a class instrument, a tool for perpetuating ruling-class domination. The social inequalities of stabilization policy are better appreciated by ordinary Americans than most economists admit, but they might usefully be laid out in detail.

There is an upper-income bias in taxation policy. A brief survey of important tax-cutting efforts to stimulate expansion—either the cuts of 1964 or those of 1981, for example—indicates that upper-middle- and upper-income taxpayers received the largest percentage reduction and the bulk of the total cut. These same groups, of course, benefit the most from the legal loopholes of the tax system, such as the ability to deduct interest payments and business expenses from their tax bills. The poor and the lower-middle class, without the benefits of tax loopholes (or even much opportunity to cheat), have lost economic ground in the tax-cutting measures of demand-side Keynesians and supply-side Conservatives. In the case of tax increases, the poor again are hit hardest. The recent increase in social security withholding taxes is a good example. Over the past few years, both the taxable base and the rate of the taxes have risen at the lower end of the income scale. (In 1989 the rate was 7.65 percent on earnings up to $51,000.) Such taxes are regressive, since they fall heaviest on lower incomes.

Low-income Americans have also lost out on the spending side. While Conservatives and Liberals (for different reasons) point to the magnitude of federal transfers to the poor and indigent, this is a massive deception. The federal government's spending in this area amounts to about the same percentage of the GNP today that it did in the pre-Keynesian 1930s.* At the same time, transfers to large farmers, businesses, and professional workers have grown. Government spending for goods, meanwhile, directly benefits the ruling class and higher-income workers. A good illustration of the upper-income and monopoly-capital bias of such expenditures is military and space spending. The recipient firms are among the largest in the nation and also the most capital- and skill-intensive. Spending funneled into

*This fact may seem startling to Americans, who are constantly bombarded with propaganda about the alleged extravagance of social spending on the poor. In reality, we currently spend only a little over 2 percent of our GNP on programs directed specifically to low-income groups. In 1938, for example, the $1.5 billion spent on various poor relief programs by federal, state, and local governments amounted to a little less than 2 percent of the GNP.

these firms strengthens monopoly power and has little or no impact on creating jobs for less skilled and lower-paid workers (see Issue 12).

Looked at in this way, government spending, even for stabilization purposes, is not neutral at all. It actually heightens class divisions in the society. Spending on low-income housing, medical care, and other social goods that would improve the poor's quality of life has always ranked very low among fiscal priorities. This is because the poor, regardless of their numbers, are not yet a powerful constituency and also because spending for certain social goods would actually create competition with the private sector. Subsidized public housing would destroy the lucrative low-income housing market in the private sector, free clinics would bankrupt private hospitals, and so on. Moreover, when the stabilization experts call for a contraction in government spending (to balance the budget or reduce aggregate demand), services and transfers to the poor are the first items sacrificed.

Although Liberals in the heyday of Keynesian policy were less inclined to cut so deeply or so obviously, the Conservative budget cutters of the Reagan years brutalized the poor. In the name of "trickle-down" economics, poor children were told that catsup now qualified as a vegetable in the school lunch program, and the unskilled were told that there were plenty of jobs in most newspapers' classified sections. And all social service budgets were chopped.

Monetary policy is equally selective and unfair in its class effects. For instance, the 1982 pursuit of high interest rates (a tight money policy) as an anti-inflation tool especially burdened the working class. For consumers, high interest rates mean that greater portions of their income must be paid for such necessities as home mortgages and for the "luxuries" provided by credit buying. Upper-income groups, of course, face the same interest rates, but their burdens are a much smaller proportion of their income and more easily borne without sacrifice of their living standards. Meanwhile, for workers, tight money translates into reduced business output and fewer jobs or lower pay.

Thus stabilization policy perpetuates and accentuates the normal class inequalities of capitalism. Expansionary policy never benefits the poor as much as the rich. And contraction always demands that the least affluent American citizens must tighten their belts the most. The normal exploitative tendencies of traditional capitalism are merely reinforced under both Liberal and Conservative approaches.

Apart from the inherent injustices of stabilization policy, there is also the problem of the irrational production and consumption that it encourages. As American capitalism has steadily enlarged its productive capacity—or, in Paul Baran and Paul Sweezy's analysis, its ability to produce surplus—it has had to develop equivalent devices to absorb the surplus. Leaving government aside for a minute, the private sector has devised a number of important ways to "waste" (absorb) output. Developing socially useless goods (hygienic and cosmetic goods come to mind) and expending considerable resources to distribute, advertise, and sell these goods help create jobs and income, but such activities do not elevate society much. Yet this needless and irrational production and consumption, with the attendant creation of needless and alienated labor, do absorb the surplus.

Government spending has pushed along the absorption of surplus through irrational means. Presently, we are spending well over $300 billion a year on military goods—a beautiful way to absorb the surplus. We build machines that have no social usefulness, do not compete with private enterprise, and hopefully will be quickly outmoded so that we can build more. However, people are put to work, corporations earn profits, and the GNP is increased by the spending.

Rather than reconstructing a stable economy, uncritical and unplanned government spending policy has reinforced the irrational production and consumption patterns of a capitalist system.

With government spending now restrained by the force of supply-side tax and expenditure cutting, it would be erroneous to conclude that government has ceased contributing to productive irrationality. By cutting corporate taxes and reducing other burdens on the private sector, encouragement of irrational production and investment decisions has shifted from the spending side of the government budget to the revenue side. The technique differs, but the outcome is the same: more socially useless goods and a more meaningless life for consumers and workers.

THE EMERGING CONTRADICTION

Overall, the past thirty years of public policy have heightened internal capitalist contradictions. The unequal distribution of benefits and losses has produced growing conflicts—big business versus little business, capital versus labor, worker versus worker, worker versus nonworker, and always, rich versus poor. And overarching everything is the mounting evidence that government cannot deliver on any of its promises of full employment, growth, and price stability.

The result is a growing public reaction against Liberal government. The temporary rise of worn-out laissez-faire economics, however, may have one positive effect: The Conservatives will reveal the class-biased nature of capitalism much more quickly. Consequently Americans may finally be willing to go beyond the narrow and oppressive economics of their past. When the Conservative ideology fails, as it must, and the Keynesian alternative remains discredited, we will be forced to consider an economic and social agenda we have evaded thus far. Under these circumstances, we will go beyond merely "stabilizing" the economy to reorganizing it and planning it so that oppression and irrationality no longer exist.

Government Deficits and Policy Choices

Does the Size of the Federal Debt Really Matter?

When national debts have once been accumulated to a certain degree, there is scarce, I believe, a single instance of their having been fairly and completely paid. The liberation of the public revenue, if it has ever been brought about at all, has always been brought about by a bankruptcy; sometimes by an avowed one, but always by a real one, though frequently by a pretended payment.

Adam Smith, The Wealth of Nations, *1776*

A decline in income due to a decline in the level of employment, if it goes far, may even cause consumption to exceed income not only by individuals and institutions using up the financial reserves which they have accumulated in better times, but also by Government, which will be liable, willingly or unwillingly, to run a budgetary deficit.

John Maynard Keynes, The General Theory of Employment, Interest, and Money, *1935*

My sum total of economic knowledge is Econ 101 and 102 when I went to college. I've listened to all the Nobel Prize winners for years but I still don't know how we can get along with $200 billion deficits.

Senator Robert Packwood, 1986

Consider the Gramm-Rudman Bill. . . . It is a brainless and gutless piece of legislation. Nearly every professional economist I know agrees with that.

Robert M. Solow, 1985

What about raising taxes? *Read my lips:* — — —

Presidential candidate George Bush, 1988

THE PROBLEM

Over the past six decades, majority economic and political thinking on the question of government deficits has undergone a 360-degree swing. The prevailing view in the early 1930s, which had been held as long as economists had been speaking out on the subject, was that government budgets should be balanced annually. Experience had shown that when governments financed spending by printing new money or by borrowing, general economic misfortunes such as inflation, currency devaluation, and general financial instability tended to follow. Ironically, FDR campaigned hard against Herbert Hoover in 1932, lambasting his "spendthrift" opponent for running deficits in the previous two years of depression.

The growing popularity of John Maynard Keynes's ideas in the 1930s and 1940s, along with the actual experience of watching budget deficits grow precisely as the economic gloom of depression receded, caused a shift in opinion. Few economists by the 1960s seriously advocated an annually balanced federal budget. A number talked about cyclically balanced budgets, in which expenditures and revenues should reach parity over a complete business cycle. The focus on the budget in such an approach was to use deficits to finance needed economic expansion while surpluses naturally accumulated during periods of prosperity. Clearly related to this view was "functional finance," which showed no real concern in any accounting sense for balance or imbalance at all but focused exclusively on using debts or surpluses as policy tools. To the functional finance theorists, there was no fundamental limitation on government's capacity to create and finance deficits, regardless of the size of the debt.

By the 1980s, the sudden explosion of the federal debt forced a change in majority economic thinking again. As Table 11.1 shows, both debt as a share of GNP and interest payments as a percent of GNP moved sharply upward. With debt and interest outlays on the debt growing faster than national output and also seeming to accompany an inflationary period of high unemployment and slow growth, many economists (mostly Conservatives at first but soon joined by many Liberals) began to believe that deficits did have an adverse effect on the general economy. Needless to say, Conservatives have been increasingly vulnerable to Liberal criticism on the debt and deficit issues. The Reagan-Bush administrations, irrespective of their official condemnation of deficits and their posturing

TABLE 11.1   Measures of the Federal Debt

Year	Public Debt (billions of current $)	Real Debt (billions of 1967 $)	Debt (% of GNP)	Interest (% of GNP)
1929	16.3	31.9	16	0.7
1940	50.9	121.2	51	1.1
1946	259.5	443.6	124	2.0
1960	290.9	327.9	57	1.2
1972	425.4	339.5	36	1.2
1976	619.3	363.3	36	1.7
1980	914.3	370.5	35	2.4
1982	1,140.9	394.6	37	2.7
1986	1,950.0	590.9	46	4.8
1990 (est.)	3,100.0	920.0	55	5.2

Source: Statistical Abstract of the United States, 1985, Economic Report of the President, 1990, and author's estimates.

on behalf of spending restraint on budget balance, ran up, in the 1980s, the greatest deficits in American history—nearly tripling the national debt (see Figure 11.1). To be sure, their defenders will correctly point out that Congress collaborated with the debt explosion too, but the irony of supposedly Conservative administrations being the most profligate is not lost on many observers.

In the mid-1980s, as annual deficits mounted, pressure built for passage of legal restraints on government's capacity to create debt. In its strongest form, this pressure expressed itself as a proposed constitutional amendment that would require annually balanced federal budgets. Whether or not such an amendment will ever be passed remains to be seen; however, Congress, responding to the popular pressure for budget balance and alarmed by its own, as well as the president's inability to slow the flood of red ink, passed its own version of budget balancing in late 1985. President Reagan quickly signed the Gramm-Rudman-Hollings Act into law. Under the act, a schedule was laid out for obtaining annual budget balance by 1991, with absolute deficit limits imposed beginning with the fiscal 1987 budget. Should budgets come in at higher-than-allowed deficits, the act called for arbitrary across-the-board cuts by the percentage of the excess deficit to all spending categories except social security.

FIGURE 11.1   Federal Budget Surplus or Deficit: 1935 to 1987

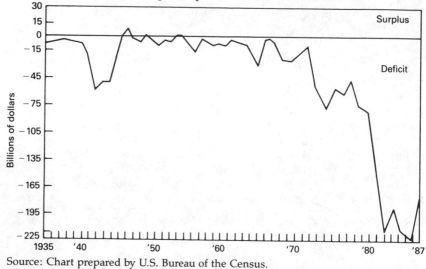

Source: Chart prepared by U.S. Bureau of the Census.

Few economists, Conservative or Liberal, expressed much satisfaction with Gramm-Rudman-Hollings' automatic, across-the-board cutting of spending to meet deficit targets. Indeed, even the constitutionality of the act was uncertain. Critics maintained Congress had acted in a cowardly fashion. Unable to decide politically *what* should be cut when the voting public seemed to be clamoring for *something* to be cut, Congress set up machinery to cut *everything* in equal proportions (except, of course, social security).

The Solomon-like wisdom of this approach to balancing budgets was certainly not economic logic—whatever the ideological paradigm—at its best. Conservatives worried about defense spending cuts and insufficient cuts in social spending. The distinct possibility that tax increases and not spending cuts would ultimately be used to meet deficit targets was another Conservative concern. Liberals and Radicals, on the other hand, saw the imposed cuts in social spending as "balancing the budget on the backs of the poor."

After passage of the Gramm-Rudman-Hollings act, the debt and deficit debate briefly cooled, but, following the Black Monday "meltdown" of the stock market on October 19, 1987, the debate reopened. Most postmortems of the securities market crash held that loss of investor faith was traceable to America's *double deficits*: the persistent federal deficit and the equally persistent deficit in international trade balances. However, as memory of Black Monday receded, so too did the urgency of the deficit issue; it got little attention in the Bush-Dukakis campaign of 1988. The deficit question, of course, didn't really go away. It merely waited in the wings during the Bush presidency, periodically appearing at center stage whenever taxation, budgetary, or spending debates boiled up in Congress or rose as an issue between Congress and the president. The final chapter is yet to be written. While there is fair agreement among all ideological shades that deficits do matter and that the heyday of "functional finance" is over, there is wide disagreement on the precise consequences of deficits, on their real significance, and on how they might be eliminated.

SYNOPSIS

Conservatives oppose government budget imbalance on the grounds that it is inherently destabilizing, producing inflation, rising interest rates, and reduced private investment. Furthermore, the discretionary nature of demand-management fiscal policy, which they see as the source of the rising debt, is singled out as particularly unwise. Liberals, although concerned with recent trends in debt growth (which they see as the result of Conservative management), generally view the debt as a tool of fiscal management. Radicals see the debt issue as a reflection of the economy's general inability to realize surplus value. They point not only to the growth of public debt to support this view but also to the even faster growth of private debt.

Anticipating the Arguments

- What is the logic of the Conservative argument that links budgetary deficits with inflationary pressures?
- Explain the Liberal argument that it isn't the size of the deficit that is important, but the way in which the deficit is acquired.
- Why do Radicals maintain that eliminating the deficit is *impossible*?

The Conservative Argument

If there is a particular gauge of the failure of demand-management policies, it must be the federal debt. The growth of the debt and a general indifference to this growth was, until comparatively recently, an aspect of Liberal doctrine that was scarcely ever criticized. Introductory economics textbooks devoted a few pages to discussion of federal debt but quickly moved on to other topics, leaving the distinct impression that "debt doesn't matter." In fact, the debt does matter. Not only is it the undesirable outcome of wrong policy choices, but annual operating deficits by the federal government and mounting aggregate debt also throttle an economy, encouraging inflation and general economic stagnation.

Although Liberals have little understanding of the real problems posed by growing deficits, they are quick to point out that much of the current federal debt was acquired during a Conservative presidency. The implication is that what Conservatives say on the debt question is really just "hot air." The charge is inaccurate and begs the evidence. Although the federal debt more than doubled during Reagan's years in office, this debt explosion was actually the result of pre-Reagan fiscal excesses and the reluctance of a Liberal Congress to cut federal spending. As much as ever, budget balance remains the central objective of Conservative fiscal thinking and the debt expansion during the Reagan presidency—whatever its sources—does not change this.

DEFICITS AS A SOURCE FOR INFLATION AND UNEMPLOYMENT

One of the more objectionable features of government's running high and persistent annual deficits is its inherent inflationary effect. When government spends more for goods and transfers than it collects in taxes, it increases the total demand for all goods produced in the economy. If an increase in the supply of goods equal to the increase in government-generated demand was instantaneously forthcoming, there would be no problem: more demand, more goods, prices unchanged. However, this is not how an economy works. Even in an underemployed economy capable of producing a greater output by simply adding productive resources, there is bound to be some *demand-pull* inflation as the existing output is bid upward in price. When the economy is operating near full-employment levels, as it was through most of the 1960s and the early 1970s, and when government is at the same time piling up large annual deficits, the demand-pull pressure on prices is very much greater. Approaching the outer limits of the society's actual productive ability, demand increases cannot by themselves raise production.

Apart from their demand effect, deficits also have an inflationary effect through the money supply. Deficits must, after all, be financed. Two options are open: Bonds may be sold to financial institutions and the general public (which creates its own special problems, as we shall presently see), or the Federal Reserve System may purchase the new securities and in turn increase the Treasury's account, providing the government with funds to pay its mounting bills. When the latter takes place, as it will when the Fed attempts to complement an expansionary fiscal policy with an accommodative (and expansionary) monetary policy, new money is created.

To comprehend the effect of monetizing the debt, we need simply understand the traditional explanation of inflation: "too many dollars chasing too few goods."

The long-term growth of output and employment in any economy depends on the society's utilization of resources. Prices are nothing more than the measure by which money is exchanged for commodities. Accordingly, the general tendency of prices in any society will be determined by changes in the stock of money available for transactions. The stock of money, of course, must increase or decrease as the general level of economic output expands or contracts. A relative decrease in money stock compared to output must produce general price reductions. A money expansion rate above the rate of increase in output will lead to price expansion. Quite simply, more money does not and cannot by itself create more goods. Instead, it will be spent on the available goods at higher prices.

This analysis of the fundamental cause of inflation is amply supported by evidence. Every significant inflationary episode in U.S. history has followed excessive growth in the supply of money. However, neither logic nor the evidence has succeeded in deflecting modern state policy from pursuing an inflationary course. As we indicated in our discussions of stabilization policy and unemployment, public policy has been committed too long to the Keynesian belief that high levels of output can be created and maintained by manipulating aggregate demand. Through the 1960s and 1970s, deficits were the intended outcome of fiscal policy. Their excess demand effects were enlarged as the Fed, often pursuing an easy money policy, monetized the deficits.

Eventually, the economy was seized by an inflationary episode it could not control. The sequence of events producing the stagflation of the mid- and late 1970s should be carefully understood. The Conservative analysis of how underlying economic forces are affected runs as follows: The immediate impact of expansionary monetary and fiscal policy will probably be to induce new business investment and additional consumer spending. Thus an increase in output and employment may occur. However, the expansion is only temporary at best. Tricked by a sudden increase in earnings, businesses and consumers have overspent and overborrowed. While money income has risen, their "real" situation has not improved; indeed, it has probably worsened if they have overspent. Over time, however, people learn. Anticipated discretionary actions by monetary and fiscal authorities merely induce businesses and consumers, who are not stupid after all, to take any action they see fit to protect themselves. Their *rational expectations* negate the impact of the authorities' policies. Expansion of the money supply over time no longer stimulates economic expansion (even temporarily); it merely fuels demand inflation without any employment benefits. In fact, unemployment gets worse. The situation is a bit like a kitten chasing its tail. Excess demand inflation (aided by other Liberal tinkerings with the market) lowers real income and demand for goods, which in turn lower employment. More economic intervention is therefore required to offset these employment losses. This in turn generates more inflationary pressures, which consequently lead to more unemployment. The more the kitten tries to catch its tail, the faster it must run.

CROWDING OUT: THE IMPACT OF DEFICITS ON INVESTMENT AND BUSINESS

As noted earlier, the monetary authorities do have an option other than monetizing the debt. They can sell new government bonds, financing government's deficit spending out of private savings. While this is certainly less inflationary, it has equally undesirable effects. When government goes into funds markets as a borrower, it competes with private borrowers. With increased competition among all borrowers—government as well as private seekers of investment funds—interest rates (the price of borrowing) are pushed upward. For business borrowers, the cost of obtaining funds rises. The result is to *crowd out* some private business investment that would otherwise have taken place at a lower interest rate.

The magnitude of the crowding out effect is a matter of some debate. A few economists hold that a dollar of government borrowing squeezes out a dollar of private investment. But even if the outcome is much smaller, government borrowing adversely affects the productive base of the economy, which is, after all, the real determinant of output and employment.

DEFICITS AND TRADE BALANCES

By the early 1980s, it was apparent that the high and rising federal deficits had yet another undesirable consequence: They were adversely affecting our international trade position. We shall examine this problem in detail in Issue 15, so a brief outline here will suffice.

Through the 1970s and early 1980s, accompanying both the deficits and the deficit-generated inflationary pressures, was a steady upward push in interest rates. From the perspective of lenders around the world, the comparatively high American interest rates made investment in all kinds of U.S. securities highly desirable. Indeed, a large portion of the new government bond issues, floated to finance the swelling debt, were purchased abroad. To buy American securities, it was essential to obtain American dollars. The resulting demand for dollars pushed upward the price of our currency vis-à-vis other world currencies. With a strong and strengthening dollar (some would call it an overvalued dollar), American goods sold at relatively higher prices in foreign markets, while foreign goods sold relatively inexpensively in our own domestic markets. With imports rising and exports falling, the balance of trade turned decidedly against the United States.

While it is not accurate to lay all our trade problems at the deficit door, it is obvious that insofar as deficit spending and deficit financing have an upward effect on interest rates, they helped create an artificially strong dollar, which translated directly into a worsening international trade position.

DEFICITS DO MATTER

From the foregoing arguments, it should be clear that deficits have an extraordinary impact on the contemporary economy. Paradoxically, they bring about the opposite of their intended effects. Rather than leading to a demand-powered expansion of output and employment, as Liberals have long claimed, they lead in the other direction toward inflation, rising interest rates, dwindling investment, and ultimately to lower levels of output and employment. Given the political nature of many of the economic decisions that increase government spending and deficits, it is difficult to create a balanced budget through the normal legislative budgetary process. Far too many powerful voting interests have personal stakes in keeping spending high and thus keeping deficits high. Too many candidates for high political office have learned that the briefly stimulative effects of a "political fiscal policy" that pumps up demand just before election time can assure victory at the polls.

The only solution is to establish a firm set of rules with regard to government finance. The passage of a constitutional amendment requiring annual budget balance, except in times of war and extreme national emergency, would end the abuses of discretionary fiscal policy and expedient political decision making that combine to create chronic deficits and bring on economic instability.

The Liberal Argument

Despite the fact that the Reagan years, when Conservative policy influence was at its greatest, saw the near tripling of the federal debt, Conservatives still hold to the view that deficits are a profoundly evil economic undertaking. Nevertheless, they are right in stressing that "deficits do matter." What they do not seem to understand, however, is that they matter in *how* and *why* they come into being in the first place. *Some deficits matter much more than others.*

PUTTING THE SIZE OF THE DEBT IN PERSPECTIVE

The recent focus on the deficit problem has been stimulated by public concern for both the size and the growth of the public debt. However, it is important to understand what the numbers really say. As Table 11.1 indicated, the *real* (or constant dollar) growth of the debt before its explosion during the Reagan years was substantially less than its *nominal* (or current dollar) growth. In constant dollars, the debt was about the same in 1981 as it had been at the end of World War II. As a percent of GNP, total debt was vastly smaller in 1981 than in 1946. Thus the argument that the growth of the debt was altering the American economic landscape is not very convincing, since the so-called spendthrift 1960s and 1970s did not have any impact on the real (as opposed to the nominal or dollar) level of federal debt.

The other misplaced emphasis of the Conservative argument, with regard to pre-Reagan debt accumulations, is to view the debt as a cause rather than the result of general economic conditions. The simple fact is that a troubled economy produces deficits, not vice versa.

UNDERSTANDING WHERE THE DEBT COMES FROM

Conservative analyses of deficits make little effort to distinguish among different sources or causes of a given deficit. Actually two major but quite different causes for the federal government's running a deficit are identifiable. First, there are deficits that are directly the result of a general economic slump. When recession strikes, government revenues decrease as taxable income falls, but expenditures rise automatically as larger numbers of the public begin drawing unemployment benefits and various other transfer payments (including subsidies to business) grow. Even if additional expenditures were not made, a gap between revenues and expenditures would develop since government outlays were planned before the slump and were based on anticipated revenues. This is called a *cyclical budget deficit*. It is estimated that every time the unemployment rate rises by one percentage point in a recession, the loss of revenues and the automatic rise in outlays create a $40 to $50 billion revenue-expenditure gap.

A second, and quite different, source of debt growth may come from a *structural budget deficit*. Structural deficits arise from some discretionary redirection of fiscal policy—the passage of a tax cut (decreasing revenue collections) or the introduction of a huge public works or military spending program (increasing outlays), for instance. Structural deficits may develop as the result of either wise or unwise policy-making. They may also result from external conditions over which policymakers have no (or very little) control, as in the case of World War II and Vietnam spending.

With a little reflection, it should be obvious that it is essential to know whether a given deficit is the result of cyclical or structural events. Clearly, an attempt to balance a budget in a period of cyclical downturn—either by raising taxes or by reducing government outlays to the needy—is both economic and political foolishness that could make downturns worse and destabilize political institutions. In failing to distinguish between types of deficits and in persistently calling for a constitutional amendment requiring a balanced budget, Conservatives are proposing the most destructive possible approach to government budgeting.

While Conservatives oppose all deficits, it is obvious that most of their attack is directed against structural deficits because they feel any manipulation of government revenues and expenditures for the purpose of demand management is wrong. Their conclusion is easily stated: Deficits, purely and simply, cause inflation and discourage investment. That judgment, however, is not unequivocally supported by theory or empirical evidence.

Consider an economy that has slumped into recession. A structural deficit acquired when an economy is undergoing a cyclical downturn or when substantial underemployment of available resources exists need not create demand-powered inflation. The expansion of total demand resulting from a consciously developed structural deficit under these conditions can put the unemployed back to work and reemploy unused productive capacity without excessively bidding up wage and resource prices. This was the case in the early and mid-1960s. The moderate deficits of the Kennedy and Johnson years (before Vietnam War spending generated demand-inflation pressures) lowered unemployment and stimulated the economy without pumping up prices. Moreover, as we noted in the last issue, most of the inflationary pressure that built up in the late 1970s came not from the demand side and government deficits but from supply-side shocks and cost-push inflationary effects. The Conservative view that all inflation results from excess demand and that government deficits are the primary source for excess demand is just not supported if the events of the 1970s are honestly reported and evaluated.

Structural deficits do not necessarily and under all conditions discourage or "crowd out" private investment demand that might otherwise be forthcoming. If crowding out exists at all, it can take place only when an economy is near full employment and is utilizing virtually all of a fixed stock of investable funds. At any point below this level, "crowding in" is a much greater likelihood, with private investment rising as expansionary fiscal policy puts unemployed resources back to work. As output rises, new investment opportunities develop; they do not disappear.

Conservative logic is empirically contradicted by recent events when Conservatives were having their own way with budget making. Following Conservative reasoning, the enormous deficits following their "supply-side" tax cuts in 1981 that were not matched by spending reductions should have generated enormous inflationary pressures. With the largest structural deficits in American history, we might also have expected the greatest price inflation. In actuality, prices did not rise very much. As any good Keynesian would have predicted, the economy expanded, and the cyclical deficit actually shrank.

Given an understanding of the foregoing points, Liberals are not about to cave in to Conservative and popular pressures and dispatch deficit spending to the junkyard of ill-conceived economic policies. Quite to the contrary of Conservative allegations, Liberals have always believed that deficits matter. They matter precisely because, when well planned and executed, they provide an important tool of economic management. However, Liberals also believe that deficits matter when they are piled up as the result of badly executed policies. The defense of deficit spending under certain conditions can in no way be extended to defend the deficits of the Reagan-Bush years.

THE REAGAN DEBT FAILURE AND THE
BALANCED BUDGET ARGUMENT EXAMINED

The so-called Reagan deficits need to be examined for a number of reasons. First of all, what was their impact on the economy? And second, how did these deficits differ from the deficit spending that Liberals are willing to defend?

Regarding the first question, it is obvious that the loose fiscal policy of the Reagan years did not reflect a very rational approach to macroeconomic management. The near-tripling of the federal debt over eight years did power the economy out of the 1981–1983 recession, but unevenly and with lingering, troublesome side effects. This occurred because Reagan's fiscal policies lacked a clear focus and were uncoordinated with monetary policy. As the federal budget was hemorrhaging from supply-side tax cuts, the administration encouraged a tight monetary policy to keep down the expected inflationary pressures. The effect was a bit like driving a car by depressing the accelerator and the brake at the same time. The car might move with some degree of control, but the equipment is being worn out. Suddenly it became apparent that as recession lifted and prices held steady, a new problem had arisen. The higher interest rates resulting from the tight money policy had created a very strong dollar (that is, the high return on U.S. dollars put the dollar in great demand relative to other world currencies). As other currency values fell relative to the dollar, dollars bought more foreign goods, and domestically produced goods, denominated in dollars, cost more when sold overseas and paid for in cheaper foreign currencies. (We shall examine this problem in more detail in Issue 15.)

Conservatives maintain that the high interest policy was the direct result of deficits and deficit-inspired inflation. That is true only insofar as a high interest rate policy was the ill-chosen Conservative reaction to the nonexistent problem of deficit-inspired inflation. Conservatives had themselves to blame for a strong dollar and the resulting damage it caused to the economy. Ironically, under Conservative mismanagement, the nation succeeded in acquiring two very large deficits—the exploding federal debt and an international trade deficit. Paradoxically, the latter deficit served to negate many of the potentially positive effects of the former. The stimulative gains of an expansionary fiscal policy (even if it was a fiscal policy Conservatives didn't want or understand) were offset by demand leakages resulting from a flood of foreign goods into American markets.

Whether the Conservative deficits were well planned or not is, of course, not the critical question. Nor is it really the first question we should ask. The question that reveals the truly important differences between Liberal and Conservative approaches to deficits is: Why would Conservatives, who advocate budget balance, ever become associated with the greatest debt explosion in American history?

To unravel the question we need only remember the sources of the expanding deficit, the sequence of events that produced it, and the ultimate objectives of Conservative macroeconomic policy. The source of the Reagan deficit is no mystery. It resulted from two developments that were a critical part of the Conservative program and, when put in place, were bound to create a highly irrational fiscal strategy. As noted earlier, structural deficits could result from well-conceived programs or from wrongheadedness. In the case of the Reagan program, the wrongheadedness is abundantly clear.

The first part of the Reagan fiscal policy produced the personal and business tax cuts of 1981–1983 and a gaping hemorrhage on the revenue side of the budget. The second part of the strategy was the incredible expansion of federal outlays resulting from a 50 percent or greater annual increase in military spending. Although social spending and entitlement programs (for example, social security) are usually singled out as the cause of growing debts, the charge obscures the fact that these programs, under the heaviest budget-cutting pressures, have shrunk as a share of the federal budget.

But wasn't the deficit-expanding effect of cutting taxes and raising spending understood? The answer is yes. It appears that the deficits were acquired by design. Only by making deficits and the size of the debt obnoxious would it be possible eventually to cap deficit spending with a balanced budget amendment. The sequence of events leading to two trillion dollars of red ink should be understood. *First*, the tax cuts were obtained. *Second*, in the name of defense, military spending was increased. *Third*, growing deficits were accomplished. By giving people something good first—a tax cut and an improved defense posture—it became obvious that the only way the good things could be kept and not have the bad effects of deficits was to cut deeply into government social programs.

Some will say this is ascribing too much perversity and manipulativeness to Conservative politicians and economists. But it is the only explanation that makes sense if ultimate policy goals are to both shrink the size of government and neutralize fiscal policy by requiring a balanced budget. In other words, the Reagan red ink was not accidental nor inherited but purposely created to frighten the nation into accepting a smaller, neutralized role for government in the economy.

As of this writing, it remains to be seen if the strategy has worked. Opinion polls indicate strong public support for a balanced budget amendment, and Congress has targeted the early 1990s for requiring annual budget balance. From the Liberal point of view there is much to worry about. As we pointed out in the last issue, neutralization of federal fiscal policy would return us to being tossed about willy-nilly by the business cycle. Instead of being able to lean against the winds of cyclical change, government would be required by constitutional law to push in the same direction. Taxes would rise and government spending would fall precisely when demand increases would be needed to offset a slump. And it is at least theoretically possible that an economic expansion could become an inflationary episode as increased tax collections are used to finance greater-than-needed public expenditures. For most Liberals, a legally required balanced budget is a leap back in time to an earlier, Neanderthal era of economic thinking.

The Radical Argument

As we discussed in the previous two issues, the current stage of capitalist crisis may be distinguished from previous crises by the central role government has come to play in the economy. The other side of the past six decades' efforts to use government both as an agent to make up chronic deficiencies in the demand for goods and to lower business production costs has been the steady increase of government deficits. The current deficit crisis and the problems it imposes serve as a measure of the failure of the belief that the normal stagnation tendencies of capitalism can be corrected by government actions.

REACHING THE OUTER LIMITS
OF POLICY MANAGEMENT

Keynesians, as we have seen, perceived that the capitalist system could continue to obtain profits only so long as the demand for goods was sustained at high levels. Doubters simply disappeared as the levels of demand were pumped up first by World War II deficit spending and later by the deficits of the 1960s. Rather than competing with

TABLE 11.2   Government in the Economy, 1903–1989

Year	GNP (billions of dollars)	All Government Spending (billions of dollars)	Government Spending as a Percent of GNP
1903	23.0	1.7	7.4
1913	40.0	3.1	7.7
1929	103.4	10.3	9.9
1939	90.8	17.6	19.4
1949	258.0	59.3	22.9
1959	486.5	131.0	26.9
1969	944.0	256.8	30.4
1979	2,417.8	750.8	31.1
1989	5,233.2	1778.4	33.9

Source: Economic Report of the President, 1990.

the private sector, as classical and neoclassical theory held, government spending (by all levels of government) reduced the pressures of
chronic unemployment and excess capacity. It absorbed output and
made the private realization of surplus value possible. As Table 11.2
shows, both the absolute magnitude of this spending and government outlays as a share of GNP have continued to grow. Absorbing a
mere 7.4 percent of national output in 1903, the government now
accounts for more than one-third of the GNP. As we saw in the previous two issues, the expansion of government spending did slow the
system's deterioration into crisis for a while, and although it seemed
to work, no one talked much about government deficits. But by the
late 1970s, deficits were seen as a source of trouble.

Of course, the trouble is that government spending in general
and deficits in particular increase demand, but at the same time raise
costs to businesses, squeezing their profits. As we saw in the last two
issues, the expansionary fiscal policy of the 1960s triggered upward
pressures on the prices of resources and on wages. The present Conservative effort (and the efforts of some Liberals) to focus on these bad
effects of activist fiscal policy and its resulting deficits merely reflects
a redirection of American policy thinking away from the "demand
solution" toward searches for a "cost solution" for sustaining profits.
It does not represent a theoretical breakthrough for capitalism.

The recent flurry of interest in Conservative supply-side solutions to the capitalist problem is revealing for two reasons. First of all, the demand-oriented policies of the Keynesian era have finally run their course. Government spending must be financed either out of growing deficits or by rising tax collections. The former method is inflationary and is severely testing the limits of the financial structure to carry the burden of debt, especially since the private sector is expanding its borrowing even more swiftly than government. The latter method pushes the taxpayer to the wall. At any rate, both inflation and rising taxes as ways of financing growing government spending are no longer acceptable policy alternatives. The capitalist system, consequently, has reached the limits of fiscal expansionism as a device for realizing surplus value.

Second, the supply-side approach is a bold and naked effort to pick up the pieces of the demand-side failure. The supply-side actions to cut social spending and to end heavy taxation of the rich and giant corporations are nothing more than an effort to maintain corporate profits by reducing the well-being of practically everyone but the very wealthy. The supply-sider wants not only to reduce taxes and social spending, but also to roll back wages, permit monopoly power, and end consumer, job, and environmental protection. All such programs, it is argued, interfere with businesses' ability to invest, expand, and make profits. Of course, the supply-siders are right: Business does need greater freedom (read: "ability to exploit") if it is to survive the growing profit squeeze. But if business survives this way, many people will not.

Yet there remains an irony in the supply-side emphasis on the "cost" effects of maintaining high levels of aggregate demand. Like a junkie hooked on drugs, giving up government deficits is difficult, probably impossible, regardless of the degree of human discomfort we are willing to impose on the general population. The fact is that enormous amounts of government spending are not demand-based at all but are directed toward the cost side. Spending has grown in a number of ways that are clearly aimed at lowering business operating costs and expanding profits. Military spending, taking up a third of all federal outlays, is, among other things, a kind of subsidy to many very large American corporations. Meanwhile, building highways, subsidizing education, even taking up most of the costs of maintaining adequate retirement and health programs for the elderly, which firms might have to pay for if social security did not, all have the effect of lowering business costs. Thus even Conservatives committed to balanced budgets have little real-world success in lowering government expenditures and balancing budgets. To make the irony a bit clearer: Like a junkie, the economy needs fiscal fixes to get high, but also it needs them just to stay even.

THE MISPLACED FOCUS ON FEDERAL DEFICITS

The attention directed by both Liberals and Conservatives to the size and growth of the federal debt, predictable as it may be, obscures the real problems of the system, of which the debt, like the growth of government in general, is only a symptom.

By looking only at the federal deficit, we are deflected from looking at other types of borrowing. The result is a misleading impression because the federal debt amounts to only a small part of total borrowing in the United States, which includes consumer debt, mortgage debt, corporate debt, and state and local government debt as well. In fact, in 1989, federal debt, even with its explosion in the 1980s, amounted to less than 15 percent of all outstanding debt. Since borrowing by consumers, businesses, and other government units has precisely the same result as federal borrowing in powering demand, the emphasis on the federal share of debt is especially myopic. More to the point, as Table 11.3 illustrates, between 1960 and 1980, the period most frequently cited by Conservatives as that in which federal debt expansion first created and then fueled a destructive inflationary spiral, the federal debt grew more slowly than any other component of the nation's total debt. While Conservatives are essentially correct in arguing that borrowing creates "too many dollars chasing too few goods" and thus, sooner or later, inflationary pressures, they focus on only one small slice of the debt pie. Even if the federal budget were balanced, it would not halt the debt-driven growth of demand.

The Conservative view that federal deficits must be brought under control (a position also supported by many Liberals—though usually for quite different reasons) focuses only on the "too many dollars" aspect of the problem. These theorists do not understand that doing the reverse of what seems to cause inflation or raise interest rates will not necessarily result in relatively falling prices and interest rates. The fact is that tightening up on debts (federal as well as other)

TABLE 11.3   Outstanding American Debt, 1960–1989 (in billions of dollars)

Year	Consumer Debt	Mortgage Debt	Corporate Debt	State and Local Government Debt	Federal Debt	GNP
1960	65	207	939	70	284	515
1965	103	333	1349	100	313	705
1970	143	474	2084	144	371	1016
1975	223	802	3444	220	533	1598
1980	385	1446	5471	336	907	2732
1985	592	2303	9400	569	1821	4015
1989	772	3453	12,000*	720*	2931	5233
change, 1960–1980	590%	698%	583%	480%	319%	430%
change, 1980–1989	101%	139%	119%	114%	224%	92%
change, 1960–1989	1087%	1568%	1178%	928%	932%	916%

*Estimated
Source: *Statistical Abstract of the United States, 1989,* and *Economic Report of the President, 1990.*

will reduce the number of dollars chasing goods. However, as we saw in the late 1970s and early 1980s (Issue 9), it does not necessarily reduce price pressures. True, rising demand may bid up prices initially, but prices may stay up as a result of businesses continuing old and inefficient (high cost per unit of production) operations. After all, reducing demand by lowering federal deficits will not necessarily signal to business an impending improvement in general economic conditions. It will not induce them to modernize their production operations and lower their costs by taking on additional investments. There would be little point in adding plant and equipment that might not be used precisely because demand was being restricted. Only by bringing the economy virtually to its knees, through a deep recession that created enormous excess capacity, was the strong upward pressure on prices halted in the early 1980s. When "few" dollars are chasing whatever goods are available, it is elemental that prices must and do come down.

Government, with its persistent expansion of debt, must be seen for what it really is — simply one aspect of the fundamental contradiction that challenges a capitalist, production-for-profit economy. The recurring crisis of production outstripping consumption has not ceased in our time. This tendency has merely taken new forms, with the contradiction manifesting itself in the battle over government budgets and fiscal and monetary policy. Indeed, the modern capitalist state is a proxy for capitalism itself. The state budget is the battleground among contending groups in the capitalist economy.

Yet it is a battleground on which victory is unobtainable. We have learned over the past six decades that when overproduction appears (or demand lags), as it periodically does, we may offset it by increasing demand (through government and private borrowing). Indeed, a measure of our reliance upon debt to "float" the economy is illustrated in Table 11.3: Every category of debt, public and private, has grown faster since 1960 than national output (GNP). We have also learned that increasing demand raises costs to firms by stimulating wage and resource price increases. The only cure to the resulting inflation is a full-blown economic slump that will force wages and costs down, a slump that is very likely deeper and more protracted than would have occurred if demand had not been stimulated in the first place.

In conclusion then, Radicals are not confused about what federal deficits are or what they can and cannot do. First of all, deficits are not the problem. Second, and herein resides an important irony, neither deficits nor budget balancing offers any long-run solution to the chronic problems of a production-for-profit economic system.

Unemployment

Are We Overstating the Problem of Joblessness?

Once I built a railroad, made it run
Made it race against time
Once I built a railroad, now its done
Brother can you spare a dime?

Popular song by Jay Gorney, 1932

Capitalism forms an industrial reserve army that belongs to capital quite as absolute as if the latter had bred it at its own cost. Independently of the limits of the actual increase of population, it . . . creates a mass of human material always ready for exploitation.

Karl Marx, 1867

The damage that high unemployment does to economic efficiency is enormous and inadequately appreciated. By contrast, the harm inflation inflicts on the economy is often exaggerated.

Alan S. Blinder, 1987

THE PROBLEM

Time was, not so very long ago, when economists and politicians talked earnestly and knowingly about *full employment*. That was, of course, before the inflationary binge of the late 1970s displaced unemployment as the nation's number one problem. It was before extensive changes in the American industrial structure caused wholesale layoffs as well as hiring stagnation in our heavy industrial base. And, it was before we became accustomed to a much higher unemployment rate as the "normal" state of economic affairs. Probably the last official reference to full employment was the passage of the Humphrey-Hawkins Full Employment and Balanced Growth Act of 1978. That now-forgotten act targeted full employment as 4 percent unemployment and mandated the target to be obtained through appropriate government policy by 1983. As Figure 12.1 indicates, a 4 percent unemployment target was not unreasonable by the standards of the 1950s and 1960s, but, good years and bad, we have never had less than 5 percent unemployed since 1973 and have actually averaged about 7.5 percent since the passage of Humphrey-Hawkins. Small wonder that the average reader is not likely to have much familiarity with this act. Indeed, within a year of its passage, its targets were "postponed" until 1988, and were forgotten altogether during the Reagan-Bush presidencies.

Rather than focusing on full-employment targets, we have begun worrying about chronic unemployment. Yet for all of the attention the unemployment rates of the last two decades have received, there is little consensus in the economics profession on appropriate strategies to deal with the problem.

The conventional economic analysis of unemployment as it has been taught for many decades in introductory economics courses starts by identifying three very different unemployment categories: frictional unemployment, cyclical unemployment, and structural unemployment.

Frictional unemployment arises mostly from the normal movement of new workers or the reentry of older workers into the labor force, as well as the largely voluntary employment shifts that occur as workers move from job to job according to their own desires. As might be expected, most economists do not view frictional joblessness as much of a problem because few of the unemployed actually fall into this category and also because such unemployment is really considered the by-product of a free labor market. *Cyclical unemployment*, which has been the focus of most

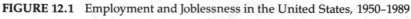

FIGURE 12.1   Employment and Joblessness in the United States, 1950–1989

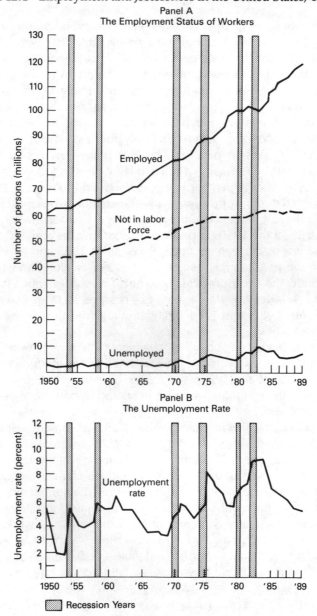

Source: Economic Report of the President, 1990.

of our references to unemployment so far, is joblessness as a direct consequence of a downturn in general business conditions. As an economy undergoes contraction, such as during the Great Depression or ordinary business recessions, the demand for goods falls, and with it the demand for labor. This "lack-of-demand" unemployment can be cured—either through public policy efforts that might rejuvenate the economy or through the ordinary improvement of economic conditions.

Structural unemployment is caused by changes in the fundamental conditions that undergird labor markets, when there is a mismatch between the supply of available labor at its existing skill levels *and* the demand for such labor. It is most frequently associated with such developments as the introduction of automated production methods, the elimination of jobs due to changes in skill requirements, the permanent decline of an industry, or the geographic relocation of jobs within a firm or industry (domestically or internationally). Until comparatively recently, structural unemployment was not considered to be a long-term problem because economic theory, as well as real-world experience, showed that labor markets would sooner or later readjust. Previously useful, but now redundant, labor would simply suffer a fall in wages until it could again be profitably employed at its former rates (if, indeed, that was possible) or the labor itself would move from low-demand to high-demand employment situations. All of this was expected to take place within the context of a naturally increasing demand for labor that a growing economy would generate. For example, we did not worry at the time nor have we worried since about what happened to carriage makers who lost their jobs as the result of the rise of the auto industry. However, by the 1960s, it was becoming apparent that structural unemployment was neither as temporary nor as self-correcting as theory and historical experience suggested.

Of the three types of unemployment, cyclical unemployment has usually been considered the principal cause for joblessness. With the coming of Keynesian analysis, there briefly blossomed (as we explained from a slightly different perspective in Issues 9 and 10) the notion that unemployment could be cured—and full employment created—by the introduction of appropriate countercyclical policy. However, even Liberals backed off from this position when they were confronted with the high unemployment rates of the 1980s. Cyclical, or lack-of-demand, explanations of joblessness in the middle and late 1980s made little sense when the economy was prospering and undergoing the longest peacetime expansion in its history.

This situation raised numerous questions. If, through the process of logical elimination, we are left with only structural explanations for our current unemployment, what precisely is it in the structure of labor markets that has changed over time to cause this condition? Are the structural changes susceptible to policy solutions? Are we better served by allowing the structural conditions to work themselves out? Indeed, is it possible that we are making too much of our current unemployment problems?

SYNOPSIS

Conservatives see the present unemployment problem as largely the result of government efforts to manage labor markets. They therefore advocate minimum government involvement as the only long-run solution to joblessness. Liberal arguments hold that much of our current unemployment is beyond the reach of usual stabilization policy tools. Thus new and enlarged job programs are necessary to remove the "structural" limitations of the economy that have created chronic unemployment. For Radicals, unemployment is characteristic of capitalism, a natural outgrowth of the system's tendency to produce surplus labor.

Anticipating the Arguments

- How, according to Conservatives, have government actions increased unemployment?
- What do Liberals mean by "structural unemployment," and how would they cure it?
- Why do Radicals believe that high levels of unemployment are characteristic of a capitalist system?

The Conservative Argument

From the Conservative point of view, unemployment is logically unnecessary. In an economy left to its own devices, involuntary unemployment can result only from short-run market readjustments. Over the long term, as prices, wages, and output adjust, there is work for all at wages commensurate with their productive contributions. Individuals who value their labor higher than the market does, higher than its actual contribution to output, or who simply prefer leisure to work may be jobless; however, their unemployment is voluntary and not a fundamental problem demanding policymakers' attention. At least, this would be the situation if labor markets were free of the interventions or "stickiness" and inefficiencies that abound in a world of Liberal social engineering, powerful labor unions, big government, and popular expectations that individuals have the right to a certain level of wages irrespective of these individuals' actual contributions to production. Alas, however, the Conservative critique of "the unemployment problem" must begin with the world as it is.

A RISING "NATURAL RATE OF UNEMPLOYMENT"

At all times, a "natural rate of unemployment" exists. By definition, this natural rate is more or less equal to the sum of the frictional and structural unemployment in the economy at any particular time. It is the minimum unemployment level consistent with price stability. Any effort to lower existing "natural rate" joblessness would trigger inflationary wage and price pressures (because efforts to raise demand for workers will not create jobs for the frictionally or structurally unemployed but *will* bid up the wages of those presently employed).

Looked at this way, the natural rate of unemployment—what some economists consider "full-employment unemployment"—is principally determined by structural conditions within the economy that affect the matching up of labor demand and labor supply. Of course, in an idealized economic world, in which wages and prices are perfectly flexible and workers are perfectly free to go wherever they desire in search of work, the natural rate would always tend to be near zero.

In our era, the natural rate of unemployment has been rising, perhaps to as much as 7 or 8 percent of the labor force currently. The source of the problem is not really surprising, and it certainly is not proof that "capitalism doesn't work." Rather it reflects how our economic system has been adversely affected by a variety of measures originally intended to improve on the market economy's performance. The natural rate of unemployment is high and rising because prices and wages *are not* flexible and because labor *is not* very mobile.

The lack of wage flexibility and labor mobility are the results of past Liberal efforts to intervene in the economy. However, presently concerned about rising "chronic" unemployment, they propose elaborate solutions that will guarantee greater unemployment and greater resource misallocation. To see the point, we need only examine a few of their past efforts.

THE RECORD OF A FAILED EMPLOYMENT POLICY

To understand how labor markets have been made less mobile and less flexible and therefore characterized by a rising natural rate of unemployment, we shall look at four areas of Liberal tinkering: support of unions, social legislation, antidiscrimination efforts, and actions to offset technological displacements.

Liberal support for labor unions in this century, while benefiting some workers, has cost many their jobs. Unions, by instinct and design, restrict the number of jobs as they force wages up for their members. The older craft unions specifically used the tactic of exclusion in forcing higher wages. By having long periods of apprenticeship and limiting the number of apprentices, unions in the building trades, for instance, purposely reduced the supply of available labor. This kept carpenters', masons', and hod carriers' wages up, but it also kept large numbers of would-be workers out of the labor force. Large industrial unions also reduce employment. By imposing on management an industry wage that is higher than would otherwise prevail in a free labor market, the industry's total demand for labor is reduced. The union succeeds in keeping the wages of its members high, but unemployment — among union and nonunion workers — is increased.

Legally mandated social legislation also depresses employment. Ironically, many of those programs aimed specifically at the poorest and least secure workers have worsened rather than improved their lot. For instance, Liberals invariably cite the passage of minimum-wage laws as one of their greatest triumphs; yet such laws have probably had the largest negative impact on employment of all of their social engineering endeavors. Setting minimum-wage rates above a market-determined wage has two immediate effects. First, more individuals enter the labor market, now willing to work at the higher wage, whereas before they opted for leisure. Second, the number of jobs available is reduced because employers cut back their hiring. Whereas minimum-wage legislation has been defended by Liberals as a boon to the less skilled workers, it has actually had the opposite effect. The least skilled jobs, those with the lowest marginal contribution to a firm's earnings, must be the first eliminated as the result of raising the minimum-wage floor. Thus part-time employment for teenagers and unskilled factory work for women and minorities have declined as the minimum wage advanced.*

Two other popular pieces of social legislation—unemployment insurance and social security—illustrate various ways that well-intended proworker efforts raise the natural rate of unemployment. With greatly improved unemployment benefits, the pain of joblessness is cushioned. However, the benefits also serve to subsidize and, therefore, extend the period of search for a new job. They also invite entry of some workers into the labor force purely to obtain the benefits. Social security, meanwhile, works in a slightly different way to increase joblessness. With employers required to pay half of the contributions, social security amounts, from an employer's point of view, to a job tax and a hiring disincentive.

Regarding antidiscrimination actions, one example of how an imposed hiring and remuneration policy can increase unemployment should suffice. Consider the recent "comparable pay for comparable work" argument. According to this doctrine, jobs traditionally filled by women and paying low wages would be priced upward toward wage levels of allegedly "similar" jobs traditionally filled by men. This is the most recent Liberal and Radical delusion about how to cure "discrimination." Never mind that there is no other mechanism than the market itself to determine "worth"; reformers plan to impose wages on the basis of their own views of equity. The result, if such a program is actually developed, will be to increase unemployment because many workers' wages will simply be greater than the value of their contributions to the firm. In the end women are likely to be the real losers.

Discrimination may exist in the larger society, but free markets are the ultimate destroyer of such a practice. The reason is simple: Employers who discriminate, thereby excluding certain elements

*Admittedly, in recent years, the minimum-wage law has actually had the effect of increasing the number of jobs, but not because of its authors' intentions. With the minimum wage constant at $3.35 per hour since 1981 and with the real value of this wage falling as price levels rose, the minimum wage, as a benchmark for minimum hiring rates, fell. This served to keep real wage rates lower. But this was not the case in the 1950s, 1960s, and early 1970s. And most important, it will not be the case in the future because we have moved once again to raise the minimum wage.

of the work force (minorities or women, for instance) from certain jobs, reduce their supply of available labor. This reduction in labor supply drives up their labor costs and diminishes their profitability. The market takes no prisoners when irrational choices lead to non-economic outcomes.

The fourth area to consider is Liberal tinkering to cushion job losses from technological progress. Periodic and quite natural shifts in the economy's structure produce short-run unemployment from time to time. Buggy makers do not become auto workers overnight, and auto workers cannot immediately be transformed into computer specialists. However, it is possible to make a temporarily bad employment situation permanently worse. Recent declining employment in the old, moribund basic industries—steel, automobiles, and farm machinery, for instance—has encouraged Liberals to call for special aid programs for the hard-hit industrial centers of the Northeast and Midwest and for direct aid to the old, failing industries. Such assistance may in fact lower unemployment for a time, just as aid to buggy makers would have softened the unemployment effects of Henry Ford's Model T production. But it also has the socially undesirable effect of halting economic change. By subsidizing antiquated, inefficient industries, we must tax the vital sectors in the economy. Detroit and Gary are kept afloat, but jobs are reduced in the high-tech centers of Texas, California, and Massachusetts.

The Liberal proposal for special job programs to deal with varieties of structural unemployment traceable to technological change is both unnecessary and counterproductive. Despite three decades of federal expenditures for the education of young people, the retraining of older workers, and elaborate public service programs, as well as affirmative action programs to increase the employment of minorities and women, there is virtually no evidence that significant numbers of would-be workers have been helped. In fact, the tax bill for funding and operating these programs has probably had a negative impact on jobs, because private-sector funds had to be shifted to these unemployment efforts.

If Americans find the present natural rate of unemployment to be higher than they would like, we possess the means to lower it. Freeing up labor markets, reducing union power, eliminating costly and counterproductive social engineering programs, and letting the chips of technological change fall where they may would go a long way toward ending the present mismatch between labor demand and labor supply.

THE UNEMPLOYMENT PROBLEM IS OVERSTATED

Unemployment is certainly higher than it should be and than it would be without current government policies; however, the level of joblessness is overstated rather than understated. The overreaction to unemployment statistics has also directed attention away from recent positive employment developments. Even with the high unemployment statistics of recent years, the number of employed workers has been growing steadily. Between 1980 and 1983, all supposedly high unemployment years, the total number of employed workers grew by 15 percent, from 99 million to 115 million.

If we recognize the obvious vitality of the economy and, at the same time, understand the forces that produce a high natural rate of unemployment, the present reported levels of unemployment may be put in a more balanced perspective. Quite simply, their urgency diminishes.

There is the possibility that entirely natural events in the near future will begin to lower unemployment rates. The demographic profile of the American work force indicates that it is aging quickly. The "baby boomers"—who in sheer numbers contributed to a high natural unemployment rate—are moving steadily toward retirement. The number of new entrants to replace these workers is comparatively small, and there are no signs that this trend will soon change. Already serious labor shortages are apparent in many regions of the country, particularly in the lower-skilled, entry-level positions. These labor shortages will continue as the years pass. Indeed, a fair number of economists are arguing that policymakers and the public have the entire "employment problem" backwards. According to this view, the nation's long-term employment difficulties will be a matter of insufficient numbers of potential workers, not insufficient jobs. Lest this state of affairs be taken as a cause for rejoicing, we should remember that a smaller labor force, *ceteris paribus*, will also mean a smaller national output. Rather than worrying about how we can absorb the presently unemployed, we might be better served by figuring out how in the near future we intend to produce more with less labor.

The Liberal Argument

Liberals also know that a "natural rate of unemployment" exists. They further understand that public policy efforts to drive this unemployment rate lower through ordinary economic expansion (stimulative fiscal or monetary policy, for instance) stand a good chance of producing inflationary side effects. However, a true Liberal regrets the use of the word "natural," in describing any unemployment condition because it suggests that the unemployment rate is somehow acceptable or simply beyond our capacity to deal with. Such is not the case.

Having argued earlier (in Issue 9) that cyclical (lack-of-demand) unemployment is self-correcting and unworthy of economists' attention, Conservatives continue to repudiate the available empirical evidence by contending that structural unemployment is also self-correcting. Presumably, if the economic policymakers act as if unemployment does not exist, it will simply go away. Such slavish commitment to the principles and processes of laissez-faire markets was perhaps possible a century ago, when the consequences were much smaller. However, indifference to chronic unemployment today is, on the one hand, an unacceptable political strategy and, on the other, the source of incredible human and social costs that are disruptive of the nation's economy.

THE HIGH COST OF JOBLESSNESS

Failure to deal with the unemployment problem will be a considerable cost for America—in both human and economic terms. In human terms, chronic unemployment erodes morale and self-esteem. Studies indicate that periods of prolonged unemployment destroy incentives and interest in work, even when the worker is later reemployed. Without employment, personal behavior patterns become erratic, leading to increased marital and family problems and greater child abuse. Unemployment also increases morbidity, mental illness, and crime. According to one study, a 1 percent increase in the unemployment rate will be associated with 37,000 deaths (including 20,000 heart attacks); 920 suicides; 650 homicides; 4,000 state mental hospital admissions; and 3,300 state prison admissions.* While it may be difficult (but not impossible) to put precise price tags on these human costs, we can measure the external or social costs of unemployment that result from (1) reduced tax collection, (2) rising unemployment insurance outlays, and (3) greater plant closings. When all these costs of permitting chronic unemployment are considered, the costs of special job programs to eliminate or reduce unemployment become insignificant.

THE EXTENT OF STRUCTURAL UNEMPLOYMENT

Of the almost 12 million Americans out of work in late 1982, a large share owed their joblessness to the recession engineered by the Reagan administration. Their unemployment was the "cost" of Reaganomics, the ruthless application of monetary brakes and budget cutting aimed at drying up inflation. About 5 million of these unemployed would find work by 1985. While their forced idleness was painful and largely unnecessary, it was not hopeless. For the others, however, even the return of good times have made little difference. Their unemployment was not the result of insufficient demand; rather it was the result of subtle institutional changes in the American economy. The problems of unemployment require a new approach. Not only do we need policies to cure lack-of-demand joblessness, but we must recognize that some unemployment is chronic and not responsive to demand increases.

Since World War II, the American economy has enjoyed, with a few brief interruptions, phenomenal economic growth; however, the expansion has produced important technological changes and regional economic shifts that have contributed to national unemployment. The demand for older jobs and skills has declined as new goods and production techniques have revolutionized labor. At the same time, the geographic distribution of manufacturing has been altered. Meanwhile, the old employment bulwarks—steel, autos, and construction, for example—are undergoing a deep structural decline, both as employers and as contributors to the nation's output, which

*Barry Bluestone, Bennett Harrison, and Lawrence Baker, *Corporate Flight: The Causes and Consequences of Economic Dislocation* (Washington D.C.: Progressive Alliance, 1981), p. 20.

few observers believe will soon reverse. The result has been to change
the structure of labor markets.

Here are some examples of these structural shifts:

1. The continued decline in agricultural employment as farm production was increasingly mechanized.
2. The increased use of more and more sophisticated technology in
   industrial production, thus reducing the relative demand for
   industrial labor in general and unskilled labor in particular.
3. The migration of many businesses and factories from the inner
   cities to suburban locations.
4. The greater concentration of economic activity in large metropoli-
   tan areas and the decline of employment in smaller cities.
5. The shift in the geographic location of industry to the West and
   South as new industries grew up in these areas and old plants left
   the industrial Northeast.
6. The sectoral shift in employment patterns as service industries
   and government increased employment and the old employers —
   in manufacturing, transportation, mining, and construction —
   declined. (In 1950, manufacturing, transportation, mining, and
   construction employed more than half the work force; by 1990,
   these industries employed less than a third. Over the same period,
   service and government employment grew from 25 percent to over
   40 percent of all employment.)

Across the nation, the structural changes in employment produced large pockets of chronic unemployment. Since most of those
unemployed lacked sufficient skills, economic expansion of the economy had little effect on their work status. Pumping up aggregate
demand would not have much effect on an unemployed railroad worker in Altoona, Pennsylvania, an out-of-work miner in Kentucky, or
an ex-steelworker in Gary, Indiana.

Changes in the composition of the labor force have added to the
structural problems. Beginning in the 1960s, larger numbers of
women began to look for work. Most of these new entrants possessed
minimal skills and took, when they could get them, low-paying jobs
in the service sector with little employment security. Many of the
female job seekers were extremely immobile. Many were wives and
mothers who had to seek work near their homes, which added a further restriction to their general lack of skills in obtaining work. Mean-

FIGURE 12.2   Profile of the Nation's Unemployed, 1972–1989

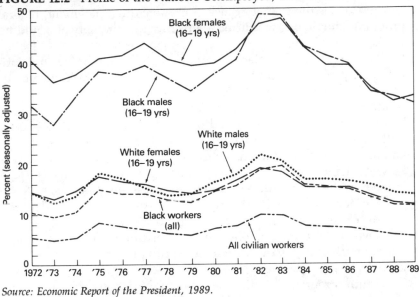

Source: *Economic Report of the President, 1989.*

while, the entrance into the job market of the large number of people born in the post–World War II baby boom increased unemployment. As with women, many of the youthful job seekers did not meet the new employment demands. For urban, primarily black, youths, there were virtually no jobs at all. They had no desired skills and did not live near or have access to the few unskilled jobs available. As Figure 12.2 shows, the gap between blacks' and whites' employment opportunities has remained wide – and many would argue is widening.

A LIBERAL PROGRAM

As we have noted, structural unemployment and joblessness resulting from changes in the composition of the work force are not responsive to efforts to pump up aggregate demand. Instead, specific job-creating programs are necessary to provide full employment. However, unlike the make-work measures of the past (such as WPA in the 1930s), these programs should not be mere band-aids. Since lack of skills is the primary cause of chronic unemployment, federal programs should be constructed to improve the hirability of would-be workers.

The urgency of implementing a variety of retraining and job-incentive programs is underscored by a number of developments. In an era of persistent fiscal crisis, getting the jobless back to work produces real social savings as initial program costs are quickly offset by the taxes the newly employed pay and by the reduction of social outlays directly related to their unemployed condition (that is, welfare and unemployment compensation). And the nation needs these workers. As demographic evidence indicates, we face a serious shortage of labor in the not-too-distant future. Accordingly, it becomes all the more important to provide the training and discipline required for the chronically unemployed to become employable.

Several job programs offer real opportunities for the so-called unemployables to join the labor force: youth programs, public service jobs, and wage subsidies.

Youth Programs With unemployment among teenagers the highest of all groups (14 percent among white teenage males and 33 percent among black teenage males, compared to an overall 5.2 percent rate), youth unemployment demands special attention. Teenagers account for about one-fourth of all the unemployed. Most teenage unemployment, especially among blacks, is found in urban areas. Also, among the teenage unemployed there is a high educational dropout rate. Thus employment programs for this group should be urban in focus and organized to encourage completion of public education. While learning useful skills, many youths will learn the workplace discipline that is necessary for retaining employment. A long-run improvement of youth unemployment problems is fairly certain as the past decade's declining birth rate makes itself felt in labor markets. With a modest job program now, youthful unemployment can be brought under control.

Public Service Jobs Beginning in 1973, the Comprehensive Employment and Training Act (CETA) instituted federal funding for local government hiring of public workers for limited employment periods. Rather than creating an overloaded federal bureaucracy, this approach allowed local communities to set and meet their own public service needs. Workers, meanwhile, obtained important on-the-job experience before their CETA employment ended. The cancellation of these programs during the years of Reaganomics has been a harsh blow to workers lacking skills.

Wage Subsidies   A third approach to chronic unemployment is to subsidize private-sector employment of the unskilled. The bonus paid to private corporations is intended to offset the expected lower productivity of workers in this program.

Be aware that the emphasis on retraining and upgrading skills in both public- and private-sector programs will not immediately affect structural unemployment; nevertheless, over time the effects on improving workers' job opportunities and their productivity should be evident in reduced chronic unemployment. However, real changes will be seen only if the commitment to these programs is much greater than at present. Largely a victim of budget-tightening pressures, the employment program that started with great promise has been scaled down to a fraction of what was originally proposed. This amounts to reversing our national commitment to full employment. Unless our full-employment goals are reaffirmed, chronic unemployment will grow, and the nation will be denied the contribution that these would-be workers could make.

The Radical Argument

Both Conservatives and Liberals misunderstand the role of unemployment in a capitalist society. To the Conservative advocating a free market economy, there would be virtually no unemployment if the market were to work freely; that is, unimpeded by government action, labor unions, and so on. To the Liberal, unemployment is at least a periodic, and perhaps chronic, condition of capitalist economies, but it can be controlled by "enlightened" public policy. Neither position sees unemployment as central to capitalist organization, as necessary to the actual functioning of the system. The simple fact is that capitalism, regulated or unregulated, cannot help but create unemployment.

UNEMPLOYMENT: CAPITALISM AS USUAL

As capitalists accumulate and successfully translate past labor into what they see as profit-producing capital and investment, the need for an absolute or growing volume of labor diminishes. This must be true by simple definition. The object of capital development is to increase production without increased (or with decreased) costs. Labor-saving machinery is cost-saving machinery only because labor is paid less per unit of output. More output can be obtained by employing more capital and less labor. Thus increased capitalization and technological growth, all things being equal, must produce growing surplus labor. This is the historical tendency of capitalism

The growth of unemployment tends to be in recessionary clusters rather than in a steady, unbroken upward movement; however, the overall unemployment trend is up over a period of time. Since the mid-1950s we have seen the official unemployment rates (themselves statistical understatements of the problem) move relentlessly higher even in comparatively "good" years. In other words, the percentage of the labor force in what Marx called "the reserve army of the unemployed" is constantly expanding. No doubt this unemployment would have been even higher in the past had not government pursued expansionary policies. In other words, the situation has been getting progressively worse despite elaborate governmental efforts to hold unemployment down. Neither the free market nor Keynesian tinkering halts this tendency.

The failure of expansionary fiscal policy to deal with the problem of chronic unemployment is particularly evident if we go back to the tax cut of 1964. This was perhaps the first self-consciously Keynesian effort to use fiscal policy to reduce unemployment (then at 5 or 6 percent). The $11 billion Kennedy-Johnson tax reduction did spur business investment and increase national output. Between 1964 and 1966, investment increased by over 22 percent—more than twice the rate of the previous two years. The gross national product grew by 13 percent during the same period, compared to a growth rate of less than 10 percent in the earlier period. However, reported unemployment fell by only 900,000 between 1964 and 1966, despite the fact that government alone increased its payroll by 1.7 million persons. Thus any real reduction in unemployment came not from tax cutting à la Keynes but from good old government hiring.

An additional case against the supposed effectiveness of "full-employment" fiscal policy is the hyperexpansion of government spending that took place during the Vietnam War. Although government policy during the war may now be represented by Liberals as unintended and undesired (in other words, determined on political rather than economic grounds), it did not result in the employment growth that modern Keynesians associate with expansionary fiscal policy. Between 1966 and 1969, during the height of war appropriations, unemployment fell by less than 100,000. Meanwhile direct government employment added an additional 1.6 million to public payrolls. Direct government hiring, not private-sector job growth, brought unemployment rates down during the middle and late 1960s.

The point of these examples should not be misunderstood. Fiscal expansionism does create demand for workers. After the 1964 tax cut, during the Vietnam War boom, and after the 1981 Reagan tax cut, unemployment rates did fall a bit. But in each case, "normal unemployment" (what Conservatives euphemistically call the "natural" rate of unemployment) leveled off at a higher level: 3.5 percent in the mid-1960s; 5 percent in the early 1970s; and 7 percent or more in the mid-1980s. What was happening was that "full employment" was being achieved at successively higher levels of normal unemployment, with the pressures of an expanding economy having no useful effect on many workers who were falling out of the employable labor force altogether.

CAPITALISM BENEFITS FROM UNEMPLOYMENT

Political rhetoric to the contrary, the fact is that capitalism benefits from surplus labor—at least to a certain degree. Surplus labor usually forces wages downward or at least slows upward pressures. Workers compete with one another, and employers have a pleasant buyer's market. Even the prospects of important union wage gains are diminished by the competitive threat of the swelling ranks of unemployed. Recently, corporations have shamelessly used the specter of growing unemployment to force the labor union elite of the working class to sign new contracts with "givebacks." Wage gains and fringe benefits struggled for in the past were wiped out as rising unemployment weakened the unions' bargaining position. The old-line management bargaining tactic of "take it or leave it" was once again successful.

The Conservative Reagan Congress allowed the consumer price indexing of minimum-wage rates to lapse. By 1990, the $3.40 minimum wage was equal to a mere $1.20 in 1975 dollars. Since the minimum wage in 1975 had been $2.10, this represented a 40 percent real-wage reduction. The logic for holding down the minimum wage for millions of American workers not protected by unions was the usual Conservative line: Higher minimum wages would only cause greater unemployment.

Aside from using unemployment to hold down workers' wages, joblessness also was used to pump up business subsidies. In typical "trickle-down" reasoning, the enterprise-zone program was launched in 1982. In seventy-five designated inner cities, corporations were granted tax reductions and allowed to hire at less than the legal minimum wage. The justification: Jobs would be created for the "unemployables"; the effect: greater profits for corporations while plain old exploitation grew.

UNDERSTATING THE PROBLEM

Bad as it appears to be, our unemployment problem is really much worse than we realize because we understate the number of unemployed in at least four ways. First, the average annual rate does not show the number of people affected by some type of annual unemployment. For instance, in 1987 at least 30 million Americans experienced some unemployment during the year. Looked at this way, unemployment touched almost 35 percent of the American workforce during the year. Even if the unemployed suffered only a week or two of lost labor, the effect could be devastating on savings, retirement plans, and the educational hopes of the worker's children. Second, our statistics tend to overestimate the actual number employed. In 1985, the "employed" included 16 million Americans who worked only part-time and another 1.5 million who fell into an "unpaid family labor" category. Such calculations expand the total "employed" category but do not show how slight their employment is. Third, official statistics do not indicate the underemployed. At least 8 million full-time workers earn wages below the official poverty income level. Fourth, the "unemployed" category does not include workers who are "not presently looking for a job," although they may be people who want jobs but have given up looking. How many people have given up looking? No accurate figures are available, but it is estimated that if this group were added to our known unemployment, the more than 7.1 percent average annual rate during the 1980s easily would have reached 12 to 14 percent.

It is important to understand not only the real size but also the composition of unemployment in the United States. Clearly, job possibilities are poorer if one is black, female, or young. This discrimination in employment is not surprising. Basically, it reflects the general contraction of labor markets and the resulting exclusion of newcomers. On the one hand, such discrimination has served the system well, because many of the unemployed are not visible but hidden away in the ghetto or home. On the other hand, obvious discrimination of this kind creates considerable political development among the affected groups, who quite consciously and correctly see themselves as an exploited class. Liberals, aware of this tendency, have proposed make-work and on-the-job-training programs aimed at quashing the discontent of the hard-core unemployed. But such programs have no long-run effect on improving employment.

There is obviously a limit to how large the surplus labor army can grow—not just an economic limit but a political one. Unemployment breeds contempt for the existing order and sows the seeds of revolution. Therefore, capitalism faces the constant problem of devising expensive "legitimation" schemes. Ironically, given our soak-the-poor tax structure and the present fiscal crisis, employed workers are increasingly burdened by taxes to support unemployed workers. This situation has so far only set workers against nonworkers, rather than uniting all against the system that oppresses them.

In any case, modern public policy can do nothing about the threat of long-term unemployment. Short-run manipulation and trade-offs with inflation (see the previous issue) are possible, but the structural foundations of capitalist unemployment remain. Nor do special job-creating programs for the chronically unemployed offer a long-run solution. At best, they only buy a little time through deceptive but unfulfilled promises of future jobs. Small wonder that officials have no wish to tabulate all the unemployed. But their statistical manipulation does not change the historical tendency of capitalism.

Military Spending
What Happens If Peace Breaks Out?

In the councils of government, we guard against the acquisition of unwarranted influence, whether sought or unsought, by the military-industrial complex. The potential for the disastrous rise of misplaced power exists and will exist.
Dwight D. Eisenhower, 1961

Today it is more likely that the military requirement is the result of joint participation of military and industrial personnel, and it is not unusual for industry's solution to be a key factor. Indeed, there are highly placed military men who sincerely feel that industry is currently setting the pace in the research and development of new weapons systems.
Peter Schenck, Raytheon Corporation, 1969

National solid waste treatment program = $43.5 billion = B-1 bomber program
Total environmental cleanup = $105.2 billion = New weapons systems in development or procurement
To eliminate hunger in America = $5 billion = C-5A aircraft program
Seymour Melman, National Cochairman of SANE, 1974

The Peace Dividend is not some huge sum like "the sweepstakes" that just falls in our lap.
Donald Regan, former Reagan cabinet member, 1989

THE PROBLEM

For more than four decades, the cold war has loomed as a constant among our political realities. However, it has also had considerable economic implications. Between 1945 and 1990, spending for war and threats of war absorbed almost $4 trillion of national output. With few exceptions, America has committed, year in and year out, between 6 and 8 percent of its GNP to national defense. During the 1980s, military spending ascended to heretofore unheard-of peacetime heights, as the Reagan administration maintained that the U.S. military establishment had to catch up with the Russians and be updated for its new international responsibilities. Indeed, as critics pointed out, the "upscaling" of the military in the 1980s was just about equal to the increase in annual federal deficits during the same period. Some argued that we simply could not afford such outlays; others held we couldn't afford not to undertake such expenditures.

Whether or not the national defense that we got was what we needed, or whether we got our money's worth out of each defense dollar spent, our defense spending has had an important *opportunity cost*. The 6 to 8 percent of the GNP going to military outlays could not be used for other things that we might have produced and consumed as a nation. Not even the most ardent advocates of a "strong America" would argue against the observation that the cold war has imposed a heavy economic burden on the nation. The extent of the burden is illustrated in Table 13.1.

In the late 1980s, however, what had seemed to be a permanent political condition showed signs of changing. With Gorbachev's introduction of *glasnost* and *perestroika* as internal Soviet political and economic programs and the USSR's shift toward certain unilateral military and political pullbacks, the old dual superpower confrontation seemed to ebb. There was also a growing rapprochement between the United States and China and, in late 1989, the collapse of the Iron Curtain in Eastern Europe as one after another former Soviet satellites repudiated communism. Almost overnight, Americans were confronted by a startling new global political environment. The sudden sweep of events raised a perplexing question: *What would we do if peace actually broke out?*

To be sure, there were those who talked glowingly about the possibility of a "peace dividend."* In a non–cold war setting, a significant portion

---

*These same arguments arose toward the end of the Vietnam War. If that experience is at all relevant, those who argue that there will be no peace dividend have the force of history on their side. The end of hostilities in Vietnam did not present the nation with a budget bulge it could devote to other uses.

TABLE 13.1   National Defense Spending, Selected Years, 1939–1990 (billions of dollars)

Year	Amount	Year	Amount
1939	$ 1.9	1976	$ 86.8
1944	84.4	1977	94.3
1949	13.2	1978	110.0
1955	38.4	1979	123.9
1960	44.5	1980	133.9
1965	49.4	1981	157.5
1966	60.3	1982	185.3
1967	71.5	1983	209.9
1968	76.9	1984	227.4
1969	76.3	1985	252.7
1970	73.5	1986	273.4
1971	70.2	1987	281.9
1972	73.5	1988	290.4
1973	73.5	1989	298.3
1974	77.0	1990*	303.0
1975	86.8		

*Estimate
Source: Economic Report of the President, 1990.

of anticipated national defense outlays could now be used for everything from a defense of the environment, to rebuilding the nation's infrastructure, to expanding social outlays, to reducing deficits and the debt. *Or so the argument went.* However, forty years of cold war spending had institutionalized the defense budget. Whole segments of the economy and large regions of the country have come to depend on war, or at least threats of and preparations for war. Industries and regions whose entire economic foundation rested on national defense expenditures, regardless of the longer-term political attractiveness of peace, saw, in the short term, real economic difficulties developing. Swords are not easily beaten into plowshares, and peace—if it really were to break out—could be very disruptive.

As of this writing, there are also those who are not yet convinced that the cold war is truly over. Accordingly, they argue that it remains as crucial as ever—perhaps even more so—that the United States maintain its military strength. Events will determine whether or not this view has merit. However, if the cold war tensions continue to ebb, pressures within and without the nation demanding a military pullback will be virtually irresistible. Consequently, the United States will have no alternative but to determine whether or not we can afford peace.

SYNOPSIS

The Conservative argument maintains that defense spending, although probably characterized by some waste, is necessary for national security. Liberals have been divided on military spending, with some opposing the growth of a powerful military-industrial complex and urging that war spending be shifted to social goods, while others, like the Conservatives, have argued for the necessity of a large arms budget. The Radical argument holds that our economy depends on war for profit and maintaining high levels of demand and that shifting this spending to other areas is politically and economically impossible under the present system.

Anticipating the Arguments

- On what grounds do Conservatives exempt defense spending from arguments they offer against other dimensions of government economic activity?
- What do Liberals mean by their argument that defense spending develops "its own constituency" within the economy? How does this constituency act to protect defense expenditures and even waste?
- Why do Radicals believe that large defense budgets are necessary in a capitalist society?

The Conservative Argument

By any rational calculus, war is wasteful and uneconomical. Human labor and physical resources are used not for production but for destruction. Markets are distorted, shortages develop, and the price mechanism fails to direct resource allocation properly. The production of war goods, meanwhile, subtracts from the society's accumulation of capital and its social and private wealth. All of this should be obvious. Yet predominant in most discussions of military spending, or the so-called military-industrial complex, is the charge that war is necessary or that war is *good* for the economy. Needless to say, this argument is usually advanced by critics of capitalism. It is demonstrably false, but proving logically that war is not essential to a capitalist economy is not the end of the matter. War and threats of war are a reality today. War spending, therefore, is not a function of limited capitalist economic options. It is a necessary political and societal response to an external threat—in this case, the protection of American capitalism and democracy from the threat of international communism.

COLD WAR SPENDING HAS
NOT BEEN A MISTAKE

A common Liberal argument holds that the defense spending of the 1980s was a monumental mistake—unnecessary in terms of military and defense realities and so excessive as to be the principal cause for current debt, deficit, and public finance problems. The charge is a massive overstatement, but its real weakness is that it overlooks some fundamental realities of the past couple of decades. Modern military equipment *is* very expensive. The high technological and capital costs of the nuclear age, however, reflect requirements that have changed a good deal since soldiers threw rocks and spears at one another. It must be remembered too that the limits on military spending are not being determined by how much we want to spend but by how much our adversaries force us to spend for adequate defense. More important, though, is the fact that defense spending, while recently rising to meet real defense needs, is relatively small by past standards.

In 1990, the defense budget ran to $303 billion, or about 28 percent of total federal outlays. This was up from the 24 percent share in 1980, when the nation was being stripped of its military strength, but it was well below the 40 percent share in the Vietnam War year 1970. In fact, as Figure 13.1 indicates, between 1970 and 1980, proportional defense spending had been steadily declining, while human resource outlays rose from 37 percent to 52 percent of the budget. During the 1980s, defense spending's share rose only modestly. As a share of the nation's total output, 1985 defense spending was a scant 8 percent. Compare this with, say, 1922. The United States was then at peace, pursuing a foreign policy of isolation, blissfully allowing its army and navy to grow obsolete, and beginning a long period of economic prosperity. Nevertheless, the $1.2 billion spent on defense that year

FIGURE 13.1 Federal Expenditures by Type, 1947–1989

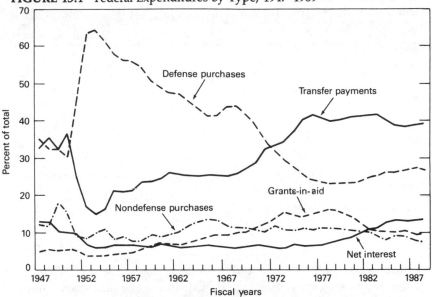

Note: Data are on a national income and product accounts basis. Total expenditures includes subsidies less current surplus of government enterprises and wage accruals less disbursements, not shown separately.
Source: Economic Report of the President, 1989, p. 83.

still amounted to 2 percent of our GNP and 35 percent of federal expenditures. The facts simply don't support the alarmist claims of those who oppose defense spending. (One might ask, parenthetically, why these opponents attack military spending—which has been small and until recently has been growing relatively smaller—while showing little concern about government spending in other areas.)

Defense is primarily a function of how one's adversary reacts; therefore, it is important to ask what the Soviet Union is doing. According to estimates of the Department of Defense and private researchers, the Russians have been devoting about 10 to 12 percent of their GNP to military outlays. Such an effort is about twice as great as ours in terms of the share of GNP. As Table 13.2 shows, the Soviet

TABLE 13.2 Constant (1978) Dollar Outlays for Defense by the United States and the USSR, 1971–1980 (in billions)

Year	USA	USSR	USSR Advantage
1971	118	120	+12
1972	117	134	+17
1973	112	140	+28
1974	112	147	+35
1975	109	151	+42
1976	103	158	+55
1977	108	159	+51
1978	108	161	+53
1979	112	166	+54
1980	129	169	+40

Source: Statistical Abstract of the United States, 1984.

Union consistently outspent the United States during the 1970s, acquiring a dangerous advantage in ICBMs, missile warheads, missile submarines, tanks, and virtually all other indicators of military strength. This, and this alone, has been the determinant of our own recent decision to increase defense spending.

As to whether or not changing international conditions can necessarily be interpreted first, as "an end to the cold war," and second, proof that we can disarm, Conservatives generally remain unconvinced. The 180-degree turn of China from reform to reaction in the Beijing Spring of 1989 shows the unpredictability of "trends" in communist countries. Moreover, even if the United States and the Soviet Union could end their cold war confrontation, this would not eliminate the need for military preparedness. While we have never faced off militarily against the USSR, we have been drawn into other conflicts over the past four decades, and the world as a whole has experienced over sixty such identifiable conflicts during this period, many of which the United States could have been drawn into to protect its own citizens or interests. Finally, we should remember the lessons of history. In the past, precisely as nations began to think and act as if wars were "impossible," forces and personalities emerged that sooner or later made war inevitable.

ACCEPTING THE HIGH COST OF DEFENSE

A second charge leveled at military spending is that it is inefficient. This is somewhat harder to refute because there is evidence of cost overruns and technological failures. The difficulty is calculating efficiency in making military hardware. The production and sale of sophisticated war goods cannot take place in a competitive market; things have changed since Lincoln's secretary of war took bids on horse blankets and salt pork. No rational executive will risk capital by speculating in the tank or missile business.

Secrecy, complex technology, and capital demands set constraints on the supply side of the military market, while the demand side is limited to a single domestic buyer and a few overseas purchasers. Given the reality of monopoly in the supply and purchase of military goods, the record of waste does not seem extraordinary. (One might ask again why critics single out the inefficiency of military spending but neglect to apply the same standards to government purchases from other industries. Is there no waste in highway construction or in federally funded and managed urban renewal and housing projects? Of course war is a waste, but the charge of economic inefficiency is another matter.)

To be sure, Conservatives do not defend inefficiency. Nor do they in any way defend instances of corruption and graft in the procurement of weapons. Neither should be allowed. But the military has no greater guilt than other sectors that deal with the government. Such problems are not unique to the alleged "military-industrial complex."

A final word might be said on behalf of indirect benefits from the military budget. Despite the ultimate waste of war and some probable inefficiency in procurement and production, defense spending has produced useful inventions and innovations. Military research and development has made possible, among many other things, Boeing 707s and 747s, our satellite communications network, and the transistor.

Lest readers mistakenly conclude that the Conservatives' position on military spending is inconsistent with their attitude toward government, it should be emphasized that war and defense are decisions that transcend the marketplace. A permanent war economy certainly extends government into areas of social activity better left to the

304 Problems of Aggregate Economic Policy

people. This issue calls for vigilance, but defense of the society is essential. This stubborn fact is totally ignored by the opponents of defense spending.

THE PEACE DIVIDEND FOLLY

Following a frequently forgotten variation of a well-known rule—that invention may be the mother of necessity as surely as being its offspring—Liberals have *invented* the "peace dividend" argument to justify the *necessity* of their own social agenda. Constrained as we are as a nation by the fiscal realities and crises of our time, where better to find the resources for massive social engineering and social welfare outlays than in a military budget Liberals now see as essentially unnecessary.

The peace dividend, if it did exist or ever comes to exist, must not become a kind of Trojan horse that undoes our economy in the guise of helping it. If we finally scale down our military expenditures, we must be careful that these savings are not used as a lever to create greater federal spending in other areas. If there is to be a peace dividend, it must be payed to the taxpaying citizen and not to government.

The Liberal Argument

Conservatives correctly maintain that adequate military defense is not a matter of purely economic choice nor of frivolous luxury. It is an outlay that must be made and that must be appropriate as determined by the real threats confronting a nation. Liberals have generally supported this position during the cold war years, although they have long worried about the symbiotic relationship that has developed between the Pentagon and broad areas of the American economy. Moreover, Liberals have often believed, especially in recent years, that the defense bill has been higher than necessary, both in terms of the total amounts we have authorized to be spent and the actual prices paid for hardware. Contemporary shifts in the world, however, now provide the United States with the possibility of reassessing *necessary* national defense outlays, with the probable outcome that we will find adequate protection can be obtained with a greatly reduced defense budget. The reduction of cold war tensions after *glasnost* and *pere-*

stroika, the prospect of cutting back strategic arms and tactical forces through bilateral agreements with the Soviet Union, as well as a reassessment our own national interests in the world will surely maintain a steady downward pressure on defense outlays.

WASTEFUL SPENDING STRATEGIES

Before turning to the larger question of whether a general reduction in defense spending is possible and what problems exist if we move in that direction, we must address a more arcane problem first: How can we get an appropriate defense at a reasonable price? Liberals know that modern technology is expensive, but they believe it is more expensive than it should be. This is the combined result of procuring weapons whose use is ill-planned and paying excessive amounts for weapons systems we really do not need.

Classic among the ill-planned defense strategies has been the Strategic Defense Initiative (SDI), or "Star Wars," as it has been better known. This system of placing "defensive" satellites in orbit with the capacity to destroy enemy missiles by means of an on-board laser cannon has been regularly funded in its development stages for more than six years. Never mind that most of the scientific community maintains that we simply do not have the technological know-how to do what SDI claims to do. Never mind that this "defensive weapon" looks very much like an offensive threat to any nation that does not possess it. Never mind that even if the technology did exist to make such a weapon, it would be negated by the similar technology of a foe who would put up their own satellites.

The SDI case is not exceptional — except perhaps in its sci-fi overtones. For a very long time, Americans have been paying for weapons whose battlefield capabilities are well below what was promised. During the "low-budget" defense years between 1953 and 1965, more than $10 billion was spent on weapons that proved useless. In the exploding defense budget of the 1980s, monies were included for the M-1 tank (cost: $2.5 million each); the F-18 bomber (cost: $32 million each); and the B-1 bomber (cost: unknown, but some experts estimate that the first fleet of 100 would go at nearly $1 billion each). These outlays were proposed despite the fact that all three of these systems had important critics within the military who doubted the actual future effectiveness of the weapons. Included also in the early 1980s budgets was continued development funding for the Sergeant York antiair-craft cannon, an item finally dumped by the Defense Department in 1985 as "totally unbattleworthy"—after $1.8 billion had been spent on the project.

Even if most of the weapons procured eventually prove out on the battlefield, there is the incredible problem of cost effectiveness in their development and procurement. Awarded handsome cost-plus contracts, prime contractors have a long record of continually piling up cost overruns that have tripled or quadrupled original estimates for weapons systems. The M-1 tank was originally programmed to be built at one-tenth its current delivery price. Defense contractors have little or no reason to maintain cost efficiency in weapons production. Indeed, being efficient would reduce the contractors' gross revenues and, with fixed profit formulas, reduce their total profits. In some instances, as illustrated by the discovery in 1985 that General Dynamics was fraudulently billing the Defense Department for work not actually done, defense contractors have gone beyond mere ineffi-ciency and involved themselves in theft of public monies.

Despite the undeniable record of waste and mismanagement that characterizes military goods procurement, Pentagon budgets have long remained sacrosanct. No part of the federal budget enjoys such intensive congressional and industrial lobbying. The public is fed a steady diet of information and misinformation about new and won-derful weapons systems, missile gaps, and the intentions of our adversaries. Behind the patriotic appeal is the simple matter of dollars and cents. A great many giant American corporations are dependent for their existence on military orders. Lockheed, General Dynamics, McDonnell-Douglas, Rockwell International, Raytheon, and Ling-Temco-Vought—all among the nation's top hundred manu-facturers—have depended on national defense spending for more than half their total sales for over twenty years. To a lesser degree, dozens of other firms feed at the Pentagon trough.

Naturally, the military economy affects many citizens. Some 7 percent of all employed Americans work in defense industries; over 20 percent of all manufacturing personnel are involved directly in producing military hardware. In states such as Connecticut, Califor-nia, and Washington, about 40 percent of the manufacturing workers are in defense-related industries.

The military-industrial complex is not limited to prime suppliers and their employees. In any area of the country where defense spending is large, the community sees itself as having a stake in the defense budget. In a single city or community, loss of a defense plant has unemployment ripple effects throughout the local economy. When the Air Force announced a plan to close its early-warning system in Duluth, Minnesota, the owner of a local frozen pizza company led an entourage of outraged citizens to Washington. When Rockwell International was lobbying for its B-1, they contacted some 5,000 subcontractors in forty states, asking them to write to members of Congress on behalf of the big bomber.

As a result of the great dependence of so many firms and individuals on military spending, it is politically difficult, perhaps impossible, for the waste in defense spending to be examined honestly and openly. Quite apart from the morality of war and the real needs of defense, the military budget also means jobs and profits. Unless we can step back and look objectively past our personal interests in jobs and income, defense budgets will remain beyond critical economic examination.

GETTING DEFENSE
SPENDING UNDER CONTROL

Given the wastefulness of much of our military spending as well as the fact that all spending—good or bad—eventually becomes politically entrenched, the present diminishing of cold war tensions offers some benefits to a nation and a world heavily burdened by the opportunity costs of military outlays. An improved relationship with the Soviet Union will, over time, erode the political clout of the military-industrial complex. Accordingly, budget cutting will become more politically acceptable, perhaps even to the point where *only* defense considerations are the basis for defense expenditures.

While a greater degree of rapprochement with the USSR will not end our need for military outlays (Conservatives are correct in stating that there are many nations other than the Soviet Union with whom we might come into conflict), it should reduce the need for the more exotic and expensive weapons systems such as SDI. In other words, if the potential for USA–USSR conflict is reduced (matched, of course, by disarmament actions on both nations' parts), then there will be a consequent reduction in military spending simply because a less sophisticated and extensive arsenal is less costly.

Indeed, another layer of cost cutting is possible if the United States moves away from its role of paying the defense burden of most of the non-Communist world. Remove the cold war scenario and add to the picture the vibrant economies of Europe, Japan, and Korea and then ask: Why must the United States pick up most of the defense costs of these nations as we have done for so long during the cold war years? Cost cutting accomplished by pulling back to a military posture consistent with our real economic interests is eminently sensible under any situation. It becomes even more so if we understand that our present worldwide military position amounts to subsidizing nations that are currently outperforming us in international markets.

THE GAINS FROM PEACE

Spending for war, whether deemed necessary or unnecessary, always involves an opportunity cost. The $4 trillion that did not go to improve education, expand peaceful productive investment, or rebuild bridges, highways, and cities is the opportunity cost of spending $4 trillion on defense over the past four decades. Just as we have been diminished as a nation by allocating resources to war, so too could we be uplifted in the future by shifting defense savings to useful social purposes. The possible social gains from reduced defense outlays may not be as large as some might imagine however. First of all, the military budget will never be reduced to zero. Second, the phaseout period of weapons systems will take time. Third, the redevelopment and reemployment of military-directed resources to nonmilitary uses will require a fair amount of budgetary support.

However, over time, the fading away of the cold war must mean a gradual shift from "guns" to "butter" on the nation's production possibilities curve. Some will find the shift threatening simply because it is unaccustomed. But most Americans, Liberals and Conservatives alike, should eventually recognize that the other options— war or constant spending in anticipation of war—are an awful waste of resources.

The Radical Argument

Before we start congratulating ourselves that the cold war is over and begin celebrating the impending reduction of military budgets, we must go back and obtain a better understanding of the causes and effects of the last four decades of bloated defense budgets. Free of the mystifications that enshroud cold war discussions, the long debate over whether we can afford preparations for war becomes transformed into a more relevant argument: *Can we afford peace?*

America's high levels of military spending are not simply the consequence of maintaining an "adequate" defensive position, as Conservatives argue. Nor, as Liberals would have it, are they the largely accidental result of efforts by a self-aggrandizing, and small political clique known as the military-industrial complex. Such explanations of the magnitude of military spending are essential for Liberals and Conservatives because their own conventional analyses, as well as common sense, sustains a different view: Namely, that any society is diminished by allocating fundamentally limited resources to war uses rather than to genuinely productive tasks. Accidental and noneconomic justifications for the high levels of military expenditures not only avoids contradictions between reality and cold warrior logic, but also provides a smokescreen to hide the crucial role defense spending plays in a production-for-profit economy. It therefore hides the fact that military outlays and preparation for war have long been essential to American capitalist development.

First of all, high levels of defense spending have been the other side of a cold war strategy that has identified American economic and political stability as dependent on our capacity to keep a sizable proportion of the world within the capitalist orbit and under the domination of American capitalist interests. Second, military expenditures have also served the useful purpose of enlarging government's role in the economy, thereby sustaining high levels of demand for goods on the one hand, while providing profitability to certain crucial sectors of the economy on the other. And, third, defense spending and the excessive patriotism it both generated and benefitted from have been useful devices for deflecting American consciousness away from many of the internal contradictions of a production-for-profit economy.

CONTAINMENT AND HEGEMONY
IN THE WORLD

Since the cold war commenced in the late 1940s, the United States has pursued a two-pronged economic and military policy: containment and hegemony. *Containment* has had the specific purpose of limiting or negating the influence of the Soviet Union in the world. It has required the development of expensive and elaborate strategic weapons to maintain a "balance of terror" with regard to potential direct confrontations between the two superpowers. On the other hand, it has demanded the maintenance of political alliances and expensive military commitments along communism's borders to contain Soviet influence. *Hegemony* has meant building and sustaining American dominance in the non-Communist world.

Regardless of how one might evaluate the wisdom of these policies in terms of their effects on heightening worldwide tensions, there is little denying the eagerness of the United States in their pursuit. Correctly or not, the United States has believed that the domestic security of the nation depended on simultaneously negating what was perceived as a worldwide Communist threat and acting as defender of the "free world." Selfless as all this may sound, this strategy—at least with regard to its hegemonic dimensions—has in fact been quite self-serving. The "free world," of course, has always been that part of the globe where American corporations or those of our allies had substantial interests to protect. Ordinarily, it has included nations that are sources of critical raw materials, locations of important capital investment, or actual or potential markets for goods. Freedom—other than freedom of business to manufacture and sell profitably and to obtain resources cheaply—has never really figured very prominently in American cold war policy-making. Friendly repressive regimes, such as those in Chile or South Korea, have always been welcome allies in the strategies of containment and hegemony.

That the United States has been firmly committed to these strategies cannot be doubted. Above and beyond the expense of an anti-Communist entente, there has been the national willingness, from time to time, to invest its young men and wealth in wars that threatened American hegemony. In the case of Vietnam, most reasonable observers would agree that the costs greatly exceeded any gains. Such spending in a war we didn't even win indicates that capitalist "defensive" policies are not rational. Nonetheless, in terms of the system's views of its overseas needs, military waste is essential, even when the waste is a crushing blow to the nation's economy and people.

PROPPING UP THE DOMESTIC ECONOMY

Apart from making the world safe for capitalism, there has been the chronic problem of keeping a production-for-profit system healthy at home. Here, too, military spending has been especially attractive.

In a macroeconomic sense, military outlays have had a beneficial effect on business balance sheets. Many firms and some entire industries are wholly dependent on the Pentagon budget for their profit margins. This is not simply a matter of firms that do 50 percent or more of their business with the government. Large companies such as General Motors, General Electric, Ford, and Chrysler—that gain less than 20 percent of their sales from military contracts—depend on these contracts for the lion's share of the profits they earn in the United States.

The military budget has also acted as an important crutch for the macroeconomy. The chronic capitalist problem of maintaining sufficient levels of aggregate demand has required, as we have seen in earlier issues, a high order of government spending. Military outlays, of course, are the perfect type of government expenditure. They in no way compete with private-sector production and profit-making activities, and, more important, they are an area of expanded government activity that every patriotic citizen can enthusiastically support. Moreover, military spending is a virtually endless spending source. Limits on the number of highways, hospitals, and schools a society needs clearly exist, but if a nation wants to be "'adequately prepared" for war, there is no limit on the military material and technology it can justify purchasing.

Neither Liberals nor Conservatives have honestly faced up to the macroeconomic benefits war spending bestows on a stumbling economy. Liberals rarely point out that it was not the elegant theories of Lord Keynes that led our economy out of the Depression. It was massive wartime spending, not the purchase of social goods, that pumped up aggregate demand and created full employment. While social spending might have had the same effect—at least in theory— the point to remember is that war spending was the route the nation followed. Nor has it altered that course. Conservatives, meanwhile, who disavow any desire to use any type of spending for the purposes of "stimulating demand" and who maintain the importance of a balanced budget in fiscal matters, have been the prime movers in the recent expansion of military spending—even though these spending increases have largely been the cause for our failure to obtain a balanced budget.

Military spending, from the corporate point of view, is especially attractive *because* it is wasteful. In other words, it produces income and profits while doing nothing to improve or change the society's stock of consumable goods. There is no need to worry about gluts of commodities that will sooner or later be blown up or abandoned. Social spending, on the other hand, is particularly disruptive. In producing certain goods (public power or public housing, for instance), it competes directly with the private sector. Too extensive social outlays also interfere with labor markets, driving labor costs upward.

The benefits of military outlays have not been lost on American workers either. Defense spending has meant jobs for millions of workers. The argument that these same outlays, made for peaceful purposes, would also create jobs is generally unconvincing to labor. From workers' perspectives, peace would create problems of job dislocations and retraining, at least for those many workers who are presently employed in the military-industrial complex. As a result, the reality of defense jobs *now* versus the possibility of unemployment under peacetime conditions has long been recognized by most workers and their unions as the real policy choice in the defense debate. And, for the most part, they have voted their interests accordingly.

GETTING BEYOND THE DELUSION

Apart from the direct benefits to certain segments of American labor, defense spending and the cold war rhetoric that has accompanied it has worked to galvanize Americans in a crusade against communism and on behalf of the American economic and social system. In such an atmosphere, critical examination of and opposition to the more objectionable economic and social outcomes of capitalism have been avoided. As a result, the capitalist system has reaped an important political advantage at home by erecting and maintaining the image of communism as a massive external threat.

However, shifts in America's relative economic position in the world, as well as changes within the Communist bloc, have begun to pull back the cold war curtain and reveal some fundamental defects in the popular belief that defense spending is in the interest of all Americans.

In America, the growing power of the military-industrial complex aggravates the problems of ordinary citizens in an already troubled economy. Military spending, going primarily as it does to large firms, strengthens monopoly power. Since most war suppliers also produce civilian goods, monopoly pricing power is enhanced in the market for civilian goods as well. Meanwhile, since war production is capital-intensive and complex in its technology, each defense dollar spent produces very few employment gains. Among the hard-core unemployed, military outlays produce no job gains at all. Even for skilled workers, military purchasing and the arms industry are having a declining impact. Thus the long-enjoyed "jobs effect" of military spending is on the wane.

If Americans can better understand the phony ideological arguments on which the military-industrial complex has been built and perpetuates itself, they can appreciate its real economic effects. Contrary to Liberal rhetoric, however, there are few possibilities of simply shifting public outlays to other areas; at least, there are few possibilities without restructuring the entire economy and society. War is waste, but capitalism depends on waste. The capitalist system is inherently unable to opt for rational and humane production.

For their part, Radicals welcome any cooling off of the cold war and any associated reduction in military spending. Such a development would do much to demystify the nature and operations of the American economic system and would open the possibility for reforming it. Given the erosion of American economic power in the world, changing perceptions of the "Communist threat," and the abiding fiscal crisis that haunts the United States, such a turn of events is not impossible. However, given what is at stake, defenders of a production-for-profit system cannot be taken very seriously when they pose as ardent champions of quickly ending the cold war.

_____

The Social Budget
How Long Can We Afford Our Social Security System?

Among our objectives I place the security of men, women
and children of the nation first.... Hence I am looking for a
sound means which I can recommend to provide security
against several of the great disturbing factors in life —
especially those which relate to unemployment and old age.
Franklin D. Roosevelt, June 8, 1934

All in all, Social Security is an excellent example of Director's
Law in operation, namely, "Public expenditures are made for
the primary benefit of the middle class, and financed with
taxes which are borne in considerable part by the poor and
the rich."
Milton Friedman, 1980

The elderly now enjoy the lowest poverty rate of any age
group.
Peter G. Peterson, Former Secretary of Commerce, 1987

If the Social Security system is in trouble it is because it is
being used as a justification for placing heavy and regressive
taxes on those least able to pay.
Senator Daniel P. Moynihan, 1990

THE PROBLEM

The second largest expenditure item in the federal budget, after national defense, is social security, amounting to about $250 billion in 1990.* Created in 1935 in the depths of the Great Depression, the social security system epitomized the New Deal era's commitment to maintaining individuals' social welfare. As the years have passed, the social security system—its benefits, coverage, and place within a growing federal welfare structure—has undergone great changes, but it has not lost its premier position within the federal social budget. However, the American social security system is in trouble.

In the early 1980s, the problem seemed to be quite immediate and caused considerable scurrying to find a short-term solution. Between 1975 and 1983, social security and Medicare outlays had approximately doubled. This sudden surge in transfer payments was directly traceable to a number of developments: inflation (which meant that payments, indexed as they were to cost-of-living increases, had to rise), the enlargement of certain individual benefits, and the increased number of recipients in an aging and longer-living American population. The increase in outlays came precisely as the nation slipped into a serious fiscal crisis. After a brief political debate in the early 1980s over whether the nation could afford its social security system in a time of growing and chronic federal deficits, the immediate funding problems, at least for the time being, were postponed through a combination of increasing participant contributions, shifting trust funds within the various social security programs to cover accounts that were facing imminent exhaustion, and some minor reductions in social security benefits.

The short-term solutions, however, did not address long-run demographic trends that promised to undermine the system's ability to meet its obligations. Increased life expectancy, the eventual retirement of the "baby boomers" of the 1950s and 1960s in the first couple of decades of the twenty-first century, and the relatively low recent birth rate will together eventually produce a ratio of beneficiaries to contributors that must cause funding difficulties. In fact, the rise in this ratio is well under way. In the 1950s, there were seventeen employed persons for each social

---

*Actually, if another $95 billion for Medicare were added, old age outlays would be the *largest* budget item.

FIGURE 14.1 Projected Beneficiaries per Hundred Covered Workers, 1980–2050

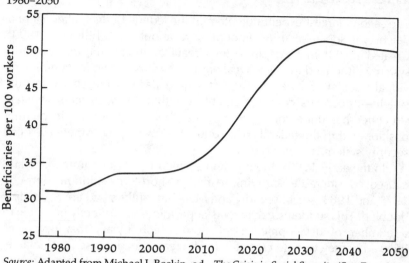

Source: Adapted from Michael J. Boskin, ed., *The Crisis in Social Security* (San Francisco: Institute for Contemporary Studies, 1977), p. 8.

security recipient. By the 1970s, there were only about three. Estimates (assuming no important changes in the law) project that by the third decade of the twenty-first century, there will be about two workers for each retiree (see Figure 14.1).

The problem posed by these trends is obvious: Just how shall we pay for our social security system? As the system was initially explained by President Roosevelt in 1935, it was to be operated like a giant insurance policy. Contributions would flow into trust funds from which workers would receive payments more or less based on what they and their employers had actually contributed. For years, the trust funds bulged deceptively, with more paid in annually than was paid out in benefits.

As time passed, however, several of the original social security premises were changed or abandoned. First, the original self-funding approach was gradually replaced by paying current retirees out of current tax collections.* Second, benefits were disconnected from the amounts actually paid into social security by individuals. Third, the benefits were expanded very greatly—far beyond an actuarial projection of payroll tax payments by individuals and employers. What does all this mean? Quite simply, it means that current tax revenues, including current social security taxes, essentially pay current benefits. Or, to be very blunt, two unknown young readers of this book can look forward to the day when they shall be supporting the author out of their current social security and general tax payments.

Can we continue to operate the social security system as we have known it? Does our generosity need to be tempered by a new economic reality? Must we abandon altogether our commitment to sustaining the elderly and the infirm? The brewing fight over this biggest slice of our social budget pie promises to break out at any time, not only setting ideology against ideology but age group against age group.

SYNOPSIS

Conservatives maintain that the defenders of the social security system have fraudulently promised elderly Americans a retirement income that simply cannot be afforded by the nation. Meanwhile, the very concept of an "involuntary" social security program erodes individuals' rights and operates as a drag on the entire economy in its discouraging of private savings. Liberals respond that social security is both a solemn promise and the only protection that many have from abject poverty in their declining years. Liberals also argue that the fear of the social security system's going bankrupt is a pure scare tactic used by its opponents. Radicals see the eventual sacrificing of the social security system as an illustration of the fiscal crisis confronting government—an inability to provide both outlays

---

*By 1975, we had reached the point where only one year's Old Age outlays exceeded that trust fund's total resources. Subsequent increases in social security taxes have changed this trend, but while the various trust funds now boast sizable surpluses, government accounting procedures have tended to offset this gain. The surpluses are used as credits against general government deficits, thus leading to a politically useful but economically dangerous understatement of current federal deficits and debt. Or, to look at the situation somewhat differently, our current funding approach to social security requires us to pay in more than we are disbursing *and* the excess is funding other government operations. But, will we be willing in the future to tax ourselves more when social security claims exceed payments?

that benefit capital *and* expenditures for people's needs. Thus social security and other social outlays must be reduced constantly.

Anticipating the Arguments

- On the basis of what evidence do Conservatives maintain we cannot "afford" the social security program?
- How do Conservatives and Liberals disagree on the question of an individual's responsibility and choice in the matter of providing for retirement?
- Why do Radicals believe that the growing attack on the social security system really masks a fundamental problem in state financing? What do they see as the cause of this problem?

The Conservative Argument

The social security system was the first and remains the biggest program in the American version of the welfare state. It is therefore appropriate to focus on the social security system in an general discussion of the social budget and the fiscal and economic crisis posed for the nation by enlarged social spending. As with most social programs, social security is an excellent example of how we have been deluded and manipulated since the incipient drift toward welfare statism began under Franklin Roosevelt. Ironically, most Americans do not understand that social security and other "giveaway" programs are pushing the national economy to the brink of disaster. It is not simply a "type" of program that Conservatives oppose for philosophical reasons. The opposition is based on plain economic sense. As we have said before, there is no free lunch. And the cost of the social security banquet, despite its immense popularity, is prohibitive.

MYTH VERSUS REALITY

The managers and political supporters of the social security system have created a number of self-serving myths that persist in spite of common sense and overwhelming evidence to the contrary. Perhaps the most enduring myth is that social security is merely an insurance program, in which government holds tax payments in a pool and then pays them out on an actuarialized basis, just as a private insurance company would. Even a catchy and inventive television commercial on behalf of the social security system perpetuates this belief when it announces: "It's your money!" Nothing could be further from the truth. We long ago abandoned the insurance-fund approach to the social security system. What remains of the old funds (Old Age Benefits, Medicare, and Disability) will be exhausted in a few years. The fact is that social security is operated on a pay-as-you-go basis; consequently, nothing is accumulated. No investment of funds is made, and there is no accumulation of interest—things that, after all, make it possible for private insurance companies to operate not only solvently but profitably.

A pay-as-you-go system means it isn't "your money" if you retire, but someone else's. Your money, meanwhile, is—or will be—going to support someone else. On the surface that may seem fair enough, as long as someone else's money is there when you have retirement needs. Okay, maybe it isn't an insurance system, but it's pretty close, right? Wrong! With retirement benefits (skipping the various nonretirement programs of social security) being paid out of current taxes *and* exceeding the actual contributions of the retiree (since benefits tend to grow much faster than contributions), it is obvious that retirees are receiving more than they themselves paid in. In other words, they are getting transfer payments from those who are productively at work. The fact is that a social security pensioner is just as certainly on "welfare" as is an AFDC mother or a food stamp recipient.

All this leads to a second myth: The retirement monies, whether provided by an insurance or a welfare system, will be there for you when it's your turn to receive. It seems fair that if you pay for someone else, someone should pay for you. However, for this to be possible, the contribution rate has to expand constantly (unless benefits are cut, which, of course, wouldn't be "fair"). Given the demographic profile of the population, the number of recipients is growing far faster than the number of contributors. The situation is a bit like the old pyramid game or chain letter: If you are near the bottom of the list, your money contribution or required number of letters expands geometrically over that required of those above you. As long as the pyramid or chain isn't broken behind you, you will do all right. But like the pyramid or chain letter, the burden for those on the bottom sooner or later becomes too great compared to the estimated rewards, and the link is broken. It is a simple political fact that the relative level of benefits for social security retirees will not be continued when contributors are faced with an excessive burden and little hope that they will ever get back anything like their contributions. There is no economic "proof" that workers in the year 2000 *won't pay* the 30 to 50 percent of their salary needed to sustain retirees at present standards, but it seems likely that such demands on workers will be politically unacceptable.

Meanwhile, the immense popularity of the social security system, as well as its economic difficulties, largely stem from another myth: The social security system was intended, by itself, to provide all of us with a comfortable standard of living when we cease working. Even by Franklin Roosevelt's liberal standards, social security was supposed only to provide "safeguards from misfortune." Framers of the act did not have in mind sending retirees to Florida condos to bask in the sun. Social security was only to protect the very poor and elderly from total destitution. It was, for the more fortunate, to be a small bonus to their personal retirement savings. At any rate, except for the very poor, benefits were to equal what the individual had paid in, which in the 1930s and 1940s wasn't very much. All that has changed today. Many Americans see their social security benefits— which far exceed their contributions—as their entire retirement program. They believe that social security is both a substitute for savings and a reason not to save (more on this later).

UNDESIRED EFFECTS

Because of the persuasiveness of the mythology, there is practically universal acceptance by Americans of the social security system. People who ordinarily grumble about "welfare queens" driving Cadillacs and who would never accept food stamps accept social security payments without a second thought. Moreover, the elderly see social security as a right and are quite willing to vote against any honest politician who has the audacity to question either the philosophy or the economics of the system. Acting as a powerful political lobby, they make ending the program impossible and reducing the system's actual benefits practically impossible. As a result, this political lobby of kindly but uninformed elderly people keeps pushing social security and ultimately the entire economy along the road to disaster. Only serious reeducation can halt this trend.

One of the first educational steps is to see that the social security system is really a tax system, and the very worst kind of tax system at that. As presently funded, individuals who are covered by social security pay a flat 7.65 percent rate on the first $51,000 of income earned. After $51,000, no taxes are paid. This is a regressive tax, falling more heavily on low-income earners than high-income individuals. The irony is that the low wage earners, who most desperately depend on social security, accordingly must pay a higher proportion of their current incomes.

Another disadvantage of the taxation method is that it discourages job creation. With employers required to match the employee's contribution rate, employers find it advantageous to hire fewer workers. This may occur in one of two ways. First, each worker represents a hidden tax payment because employers are required to match employee contributions. By keeping numbers of workers down, taxes and costs are lowered. Second, where employers are already paying the maximum tax because workers are at their maximum wage for paying social security contributions, it is more desirable to require more work from present workers (and pay more in wages) than to hire new workers and pay the additional employment tax. The macroeconomic effects of such a tax system in reducing employment are obvious, but rarely has a Liberal demand manager come forth to criticize these arrangements.

A second economic fact to be recognized is the unfairness of the benefits. Payments are determined neither by the amount paid in nor by the individual's needs. While some limits to benefits are set according to lifetime contributions to the system, the benefit schedule is connected only loosely to real contribution rates. To a considerable extent, conditions totally unconnected to either need or contributions determine payments to the social security recipient. Married persons have greater benefits than the unmarried. A widow who never worked is able to get her late husband's pension. Those who choose to work past the mandated retirement age give up their benefits as long as they work; thus they are penalized for being diligent. Meanwhile, more than 30 percent of all Americans are excluded entirely from social security. It is difficult to defend such benefit arrangements. Part insurance in philosophy and part welfare, the benefit program is both unfair to the needy and inequitable to the contributor. Welfare to the truly indigent is perfectly acceptable to a Conservative.

Even a system by which a contributor received benefits equal to his or her contribution can be defended logically (as long as the contributions are voluntary). However, we have neither.

An undesirable macroeconomic outcome of the social security program has been its impact on savings. As we noted before, the initial object of social security was to provide a bare cushion for those who lost their savings in the Depression years. However, as the coverage and benefits of the program—not just old age benefits but everything from educational to health benefits—has grown, social security has increasingly been treated as a substitute for personal savings. According to studies by Martin Feldstein, social security depresses personal savings by 30 to 50 percent. The social security "contributions" collected by the government are not saved but rather spent on a pay-as-you-go basis. Thus government-forced saving (in withheld contributions) does not replace lost personal savings. The macroeconomic effect of dwindling savings rates is not difficult to estimate. It denies the nation the fund of savings that would otherwise be available for expanded investment. More consumption and less savings mean less capital. Accordingly, with investment lowered, employment is lowered and unemployment increased. The negative macroeconomic impact of social security cannot be overlooked. Feldstein and others estimate the drag on the GNP to be very great. National output may be reduced by as much as 15 to 20 percent as a result of social security's discouragement of savings.

WHAT THE NUMBERS TELL US

Despite compelling arguments about the unfair taxing and compensation aspects of social security and its drag effect on GNP, the bottom line on the social security question is much simpler. It cannot continue to work because (1) there will be too many recipients, (2) benefits are too liberal, and (3) there are too few potential contributors down the road. In other words, it will collapse, not because of any Conservative theoretical criticism, but because it cannot pay its own way.

Therefore, we face three options: (1) Close down the social security system, (2) drastically scale down the benefit structure, or (3) wait for its collapse. Conservatives, naturally, would prefer the first alternative, but recognizing that such a step could, at best, come only over time, the second scenario seems most likely in the short haul. Quite simply, we must begin to shrink the social security system to what it was intended to be—a hedge against personal financial catastrophe and not a guaranteed retirement equal to ordinary living standards. To get individuals to save for their own retirement, the government might legitimately operate its own *voluntary* system of collecting employee contributions (employers should not be forced to pay social security benefits or any other retirement contributions unless they choose to do so as an ordinary aspect of wage considerations). Regardless of whether the retirement program is government-operated or carried on by private insurance companies, employee contributions should be seen as savings that grow in value as interest from loaning accumulates. Moreover, an individual's retirement income becomes properly a function of what she or he has decided to save and not a matter of what others think is appropriate. Those unwilling to save for their "golden years" may be paid a very minimum maintenance after they have ceased work, but that is properly a welfare and not a retirement insurance consideration.

Space prohibits extending the present social security analogy to the entire welfare system, but it should be obvious from the preceding arguments that what is wrong with social security is equally wrong with other components of the social budget. We face a modern-day fiscal crisis of exploding outlays and shrinking ability to pay. The question is not *whether* social outlays will be cut but *how* and *how soon*.

The Liberal Argument

Conservatives are correct when they assert that the social security system is the showpiece and the keystone of American social legislation. They are dead wrong, however, when they claim that if this is the case it "proves" the foolishness of government efforts to maintain minimum social welfare conditions. The Conservative allegation with regard to the "bankruptcy" of social security financing and their charge that we simply cannot afford the excessive benefits of social security are misrepresentations of the facts.

THE IMPORTANCE OF SOCIAL SECURITY

Steeped as it is in the philosophy of voluntaristic and individualistic social behavior, the Conservative argument preaches that it is each person's responsibility to provide for his or her old age or illness. Their arguments, however, fail to point out that this was precisely the kind of social philosophy that prevailed before the New Deal era and before social security. Such an individualistic approach to national social welfare was found wanting at that time, and nothing has happened to change the situation. Even in the best of times, the average industrial worker had only the most limited opportunity to set aside a "nest egg" for his or her retirement years. Indeed, most workers in the pre–New Deal era worked until they were physically unable to go on any longer or, more likely, until they were fired by bosses interested in hiring younger, more productive workers. The "declining years" of an elderly worker were often spent in the back bedroom of a son's or daughter's home. This "extended family" condition has received praise lately from Conservative social theorists such as George Gilder, who emphasize the values of family and togetherness. Reality was usually different, however. Having an old person live with you meant, sooner or later, increased medical bills for the family and almost always long hours of tending the elderly when they became bedridden. Not many who had to go through this experience—neither the old parent nor the children—found life quite so idyllic as modern exponents of the extended family make it seem.

For other poor workers, without savings and without family, there was the grim prospect of wasting away in a public institution. "Going to the poorhouse" was not just gallows humor among workers; it was a very real possibility. Usually located on the outskirts of a city, "county homes" and "state homes" had an exquisite institutional ugliness. Workers usually lived dormitory-style; thus husband and wife were separated save for an occasional walk on the premises. The food was of equal quality and quantity to the fare offered at the county jail. There were few social programs for residents to enjoy, just utter boredom until the end.

While Conservatives anguish over the adverse effects of social security on private savings habits, their concerns overlook the fact that few American workers were able to save anyway. After the social security system was instituted, saving was not only possible but required, as workers and their employers put income aside in trust funds.

For those workers who did succeed in putting away some savings for their later years, the Great Depression of the 1930s demonstrated that there was little virtue in voluntary frugality. As the stock market crashed and banking and financial institutions went under, the elderly of the era watched their savings vanish. Practically overnight, the diligent citizen who had planned ahead for retirement was no better off than the poorest worker or the most profligate. This was the situation when the Social Security Act was passed in 1935. Far from being a destructive "giveaway," it was a very modest attempt to pull millions of elderly Americans out of the terrible insecurity of economic dependency. Conservatives represent social security as a step into the collectivist state; the irony is that it returned many elderly people to a condition of economic self-sufficiency and individualism.

The social security system has been broadened since 1935. First, many additional workers and their dependents came to be covered under the law. Second, the social security system was extended to provide health and disability benefits. Third, the payments under social security provisions were enlarged. As a result, Americans came to rely on social security to handle the economic problems of their retirement years. It became part of a new social contract between government and its citizens, and it is almost universally popular.

It would be wrong to conclude, as Conservatives suggest, that we no longer need social security, that the modern-day affluence of Americans would allow a private and voluntary accumulation of savings that would be a "better deal" for workers than the social security system. Comparisons with private pension programs are downright misleading. No private insurance company can offer—regardless of the price—a retirement package that includes a pension, health insurance, disability, and life insurance where the benefits are protected from inflation, are mostly tax-free, and would not be lost nor reduced if contributions were temporarily interrupted should the contributor lose his or her job.

BALANCING THE BUDGET ON RETIREES' BACKS

The Conservative attitude toward social security is another dimension of their budget-balancing preoccupation, but in this case it misses the point altogether. In fact, Conservatives know full well that their charges of social security profligacy and bankruptcy have been merely a smoke screen for other objectives. When the social security system faced a short-term funding crisis in the early 1980s, Conservatives, arguing that the crisis "proved" the system was bankrupt, succeeded in increasing social security taxes while lowering some benefits. Pretending that these reforms were needed only to permit the system to be solvent and self-funding, the Reagan administration had other plans for the suddenly swelling trust fund accounts.

Conservatives pose as "fiscal realists" in discussing the funding problems of the social security system, but they rarely mention the "creative accounting" devices the Reagan reforms of the 1980s built into the system. Precisely as the Reagan administration was cutting income taxes for the well-to-do, they raised social security withholding taxes. For those with incomes below $50,000, social security contributions went up by nearly 50 percent during the last half of the 1980s. For many taxpayers these increased contributions overwhelmed any real income tax reduction gains. Deceptive as this was, the matter did not end there. The increased social security contributions quickly filled the depleted trust fund accounts and produced, on paper at least, a growing surplus. However, the social security surplus was not carried on government's books separately, but went into the general tax collections. There it was used to reduce, again on paper, the size of annual government deficits. The effect of all of this has been to impose a special tax on the less well-to-do to reduce the deficit and to create a situation where social security is, in a practical way, more impoverished than it was before the 1983 Reagan reforms. Of course, the ultimate "bankrupting" of the social security system would produce few laments among Conservatives, since the destruction of social security remains their professed goal.

WE CAN AFFORD IT

The short-run social security crisis of the early 1980s was headed off by some "quick fixes": raising maximum contribution levels (individual payments have doubled since 1983), postponing a cost-of-living increase, and taxing benefits paid to high-income households. Liberals agree with Conservatives that these are not long-term solutions. However, best estimates now suggest that they should get us through until the 2020s. Consequently, despite the shrillness of the Conservative assault on social security, the problem is certainly not as pressing as it appeared to be in the early 1980s.

However, we are still left with the long-run problem. Can a smaller pool of workers sustain a growing pool of retirees without producing an unfair *intergenerational redistribution of income* that is eventually going to be politically rejected by those paying the transfers? Two strategies would ease the problem. First, the United States must maintain a steady, high rate of real economic growth (certainly better growth performance than experienced during the Reagan-Bush "boom" of the 1980s). An expanding economy, as Reagan's own 1983 study of the social security system stated, would provide the foundation for continued funding of the system pretty much as it currently exists. While, even with such growth, workers will have to transfer greater amounts to retirees, the rising incomes of the contributors will ease the pain of larger outlays. Moreover, before they reject the social security system, those making the transfer payments would be well served considering the alternative: the substantial costs they themselves might have to pay to sustain a retired parent or grandparent if no social security system existed.

The second strategy requires taking social security out of politics or vice versa. By organizing the system as a separate independent agency, the tendency to bribe elderly voters with irresponsibly expensive short-term benefits would be removed from congressional and presidential politics. The system should be removed from its Health and Human Services cabinet department and organized as a separate independent board, perhaps similar to the Federal Reserve System. The point of such an effort is to return social security to its earlier nonpartisan place.

Of course, Liberals understand that social security is really a "stalking horse" for the entire social welfare structure. Conservatives may be willing to "save" social security if other social programs are sacrificed, or they may be willing to accept a trimmed-down social security program. The Conservative view rests on the assumption that we, as a people, can no longer pay for the levels of social welfare we accepted as "right and proper" a couple of decades ago. Liberals reject such a view.

The Radical Argument

The current crisis in the American social security system cannot be understood apart from the general fiscal crisis that grips the government budgets of all modern capitalist economies. From the Radical perspective, we must go beyond the narrow and partisan claims of

Liberal and Conservative adversaries and look deeper into the fundamental relations of the state and capitalist enterprise. These real economic relationships, not merely political prejudices, set the actual limits to the growth and development of social spending.

THE STATE BUDGET WITHIN CAPITALIST ECONOMIES

Within a capitalist economic system, the object is always to employ capital and to produce goods in such a way that profits (or surplus over the costs of production) continue to rise. It should be remembered that this is not an arbitrary and doctrinaire definition. Conservatives as well as Liberals know full well that "profits are the name of the game." Conservatives, of course, maintain that government appropriation of the outcome of production (government taxes and their budgetary allocations) come *at the expense* of the private sector. In other words, what government takes and redistributes is a subtraction from what businesses would otherwise receive. Liberals, on the other hand, also see the government taxing and budgetary process as redistributive, but defend it on the grounds that either such redistribution is socially desirable or that government spending in fact generates output that would not otherwise take place (see the Liberal argument in Issue 9). Both views, however, miss the important role played by government taxing and budgeting within the modern capitalist state—they fail to grasp the central place of the state in the process of accumulating capital *and* maintaining social and economic order. In consequence, neither understands the central issues involved in the political and economic struggle over social spending in general or the social security system in particular.

If we examine the taxing and budgeting activities of modern capitalist states, it becomes apparent that they pursue two basically different objectives: *accumulation* and *legitimation*.* On the one hand, the state undertakes actions that are aimed directly at stimulating economic growth and encouraging business profits (providing for capital accumulation). On the other hand, the state attempts to create and maintain general conditions of social harmony, thus legitimating

---

*The following analysis adopts the terminology and concepts of James O'Connor, *Fiscal Crisis of the State* (New York: St. Martin's Press, 1973).

the operation of a capitalist society. If in fact the state could provide the desired levels of accumulation and legitimation at the same time, there would be no crisis. Nor, of course, would there be much reason to study economics since, in such an Alice in Wonderland world, scarcity would not exist. In the real world, however, these two objectives are competing uses for the state budget. Moreover, as we shall see, outlays for one purpose may be in direct contradiction to the goals of the other objective. The contradiction has become particularly sharp in our era of lagging capitalist growth. Presently, it is obvious that there are very real limits to the budgetary outlays that government can make in these two general areas without (1) raising to unacceptable levels the taxes on society or on certain groups within society or (2) generating excessive inflationary pressures (see Issues 10 and 11).

To see how the "accumulation" and "legitimation" functions of the capitalist state budget work, we need only dissect the budget according to these functions. First, there is a broad category of social capital outlays that either *directly* increase capitalist output (social investment) or *indirectly* lower the cost of capitalist production (social consumption). Social investment and social consumption spending add to the accumulation of capital in a variety of ways. Social investment includes outlays for roads, airports, and industrial parks; that is, outlays that increase private-sector output by having government pay for part of the investment cost. Social consumption expenditures such as education and unemployment insurance are useful to business *indirectly*, since the enterprise does not have to pay for training its workers or for sustaining them when economic conditions deteriorate. While social investment and social consumption spending primarily serve the accumulating function, it is obvious that they also work to legitimate the capitalist system. Meanwhile, certain other outlays, which we shall call social expenses, have not the slightest impact on accumulation and work only to achieve legitimation. This is the service performed by those budgetary expenditures that commonly are called "welfare"–payments to the surplus or unemployed portion of the population for the purpose of bribing them into complacency and political acceptance of the economic order.

The categories may seem confusing and, in truth, the confusion is heightened by the fact that some government outlays serve both accumulation and legitimation ends. Social security, for instance,

330 Problems of Aggregate Economic Policy

lowers the production cost of employers (by having government provide pension funds) and legitimates by sustaining otherwise "useless" workers. Nevertheless, with a little reflection it is possible to categorize government outlays according to how they serve one or both of these basic functions. Such an approach is important because it demystifies the otherwise obscure organization of the government budget. We can begin to see just what certain spending categories are intended to do.

THE GROWING FISCAL CRISIS

Viewing the budget according to the categories of accumulation and legitimation ties together nicely the Radical critique offered in the earlier issues dealing with stabilization policy, unemployment, deficits, and military spending. By looking at how the government budget is constructed according to the conflicting demands of accumulation and legitimation, we can gain insight into the problems of modern macroeconomic policy-making. The issue of social security becomes understood in the context of a much larger political and economic crisis.

The general fiscal crisis of the modern capitalist state (within which the social security crisis is but one small element) can be put simply enough: There are rising demands for government outlays and a dwindling capacity or willingness to pay for such outlays through taxes. Thus the crisis takes several forms. First, there is the problem of rising accumulation and legitimation demands. In the current period of economic stagnation, business (in particular the big-business or monopoly sector) requires greater outlays (or what amounts to the same thing, tax cuts) to lower production costs and facilitate capital accumulation. Thus farm subsidies and business "investment credit" programs have continued to expand. Some direct aids to business—such as the "enterprise-zone" concept—have been presented inaccurately, as if they were really aid to the unemployed worker. Meanwhile, with chronically high unemployment and a stagnation of real income growth, there has been a rise in legitimation claims.

Second, with claims rising, there has been steady pressure for tax increases. This has stimulated a considerable number of taxpayer revolts such as California's Proposition 13 and dozens of similar efforts to force down taxes. Ronald Reagan's victory in 1980, perhaps more than anything else, signaled a popular reaction among tax-payers to hold down spending and even to cut it back. Yet when we look at the fiscal restraint actually produced by the tax revolts and by Reagan's victory, we find that few ordinary people have benefitted.

The budgetary cuts forced by the fiscal crisis have come primarily from the "legitimation" activities of government. Using Marxist terminology, the budget has become increasingly an instrument of class oppression and domination. Thus budgetary actions that mainly benefit big business' and upper-income groups' abilities to accumulate profits and capital have been protected or have actually expanded, while budget items aimed at maintaining a minimum level of personal well-being have been sacrificed. Quite simply, it is *first* a matter of profits for General Motors and IBM. Conservatives, with their supply-side and trickle-down theories, have been surprisingly honest in putting forth this objective. Even more surprisingly, people who have nothing to gain from such an approach have accepted this nonsense, but only up to a point. Social security is a good example of how the fiscal crisis can explode into a serious political crisis.

SOCIAL SECURITY AND THE FISCAL CRISIS

The recent shrinkage of purely "legitimation" outlays within the budget, while painful to welfare recipients, never held out much possibility for solving the fiscal crisis. Our outlays for the poor always have been too small to provide a significant amount of savings that can be transferred to needed accumulation activities. Moreover, even the wildest-eyed supply-sider knows at heart that literally "starving the poor to death" would bring more political chaos than the system could handle. After all, some minimum outlay must be made for legitimation.

Social security, with its $200 to $300 billion in outlays each year, is certainly a more attractive area from which to obtain accumulation gains. Because "everybody" pays into social security and receives its benefits, the class nature of raiding social security is not so immediately obvious. If we look beneath the surface, however, we find that the social security problem is a good illustration of the basic class nature of government spending and taxing.

On the revenue side, social security taxes are collected only on earned income. No taxes are paid from income received from rents,

interest, and dividends. Thus the owners of wealth and property are
exempted from any payments. The payroll tax itself is regressive, with
a constant percentage levied from the first dollar up to a maximum
earned-income level. The result is that low-income groups must pay
a higher proportion of their income in social security taxes. Currently
these people are told that the social security system can be saved only
by making the tax more regressive, that is, by raising their percentage
contribution (and modestly expanding the taxable income level) or by
taxing the benefits actually received. This regressive tax structure is
encouraged by the fiction that social security is self-funding, or that
you get according to what you pay in. By keeping the self-funding
myth alive, workers are told that they can get only what they pay for.
If the various trust funds go bankrupt, contributions must increase or
benefits must go down. This successfully evades the questions of
guaranteeing minimum retirement benefits irrespective of contributions and of establishing minimum welfare standards for the elderly
and the ill. It maintains the capitalist faith that we are responsible
only for ourselves and not for others.

Class bias also appears on the benefits side of the social security
system. Proposals to lengthen the period for retirement eligibility
work against the low-income production worker whose ability to
work productively is diminished by the physical demands of his or
her job. Being forced into early retirement because of health means
accepting greatly reduced benefits for the rest of one's life. Meanwhile, well-to-do professionals, who do not suffer from health-
damaging employment, are permitted to collect benefits *and* earned
income after retirement age has been reached.

The assault on the social security system reveals much about
capitalism in general and about the current crisis of the capitalist
order in particular. First, by attacking social security as well as such
traditional "legitimation" functions as welfare spending, the
defenders of capitalism reveal just how far and how deep the fiscal crisis has developed. The trade-off between accumulation and legitimation activities by the state has become quite severe, revealing a much
greater problem certainly than well-meaning Liberal defenders of
social security understand. Second, both the attack on social security
and the proposed compromises to save it amount to a new "disciplining" of the working population. Even with its many flaws, social security has been an important social welfare program and has been

immensely popular with most Americans. Its promise far exceeded its delivery, but it did create a widely held belief that society would indeed protect individuals. Reneging on social security sends the signal that this commitment will no longer be honored. Whether Americans are willing to accept this new discipline of reduced social welfare remains to be seen, but the old Liberal public policy that delivered both extensive accumulation and legitimation outlays is being undone.

America in the World
What Limits Does the New International Economy Impose?

Under a system of a perfectly free commerce, each country
naturally devotes its capital and labor to such employments as
are most beneficial to each. This pursuit of individual advantage
is admirably connected with the universal good of the whole.

David Ricardo, 1817

If nations can learn to provide themselves with full employment by their domestic policy . . . international trade would
cease to be what it is, namely, a desperate expedient to maintain employment at home by forcing sales on foreign markets
and restricting purchases which if successful will merely shift
the problem of unemployment to the neighbor.

John Maynard Keynes, 1936

On the whole, capitalism is growing far more rapidly than
before; but this growth is not only becoming more and more
uneven in general, its unevenness also manifests itself, in
particular, in the decay of countries richest in capital.

V.I. Lenin, 1916

Japanese and German automobile companies have converted
Detroit executives from card-carrying free traders to lobbyists
for protection to their markets.

Paul Samuelson, 1980

Given a level playing field, the U.S. can outcompete anybody,
anytime, anywhere.

James Baker, Secretary of the Treasury, 1988

THE PROBLEM

Thus far our survey of contemporary economic issues has centered almost exclusively on purely domestic concerns. Now we must add a missing dimension: *the world*. Until comparatively recently, Americans have not paid much attention to international economic affairs. From the end of World War II to the 1970s, the preeminent position of America in both international trade and finance was pretty much taken for granted by Americans (and by most of the rest of the world too), very much as we took for granted our international political preeminence. Unlike many nations whose very existence depended on foreign trade and commerce, American imports and exports of goods had never been very large, not amounting to much more than 6 percent of our gross national product. As one economist observed of the American tendency to worry little about matters of foreign trade and finance, to do otherwise "would be to let the tail wag the dog."*

To understand how we have moved away from our earlier insular, unconcerned attitude toward the rest of the world and to pondering the impact of international events on the domestic American economy, we need only look at the following chain of representative events over the past two decades:

The Vietnam War (or at least our participation in it) ends in 1973 as an American defeat with a corresponding loss of self- and worldwide esteem of America's preeminence in global politics.

In 1973 and 1977, the United States is ravaged (as is Europe) by an energy shortage and rising energy costs precipitated by oil embargoes initiated by OPEC.

Beginning in 1976, the United States commences an uninterrupted period of annual trade deficits (see Figures 15.1 and 15.2).

In 1985, the United States, for the first time since just before World War I, becomes a net debtor nation, owing more to the rest of the world than is owed to it.

In early 1987, the United States becomes the largest debtor nation in the world.

*Campbell R. McConnell, *Economics: Principles, Problems, and Policies*, 7th ed. (New York: McGraw-Hill, 1977), p. 918.

FIGURE 15.1   Exports and Imports as a Percent of GNP, 1929–1985

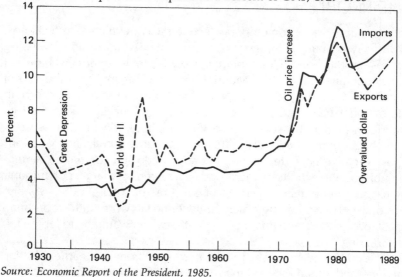

Source: *Economic Report of the President, 1985.*

On "Black Monday," October 19, 1987, the New York Stock Exchange
suffers its biggest one-day loss, and American and world financial
markets undergo a short-lived, but thoroughly frightening, panic.
Causes of this crisis are generally held to be America's "double
deficits"—a federal deficit of about $200 billion for the year and an
annual trade deficit of about the same amount.

In October 1989, in a scarcely noted move, a Japanese investment group,
Mitsubishi, buys Rockefeller Center in Manhattan, long an architec-
tural symbol of American achievement in enterprise, commerce, and
technology.

What these and other events showed was that (1) the long-held American
economic and political preeminence in the world was in retreat; (2) we
now depended more on the world for trade (but were also chronically
buying more than we were selling); and (3) the conditions of our domestic

FIGURE 15.2   U.S. International Transaction Balances: 1970 to 1986

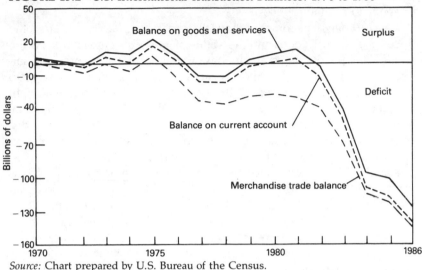

Source: Chart prepared by U.S. Bureau of the Census.

well-being were intricately connected to our international trade and financial condition. Alas, the tail was wagging the dog.

To understand the nature of domestic-international interconnectedness and to appreciate the constraints our international situation places on the domestic economy, we need to comprehend at the outset how international trade takes place.

Although discussions of international economic issues invariably become quite complicated, mastery of the fundamental reasoning involved is easier than many noneconomists realize. The conditions affecting trade among nations are not very different from the conditions affecting trade among individuals in a simple market. Just as an individual's ability to sell his or her goods is basically determined by (1) the price of the goods and (2) the ability and willingness of buyers to pay that price, so it is with exports and imports. Whatever America or any other exporting nation is able to sell to the rest of the world is determined by the prices that must be charged for their exported goods and by foreign purchasers' willingness and ability to pay such prices. Similarly, the amount of goods we buy from abroad (import) depends on the prices we are charged and our willingness or ability to pay these prices.

Accordingly, it becomes obvious that the various factors that affect the prices of a nation's goods and the ability of world buyers to purchase the goods at the prices offered are the basic variables in determining any particular nation's export or import position. Some examples may serve to make the point a bit clearer. All things being equal, anything that might raise the price of American goods relative to the prices being charged by other (non-American) sellers of the same good would obviously discourage foreign purchases of American products. Higher production costs, resulting from rising factor prices, various production inefficiencies, or a general domestic inflation would raise the prices of exports. And, as we saw earlier in our examination of the federal deficit, so too could an international exchange rate situation where the exporting nation's currency is strong (high-priced) relative to importing nations' currencies.* The operation of such forces in pushing our export prices upward would likely lead to a decline of American exports. And what makes exports unattractive to foreigners usually makes imports attractive at home. With foreign goods cheaper than American goods, American consumers would also choose to buy foreign products. In other words, our exports would be lower and our imports higher as a result of this price disparity. *Of course, the opposite would be true if our prices were relatively lower than prices charged by the rest of the world* (that is, our exports higher and our imports lower as a result of this type of price disparity).

However, even if our prices were competitive with world prices (or were even lower) we could also face difficulties, at least in exporting goods, if the rest of the world was gripped by a serious recession that greatly reduced foreigners' ability to buy our goods. On the other hand, we would expect to be able to sell more in the world—as long as our prices were attractive—if the world was undergoing a high order of prosperity.

---

*A strong (relative to other nations) currency will not necessarily work against a nation's exports and balance of payments. Other factors are important, such as the relative prices of goods in the first place. However, in the mid-1980s, high interest rates in the United States led to foreigners seeking American dollars to purchase high-return American investments. The result was "an exceptionally strong dollar" even though the United States was already in a serious trade deficit situation. The higher-priced dollar meant that when U.S. goods were sold overseas, after the conversion of dollar prices to that of the local currency, they were priced quite high. The result was to depress American exports even further. Meanwhile, imported goods enjoyed, after price conversion into dollars, low prices that encouraged U.S. imports to soar.

This comparatively simple model of world trade, however, becomes more complicated when we begin to mix and match our price and demand variables. For instance, consider what will happen if American prices are relatively high compared to the rest of the world *and* we are undergoing a modest expansion in the domestic economy while most of the world economies are in a slump. U.S. exports will be relatively low because of higher prices *and* because of diminished worldwide ability to buy our goods. Meanwhile, we will import more because our capacity to purchase is fairly high and foreign goods are cheaper than American-made products. Indeed, this was precisely the real-world situation in the mid-1980s as the United States began to run up very large trade deficits.

While the mechanisms affecting exports and imports are rather easily explained, they are more complex if we look a bit deeper. What caused American prices to be higher than world prices for many products in the 1980s? What caused world economies to slump while ours expanded moderately? Most important, to what extent could we have altered the underlying forces to close our trade gap? Explanations to these and to other questions about the relative international trade and financial position of the United States are scarcely matters of universal agreement among economists, as we shall see in the following debate. However, near-unanimity exists on one point: *The U.S. economy is more firmly interconnected with the rest of the world than ever before.* As a result, our domestic economic policies—both in their immediate objectives and in their longer-term effects—must always be seen as having an international connection. Moreover, the connection is two-way: other nations can surely be expected to respond to our policy initiatives. Their actions in turn rebound back on the United States, perhaps negating or distorting the outcomes we sought with our original domestic policy. For American economic policy-makers, the world has become a much smaller and more complicated place in the past few decades.

SYNOPSIS

Conservatives argue that U.S. trade and currency problems are traceable to protectionism, pegged exchange rates, and ill-conceived domestic economic policy. Liberals oppose the Conservative remedy of free trade and floating exchange rates, maintaining that the cost in terms of jobs and industrial decline in the United States would surpass any benefits. They hold that only stimulation of the domestic economy will assure international vitality. To Radicals, the present international trade and finance problems of the United States are a gauge of the nation's decline from power and a further measure of the chronic capitalist crisis of production and distribution.

Anticipating the Arguments

- According to Conservatives, what particular economic problems are caused by protectionism?
- Why do Liberals believe that even worse problems would be caused by free trade and floating exchange rates?
- What do Radicals identify as the cause for recent U.S. balance-of-payments problems?

The Conservative Argument

Perhaps the severest test of commitment to a free and open capitalist economy arises with respect to international trade and finance. Economists, politicians, and especially business leaders who perceive the advantages of competition and the market and who ardently oppose any type of controls or intervention in domestic activities are ever-tempted to abandon their philosophy at the national borders. Perhaps it is a narrow nationalism or a basic parochialism in economic thought, but the logic of free markets is too easily abandoned when international issues are raised. For the consistent Conservative, however, there should be no exceptions. Free economic arrangements are as crucial internationally as they are domestically.

THE NECESSITY OF FREE TRADE

The first requirement for a free trade arrangement is the elimination of all tariffs, quotas, and bilateral or multilateral trade agreements that inhibit the free operation of international markets. Each nation must be free to sell its goods to any other, and each nation must be open to any other's goods. Regrettably, however, the desire for protectionism runs very deep among nations. This remnant of outmoded mercantilist philosophy persistently reappears when one nation gains a production or price advantage over another in a particular product or line of products. In the United States, it appears when firms or industries act as special-interest groups lobbying Congress to raise duties on hated imports or to set quotas on these imports. Supposedly, by limiting the ability of foreign firms to compete through price or other means, American industry's position is enhanced.

Ironically (in terms of the long-run effects), labor unions in affected industries very often ally themselves with the corporation in their lobbying effort. For example, in the 1980s, the United Steelworkers joined with the steel industry to urge import restraints on certain "specialty steel" items. From the union's point of view, the object is always to protect jobs. The real outcome is quite different, however, for several reasons.

First, protectionism is costly. It raises the prices of imported goods for all consumers or artificially holds up the price of competing domestic goods. This may mean jobs and income for steelworkers and steel companies in Gary, Indiana, but it means reduced buying power and lost jobs elsewhere. Tariffs and quotas have not protected American earnings, but have merely redistributed income and jobs and raised prices for everybody.

Second, protectionism encourages inefficiency. Without the incentive provided by competition, neither business nor labor is induced to increase productivity or to modernize production techniques. In turn, consumers must pay for an industry's protected inefficiency, which can be quite costly over time because it tends to grow cumulatively. The limits on foreign competition are very often increased as the production gaps between a vibrant overseas producer and a lethargic domestic industry grow.

Third, protectionism invites retaliation. Other nations will be induced to follow the same protectionist path if their goods are effectively priced out of our domestic markets. Thus we may find the threat of foreign steel eliminated at the cost of being unable to sell U.S. tractors in foreign markets. The ultimate result is the end of trade altogether.

Fourth, protectionism invites other undesirable tinkering with trade, exchange rates, and capital flows to effect political solutions to economic problems. For instance, Liberals would attempt to artificially improve our international balance of payments through a variety of interventions. Practically disregarding the favorable effect of inflows of foreign earnings by U.S. businesses on our balance of payments, many Liberals have incorrectly singled out the export of U.S. capital as a primary cause for balance-of-payments deficits. Their shortsighted cure is to restrict U.S. overseas investment. Beginning in 1964, through special taxes on American purchases of foreign securities, overseas investment has been discouraged. As with all protectionist actions, the effect has been counterproductive for the economy. American businesses are placed at a competitive disadvantage in world markets at precisely the time when they should be developing strength.

Free trade and free overseas movement of U.S. capital may indeed mean the end of some American industries and may throw some workers out of jobs. However, other production possibilities are opened. Let the Koreans concentrate on toy or textile production and the United States exploit its computer technology. Indeed, let each nation develop its comparative advantages so that trade between them is possible.

Milton Friedman has emphasized the significance of a commitment to free trade this way:

> There are few measures we could take that would do more to promote the cause of freedom at home and abroad. Instead of making grants to foreign governments in the name of economic aid—and thereby promoting socialism—while at the same time imposing restrictions on the products they succeed in producing—and thereby hindering free enterprise—we could assume a consistent and principled stance. We could say to the rest of the world: We believe in freedom and intend to practice it. No one can force you to be free. That is your business. But we can offer you full co-operation on equal terms to all. Our market is open to you. Sell here what you can and wish to. Use the proceeds to buy what you wish. In this way co-operation among individuals can be world wide yet free.*

THE NECESSITY OF FLOATING EXCHANGE RATES

Despite the central importance of free trade policies in developing an efficient and mutually beneficial system of international commerce,

*Milton Friedman, *Capitalism and Freedom* (Chicago: University of Chicago Press, 1962), p. 74.

free trade alone will not bring freedom to international markets. The other side of the free trade coin is the maintenance of freely floating exchange rates. Indeed, the two must proceed together.

To understand the advantages of flexible exchange rates, we need to see how they work and how pegged rates cause trading difficulties. Take two countries, the United States and Great Britain, for instance. Consider also a particular bundle of representative goods. In Britain, this bundle of goods can presently be purchased for £50, and in the United States an identical bundle costs $100. Accordingly, we can say that £50 buys $100 worth of goods, and vice versa. Thus we can conclude that in terms of a free or floating "exchange," £50 = $100, or £1 = $2, or $1 = £.5. Now consider that inflationary pressures develop in the United States, causing the dollar price of our bundle of goods to rise to $200. If the exchange rates are still floating freely, the new exchange rate will be £1 = $4. Inflation has reduced, both at home and overseas, the buying power of the dollar, which is exactly the effect we would expect of inflation. However, if the United States tried to maintain the old $2 = £1 rate, the official exchange value of dollars to pounds would be overvalued. The price of American goods in Britain would be artificially high. Rather than getting an equivalent bundle of goods for £50, Britons would get only half a bundle for their money if they bought American goods. Meanwhile, in the United States, British goods would be relatively cheaper than American goods. It would take only $2 to buy goods denominated at £1 rather than the $4 that would be required if we had a freely floating exchange rate reflecting the actual 4-to-1 dollars-to-pounds ratio. It becomes immediately obvious that pegged rates that are either above or below the real purchasing power parity (based on our identical bundles of goods) make it impossible for stability to exist in international markets. Nations with currencies that are overvalued relative to those of other nations will actually encourage a worsening balance of trade as import prices are held down and export prices are held up. And so it was for the United States during the mid- and late 1980s as certain domestic economic policies tended to produce a strong and expensive dollar. Meanwhile—and this is a strategy not lost on most nations—undervaluation of a nation's currency tends to encourage exports and discourage imports.

From the end of World War II until the 1970s, the world used a fixed exchange rate system. Under what was known as the Bretton

Woods* arrangements, the U.S. dollar replaced the traditional international unit of account – gold – as the instrument for measuring and making international payments.

To oversee these international transactions, the International Monetary Fund (IMF) was created. The pound, the franc, the mark, the yen, and all other currencies were valued by the IMF against the dollar. Thus when a nation experienced domestic inflation that raised the price of its goods relative to those of other nations, it was obliged, for international money exchange purposes, to devalue its currency in relation to the dollar. If, for instance, the British experienced an inflation that doubled the price (in pounds) of British goods, the only way to bring the inflated British currency into proper balance with unchanged dollars (and other currencies) would be to devalue the pound by one-half. Each dollar would now buy twice as many pounds and twice as much British goods as was possible before the revaluing. If the British did not devalue their currency, trading nations would shun either their products or their currency, and the domestic crisis would be worsened. To forestall short-term shortages of funds for international payments and to avoid the anarchy of devaluation wars as each nation sought to gain a brief currency advantage over others, the trading nations maintained reserve balances with the International Monetary Fund or could borrow from the fund. Meanwhile, the fund pegged currencies to the dollar, adjusting values from time to time as economic conditions within nations changed. So long as the dollar was sound, the problems of inflation or unemployment could be limited to the affected country. The system's weakness, however, was what everyone had thought to be its strength – the dollar.

During the 1950s and 1960s, the previously weakened European and Japanese economies strengthened precisely as the American economy slowed. For the United States, the pegged exchange rate meant maintaining an overvalued dollar. The result was a growing balance-of-payments deficit during the 1970s as overpriced American goods sold poorly in foreign markets while cheaper foreign goods flooded the United States. Under a pegged system, the only options to eliminate the balance-of-payments deficits were to (1) pay out gold

*Meeting at Bretton Woods, New Hampshire, toward the end of World War II, the Allied powers agreed to an "adjustable-peg" system. While exchange rates for individual currencies were pegged to the dollar, their value in dollar terms could be changed to reflect overvaluation or undervaluation.

to creditors (so long as we were on an international gold standard); (2) engineer a domestic recession to lower import demand and reduce the prices of exported goods (thus increasing export volume); (3) establish import controls; or (4) resort to an official devaluation of the nation's currency. For a variety of reasons, each of these options has such serious political or economic effects that the balance-of-payments deficit could not be eliminated. As a result, the worsening U.S. payments situation through the early 1970s was directly traceable to the Bretton Woods–IMF system of fixed exchange rates.

Furthermore, the flow of dollars into European markets and the effects of U.S. government efforts to impose exchange controls created extensive internal currency problems for all nations. The initial flood of U.S. dollars and the attempt to maintain the value of these dollars forced an unwanted inflation on many European nations as their central banks purchased all dollars presented to them. With foreigners now holding more dollars than they wanted—dollars that were believed overvalued by the old Bretton Woods pegging system—the United States was forced to take action. On August 15, 1971, President Nixon suspended the dollar's convertibility to gold. At the time, foreign dollar holdings were four times greater than the value of the U.S. gold stock, the price of which was then officially stated as $35 per ounce. Gold henceforth became a speculative commodity having no official role in international payments. It climbed to over $900 per ounce in 1980 before tumbling back to between $300 and $400 by the mid-1980s.

After the United States ceased gold conversion, there were periodic efforts to revalue the dollar under the old pegging system. However, even after several devaluations of the dollar, it became obvious that the era of fixed exchange rates was over. Each nation now let its currency "float" to whatever value the market established, and neither gold nor U.S. dollars served as the international currency. Instead, the IMF kept national payment accounts in order through a kind of "paper gold" (SDRs, special drawing rights) that were made available to members on a quota system. The value of the paper gold is based on an average of five leading nations' currencies.

The drift toward floating exchange rates was a desirable development. If practiced honestly and without the slightest tinkering by governments, floating rates allow nations to trade goods based on their real values as opposed to the manipulated values under pegged rates.

Over the long run, flexible exchange rates eliminate balance-of-payments deficits and associated problems. The market forces of supply and demand for a nation's currency create an equilibrium. Assume that two nations are trading. An excess of imports over exports in nation A will bid up the price of the currency of the exporting nation B (or lower the value of the importer's currency relative to that of the exporter). The currency of importing nation A is now devalued. However, this means that its goods are now lower-priced than before, and its exports to B will rise while its imports from B will fall until equilibrium between the two trading nations is reached.

From the point of view of most Conservatives, the abandonment of pegged exchange rates and the international gold standard have freed international trade from some of the tyrannies of the past. Gold prices may fluctuate as a matter of speculative supply and demand. In theory at least, floating exchange rates can reflect increasingly the real value of a nation's currency against that of other nations. However, this latter situation has not yet been attained. The present managed float system still allows member nations great latitude in determining their own exchange rates and in taking individual actions to bolster their currency. Until exchange rates are freely flexible and until free trade principles are generally accepted, international trade and currency crises will continue.*

INTERNATIONAL CRISIS AS FAILURE OF DOMESTIC POLICIES

The creation of free trade and freely floating rates, desirable as they are, will not protect a nation that is hell-bent to cut its own throat. The recent exchange rate and trading difficulties of the United States are the direct result of foolish domestic policies. In particular, the expansionary fiscal and monetary policies of the 1970s triggered an inflationary situation that, to our benefit, did drive the price of the dollar downward, but also caused soaring product prices (relative to the rest

*The argument on behalf of floating exchange rates presented here is the "traditional" Conservative view. It should be noted, however, that some Conservatives, led recently by Robert Mundell, favor a return to the gold standard. This view argues that tying the domestic and international monetary arrangements to a fixed gold standard will create greater stability, making it impossible for nations to export their domestic inflationary policies and to "manipulate" exchange rates to their own advantage.

of the world) that overwhelmed any exchange rate gains. The net result was a decrease in U.S. exports and a rise in U.S. imports. Moreover, in an effort to protect themselves from "importing" the American inflation, a number of our trading partners undertook contractionary economic policies at home. Correspondingly, as the German, Japanese, and other economies cooled down, the ability of the United States to sell in these nations was further reduced.

To prove the point once again that domestic policies are interconnected with international economic conditions, consider what the costs were in the 1980s as America came to grips with the chronic inflation that had gnawed deep into the economy through the 1970s. To halt the inflationary pressures, the Reagan administration had been required to use a tight money, high interest rate policy. However, the high American interest rates (and the relative stability of the United States as a place for investment) were attractive to foreign investors who now sought dollars to buy high-yield U.S. securities. Their actions bid up the price of the dollar, and with its rise, the price of American goods rose relative to foreign goods. Soon an unfavorable trade balance changed sharply for the worse. It also produced a growing pressure to return to the bad old days of protective tariffs and pegged exchange rates. The old lie—that trade balances and currency values can be manipulated as desired through public policy efforts—surfaced again.

Yet America's recent trade problems were not, at bottom, the result of flexible exchange rates and free trade, which were singled out as the culprits by some Liberals. The problems began with domestic inflation, and the problems would only ease by ending inflation—even though the means for fighting inflation might have to be even worse short-term trade deficits. At any rate, the lesson to be learned here is that we cannot separate the domestic economy, either in its general conditions or in the policies undertaken to correct these conditions, from the international economy. To avoid the spillover of domestic policy effects into world markets and back again into the domestic economy, the only certain strategy is to let domestic trends work themselves out naturally and to undertake a minimum domestic policy strategy because supposed public policy "cures" to macroeconomic problems only make the situation worse.

The Conservative position is absolutely clear with respect to efforts to set up trade barriers to protect American markets and to manipulate currency values to expand foreign sales: All such interferences with the market mechanism, despite the short-term ill effects of an unfavorable balance of trade, must be opposed if we are ever to obtain the benefits of free international trade. Painful as it may be, we must bite the bullet as the price of our past fiscal and monetary policy excesses.

The Liberal Argument

Typically, Conservatives remain detached from reality and hopelessly utopian in their advocacy of free trade: the *perfect* solution for an *imperfect* world. Although there are, theoretically, greater long-run benefits to be obtained under free trade than under protectionism, Conservatives are calling for America to act as a free trader in a very unfree international economic environment. Playing by Marquess of Queensbury rules while most of the rest of the world cheats has already cost us dearly.

A BACKGROUND TO THE
TRADE CRISIS OF THE 1980s

According to the Conservative scenario, free trade and floating exchange rates go hand in hand to produce harmony and equilibrium in international trade and finance. Quite naturally, they oppose any efforts at protection or manipulation of exchange rates. However, they don't seem to make any connection between their own domestic economic policies and the nation's recent trade deficits, preferring to blame it all on past Liberal economic policy.

In point of fact, the incredible decline of American exports and the even more incredible flood of imports after 1980 was the direct result of Conservative domestic policies that had adverse international effects for the United States *precisely because* we had followed a free trade, floating exchange rate path. The scenario went like this: The incorrect Conservative view that the late 1970s' inflationary pressures were demand-based (too much spending by government, business, and consumers) led to the adoption of a tight money policy by the Federal Reserve System. Consistent with our macroeconomic understandings, this led to rising real interest rates and eventually to a domestic recession. On the surface, the recession might have been expected to have had a stimulating effect on exports as prices of domestic goods steadied or even fell a bit. However, this did not happen. Instead, in an economic world where exchange rates had become more flexible (after the collapse of the old pegging system), high dollar interest rates in the United States suddenly became attractive to foreign investors. The demand for dollars (to invest in the United States) grew, and as demand grew, the price of the dollar rose. With the dollar now strengthening relative to other currencies, dollar-denominated goods became more expensive in foreign markets while goods denominated in yen, marks, francs, and other currencies became cheaper in the United States. The effect was to depress U.S. exports and invite an explosive increase in imports. The recessed conditions of the domestic economy, stemming as they did from the original tight money policy, were in fact worsened as many key industries were closed out of foreign markets precisely as they were being battered at home by imports.

It suddenly became apparent that domestic economic policies could have unintended international effects in a world of floating exchange rates and free trade. Of course, free traders will argue at this point that sooner or later the overvalued dollar will fall in value as exchange rates adjust. All this supposes, naturally, that exchange rates are in actual fact freely floating, and it presumes that an overvalued dollar will not continue to be propped up by a high interest rate money policy that is in place to fight domestic inflation.

Whereas it is easy for economic theorists of any political preference to dismiss protectionism as "beggar thy neighbor" economic policy, the recent protectionist sentiment, from a Liberal point of view, is perfectly explainable and not entirely without justification. What we have learned from the trade problems of the 1980s is that pursuit of free trade in a world where some nations practice free trade and maintenance of floating exchange rates while others manage their rates can lead to unacceptable economic costs. These costs destroy certain domestic industries and greatly increase American unemployment. In short, for all its theoretical attractiveness, free trade and floating exchange rates can, under certain conditions, deliver the opposite of what they promise.

THE CASE FOR MODIFIED PROTECTIONISM

As Figure 15.3 shows, U.S. tariffs have fallen steadily since World War II and stand at historic lows. Duties collected amount to less than 10

FIGURE 15.3 Major U.S. Tariff Agreements and Level of Effective Tariffs, 1910–1987

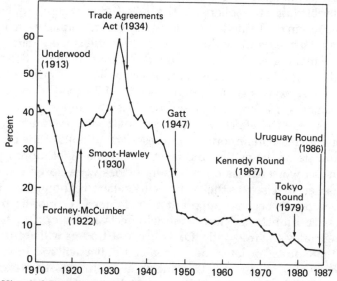

Source: *Historical Statistics of the United States* and *Statistical Abstract of the United States, 1989.*

percent of the value of imports. Forty-five years ago, duties stood at about 60 percent. Moreover, the U.S. government has conducted, since the Kennedy years, serious trade negotiations to reduce restrictive tariffs and import quotas throughout the trading world.

But reduction of trade restraints must be a two-way street. Reductions of restrictions on U.S. goods should be expected from nations desiring or obtaining benefits from the United States. Otherwise, the United States throws its doors open to foreign goods while our own goods are effectively excluded from foreign ports. Nor are tariffs and quotas the only devices nations use for creating trade advantages. The Japanese, for instance, have provided extensive governmental subsidies for their manufacturers, thus creating artificially low prices. Their notorious "dumping" of such underpriced commodities as TVs, cameras, specialty steel items, and the like must cease or the United States will be obliged to take restrictive trade actions.

When these real-world obstacles to trade are considered, it is apparent that the road to free trade is much bumpier than Conservatives admit. And apart from the difficulty of inducing all trading nations to accept the principles of free trade (which would be a minimum requirement even under Conservative logic), the serious domestic problems that might follow the hurried or reckless adoption of free trade must be considered.

First, the failure to employ protective tariffs might deal a death blow to many American industries. Among these would be firms that are critical to our capacity to defend ourselves militarily or to our continued economic well-being if world trade were interrupted in the future. In brief, the military and political significance of self-sufficiency in certain goods and raw materials would outweigh the free trade argument of greater efficiency resulting from free trade.

Second, concentrating production efforts only in industrial areas where a nation may have a comparative trade advantage would tend to create an incomplete and possibly unstable economy. As our own production mix became more specialized and concentrated, we would become more vulnerable (not stronger, as Conservatives argue) when there was any interruption in world markets. The serious impact that overseas shortages of critical goods might have domestically has been demonstrated amply by the crises caused by the OPEC energy cartel. Similarly, we might experience interruptions in the purchase of our specialized production when buyers disappeared. The result would be massive layoffs and recession at home.

Third, and closely associated with the first two points, free trade might have the effect of closing off the development of new ("infant") industries. Already-established overseas firms would enjoy marketing and capital advantages that could not be overcome. Limited tariff protection would allow new industries to emerge and mature. It is a strategy that has worked well for the Japanese, and we should profit from that lesson since it has been a costly one for the United States.

Fourth, and probably the best-known argument against absolute trade freedom, American firms might be completely priced out of certain markets by cheaper foreign labor or by foreign dumping, causing massive domestic economic upheaval and unemployment. In the short run, free trade, without any quotas or restrictions, would probably produce massive unemployment in basic industries like steel and autos, which would make our current unemployment problems in these industries look inconsequential. Even if, in the long run, new industries emerged to fill the employment gap, billions would be spent on unemployment insurance, welfare, and job retraining. Whole areas of the nation would be disrupted as our nation's production mix changed. Such costs would more than offset the efficiency advantages proposed by Conservatives.

THE NEED FOR RULES AND ENFORCEMENT

Although Conservatives are correct in pointing out the foolishness of pegged international exchange rates, whether currencies are tied to gold or to the U.S. dollar, they inaccurately see the present period as a time of largely floating rates. With the exception of the United States, most nations use "managed floating rates." That is, central banks and national governments take actions as they see fit to strengthen or weaken their currency vis-à-vis other nations. For example, by taking actions in the early 1980s to keep the yen undervalued, the Japanese enjoyed selling their commodities in the United States while keeping out the higher-priced (in yen) American goods.

As long as exchange rates are managed—and Conservatives offer no reasonable suggestions for controlling economic nationalism—free trade will be impossible. Free-trading nations such as the United States have few options except to resort to some form of protectionism when exchange rates are rigged to open such nations to a flood of imports and to shut off their export markets. The only other option is to manipulate our own exchange rates by taking actions to devalue the dollar (as we in fact did in 1985), to offset other nations' actions. However, in the long run, such action is useless unless other nations consent to our move and do not take offsetting devaluation measures.

The bottom line is that strong international agreements are necessary before freely floating exchange rates and free trade are possible. Ironically, free international trade and finance can be "free" only if the rules of the game are vigorously enforced. Unless the economic nationalism of states can be brought under control (which implies creating international administrative arrangements that really work, rather than depending on some anarchic notion of "freedom"), the benefits of free trade will always be illusory to nations that maintain truly floating exchange rates and open markets.

PUTTING THE INTERNATIONAL
ECONOMY IN PERSPECTIVE

Regardless of what happens in the development and enforcement of international "rules of the game" the United States cannot withdraw from the world economy. But we should put it in proper perspective. Probably the most significant problem posed by free trade and floating exchange rates is that the domestic economy is subordinated in international economic affairs. Policies aimed at correcting balance-of-payments and exchange problems may actually worsen domestic problems. For instance, unemployment in the United States would have to grow and an extended domestic recession would be required as the price of ending our international payments deficit.

Free traders may resolve this conflict between needed expansionary policies at home and the required contractionary actions to put our international payments in balance by glibly saying, "We must bite the bullet." Matters are not that simple. Indeed, the contraction might be so unbearable as to trigger extensive political reactions in the United States that would destroy not only our political institutions but even the market economy so beloved by Conservatives.

The necessity for strong and enforced trading and exchange rules has never been greater. The American economy is no longer dominant, nor is it insulated from the rest of the world. With the impending integration of the European economies after 1992, it will no longer be the largest of the world economies. Requiring that the rest of the world play by the rules of the "trading game" (and penalizing those who do not) is, after all, only fair, but given the degree of cheating in the past, as well as our diminished stature in the world economy, the United States may have to act unilaterally to protect itself.

The real measure of a nation's strength in international affairs is the strength of its domestic economy. Accordingly, the United States may have to undertake limited protectionism and exchange rate intervention to shield itself. Such actions, of course, must be complemented by domestic microeconomic and macroeconomic policies to stimulate investment and productivity growth; otherwise, the Conservative scenario of a nation decaying behind its own protectionist walls *is* a distinct possibility. However, we shall lose sight of the real issue as well as any control over it if the seductive logic of free trade leads to a benign neglect of the domestic economy.

The Radical Argument

Although the Conservative and Liberal scenarios of international trade and exchange problems seem to be quite different, a closer examination indicates that they are similar. Both arguments accept as a matter of fact or "right" the continued dominance of the United States in world trade. The remedies that they suggest for current problems, whether it be the free trade approach of the Conservative or the administrative emphasis of the Liberals, are intended primarily to restore and strengthen the American position. Moreover, their underestimation of the significance of international trade and finance and of the degree of crisis now existing in these areas is a dangerous error of judgment.

Capitalist nations do not trade and expand their international influence merely "to improve efficiency" or "to benefit mutually from each nation's exploitation of its comparative advantage." Profit making, pure and simple, is the engine that drives overseas trade and investment. Indeed, the overseas search for markets, cheap resources, and profitable investment is absolutely essential for any capitalist system's continued expansion. Rather than trade and international economic affairs being mere aspects of capitalism, as Conservatives and Liberals suggest, they are the *central features* of modern production-for-profit economies. The international trade and exchange crisis is thus the result of the insatiable drive of individual capitalist nations to exploit the rest of the world for their own gains.

THE RISE OF THE AMERICAN EMPIRE

Americans tend to think of themselves as reluctant internationalists drawn into world affairs only to save the rest of the world from itself. However, the facts support quite a different explanation. By the turn of the twentieth century, American capitalism had exhausted its domestic markets. The long decade of depression in the 1890s suggested to many the need for overseas expansion either to obtain markets for our surplus goods or to gain access to cheap raw materials and foreign labor. The United States steadily enlarged its world trade between the 1890s and the 1960s, exporting ever-larger amounts of expensive manufactured goods and importing greater quantities of cheap raw materials. At the same time, to secure markets and assume

TABLE 15.1   Value of Overseas U.S. Investment, Selected Years, 1880–1990
(in billions of dollars)

Year	Amount
1880	1.6
1890	2.9
1900	2.5
1914	3.5
1920	7.0
1930	17.2
1940	12.2
1950	19.0
1960	40.2
1970	75.5
1980	215.4
1990*	417.0

*Estimate
Source: U.S. Bureau of the Census, Historical Statistics of the United States and Economic Report of the President, 1990.

control over raw materials, Americans exported vast amounts of capital (see Table 15.1).

The old trading powers of Europe exhausted themselves in two world wars—wars that had been fundamentally economic wars for trade supremacy—while the United States continued to expand its overseas sales, purchases, and investment. By the 1960s, the United States, in terms of comparative development, had reached the peak of its international economic power. The rise to this height and the later fall are important and instructive enough to examine in some detail.

In 1950, U.S. gross domestic output was about equal to that of the rest of the world combined. Great Britain's output was only 13 percent of America's, while those of France, West Germany, and Japan were 10, 8, and 4 percent, respectively. During World War II, the United States, as principal supplier of arms, had accumulated almost the entire world's gold stock, as well as many other overseas assets. Our exports accounted for about one-third of all the world's exports and more than a quarter of all manufactured exports.

Meanwhile, as a result of Marshall Plan aid and other dollar grants to "free" European economies, other capitalist nations fell into a client relationship with the United States. Dependent economically on aid and trade programs and militarily (in the cold war years) on America's armed forces and mutual defense treaties (such as NATO) that were dominated by the United States, the older capitalist nations became part of the American economic sphere. At the same time, the United States expanded its penetration into the Third World, establishing a new, informal colonial system. Within this imperial system, the resource-rich remnants of the former European colonial empire in Africa and Asia joined Latin America as part of our sphere of influence. Through development aid and especially through supporting friendly repressive regimes with military assistance, the United States established a neocolonial system without resorting to the old tactic of territorial seizure.

By the late 1950s, the United States enjoyed a virtually unchallenged economic hegemony over the noncommunist world, comprising the Western European and Japanese economies and much of the Third World. Supposedly international agencies such as the International Monetary Fund, the World Bank, and the United Nations became arms of American foreign economic and political policy. Under such conditions, it is small wonder that the American dollar became the international medium of exchange and that the international financial situation of the United States appeared so secure. We could virtually dictate exchange rates, and we could hide any balance-of-payments problem by compelling foreign governments to accept and hold dollars rather than demand gold. The ultimate fall from this pinnacle of international power was to be a terrifying experience for Americans.

THE COLLAPSE OF THE EMPIRE

The fall from power was speeded by events overseas and at home. First, the Soviet challenge failed to disappear. The Soviet economy rose swiftly from the ruins of World War II. Despite the Korean War and dozens of other cold war confrontations, the power of cold war ideology in holding the American–Western European alliance together waned as Europeans reevaluated their position within the American empire. This, as much as anything, directed Europe to a more middle-ground approach.

Second, the European economies made their own rapid recoveries in the 1960s. By 1972, the combined gross domestic output of Western Europe and Japan exceeded that of the United States. Accordingly, the U.S. share of world markets declined drastically. Between 1950 and 1972, our share of passenger vehicle production fell from 82 to 29 percent; similarly, steel production fell from 55 to 20 percent and energy production from 50 to 33 percent. At the same time, other industrial nations began to claim larger shares of the American market. Finished manufactured imports increased almost 300 percent between 1965 and 1970, while U.S. exports of manufactured goods grew by only 80 percent in the same period.

Third, U.S. domination of the Third World declined. Wars of national liberation and the emergence of new regimes committed to an independent political course eroded American influence. The failure of our effort in Vietnam to stem the tide of Third World nationalism only accelerated the decline of the empire. By 1973, the United States was helpless in dealing with the OPEC embargo. In 1979, it could only stand aside quietly as Iran, perhaps one of the most crucial parts of our earlier neocolonial system, threw out its pro-American government.

Fourth, the emergence of American multinational corporations further weakened the United States. The flight of U.S. capital overseas to the expanding economies in Europe and the Third World accelerated the decline of the U.S. balance-of-payments position. The multinationals' flight left investment and employment gaps at home, with which the nation was ill prepared to deal. By 1971, the United States registered the first trade imbalance in the century, as imports exceeded exports.

LITTLE HOPE IN SIGHT

Since the early 1970s, the United States' terms of trade with the rest of the world has continued to deteriorate. The energy crisis and domestic inflation in the 1970s first priced American goods out of many foreign markets and eventually brought on a worldwide recession. As the recession ebbed in the early 1980s, the nation found itself locked in serious competition with Europe and Japan. The old specter of capitalist trade wars, which had already led to two world wars in this century, appeared once again. The United States, hampered by a strong dollar resulting from domestic efforts to get inflation under control was beset by continually worsening trade deficits through the 1980s. Faced with the loss of foreign markets and its own domestic markets to growing foreign competition, America turned increasingly toward protectionism, that long-discredited policy for protecting profits of domestic industry and for exporting a county's unemployment. Should the American protectionist effort push very far, of course, it would likely be responded to in kind by most of the rest of the world. In turn, as in the 1930s, it could be expected that world trade would dry up and all production-for-profit economies would find sales and profits falling.

From a Radical perspective, the problem has been predictable. The internationalization of capital is only a further step in capitalism's irrational development. The strength of the American overseas economic operations of the 1950s and 1960s was the result of its power to exploit the so-called free world. This country's gains were others' losses. What we saw as a normal situation was an exceptional one. As our capacity to exploit has been challenged by other capitalist economies, by the development of socialist countries, and by Third World independence, our premier position in world trade and finance has declined. As overseas growth ends, domestic contraction sets in. The specter of another worldwide capitalist depression looms larger. The crisis is, of course, a production crisis—too many goods and too few buyers. It cannot be resolved by dealing purely with money, balance of payments, and exchange rates. Rather than being the causes of our international economic crisis, our balance-of-payments and exchange problems merely reflect the basic production-distribution problem of the capitalist system. Neither free trade nor protection, and neither floating exchange rates nor pegged rates, offer a long-term solution. Conservative and Liberal solutions are equally irrelevant.

Planning versus the Market
Which Strategy Works Best?

Whenever the legislature attempts to regulate the differences
between the masters and their workmen, its counsellors are
always the masters.

Adam Smith, 1776

The world is *not* so governed from above that private and
social interests coincide. It is *not* so managed here below that
in practice they coincide. It is *not* a correct deduction from the
Principles of Economics that enlightened self-interest always
operates in the public interest.

John Maynard Keynes, 1926

In area after area of our national life, we have adopted policies
that unnecessarily threaten the integrity of the individual. . . .
There runs through them the common element: the substitution of bureaucratic organization and control for market
arrangements, the rejection of Adam Smith's great insight.

Milton Friedman, 1970

It used to seem to me that the drift of all Western countries
was toward something like socialism. But now, when I reflect
on what is happening . . . , it is not so clear. There is a sense
of return to the market, because the task of planning in a
modern economy is so complex.

Robert Heilbroner, 1986

THE PROBLEM

Throughout our examination of contemporary economic issues, there has been a consistent tension among the Conservative defense of a free and unregulated economy, the limited regulation objectives of the Liberals, and the general assault on free markets by Radicals. At issue has been the question of exactly how free or how planned the economy should be. In our closing debate, it is appropriate to deal with this question directly: Which strategy—the market or economic planning—is most likely to provide the desired outcomes?

Based on public opinion surveys, recent trends in American political rhetoric and practice, and events beyond the borders of the United States, an ordinary observer might quickly conclude that planning is in full retreat. Public support for the Keynesian social engineering efforts of the 1960s and early 1970s withered by the late 1970s, and for more than a decade, Americans have sent to Washington administrations that, at least in terms of their public posture, were emphatically promarket. Underlining this domestic trend have been recent political shifts outside the United States. The Soviet Union, long perceived by Americans as the antithesis of market economic organization, has publicly admitted the failure of its past central planning efforts and, under Gorbachev's introduction of *glasnost* and *perestroika*, moved to encourage market initiatives. Even more sweeping have been the changes in Eastern Europe, which in late 1989 saw the overturning of one Communist regime after another. Invariably the successful East European reformers (all this happened without a sweeping political revolution of the old type), while not rejecting planning completely, spoke of a desire to explore the options of a greatly expanded free market. China's introduction of "enterprise zones" and limited market economic experiments—despite being dampened by the Beijing Spring student uprising in 1989 and the brutal governmental reaction it provoked—are also viewed as a drift away from central planning principles.

Understandably, promarket advocates are quick to draw "final conclusions" on the basis of these trends. Yet, what can we really conclude with certainty? Six decades ago, in a world caught up in abject economic depression, the market system stood discredited in the eyes of many. However, market-based economics has obviously enjoyed a rebirth in recent years. The failure of the Communist bloc economies may say more about the effects of poor planning and the shortcomings of imposing ideology through the planning apparatus than about planning in general. After all, economic planning in various degrees remains alive and well in many nations, not the least of which are the highly successful cases of Japan, Sweden, France, and West Germany. Nor can we ignore the fact that economic planning efforts have deep roots in the American past.

Someone unfamiliar with American history might conclude that current economic trends are a ringing and final referendum against any effort to construct even a modestly planned economy. Such a judgment would likely be premature. Popular political belief in the possibilities of national economic planning has frequently surfaced in the past and has been translated into policy. From Alexander Hamilton's "Report on Manufactures" to Henry Clay's American Plan to Woodrow Wilson's progressive New Freedom to Franklin Roosevelt's New Deal, the United States has undergone a number of periods in which varieties of faith in central planning were applied to the nation's economy. Nor are these experiments with planning mere artifacts of a distant political past.

A little over a decade ago, a Liberal Congress enacted the Humphrey-Hawkins Full Employment and Balanced Growth Act (it passed the Senate by an overwhelming 70–19 margin). The original Humphrey-Hawkins proposal had called for the collection of national input and output data on American industry (an essential and first tool in any economic planner's toolbox) and the creation of an Economic Planning Board to set and implement national economic planning objectives. Although these particular proposals narrowly failed inclusion in the final legislation, the Humphrey-Hawkins bill did call for—though obviously without much authority—the coordination of economic policy between the president, Congress, and the Federal Reserve System and the setting of 3 percent adult unemployment as the "official" target for public policy. As Humphrey-Hawkins was debated in 1976–1978, there were those who talked about entering a "new era in American economic affairs" in which government played a central role in setting and fulfilling output and employment objectives. Times change quickly, however, and Humphrey-Hawkins has passed out of the memory of most economists and politicians.

As recently as the 1980–1983 recession, even with a staunch defender of free market economics in the White House, another vision of central planning attracted considerable attention, this time with startlingly strong support in the business community. "Industrial policy," as it was known, promised to revitalize American industry through, among other things, the creation of a federal investment bank that would act as a lender of last resort to businesses, especially those "Rustbelt" industries that were particularly hard-pressed. Some industrial policy advocates urged that the United States develop its own version of Japan's highly successful MITI (Ministry of International Trade and Industry). MITI had operated since shortly after World War II, directing Japanese industrial development and targeting winners and losers in Japan's export and domestic markets through its control over research and development funds, investment sources, and imports. However, industrial policy did have its critics in the United States, and it never developed to the point of proposing specific legislation. At any rate, its attractiveness diminished as the recession of the early 1980s lifted.

While the decade of the 1980s will doubtless be remembered for the resurgence of market economic philosophy in the United States, some observers could be excused if they wondered aloud just how deep this redirection in American economic thinking really went. After all, the scare provided by "Black Monday" in October 1987 produced all manner of pleas from members of the business and financial communities for greater "controls" over securities trading. Similarly, the savings and loan crisis of 1988–1989 triggered calls for greater regulation of American banking. And, despite the expansive arguments on behalf of deregulation in general, surveys of public attitudes indicate no diminishing of the general population's support for environmental and consumer protection activities by government. Meanwhile, for all the talk of shrinking the size of government in the economy, government spending as a percentage of GNP actually increased between 1980 and 1990. Given the cyclical nature of economic planning's popularity and its tendency to arise precisely as the general economy's performance sags, it is entirely possible that "industrial policy," "full-employment planning," or perhaps even more radical and far-reaching planning efforts simply await the next significant slump in the economy.

SYNOPSIS

For Conservatives, the adoption of national economic planning would mean the ending of capitalism as a social system and the imposition of an inefficient dictatorship in its place. Liberals, however, see planning as compatible with our mixed capitalist economy, since the essential elements of the system (private property and economic and political freedom) would actually be enhanced by the increased stability planning would provide. To be sure, Liberals advocate only a limited system of planning. Radicals, meanwhile, see present planning proposals only as efforts to maintain the present inequalities and exploitativeness of the capitalist system. To them, planning is essential, but it must be done at the level of human needs, not those of the corporation.

Anticipating the Arguments

- What is the Conservatives' fundamental philosophical disagreement with centralized planning efforts?
- How do Liberals argue that planning and a basically capitalistic economic system are compatible?
- What do Radicals mean when they call for planning "for and by people"?

The Conservative Argument

At this stage in our discussion of contemporary economic problems, the Conservative response to the idea of national economic planning should be obvious—or perhaps it would be better to say *familiar*. National economic planning, in the sense that it means nonmarket, administrative decisions on output, pricing, employment, capital, and so on, is to be opposed as vigorously as possible. Planning is the final collectivist victory over freedom and individualism. When economic and political authorities, whether they be Fascists or Communists or even well-meaning Liberals, have the power to determine all important matters in the economy, there is little else left in life that is beyond their ability to control. *Brave New World* and *Nineteen Eighty-four* are no longer merely science fiction.

The economic criticism of central planning is quickly summarized. First of all, it is profoundly inefficient in terms of theoretical economic principles. Second, empirical evidence on efforts at national economic planning (which is abundant) proves that such planning is ineffective.

NATIONAL PLANNING:
THEORETICALLY INEFFICIENT

As we know, under a market system, prices are the signals for economic activity. The decision to produce a particular good can be calculated both in terms of the actual production costs of labor, capital, or resources and in terms of what that particular good costs compared to other goods. As long as the market designates the prices of the factors of production (labor, capital, and resources) and the prices of final goods, we have a rational calculus. As consumers or producers, we can make choices based on a steady and reliable set of indicators. This is not to say that prices will not fluctuate. Of course they will. They are supposed to fluctuate to show changes in demand and supply and thus changes in the cost structure or in consumer satisfaction.

Far from being anarchy, the market *is* a planning mechanism. The market works like a system and, as Adam Smith observed in an essay on astronomy written long before his *Wealth of Nations*, "A system is like a little machine." Like a machine, a "market-planned" economy has regulators that keep it in balance.

Administrative planning, on the other hand, has no natural internal or external checks on its effectiveness. In an administered economy, levels of output, employment, and the mix of goods are purely matters of political determination. It is not really important whether these goals are set by commissars, Harvard economists, or the duly elected representatives of the people; they are the result of human judgments. They reflect particular individual or collective biases. Not even a computer can tell what output and employment goals are "correct" unless it is programmed (by humans) to respond to certain criteria (selected by humans).

Defenders of planning may point out that high levels of growth and employment have been attained in certain planned economies. There is some truth to this, but the argument misses the point. Administrative planning in the Soviet Union during World War II and immediately afterward, and in developing nations more recently, was bound to have some success because of these nations' very primitive level of economic development. When you have nothing and plan something, you can hardly lose, especially if you have authoritarian control over the labor force. It is quite another matter, however, to maintain efficient administrative planning in an advanced, complex economy. This, of course, is exactly what the Russians, the East Europeans, and, to some extent, the Chinese discovered in the 1980s, as decades of inefficient planning brought economic growth to a standstill and discredited communism as an economic and political system.

Like market economies, most administered economies use prices to direct economic activity toward predetermined goals. But it should be remembered that these prices, like the goals themselves, are administratively determined. Prices, therefore, do not reflect costs as we speak of them but are merely a rationing technique used to direct labor, capital, output, and, ultimately, social behavior toward certain imposed objectives.

Space prohibits a more detailed theoretical attack on the output and pricing behavior of planned economies, but a brief survey of some of the problems encountered by them may demonstrate the essence of the Conservative critique.

NATIONAL PLANNING: INEFFECTIVE IN PRACTICE

The Soviet Union is a striking example of what can happen when economic mechanisms are subordinated to clearly political objectives. Not unlike the implied long-run objectives of the Humphrey-Hawkins Act, Soviet goals, at least up to the Gorbachev reforms, also included full employment, enforced price stability, and specific production targets for certain goods.

In the Soviet case, full employment means a job for everyone. In an authoritarian collectivist society, this was not a great problem, but there is a big difference between putting people in jobs and having them perform productively. For instance, Soviet plant managers, given output goals by state planners (which were to be met or else), often feared a shortage of labor in the future and so "hoarded" workers. On other occasions, they had to hire labor as directed by state authorities, whether or not they needed it. In either case, the workers in question were underemployed. In terms of economic analysis, the result is obvious: inefficiency. Workers are hired without any view to their productivity. Wages are set by state planners, who have little or no knowledge of costs of production at a plant. Thus managers may reach their output targets, with workers "fully employed," but the actual cost of goods (as reckoned by alternative uses of labor and capital) may be much higher than the planners can cover in setting a price. In real terms this means that the whole society must pay the actual costs by forgoing other goods. An inefficiently made tractor may "cost" many thousands of nonproduced consumer items.

The tendency to think only in output (quantitative) terms has qualitative effects, too. Production rushed to meet a planner's goal may encourage defective and shoddy manufacture. Quick and flexible adaptation of production to meet changes in goals is very difficult. Planners lack the signals of prices based on supply and demand to tell them when and how to change the production mix. Plans become rigid, at both the plant and planning levels.

In the Soviet Union many of the worst features of central planning were eliminated over time. The introduction of linear programming, input-output analysis, and, finally, the computer did improve the accumulation and flow of information. The incredible lapses of mind that had led to the production of motor vehicle engines and chassis but not the needed ball bearings for their wheels had generally disappeared by the 1980s. In fact, Soviet industry had achieved a measure of technological success in some cases (for example, space-related industries). However, as Gorbachev took over, the overall microeconomic decision-making process remained bogged down by the political administration of prices and wages and by mind-boggling distributional inadequacies. Even after years of sacrifice to build the industrial base of the society, ordinary Russians remained as they had always been—the balancing item in the central plan ledger. The errors of planners, even those with computers, were still to be paid for in relinquished consumer goods and in a scarcely improving standard of living.

In what has to be considered the ultimate rejection of the central planning concept, Gorbachev initiated a variety of economic and political reforms aimed at dislodging the central planning bureaucracy and encouraging a degree of market freedom and even political freedom. Generally, Conservatives remain doubtful about the final course of events in the USSR. Abandoning the tenets of Marxism and the habits of socialist authoritarianism will not be easy. Once entrenched, the patterns of thought and action that naturally oppose individual freedom and free economic and political expression are difficult to dislodge. But the essential point remains: *The foremost model of the centrally planned, authoritarian state has been deemed a failure*—not just on the basis of its own performance, but in the opinion of its own leaders.

PUTTING PLANNING WITHIN
AN AMERICAN CONTEXT

Critics will argue that the Soviet case is irrelevant to any planning situation affecting the United States. They will maintain, of course, that American "mixed capitalism"—a combination of a dependence on the market and appropriate interventions to correct the market—is much different from a fully planned, authoritarian economic system. To Conservatives, though, the threat of planning is quite real. Talk of national economic planning goes back a long way in American history, and, as is evident in day-to-day government reaction to the issues discussed in this book, the tendency toward collectivist solutions to all economic problems, although diminishing a bit lately, remains strong. History shows that, once commenced, the march toward collectivism is hard to reverse. Today we may be talking merely of obtaining additional data for national planning or making "full employment" a law. Tomorrow, the managed-economy objectives may be more personal to all of us—determining where we live, where we work, what we buy, and so on.

Conservatives are not anarchists. Indeed, they believe in planning, and today we have a high order of acceptable planning in the economy. This planning, however, is a function of individual choices collectively expressed in the market. As Milton Friedman has observed:

> Fundamentally, there are only two ways of coordinating the economic activities of millions. One is central direction involving the use of coercion—the technique of the army and of the modern totalitarian state. The other is voluntary cooperation of individuals—the technique of the market place. . . . Exchange can bring about coordination without coercion.*

The present in-between, never-never land of mixed American capitalism cannot continue long. *We must go either one way or the other in the future.*

The Liberal Argument

The public furor created by discussions of planning arises out of ignorance. Planning as envisioned in the original Humphrey-Hawkins proposal or in many of the "industrial policy" proposals of a few years ago, irrespective of our recent policy turn toward deregulation and "minimum government," was not a sharp divergence from the past. It was basically an elaboration of the principles laid out, but not specifically implemented, in the Employment Act of 1946. Nor is

---

*Milton Friedman, *Capitalism and Freedom* (Chicago: University of Chicago Press, 1962), p. 13.

planning in general at all new to the American economy. After all, the government budget is not constructed without calculating the impact of its spending and taxing, nor does Exxon make annual profits of more than $4 billion accidentally. Regrettably, planning calls up the image of a Soviet-type society, when in fact it is essential for the improvement of our own democratic capitalism. The type of planning being given serious consideration at present is not an Orwellian nightmare where "Big Brother is watching you." Aside from creating jobs and improving efficiency, it is not intended to alter American life very much at all. In fact, planning is intended to protect, as much as possible, the conditions to which we have become accustomed.

IN DEFENSE OF PLANNING

At this point in our discussion, the Liberal defense of planning need not be lengthy. The necessity for some type of general control mechanism has been evident in all our comments on contemporary policy issues. A shift toward self-conscious national planning, however, would be a major effort to integrate the separate planning and control efforts on which we now depend.

The need for an integrated governmental planning operation will be accepted sooner or later. The crises of energy, the environment, unemployment, inflation, and public finance cannot be dealt with continually via ad hoc policy-making. The multiplication and lack of integration of these separate efforts are wasteful and counterproductive. For instance, an energy conservation policy constructed without specific commitment to employment and price objectives may save us fuel but cost us jobs and investment, or may have disastrous environmental effects. The great virtue of national planning is that it recognizes the interconnection of all economic problems and hence seeks solutions in a broad rather than narrow way.

For instance, collection of adequate production data would make it possible to target general objectives in the economy—say, a certain acceptable level of economic growth in particular industries. In turn, balance can be created among industries, such as that needed between developing public transportation on the one hand and sustaining the private automobile industry on the other.

As a rule, coercion would not be necessary to assure that targets are attained. Careful use of tax-subsidy incentives and participation by capital and labor in the planning process could generate a high order of consensus among the constituent parts of the economy. Meanwhile, with government acting positively as a guarantor of jobs in the last resort, the persistent unemployment problem could be laid to rest.

Of course, we must expect crises from time to time, and mere targets or gentle nudging will not always be enough. War, oil embargoes, and international economic difficulties beyond our control may necessitate some coercive use of planning. Such situations may demand rationing of goods, rigorous wage and price controls, or perhaps more. However, in the face of serious crisis, the nation would have no alternative—any more than it had an alternative to rationing and controls during World War II.

Conservative defenders of the market philosophy invariably argue that planning always fails. Usually they dredge up the Soviet Union as the classic planning failure, or they turn to past, ill-conceived American efforts such as Richard Nixon's attempts in the 1970s to maintain wage and price controls. And then there is China— once a rigidly planned and controlled economy, now experimenting with market capitalism. However, Conservatives neatly avoid the planning successes. The inherent failure of planning will come as a considerable surprise to the French, the Germans, the Scandinavians, and the Japanese—all of whom have relied on some form of planning to produce economic miracles over the past three or four decades. Indeed, Japan has been particularly instructive to American business leaders, who are increasingly aware that Japan's industrial policy of subsidizing and directing key segments of its economy has made its economy more dynamic than our own. Many U.S. leaders have recently begun advocating adaptation of certain elements of Japanese planning for the American economy.

As two Liberal defenders of planning, Robert Heilbroner and Lester Thurow, have observed:

> Planning may well be to our era what the discovery of the Keynesian explanation of depression was to the era of the 1930s. Keynesian policies did not solve the economic difficulties of that era by any matter of means, but they did get us through a period that threatened to plunge us into very serious social and political trouble. Perhaps the proper estimate of planning is much the same. We should not realistically hope that it will

solve many of the problems that beset our times—problems of technology, of bureaucracy, of a terrible division of the world between rich and poor—but planning may nevertheless get us through this period of drift and disappointment. That would be quite enough.*

The Liberal who is challenged to defend planning in principle and practice has only one answer: "Given where we are, is there any other way?"

PLANNING AND CAPITALISM

We cannot leave this topic without taking up the Conservative charge that planning means the end of capitalism. If by capitalism the Conservatives mean the quaint little world of Adam Smith where everyone haggled and sold freely and equally, that world passed out of existence a very long time ago—if, in fact, it ever existed. The tragicomic Conservative defenders of individualism and freedom have failed to adapt these values to a highly complex technological world. The mutual economic interdependence of people, nations, and institutions does not allow us to talk of freedom in such a simplistic sense. The freedom to be poor, the freedom to starve, or the freedom to collapse into social anarchy is really the long-run outcome of efforts to return to a marketplace mentality.

Contrary to the Conservative outlook, planning is not necessarily communism, nor is it authoritarianism of any special breed. Planning is essential to maintaining the American democratic capitalist tradition. To the Liberal, of course, "democratic" is much more important than "capitalist" in a generic sense. The economic experience of the United States and all other basically "capitalist" countries indicates quite clearly that only planning can save the private-property, production-for-profit system from self-destruction.

Although he has not always been in the mainstream of Liberal opinion, John Kenneth Galbraith's observations of over two decades ago fairly represent the Liberal position today. After weighing the growing problems of American industrial society, Galbraith concluded:

> It is through the state that the society must assert the superior claim of aesthetic over economic goals and particularly of environment over cost.

*Robert Heilbroner and Lester Thurow, *The Economic Problem Newsletter* (Englewood Cliffs, N.J.: Prentice-Hall, Spring 1976), p. 3.

It is to the state we must look for freedom of individual choice as to toil. . . . If the state is to serve these ends, the scientific and educational estate and larger intellectual community must be aware of their power and their opportunity and they must use them. There is no one else.*

The Radical Argument

Despite the current Conservative celebration of a renaissance of "free market" thought and practice, capitalism has for a considerable period of time moved inexorably toward greater central control. Although there is much debate on how close we really are to a formally planned and controlled economy, Radicals would generally agree that it is the next great leap in capitalist development. From laissez-faire to monopoly capitalism to state-corporate regulation to formal planning—capitalism runs its course in its effort to secure profit and protect itself. The obvious irony, of course, is that planned capitalism is a contradiction in terms. As the basic economics textbooks tell us, capitalism emerged as a totally free economic philosophy. However, it ends as a totally authoritarian one.

CAPITALISM NEEDS PLANNING

Ideologies, even after they have proved worthless, die hard, often convulsively. It remains to be seen how the outmoded rhetoric of laissez-faire or even the more sophisticated mixed-economy philosophies will pass into history. They are deeply rooted in the individual practice and thought of American citizens, and their public defenders are still loud and shrill. Nevertheless, as our discussions of other contemporary issues should indicate, the use of government intervention in the economy is apparent everywhere.

This process is not really very new. It originated in the late nineteenth-century response to the growing crises of American capitalism. Troubled by periodic panics or recessions (in 1873, 1885, 1893, and 1907), chronic excess capacity and overproduction, and anarchic market conditions, and threatened by increasingly radicalized labor strife, American capitalism depended more and more on state intervention. We have elaborated on these interventions in our discussions of stabilization policy, government deficits, unemployment, and

*John K. Galbraith, *The New Industrial State* (Boston: Houghton Mifflin, 1967), p. 335.

international trade. As the state became a partner in supporting business, American corporations enlarged their monopoly powers through concentration and control.

This growth of state-corporate integration has been euphemistically termed the "mixed economy" in economics texts. Uninformed Conservatives attacked this integration as the domination of business by the state, without even stopping to ask just whose interests the state represented. They fail to see that, quite as Marx specified, "the State is the form in which the individuals of the ruling class assert their common interests."

Capitalist production has proved to be extraordinarily rational in a microeconomic sense. The organization of production, labor, and capital for any particular firm is governed by economic rules of behavior (we call it "the price system") that, for an individual entrepreneur, give key signals on how best to attain profit objectives. Yet, in totality, the capitalist system is irrational. Though the actions of any given firm are rationally "planned" or calculated with profit in mind, the actions of all firms taken together produce macroeconomic and social disorder. There is a lack of coordination and integration, even among monopolistic capitalists, in dealing with different industries and different sectors of the economy. Rational control of the whole labor force, of total output, and of investment alternatives is lacking.

The boom-bust rhythm of the business cycle, although recently muted when compared to the past, is still evident—but with a difference. Today's highly integrated and automated production is extremely vulnerable to even the slightest variations in sales, profits, and output. In the past, when industry was predominantly labor-intensive, a business downturn amounted mainly to sending the workers home with empty pay envelopes and waiting until things got better. Today, with greater capital usage and production on an international scale, nonproduction presents a firm with greater losses. These, in turn, affect financial markets and the international structure of business.

Moreover, modern capitalism has so penetrated the world that it is limited in its ability to acquire new markets, so essential to its survival. At the same time, as we have noted repeatedly before, capitalist production can be carried on at higher output levels using less labor power. As a result, the crowning irrationality of the system is that it can produce more and more, but labor becomes increasingly redundant and markets harder to find.

The chronic tendency toward unemployment and excess capacity, the steady threat of inflation, and the worsening balance-of-trade situation leave few options for American capitalism. As the Liberal John Kenneth Galbraith has argued for years, the next step in capitalist development is to transcend the market and modern Keynesian efforts to correct it and to move straight toward direct economic planning and controls. Only through such efforts can capitalist irrationality be controlled. Planning presents possibilities for reorganizing the capitalist processes of production and accumulation and at the same time can "legitimize" or bring order to labor markets.

PLANNING FOR PROFITS, NOT PEOPLE

The name of the game in capitalism is profits, and the name does not change when capitalist systems adopt centralist planning techniques. Two examples are worth noting.

The Liberal effort at central planning for full employment in the Humphrey-Hawkins debates in the mid-1970s (and there is little reason to believe that die-hard Liberals have changed their positions much) called for specific government planning actions. First, government output "recommendations" were to act as a general guide to business in undertaking specific investment and output decisions. This "indicative" planning can show beforehand where shortages and bottlenecks might appear; it presupposes that rational capitalists will take actions to eliminate such problems. The second aspect of this planning would be selective tax cutting to induce business to move toward certain production goals. This "tax-cutting planning" is really only a dressed-up version of modern Keynesianism. Accordingly, it has, built in, all of the problems associated with trying to generate employment increases by pumping up aggregate demand (see Issues 9, 10, and 11). As we have seen, this may produce short-run profits, but it also generates longer-run cost pressures. Sooner or later, in the form of inflationary real-wage reductions or imposed wage controls, workers end up paying for the profits with lowered real wages. If the planning is extensive enough, it may put millions back to work, but only by lowering the real living standards of American workers. The classical economic doctrine of the "iron law of wages" (that incomes should equal subsistence) would be reintroduced through tax transfers and wage controls.

A more blatant profits-first approach to planning, attractive to some Liberals and even a few Conservatives, surfaced in the so-called industrial policy debate. The inspiration that has attracted a number of business leaders to endorse joint government-business coordination of investment, labor policy, and trade policy to "halt the deindustrialization of America" is pure greed. Presumably, an effective industrial policy would determine winners and losers among American enterprises (since surely not everyone can be a winner), very much as the Japanese have done over the past twenty or thirty years. Industrial policy is obviously popular with present losers, those whose profits have fallen in the perpetual capitalist game of survival. Industrial policy promises improved profits for the losers by either insulating them from competition (thus raising their sales) or lowering their investment and even their labor costs.

In the short run, industrial policy efforts could indeed raise profits, but with little or no gain for ordinary workers or consumers. Goods prices would have to rise if tariffs or quotas were used to protect certain threatened industries. Increased government investment subsidies, as noted earlier, must eventually be translated into losses of consumer buying power either via inflation or tax increases. In all of this, labor will be expected to be disciplined, like Japanese labor, making the sacrifices in both wages and intensified work requirements necessary for keeping costs down and profits up. Recognizing this, some industrial policy proponents have advocated that organized labor be included in the general planning procedures. While the participation of labor in the planning process has certain obvious attractions from a Radical point of view, it is necessary to recognize that most such proposals to date have included labor only as window dressing.

In both of the planning scenarios cited, profits are the central concern, and if profits are to be maintained at all, they are maintained at the cost of real losses for workers. Under such planning arrangements, the basic antagonisms and contradictions of capitalism are not eliminated. They now become embedded in the institutional apparatus of national economic planning. Planning for people's needs simply does not take place.

THE RADICAL ALTERNATIVE:
PLANNING *FOR* AND *BY* PEOPLE

Although Radicals may be divided on the means by which social planning is to be achieved—some seeing class revolution as the tool and others willing to work within the framework of traditional American political institutions—there is greater agreement on *how* such planning should proceed once it is established. Most American Radicals would reject out of hand the varieties of social planning demonstrated by such socialist nations as the Soviet Union or China. These efforts at "state planning" have lost sight of the major objective of any rational and humane planning: *people*. In these cases, plans have been developed and imposed from above by central planning or political authorities whose decisions have no more to do with workers' and consumers' needs than decisions currently made by Exxon or IBM officials.

The first and unifying rule for Radicals with regard to planning is that the planning process must begin with popular participation and must be conceived to deal with "people's problems." There are, of course, many levels of planning, from decisions pertaining to a particular plant or factory to broad national output targets. Obviously, the more distant the level of planning, the more difficult individual participation becomes. However, it does not become impossible. Recognizing that the historic Soviet and Chinese cases are examples of what can happen when planning becomes too abstracted from popular input, the object is always to keep as much of the decision making at the lower levels as possible and, when that is no longer a reasonable alternative, to devise the broader elements of the plan through as democratic means as possible.

Workers or their directly elected representatives must be the basis for local output, pricing, and workplace decisions. Such decisions, of course, must be made with an eye to the general welfare. No worker or group of workers has the right to earnings obtained by sacrificing consumers or some other group of workers. That would merely be capitalism reappearing in the disguise of socialism, and it would lead to the same kind of exploitative conditions we now live under. (Moreover, it is also apparent that recent Soviet "reforms" in their economy are leading to precisely this very outcome.) Thus it is obvious that workers must be joined by consumers in the local or lower-level planning activities. Organizing broad popular participation in the planning process will not be easy, nor is there absolute certainty that a democratically devised plan will not be guilty of error and even failure. It is comparatively easy for Conservatives and Liberals to paint a picture of chaotic planning meetings as various representatives of workers, managers, and consumers determine key economic

376 Problems of Aggregate Economic Policy

objectives. However, they miss two very important points. First, the "failures" of such planning efforts can be little worse than the current private planning "successes." Second, even at its worst, planning based on workers' and consumers' participation *is* democratic planning and *is* consistent with the professed ideals of a democratic society.

Regardless of the precise methods ultimately devised to facilitate participatory planning – and trial and error will certainly play a role in selecting planning goals – the Radical holds to a basic belief that the people must be the architects of their own society. The basic economic decisions of what is produced, how, and for whom must not be entrusted to an elite, whether they be capitalists, political commissars, or ex-commissars turned capitalist.

The late Radical economic and social historian William Appleman Williams put it this way:

> Hence the issue is not whether to decentralize the economy and politics of the country, but rather how to do so. . . . This literal reconstructing and rebuilding of American society offers the only physical and intellectual challenge capable of absorbing and giving focus to the physical and intellectual resources of the country during the next generation. . . .
>
> Throughout such a process, moreover, the participants will be educating themselves . . . for their membership in the truly human community they will be creating. In the end they will have built a physical America which will be beautiful instead of ugly, and which will facilitate human relationships instead of dividing men into separate functional elements. They will have evolved a political system which is democratic in form and social in content. And they will be prepared . . . to function as men and women who can define their own identity, and their relationships with each other, outside the confining limits of property and the bruising and destructive dynamics of the competitive marketplace. They will be ready to explore the frontier of their own humanity.*

*William A. Williams, *The Great Evasion* (Chicago: Quadrangle Books, 1964), pp. 175–176.

PART 4

CONCLUSION

Final Thoughts and Suggested Readings

Having reached the end of this volume of debates on contemporary economic issues, it is probable that the reader expects (perhaps even hopes for) the author to make his own pitch—to say straight out which of the representative paradigms is correct and which is not, perhaps to unveil his own grand program. Indeed, the opportunity is tempting. For an economist, it is practically a reflex to try to get in the last word, especially one's own last word. However, after much thought, I decided that such a conclusion would spoil the entire effort. This book was undertaken to present the differing ideological alternatives as objectively as space and writing talents allowed so that the reader would be free to make personal choices on matters of economic policy.

I can hear some readers complaining: "Cop-out! You're avoiding presenting your own preferences and your own conclusions. You've taken the easy way out of the swamp." Not so. Delivering my own final polemic would in truth be ever so easy. But the book has been about questions and choices. The reader, then, shall be left in the uncomfortable position of making a choice among the paradigms and policy questions surveyed here. And that is the way it should be.

This perspective, however, must not be misunderstood. The author has not intended to produce a "relativistic" conclusion in which any choice will do and one choice is as good as any other. The point is for the reader to make a *good* choice, and some policy choices *are* better than others. However, only a reasoned analysis of the facts and a critical study of the "truths" of this world will permit any of us to make wise choices.

The British economist Joan Robinson has said it best:

> Social life will always present mankind with a choice of evils. *No* metaphysical solution that can ever be formulated will seem satisfactory for long. The solutions offered by economists were no less delusory than those of the theologians that they displaced.
>
> All the same we must not abandon the hope that economics can make an advance towards science, or the faith that enlightenment is not useless. It is necessary to clear the decaying remnants of obsolete metaphysics out of the way before we can go forward.
>
> The first essential for economists, arguing amongst themselves, is to "very seriously," as Professor Popper says that natural scientists do, "try to avoid talking at cross purposes."*

Before we can "avoid talking at cross purposes" on economic matters, we must understand our fundamental differences in opinion and interpretation. Hopefully, this book has identified some of these important differences for the reader.

In undertaking this task, any author would be sorely tested. While trying to submerge personal biases, one also must master the biases of others. Perhaps I have not entirely succeeded on either count. Only the reader can judge. Nevertheless, such an endeavor is extremely educational. It compels one to work through unfamiliar logic and ideas and weigh them against one's own beliefs. For readers who desire to dig deeper into economic ideologies and their application to contemporary issues, the following bibliography offers some landmark readings in the respective Conservative, Liberal, and Radical schools of economic thought.

Conservative

Banfield, Edward C. *The Unheavenly City*. Boston: Little, Brown, 1970.
Buckley, William. *Up from Liberalism*. New York: Honor Books, 1959.

*Joan Robinson, *Economic Philosophy* (Garden City, N.Y.: Anchor Books, 1964), pp. 147–148.

Friedman, Milton. *Capitalism and Freedom*. Chicago: University of Chicago Press, 1962.

_____. *Free to Choose*. New York: Harcourt Brace Jovanovich, 1980.

Gilder, George. *Wealth and Power*. New York: Basic Books, 1981.

Hazlitt, Henry. *The Failure of the "New Economics": An Analysis of the Keynesian Fallacies*. New York: Van Nostrand, 1959.

Kirk, Russell. *The Conservative Mind*. Chicago: Regnery, 1954.

Klamer, Arjo. *Conversations with Economists*. Totowa, N.J.: Rowman & Allanhold, 1983.

Knight, Frank. *Freedom and Reform*. New York: Harper & Row, 1947.

Malabre, Alfred E., Jr. *Living Beyond Our Means*. New York: Vintage Books, 1987.

Marshall, Alfred. *Principles of Economics*. New York: Macmillan, 1890

Rand, Ayn. *Capitalism: The Unknown Ideal*. New York: New American Library Signet Books, 1967.

Schumpeter, Joseph. *Capitalism, Socialism, and Democracy*. New York: Harper Brothers, 1942.

Simon, William E. *A Time for Action*. New York: Berkley, 1980.

Simons, Henry C. *A Positive Program for Laissez-Faire*. Chicago: University of Chicago Press, 1934.

Smith, Adam. *An Inquiry into the Nature and Causes of the Wealth of Nations*, 1776.

Stein, Herbert. *Presidential Economics: The Making of Economic Policy from Roosevelt to Reagan and Beyond*. New York: Simon and Schuster, 1985.

Von Hayek, Friedrich. *The Road to Serfdom*. Chicago: University of Chicago Press, 1944.

Von Mises, Ludwig. *Socialism: An Economic and Sociological Analysis*. New Haven, Conn.: Yale University Press, 1959.

Liberal

Berle, Adolf A. *The Twentieth Century Capitalist Revolution*. New York: Harcourt Brace Jovanovich, 1954.

Clark, John M. *Alternative to Serfdom*. New York: Random House/Vintage Books, 1960.

_____. *Social Control of Business*. New York: McGraw-Hill, 1939.

Friedman, Benjamin. *Day of Reckoning*. New York: Random House, 1988.

Galbraith, John Kenneth. *The Affluent Society*. Boston: Houghton Mifflin, 1971.

_____. *Economics and the Public Purpose*. Boston: Houghton Mifflin, 1973.

_____. *The New Industrial State*. Boston: Houghton Mifflin, 1967.

_____. *Economics in Perspective*. Boston: Houghton Mifflin, 1987.

Hansen, Alvin. *The American Economy.* New York: McGraw-Hill, 1957.
Heilbroner, Robert. "The Future of Capitalism," in *The Limits of American Capitalism.* New York: Harper & Row, 1966.
———. *The Nature and Logic of Capitalism.* New York: Norton, 1985.
Heller, Walter W. *The Economy: Old Myths and New Realities.* New York: Norton, 1976.
Keynes, John M. *The General Theory of Employment, Interest, and Money.* New York: Harcourt Brace Jovanovich, 1936
Lekachman, Robert. *The Age of Keynes.* New York: Random House, 1966
Okun, Arthur M. *The Political Economy of Prosperity.* New York: Norton, 1970.
Reagan, Michael D. *The Managed Economy.* New York: Oxford University Press, 1963.
Reich, Robert B. *Tales of a New America.* New York: Times Books, 1987
Shonfield, Andres. *Modern Capitalism: The Changing Balance of Public and Private Power.* New York: Oxford University Press, 1965.
Thurow, Lester C. *Dangerous Currents.* New York: Random House, 1983.
———. *The Zero-Sum Society.* New York: Basic Books, 1980.
———. *The Zero-Sum Solution.* New York: Simon and Schuster, 1985.

Radical

Baran, Paul. *The Political Economy of Growth.* New York: Monthly Review Press, 1957.
———, and Paul M. Sweezy. *Monopoly Capital.* New York: Monthly Review Press, 1966
Bowles, Samuel, and Herbert Gintis. *Property, Community, and the Contradictions of Modern Social Thought.* New York: Basic Books, 1986.
———, and Richard Edwards. *Understanding Capitalism.* New York: Harper & Row, 1985.
Domhoff, William. *Who Rules America?* Englewood Cliffs, N.J.: Prentice-Hall, 1967.
Dowd, Douglas. *The Twisted Dream.* Cambridge, Mass.: Winthrop, 1974.
Duboff, Richard. *Accumulation and Capital.* Armonk, N.Y.: M.E. Sharpe, 1990.
Franklin, Raymond S. *American Capitalism: Two Visions.* New York: Random House, 1977.
Kolko, Gabriel. *Wealth and Power in America.* New York: Praeger, 1962.
Magdoff, Harry. *The Age of Imperialism.* New York: Monthly Review Press, 1967.
Mandel, Ernest. *Marxist Economic Theory.* New York: Monthly Review Press, 1967.
Marx, Karl. *Capital.* 1867.

O'Connor, James. *The Fiscal Crisis of the State.* New York: St. Martin's Press, 1973.

Robinson, Joan. *An Essay on Marxian Economics.* London: Macmillan, 1942.

Sherman, Howard. *Radical Political Economy.* New York: Basic Books, 1972.

_____. *Stagflation: A Radical Theory of Unemployment and Inflation.* New York: Harper & Row, 1976.

Strachey, John. *The Nature of Capitalist Crisis.* New York: Covici, Friede, 1933.

_____. *The Theory and Practice of Socialism.* New York: Random House, 1936.

Sweezy, Paul. *The Theory of Capitalist Development.* New York: Monthly Review Press, 1942.

Williams, William A. *The Great Evasion.* Chicago: Quadrangle Books, 1964.

Index